War Against All Puerto Ricans

War Against All Puerto Ricans

Revolution and Terror in America's Colony

NELSON A. DENIS

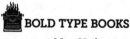

BOLD TYPE BOOKS

New York

Bold Type Books

116 East 16th Street, 8th Floor New York, NY 10003

www.boldtypebooks.org

@BoldTypeBooks

Printed in the United States of America

Originally published in hardcover and ebook in April 2015

First Trade Paperback Edition: March 2016

Published by Bold Type Books, an imprint of Perseus Books, LLC, a subsidiary of Hachette Book Group, Inc. Bold Type Books is a co-publishing venture of the Type Media Center and Perseus Books.

The Hachette Speakers Bureau provides a wide range of authors for speaking events. To find out more, go to www.hachettespeakersbureau.com or call (866) 376-6591.

The publisher is not responsible for websites (or their content) that are not owned by the publisher.

Library of Congress Cataloging-in-Publication Data

Denis, Nelson A.

  War against all Puerto Ricans : revolution and terror in America's colony / Nelson A. Denis.

  pages cm

  Includes bibliographical references and index.

  ISBN 978-1-56858-501-7 (hardcover)—ISBN 978-1-56858-502-4 (electronic)—
  ISBN 978-1-56858-561-1 (paperback)

  1. Albizu Campos, Pedro, 1891–1965. 2. Puerto Rico—History—Autonomy and independence movements. 3. Puerto Rico—Politics and government—1898–1952. 4. Nationalism—Puerto Rico—History—20th century. 5. Puerto Rico—Relations— United States. 6. United States—Relations—Puerto Rico. I. Title.

  F1975.A45D46 2015

  972.9505'2—dc23

  2014047904

ISBNs: 978-1-56858-501-7 (hardcover), 978-1-56858-502-4 (ebook), 978-1-56858-561-1 (paperback), 978-1-56858-545-1 (Spanish paperback), 978-1-56858-546-8 (Spanish ebook)

LSC-C

10 9

*For my mother, Sarah, my grandmother, Salome,
and Migdalia, who holds them in her heart.*

CONTENTS

EVENTS

There will be war to the death against all Puerto Ricans.

—E. Francis Riggs, Chief of Police of Puerto Rico

They were conquerors . . . They grabbed what they could get for the sake of what was to be got. It was just robbery with violence, aggravated murder on a grand scale . . . The conquest of the earth, which mostly means the taking it away from those who have a different complexion or slightly flatter noses than ourselves, is not a pretty thing when you look into it too much.

—Joseph Conrad, *Heart of Darkness*

PREFACE

My mother was Puerto Rican. My father was Cuban. They worked very hard, and we lived in a small but spotless apartment in New York City's Washington Heights. I was eight years old when men from the FBI banged on our door at 3 a.m. No one understood what was happening: my mother screamed, my grandmother cried, and I hid behind a curtain. The FBI agents grabbed my father and took him away; we never saw him again.

It was October 1962, the height of the Cuban Missile Crisis, and someone had denounced my father as a spy. There was no trial or administrative hearing, no evidence or due process—he was simply deported to Cuba. A few months later, in June 1963, Attorney General Robert F. Kennedy received his annual Immigration and Naturalization Service report, which stated, "Investigation of Cuban refugees increased during this year. Under this pressure, a number of Cubans alleged to be subversive departed prior to the completion of the investigations. These included . . . Antonio Denis Jordan, suspected Cuban G-2 agent in New York City."

My father was an elevator operator and a member of the janitor's union, 32BJ SEIU. He supported the Cuban Revolution and spoke in favor of it during the late 1950s. He even read *Bohemia* (a leftist magazine) and showed me the 1959 "Bohemia of Freedom" issue, with its gruesome photos of bodies massacred by Cuban dictator Fulgencio Batista. He was a Cuban patriot, but he was not a spy.

This didn't matter to the United States, which never allowed him to return. My mother raised me by herself, working in belt factories for $50 a week, and I vowed to become a lawyer so that no one would knock on our door again and rip our family apart.

As a Harvard undergraduate, I noticed a strange thing in Widener Library: it had fifty-seven miles of shelves and 3 million books, but the 1973 card catalog contained not even a single volume about Pedro Albizu Campos, the principal figure in Puerto Rican political history. I responded with my own scholarship: a study of the fraudulent constitution of Puerto Rico, which became the cover story for the 1977 *Harvard Political Review*.

Over the subsequent forty years, I have continued to research the life and death of Albizu Campos. I visited my family in Puerto Rico dozens of times, particularly in Caguas, where they helped me meet members of the Nationalist Party, a political organization deeply committed to Puerto Rican independence. Some of these Nationalists served time with Albizu in the Atlanta federal penitentiary. Others were imprisoned with him in La Princesa, a prison in San Juan. Still others were tortured in Aguadilla. All of them had vivid memories of El Maestro (the Teacher) and the revolution he ignited.

I wasn't writing a book yet; I was recovering my own past and understanding certain quirks in the Puerto Rican personality. For example, we see so many huge, surrealistic flags during the New York Puerto Rican Day Parade because all Puerto Rican flags were illegal on the island from 1948 until 1957. Even a Nobel Prize nominee, Francisco Matos Paoli, was sentenced to twenty years in La Princesa for owning one.

Over time I became a lawyer, the editorial director of *El Diario/La Prensa*, and a New York State assemblyman. This enabled me to access more people and information, but I still wasn't writing a book. And then I saw the FBI files.

The bureau kept secret dossiers on Puerto Ricans for over sixty years. There are 1.8 million pages of files about Albizu Campos, the Nationalist Party, Puerto Rico's October 1950 revolution, and over 100,000 Puerto Ricans, most of whom had no idea that they were being followed.

These files contain surveillance notes, telephone taps, bank account information, criminal and medical records, tax returns, credit card numbers, professional licenses, school transcripts, child support payments, home mortgage documents, job applications, voting and credit histories, wedding lists, sexual profiles, and neighborhood gossip. The FBI used them to monitor and control people. The bureau also used them to destroy careers. When I saw these files, I thought of my father. Infuriated, I finally decided to write this book.

I read thousands of FBI documents and hundreds of newspaper accounts; I scoured university, museum, and historical society archives. I tracked down oral histories, personal interviews, private correspondence, diaries, church registries, and old photos. I read amicus curiae briefs, congressional testimony, Senate committee reports, CIA manuals, and Defense Department contracts. I walked the streets of Puerto Rico where people had been murdered. I talked to their families. Then I started writing.

೮ನ

On October 30, 1950, a violent revolution swept through Puerto Rico: Nationalist assassins were sent to kill President Harry S. Truman; gunfights roared in eight towns; revolutionaries burned police stations, post offices, and selective service centers, representative of the US presence, to the ground.

A bloody shootout raged at the Salón Boricua barbershop—a three-hour gunfight between forty US National Guardsmen (armed with machine guns, grenades, bazookas, rifles, and carbines), the Insular Police, and one lone barber named Vidal. Puerto Rican radio stations covered the battle live and broadcast it over the entire island.

To suppress the revolution, the US Army deployed 5,000 troops and bombarded two towns—the only time in history that the United States has bombed its own citizens. They also arrested thousands of Nationalists and imprisoned their leader, Albizu Campos. While Albizu was in prison, evidence strongly indicates, the US government subjected him to lethal radiation—until it killed him.

This is not a pretty story. If it helps you to understand the world in which we live, then I have done my job. The rest is up to you.

Facts

CHAPTER 1

La Princesa

In 1808 it was a beautiful Spanish castle. In 1976, a US district court ordered it shut down forever, calling it "a notorious monument to man's inhumanity to man." By 1950 it was already a brutal prison where inmates were starved, tortured, and used for medical experiments. People called it La Princesa (the Princess), but it was actually a graveyard—designed to break men and women, to kill their spirits, to grind them into drones, then animals, then feces and ash.

The prison housed over six hundred souls; at least fifty were blind, crippled, lacked an arm, had elephantiasis, or were hunchbacked. Humans with every imaginable deformity walked about in rags, and none were excused from work of some kind or another.[1]

On the outside it looked like a quaint Spanish mission: wood and red-brick masonry and white-framed windows, nestled behind swaying palm trees and topped by a four-foot clock, a trim cupola, and a US flag. Inside it was a rectangular stone fortress, about one hundred by thirty feet, with a cement courtyard in the center ringed by cells on three sides. The fourth side was an eighteen-foot wall with a catwalk patrolled by guards with rifles and dogs.

The prison's three *galerías* (galleries) totaled 7,744 square feet and held over 400 inmates (providing less than twenty square feet per inmate); three *galeritas* (little galleries) held another 150. A quarantine gallery held the mentally deranged, and thirty *calabozos* (dungeons) held the "difficult" prisoners.

After the Nationalist revolt of October 1950, the jail became so crowded that *galería* prisoners had to sleep on the floors and in hallways and bathrooms. In the *galeritas*, two or three men slept in every bed, some of which had no mattresses and most of which had no sheets. Many of the mattresses were old, dirty, worn, and torn. Even in the *hospitalito* (the medical clinic), inmate patients had to sleep on the bare floor.

The dungeons—arranged along a hallway on the first floor, fifteen to a side, all divided by concrete partitions—were famous throughout Puerto Rico. This hallway was covered with filth, barely lit and poorly ventilated. Each row of fifteen cells shared a common roof of iron bars as thick as railroad tracks, topped with steel walkways. The guards patrolled them from opposite ends, stopping when they met in the middle to retrace their steps. It was a vantage point, like a captain's bridge: the guards could look down and see every occupant of every cell. They could also point their rifles at them.

Each dungeon held one inmate, one can of water, and one bucket for human excrement. That was all. There was no sink or toilet, no bed, mattress, or blanket, no other furniture. Prisoners slept on the floor and, after using the buckets, covered them with their shirts to combat the stink and the scarab beetles, which loved to eat from the buckets. The only air and light entered through the iron-bar ceilings, twelve feet over the prisoners' heads. A nauseating odor permeated the entire area. It floated up from the buckets, which were emptied only once every twenty-four hours.

Each morning, two forlorn prisoners and four armed guards went from cell to cell. The prisoners entered, lugged out the buckets, and emptied them into a barrel hanging from their shoulders on two wooden bars. The stench of crap and urine was suffocating. Sometimes, if they felt like it, the guards brought the inmates' breakfast at the same time the buckets were emptied.

Cell door in La Princesa

Photo courtesy of http://freephotooftheday.com/2011/12/06/
la-princesa-puerto rico-tourism-company-san-juan-puerto-rico/

Breakfast was short and simple: a cup of black coffee, *agua de arroz* (water in which rice had been boiled), and a lump of old bread. Lunch and dinner were rice and beans. Once a week the inmates received *carne molida* (ground beef) or *Spam frito* (fried Spam).

Even as they ate, the inmates fought off mosquitoes that flew down from the ceiling, rats that stole their bread, and bedbugs that migrated from cell to cell in search of warm bodies.

The dungeons were filled with sick men. After a few months in confinement—with little food, light, exercise, or fresh air—they became walking skeletons. They grew anemic, suffering from dysentery, hookworm, malaria, and scurvy. As their digestive systems shut down, they lost all desire to eat. Many inmates did not survive the dungeons.

The warden didn't care because the *calabozos* housed highly accomplished criminals: men convicted of theft, looting, arson, murder, and even cannibalism. But the most dangerous prisoners were the Nationalists, and these he did care about. The career of every prison official in La Princesa—from warden to guard—would be destroyed if the Nationalists caused any trouble, inspired prisoners to revolt, or attracted attention from the press. And so they had to be isolated. The Nationalists spent more time in the dungeons than any other group, including the murderers and cannibals.[2]

೦෨

After the October 30 revolts, mass arrests filled all the prisons with 3,000 prisoners for the next few months. This number gradually diminished as trials were held, and some prisoners (generally the better financed) were found innocent. The week before Christmas 1950, the dungeons were still stuffed to capacity. One man was insane. He counted eternally, as he had for the past six months: "47, 48, 49 . . . 47, 48, 49 . . . 47, 48, 49."

Another man sat hunched in a corner. Had he risen, he would have stood six feet tall—but he was too weak to stand. He'd been in the dungeon for over a year, weighed 110 pounds, and was starving.

A third man was only twenty years old; he had a slender, boyish body and big brown eyes guarded by long dark lashes. Two inmates had died fighting over him.

A fourth man would make a cord out of his pants and hang himself on Thanksgiving Day.

A fifth man lived with a Puerto Rico Upland gecko. He fed it dozens of bedbugs every day and let it crawl all over him. He also talked and sang to it. This man was a murderer.

US Army doctors had convinced a sixth man, named Hector, to swallow "some new pills" for a few weeks. He started vomiting and developed bloody diarrhea, then liver cancer. Hector belonged in a hospital, but La Princesa didn't want any bad publicity, so he went into the dungeons. The army doctors never returned.

Hector's neighbor was insane and smeared feces all over dungeon number seven.

Deusdedit Marrero, a social worker in dungeon number eight, was in the process of losing his mind. He had played no part in the revolution. He was at work when it broke out on October 30, and he was not a Nationalist. Unfortunately, Deusdedit was a Socialist, which was close enough for the Insular Police.[3] They arrested him in his office and sentenced him to twenty years. While still in prison, Deusdedit learned that his pregnant wife had committed suicide—and it destroyed him. When finally released, he was unable to function and became homeless.

In the ninth dungeon, Francisco Matos Paoli was a Nationalist and a prolific poet. A few friends sent him cigarettes and cigars, which he bartered with the prison guards for pencils. Paoli wrote every day. Sometimes he snuck a poem out to his fellow Nationalists. Other times he unrolled a cigar, wrote a poem, rolled it back up, and smoked the poem.

He also wrote on the floor and on every wall of his cell. Every square foot had a poem on it. The warden heard about it and made Francisco paint over the walls—but two weeks later, he had covered them with poems again.[4]

Separated from everyone, in the fifteenth dungeon, was a small man with fiery brown eyes and wet towels wrapped around his head. For several days his legs had been black, and his gums were bleeding. Fifty-nine years old and exhausted beyond measure, he paced silently up and down, always the same five steps, back and forth. One, two, three, four, five, and turn . . . an interminable shuffle between the wall and door of his cell. He had no work, no books, nothing to write on. And so he walked.

One, two, three, four, five, and turn . . .

His dungeon was next door to La Fortaleza, the governor's mansion in Old San Juan, less than two hundred feet away. The governor had been his friend and had even voted for him for the Puerto Rican legislature in 1932. This didn't help much now. The governor had ordered his arrest.

One, two, three, four, five, and turn . . .

Life had turned him into a pendulum; it had all been mathematically worked out. This shuttle back and forth in his cell comprised his entire universe. He had no other choice. His transformation into a living corpse suited his captors perfectly.

One, two, three, four, five, and turn . . .

Fourteen hours of walking: to master this art of endless movement, he'd learned to keep his head down, hands behind his back, stepping neither too fast nor too slow, every stride the same length. He'd also learned to chew tobacco and smear the nicotined saliva on his face and neck to keep the mosquitoes away.

One, two, three, four, five, and turn . . .

The heat was so stifling, he needed to take off his clothes, but he couldn't. He wrapped even more towels around his head and looked up as the guard's shadow hit the wall. He felt like an animal in a pit, watched by the hunter who had just ensnared him.

One, two, three, four, five, and turn . . .

Far away, he could hear the ocean breaking on the rocks of San Juan's harbor and the screams of demented inmates as they cried and howled in the quarantine gallery. A tropical rain splashed the iron roof nearly every day. The dungeons dripped with a stifling humidity that saturated everything, and mosquitoes invaded during every rainfall. Green mold crept along the cracks of his cell, and scarab beetles marched single file, along the mold lines, and into his bathroom bucket.

The murderer started screaming. The lunatic in dungeon seven had flung his own feces over the ceiling rail. It landed in dungeon five and frightened the Puerto Rico Upland gecko. The murderer, of course, was threatening to kill the lunatic.

One, two, three, four, five, and turn . . .

The man started walking again. It was his only world. The grass had grown thick over the grave of his youth. He was no longer a human being, no longer a man. Prison had entered him, and he had become the prison. He fought this feeling every day.

One, two, three, four, five, and turn . . .

He was a lawyer, journalist, chemical engineer, and president of the Nationalist Party. He was the first Puerto Rican to graduate from Harvard College and Harvard Law School and spoke six languages. He had served as a first lieutenant in World War I and led a company of two hundred men. He had served as president of the Cosmopolitan Club at Harvard and helped Éamon de Valera draft the constitution of the Free State of Ireland.[5]

One, two, three, four, five, and turn . . .

He would spend twenty-five years in prison—many of them in this dungeon, in the belly of La Princesa. He walked back and forth for decades, with wet towels wrapped around his head. The guards all laughed, declared him insane, and called him El Rey de las Toallas. The King of the Towels.

His name was Pedro Albizu Campos.

CHAPTER 2

Four Hundred Years of Solitude

The King of the Towels was in jail for a serious reason. He was trying to reverse four hundred years of history.

In the sun-splashed paradise of Puerto Rico, you can lie on a beach in the morning, hike through a rain forest during the day, and spend the evening exploring the ancient walls of a colonial city. The white coastal sands glitter like sugar. The water is so pristine that, from an airplane, you'll see several shades of turquoise between the shore and the deep blue of the ocean. Through the middle of the island, the Cordillera Mountains form a series of misty ridges draped in thick sierra palm and pine forest, whose foothills taper gracefully into the Caribbean. Over a thousand silver streams and rivulets gush down the mountains and rush headlong into the sea.

The world's third-longest underground river, the Río Camuy, lies under a beautiful, vast cave system—ten miles of cool limestone caverns and 220 caves—packed with dripping stalactites, giant stalagmites, and flowstone walls.

El Yunque is the only subtropical rain forest in the United States. Wreathed in clouds or framed against a cobalt sky, it rises majestically with a canopy of forest trees, plunging waterfalls, and natural swimming pools. Its 28,000 acres nourish over fifty species of orchids, as well as giant tree ferns, sierra plants, bamboo thickets, heliconia, ginger, and 225 native tree species, all thriving in an explosion of color and natural beauty. It also houses lizards, iguanas, the coquí tree frog, and seventy-nine types of birds, including the rare green-feathered Puerto Rican parrot (rarely seen outside the Puerto Rican legislature and Washington, DC).[1]

The entire island is volcanic, and its soil is very rich. It is strategically located between North and South America—the first major land mass that a Spanish galleon would encounter after a long and harrowing voyage.

For all those reasons, over four centuries, Puerto Rico became a military and political football.

❧

The abuse of the island started early. In 1493, Columbus made his second voyage to the New World with seventeen ships, 1,200 men, horses, cattle, guns, and smallpox. When he finally reached a major island, it happened to be Puerto Rico. The Taíno Indians welcomed Columbus, but they made a big mistake: they showed him some gold nuggets in a river and told him to take all he wanted.[2] Naturally, this started a gold rush.

Spain named the island Puerto Rico (meaning "rich port") and invaded with embroidered bibles and African slaves. They enslaved the Taínos as well: every Taíno over the age of fourteen had to produce a hawk's bell of gold every three months or have their hands cut off. Since they'd never seen a hawk, a horse, an armored man, or firebreathing muskets, the Taínos did as they were told.[3] To make matters worse, a strange plague (smallpox) was killing all the Taínos but sparing the Spaniards, which meant they must be gods or at least immortal. This didn't sit well with an old Taíno named Urayoán—and so, in 1511, he conducted a little experiment.

He told a lonely Spaniard named Diego Salcedo that a lake filled with virgins was waiting for him. Diego dashed right over but met a lakeful of Taíno warriors instead. After they drowned him, Urayoán watched and poked and smelled the body for three days. When Diego began to rot, Urayoán spread the news. Riots broke out all over the island, and Ponce de León shot 6,000 Taínos in order to maintain public order and respect for the queen.[4]

Three centuries later there were no Taínos left, but the situation hadn't changed much. Puerto Rico was still a political football. In 1812 the first Spanish constitution, the Cádiz Constitution, was extended to Puerto Rico, and the island became a province of Spain with the same rights as other provinces. In 1814, the Cádiz Constitution was repealed; in 1820 it was restored, and in 1823 it was abolished. In 1824 the Spanish governor was again given absolute power over Puerto Rico.

On September 23, 1868, nearly 1,000 men rose up in the town of Lares to demand independence from Spain. By midnight they'd taken over the municipal seat of government, deposed the Spanish officials, arrested the Spanish merchants, and hauled them all off to jail. They hoisted a white flag with the inscription "Libertad ó Muerte; Vive Puerto Rico Libre; Año 1868" (Liberty or Death; Free Puerto Rico Lives; Year 1868). They took the town hall and forced the parish priest to celebrate a Te Deum for the establishment of the republic. Then they declared Puerto Rico independent, installed a provisional government, and offered freedom to any slave joining their cause.

The next afternoon, the Spanish militia from nearby Pepino routed the rebels, and troops pursued them from Aguadilla to Arecibo. El Grito de Lares had ended.[5] In response to it, however, a liberal constitution was adopted in 1869, which restored Spanish citizenship to Puerto Ricans, as well as the right to representation in the Cortes Generales (the Spanish parliament).

Thirty years later, in 1897, the Spanish prime minister signed the Carta de Autonomía (Charter of Autonomy), which granted Puerto Rico the right to its own legislature, constitution, tariffs, monetary system, treasury, judiciary, and international borders. After four hundred years of colonial rule, the charter created the free Republic of Puerto Rico.[6] Elections for the new legislature were held in March 1898, and the new government was scheduled for installation in May.

On May 12, cannon blasts awakened everyone in San Juan as twelve US battleships, destroyers, and torpedo boats bombarded the city for three hours, turning the sky black with cannon smoke. Homes were hit. Streets were torn. El Morro lighthouse and La Iglesia de San José, a sixteenth-century church, were shelled repeatedly. The governor ran to Fort San Felipe del Morro to defend the island with three Ordóñez cannons, but San Juan became a ghost town as 30,000 residents fled the city, the world shattering all around them. The Spanish-American War, declared by the United States on April 25, had arrived in Puerto Rico.[7]

When US soldiers invaded the inner towns, the *New York Times* trumpeted, "Our Flag Raised in Puerto Rico."[8] As the war continued and US troops marched through the island, the Puerto Rican bourgeoisie were still buzzing about liberation, but the peasants—sick of politics, politicians, and promises, no matter what country they came from—couldn't care less. When the American soldiers passed by, local dogs barked at them and farmers kept plowing their fields. They accepted the change in sovereignty with the same fatalism with which they accepted hookworms, hurricanes, and tuberculosis.[9]

Americans were more upbeat about the matter. "Give my best love to Nannie, and do not make peace until we get Porto Rico," wrote Theodore Roosevelt to Senator Henry Cabot Lodge in 1898.[10] "Porto Rico is not forgotten," replied the senator. "We mean to have it."[11] The *New York Journal of Commerce* declared, "We must have Porto Rico," because when a "territory of that nature falls into our hands it must never be parted with."[12]

The *New York Times* noted "the commercial value of Porto Rico" and "the wisdom of taking . . . and keeping it for all time." According to the *Times*, it was "a charming winter resort," a fine naval station with "a commanding position between two continents," and "an island well worth having." In language akin to that of Rudyard Kipling's "The White Man's Burden," the *Times* concluded, "We need it as a station in the great American archipelago. . . . We are not pledged to give Porto Rico independence. . . . [I]t would be much better for her to come at once under the beneficent sway of these United States than to engage in doubtful experiments at self-government, and there is no reason to believe that her people would prefer it."[13] Even the poet Carl Sandburg, who saw active service in Puerto Rico with the 6th Illinois Infantry during the war, wrote, "For four hundred years this island had been run by a Spanish government in Madrid. Now it was to be American and it was plain that the island common people liked the idea."[14]

On July 4, 1898, in the Central Presbyterian Church of Brooklyn, the Reverend J. F. Carson read from the Holy Bible, "And Joshua took the whole land, and the land rested from war." He sermonized that "the high, the supreme business of this Republic is to end the Spanish rule in America, and if to do that it is necessary to plant the Stars and Stripes on Cuba, Porto Rico, the Philippines or Spain itself, America will do it."[15] That same night, in the Presbyterian Church of Fifth Avenue, the Reverend Robert MacKenzie prophesied, "God is calling a new power to the front. The race of which this nation is the crown . . . is now divinely thrust out to take its place as a world power."[16] Senator Albert J. Beveridge also saw a divine plan. "God has not been preparing the English-speaking and Teutonic peoples for a thousand years for nothing," he declared. "He has made us adept in government so that we may administer government amongst savages and senile peoples."[17]

On July 21, 1898, the US government issued a press release stating, "Porto Rico will be kept. . . . Once taken it will never be released. It will pass forever into the hands of the Unites States. . . . Its possession will go towards making up the heavy expense of the war to the United States. Our flag, once run up there, will float over the island permanently."[18] On the floor of the US Senate, Republican senator Joseph B. Foraker declaimed, "Porto Rico differs radically from any other people for whom we have legislated previously. . . . They have no experience which would qualify them for the great work of government with all the bureaus and departments needed by the people of Porto Rico."[19]

Within a few years, Puerto Rico would be stuffed with "bureaus and departments," becoming a base for Roosevelt's "big stick" policy in the Caribbean.[20] In fact, nearly a decade before the Spanish-American War, US President Benjamin Harrison and Secretary of State James G. Blaine had already been considering the island's value as a navy coaling station, provision center, and stepping stone to the Latin American market.[21]

Eugenio María de Hostos, the great Puerto Rican educator, summed it up as follows: "How sad and overwhelming and shameful it is to see [Puerto Rico] go from owner to owner without ever having been her own master, and to see her pass from sovereignty to sovereignty without ever ruling herself."[22]

The United States told Puerto Ricans a very different story, however. On July 29, 1898, four days after the landing of American troops, Major General Nelson Appleton Miles issued a proclamation from his military headquarters in Ponce. It was the first official public statement from the US government explaining its plans for Puerto Rico:

> The chief object of the American military forces will be to overthrow the armed authority of Spain and to give to the people of your beautiful island the largest measure of liberties consistent with military occupation.
>
> We have not come to make war against a people of a country that for centuries has been oppressed, but, on the contrary, to bring you protection, not only to yourselves but to your property, to promote your prosperity, to bestow upon you the immunities and blessings of the liberal institutions of our government . . . and to give the advantages and blessings of enlightened civilization.[23]

This "enlightened civilization" held some firm views about their neighbors. On February 22, 1899, the *New York Times* ran an article headlined "Americanizing Puerto Rico," describing Puerto Ricans as "uneducated, simple-minded and harmless people who are only interested in wine, women, music and dancing."[24] As late as 1940, *Scribner's Commentator* stated, "All Puerto Ricans are totally lacking in moral values, which is why none of them seem to mind wallowing in the most abject moral degradation."[25] In 1948, popular writers were still ranting that "Puerto Ricans are not born to be New Yorkers. They are mostly crude farmers, subject to congenital tropical diseases, physically unfit for the northern climate, unskilled, uneducated, non-English-speaking and almost impossible to assimilate and condition for healthful and useful existence in an active city of stone and steel."[26]

The most colorful (and color-conscious) opinions were voiced by the southern wing of the Democratic Party. Here are some choice words on the floor of the US Senate from Senator William B. Bate (D-TN), who had served as a major general in the Confederate Army:

What is to become of the Philippines and Porto Rico? Are they to become States with representation here from those countries, from that heterogeneous mass of mongrels that make up their citizenship? That is objectionable to the people of this country, as it ought to be, and they will call a halt to it before it is done.

Jefferson was the greatest expansionist. But neither his example nor his precedent affords any justification for expansion over territory in distant seas, over peoples incapable of self-government, over religions hostile to Christianity, and over savages addicted to head-hunting and cannibalism, as some of these islanders are.[27]

The national perception was clear: Puerto Ricans were ignorant, uncivilized, morally bankrupt, and utterly incapable of self-rule. The US would protect them, tame their savagery, manage their property, and deliver them from four hundred years of solitude.[28]

CHAPTER 3

Our Children Speak English and Spanish

Central Grammar School was a former military armory: a stone building looming over Calles San Francisco and Luna in the heart of Old San Juan. In 1908, it stood next to a chicken slaughterhouse and had a concrete yard enclosed by an iron-spiked fence, with heavy double doors that slammed shut as students walked in. Stuffed birds, monkeys, and other animals in dusty glass cages lined the long, dark hallways. No one knew how they got there or where they were going.[1]

The students wore green-and-yellow uniforms, sat in neat little rows with their hands folded, and called their teachers "Meester" and "Meeses." They started each day with the Pledge of Allegiance, then sang a patriotic ditty:

Puerto Rico is a beautiful island
It belongs to the United States
Our children speak English and Spanish
And salute our flag every day

Their flag was the Stars and Stripes, which hung in every classroom. The teachers wore starched blouses or crisp white shirts and wiped their foreheads with crumpled handkerchiefs all day. In the early 1900s, the most popular teacher was Mrs. Del Toro in Room 9 because she wore sweat pads under her arms. Every morning the strings holding them in place slipped out of the short sleeves of her starched white shirts, and she had to turn her back in order to adjust them. The children always loved that.

Then she would get down to teaching. On a given day, while displaying a chart of the major food groups, she might explain in barely comprehensible English the importance of nutrition and eating all the foods on the chart: broccoli and carrots, turnips and iceberg lettuce, plums, a large meatloaf, and other strange items. If a child remarked that none of the vegetables on the chart grew in Puerto Rico and the class laughed, Mrs. Del Toro would slam her pointer on the blackboard.

By way of punishment she might move on to mathematics, instructing the children to pull out books written entirely in English as she wrote an equation on the board: $1 / 2 = ? / 8$. "Now remember, to change the denominator of a fraction, you first divide the first denominator by the second denominator," she would explain.[2] The children would look at each other and scratch their heads, not having the faintest idea what she'd said and unable to read the English-language math books.

After lunch, Mrs. Del Toro might settle the class down with a little song.

Pollito, chicken
Gallina, hen
Lapiz, pencil
y Pluma, pen
Ventana, window
Puerta, door
Maestra, teacher
y Piso, floor

With her ruler, she would point at the chickens in the slaughterhouse across the street, at the pencil on a student's desk, at the pen on her own desk, at the window, the door, herself, and the dull wooden floor.

"Very good!" she would exclaim, then unfurl a map at the front of the room. "Today we study the geography of the United States." For the next hour, the children might memorize the names of states, cities, lakes, and rivers 2,000 miles away that they had never seen or heard of. They might learn about an "American Progress" that brought railroads, electricity, telegraph lines, Christianity, and light to that far-flung continent and drove bears, bison, and Native Americans off the map.[3]

They might learn about "Teodor Ro-se-bel," the president of the United States, and how he led the Rough Riders up San Juan Hill and shot the Spaniards and risked his life to liberate Puerto Rico.

If the children behaved, the day would end with another fun song, albeit one that no one understood.

My bonee lie sober de o chan,
My bonee lie sober de sí,
My bonee lie sober de o chan
O breen back my bonee too mi

જી

This unfortunate scenario was playing out all over the island. Within ten years of US occupation, every subject, in every class, in every public school was being taught in English. The textbooks were all written in English as well—even though none of the students and few of the teachers could understand them. Beyond the obvious plan to enrich a few well-connected US publishers and pedagogues, this represented a direct assault on four hundred years of language and culture under the guise of "civilizing a savage people."[4]

Educators like Paulo Freire, as well as sociologists and historians, have studied this "civilizing" dynamic in colonial relationships: "In the case of a colony—which by its very nature is the object of exploitation by the political power—the purpose of every colonial administration is

US pedagogy in Puerto Rico

Louis Dalrymple, *School Begins*; Illustration from *Puck* magazine, v. 44, no. 1142
(January 25, 1899), courtesy of the Library of Congress

and has always been to overcome, by all possible means, the resistance
of the subjugated power. To accomplish this goal requires the active
control by those in power of the cultural and educational systems."[5] The
president of the Puerto Rico House of Representatives, Cayetano Coll y
Cuchí, recognized it immediately. "We knew perfectly well that the soul
of a people is incarnated in its language. We would have preferred being
without a country, to losing our native tongue. On this issue we joined
battle, and my friends and I threw ourselves into the fight."[6]

It was more like trench warfare. In 1902, the Official Language Act
(a component of the US Foraker Act) declared that all insular governmental departments, courts, and public offices would use English as a
"coequal language." Then the US-appointed commissioner of public
instruction ordered that all school children must start the school day
saluting the American flag, declaiming the Pledge of Allegiance, and
singing the national anthem (in English).[7] Finally, in 1909, the commissioner decreed that speaking Spanish was "forbidden" in all public
schools and that everyone—both teachers and students—could be dis-
ciplined for violating this rule.[8]

For a while, the English attack worked. On an island where most people lived and died within a twenty-mile radius, everyone struggled to learn a language spoken a thousand miles away.

Then something akin to *The War of the Worlds* occurred. In that novel, Earth is powerless to stop an alien invasion until the humblest creatures, bacteria, destroy the aliens and save mankind from extinction. In a similar fashion, the children of Puerto Rico got fed up with bad report cards and simply stopped going to school. Even under the threat of expulsion, they still refused to attend—anything was better than going home with a D in every subject and catching a beating from their parents. In this manner, children aged six, seven, and eight succeeded where the adults failed.[9] As of 1915, English was still the official language in Puerto Rico's high schools, but Spanish was restored in the grammar schools.[10]

Coincidentally, *The War of the Worlds* was published in 1898, the same year that the United States invaded Puerto Rico.[11]

CHAPTER 4

The Green Pope

From the air, the narrow coastal plain of southern Puerto Rico looks like an irregular green ribbon. It contrasts sharply with the blue waters to the south and the craggy mountains to the north. During the early 1900s, sugar cane, many miles of it in every direction, covered the plain. A railroad cut through the cane, running parallel to the sea and linking the towns along the southern coast.

Most people lived in shacks along that railroad, in barracks and houses around the plazas of the sugar haciendas, or in company towns built near the monster cane-grinding mills. The mills were the most conspicuous landmarks: their chimneys cast long shadows over the shacks and across the cane, exhaust plumes rising hundreds of feet into the air. From far away, the workers' shacks looked regular and neat. The thatched roofs, the waving palms, and the nearness of the sea seemed almost picturesque.

Up close, however, the villages told a different story. Tin cans, paper, coconut husks, and cane trash littered the hard and dusty ground. The houses were patched with old Coca-Cola signs, boards torn from packing cases, and cardboard. Only a few were painted. Inside, large families crammed into tight living spaces. Curtains draped over laundry lines divided houses into two, three, or more sections.

These villages were all bunched around the *colonias*, the great farms of the corporations that controlled 98 percent of the cultivated land in the municipality of Santa Isabel.[1] The largest farm was Colonia Florida, with its own company store, thirty-six two-room shacks, a two-story house for the *majordomo* (overseer), and two barracks left over from the days of slavery.

In southernmost Santa Isabel a cluster of houses on the sea and along the Ponce and Guayama Railroad and the Central Canovanas Railroad link resembled hundreds of other "line" villages on the southern coast: it had six small stores, no church or post office, and no electricity or running water. Its residents' entire lives revolved around and depended on one thing: the cutting of sugar cane.

At 5 a.m., six days a week, Santa Isabel was still and barren. The roosters crowed, dogs barked, and the surf sounded softly a few hundred feet away. The shacks were shut against the night air, as an easterly breeze stirred the cane and rattled the Coca-Cola signs.

An hour later, the village came to life. Shutters swung open, and tendrils of smoke curled from outdoor stoves on which fresh coffee boiled. Men moved from the thatch shacks along the railway toward the old haciendas to get their daily work orders. Some worked as *macheteros* (sugar cane cutters); others were cultivators, seed cutters, *vagoneros* (oxcart loaders), or *fulgoneros* (railcar loaders). Every *fulgonero* hoisted more than 50,000 pounds of sugar cane onto a railway car every day with his bare hands.

Like many barrio elders, Don Tomás was a *palero* (ditch digger), the highest-skilled and best-paid job in the fields. Another old man, Don Daniel, liked to plant seed—a curious choice for such a tall man because seeding required him to bend over continuously, setting and trapping the seed (which was not a seed at all but a cutting of cane stalk) into place. Twelve-year-old Julio Feliciano Colón was a cutter, the most backbreaking work of all. Every dawn he set out to *defenderse*—to fend for himself and his family. Every evening he came home drenched from head to toe with sweat.[2]

Sugar cane cutter, also known as a machetero
Courtesy of the Library of Congress

Six days a week, Julio and a line of men stood before the cane like soldiers before an enemy. They seemed tiny but implacable, cutting fifteen-foot stalks with their machetes, each man cutting over 1,000 pounds of cane per hour. They lopped off the leaves, cut the stalks in halves or thirds, and dropped the pieces behind them. Every two or three hours, they'd load the cane onto the oxcarts. By the end of the day, the cane fragments would stick to their skin.

The cane choked off any breeze, and the soil radiated heat like an oven. Julio would sweat profusely all day as he grunted and strained alongside the oxen. Crane flies and gnats flew into his mouth when he spoke, and he spat them out like coffee grounds. Mosquitoes bit his eyelids, nostrils, lips, and gums and flew into his ears like buzzing jets. But Julio did not complain.

His father had been a *palero*, but he'd died four years earlier. Now Julio woke up and faced the cane to help feed his mother and younger brother. He hadn't planned it that way; he'd been a good student, particularly in mathematics and geography. Every few weeks the schoolmaster would raid the cane fields, grab Julio and other truant boys, and haul them back to the schoolhouse. It didn't matter; the next day, Julio would be cutting cane again.

He worked for $4 a week and spent most of it at the Colonia Florida company store, where all the food was dispensed through shaded windows, so he couldn't watch it being weighed. He knew he was being cheated.[3]

Julio ate rice and beans, salted cod, and plantains. Sometimes he was able to afford *carne molida* (ground beef). Mostly he was glad that his mother and brother had food. That was the main thing. His mother took in laundry and sewed blouses every day in their one-room shack, but she earned only fifty cents a week for her needlework.[4]

Every man in the village of Santa Isabel worked in the cane fields. They learned to use a blunt machete as toddlers, to catch land crabs as children, and to cut cane as teens. The few who managed to escape either ended up in jail or were never heard from again, as if the earth had swallowed them up.

While sweating in the fields, the men spat out mosquitos and joked to keep their spirits up. The younger ones talked of revolution. One claimed that he would kill ten Yankees, then buy new shoes. Another dreamed of buying better rum. One joked that he planned to save his money and start a child labor factory. A fourth bragged that he would marry Greta Garbo. When asked his plans for after the revolution, Don Tomás replied, "I am a *platónico*. I grow too old for the señoritas." The older men threatened to report everyone to the *majordomo*.[5]

Don Tomás explained that their revolution could never succeed because of the Green Pope, a man who sits in an office with millions of green dollars at his command. He lifts a finger and a ship starts or stops. He says a word, and a republic is bought. He sneezes and a president, general, or Supreme Court judge falls. He rubs his behind on his chair, and a revolution breaks out. Puerto Ricans, Don Tomás admonished, had to fight this man. But no one knew who or where he was. And even if they did find and kill the Green Pope, a hundred others would replace him.

‿

Don Tomás was not far off. Shortly after the US invasion, Hurricane San Ciriaco, one of the largest in Caribbean history, destroyed thousands of Puerto Rican farms and nearly the entire 1898 coffee bean crop. Of 50 million pounds, only 5 million (10 percent) were saved.[6]

American hurricane relief was strange. The United States sent no money. Instead, the following year, it outlawed all Puerto Rican currency and declared the island's peso, with a global value equal to the US dollar, to be worth only sixty American cents.[7] Every Puerto Rican lost 40 percent of his or her savings overnight.[8] Then, in 1901, a colonial land tax known as the Hollander Bill forced many small farmers to mortgage their lands with US banks.[9]

But with no laws restricting usury, interest rates were so high that within a decade, the farmers defaulted on their loans, and the banks foreclosed. These banks then turned a diversified island harvest—coffee, tobacco, sugar, pineapple, and other fruits—into a one-crop cash cow. That crop was sugar.[10]

The very first civilian governor of Puerto Rico, Charles Herbert Allen, used his brief tenure to become the King of Sugar. When he returned to the United States in 1901, he quickly installed himself as treasurer and then president of the largest sugar-refining company in the world, the American Sugar Refining Company, later known as Domino Sugar. In effect, Allen leveraged his governorship into a controlling interest in the entire island economy.[11]

In 1922, the US Supreme Court declared Puerto Rico a territory, not a state, and as such the US Constitution did not apply there. This lay the groundwork for denying any rights to work, or a minimum wage or collective bargaining granted to US citizens.[12]

In 1926, President Calvin Coolidge appointed Frederick G. Holcomb, auditor for the United Fruit Company, as auditor of the entire island of Puerto Rico.[13]

By 1930, Allen and US banking interests had converted 45 percent of all arable land in Puerto Rico into sugar plantations. These bank syndicates also owned the insular postal system, the entire coastal railroad, and the international seaport of San Juan.[14]

By 1934, every sugar cane farm in Puerto Rico belonged to one of forty-one syndicates, 80 percent of which were US owned; the four largest syndicates—Central Guánica, Central Aguirre, Fajardo Sugar, and United Porto Rico Sugar—were entirely US owned and covered over half the island's arable land.[15]

By itself, United Porto Rico Sugar owned over 16,000 acres of cane-producing land, four sugar-refining mills, warehouses, harbor facilities, port terminals, railroad cars, and more than one hundred miles of railroad.[16]

With no money, no crops, and no land, Puerto Ricans sought work in the cities. But when the island legislature enacted a minimum-wage law like the one in America, the US Supreme Court declared it unconstitutional—despite AFL-CIO president Samuel Gompers's testimony that "the salaries paid to Puerto Ricans are now less than half what they received under the Spanish."[17]

To make matters worse, US finished products—from rubber bands to radios—were priced 15 to 20 percent higher on the island than on the mainland. Again, Puerto Rico was powerless to enact any price-fixing legislation.[18]

US economic reports labeled this draining of resources from a starving population into the richest country on earth as "a favorable trade balance," and the transfer of wealth did not go unnoticed. Historian Bailey W. Diffie noted in 1931, "Land is passing into the hands of a few large corporations. . . . [T]he sugar industry, tobacco manufacturing, fruit growing, banks, railroads, public utilities, steamship lines, and many lesser businesses are completely dominated by outside capital. The men who own the sugar companies control both the Bureau of Insular Affairs and the Legislature of Puerto Rico."[19] Diffie, a professor at Yale University, also remarked that "practically every mile of public carrier railroad belongs to two companies—the American Railroad Company and the Ponce and Guayama Railroad Company, which are largely absentee owned. . . . Every trolley ride taken by a Porto Rican pays tribute to a foreign owner, about half the towns depend on absentee companies for their lights and power, and more than half the telephone calls go over wires owned by outsiders. . . . [I]t is the absentee capitalist who has made the profit."[20]

In 1929 the *American Mercury* magazine also noted, "The American economy, as introduced by the Guánica, Aguirre, Fajardo and other great *centrales* was based on the million-dollar mill and the tight control of the surrounding countryside. . . . The development of large absentee-owned sugar estates makes Porto Rico a land of beggars and millionaires, of flattering statistics and distressed realities. More and more it becomes a factory worked by peons, fought over by lawyers, bossed by absent industrialists, and clerked by politicians. It is now Uncle Sam's second largest sweatshop."[21]

∽

Back in the cane fields of Santa Isabel, Don Tomás didn't know any Yale professors or subscribe to the *American Mercury*—but he knew everything that mattered. He felt it deep in his bones. It was a tragic wisdom because he was powerless to do anything about it. His life and death, and everything in between, were controlled by the Green Pope.[22]

CHAPTER 5

A Good Career Move

Barceloneta is unique among the many Puerto Rican municipalities: it is the home of a Pfizer factory that produces all of the Viagra sold in North America. Known as Ciudad Viagra (Viagra City), the town reflects a larger relationship between the island and Big Pharma.[1] As of 2008 Puerto Rico was the world's largest shipper of pharmaceuticals, accounting for nearly 25 percent of total shipments. Sixteen of the twenty biggest-selling drugs in the United States are produced in Puerto Rico, and the profits are enormous.[2] North American sales of Viagra exceed $1 billion per year, with profit margins of roughly 90 percent per pill.[3]

Seventy years ago the town had a different industry. Every year, more than 1,000 women walked into the Hospital Municipal de Barceloneta carrying a little suitcase containing a bathrobe, underclothes, slippers, a rosary, and sometimes a Bible. Each woman would talk to a doctor, fill out a few forms, and be assigned to a bed. Two days later she'd walk out with her tiny newborn, the joy of her life.

She didn't know, however, that her tubes had been cut and that she would never have another baby. For decades the doctors in Barceloneta sterilized Puerto Rican women without their knowledge or consent.

Even if told about *la operación* (the operation), the women were not informed that it was irreversible and permanent. Over 20,000 women were sterilized in this one town.[4] This scenario was repeated throughout Puerto Rico until—at its high point—one-third of the women on the island had been sterilized and Puerto Rico had the highest incidence of female sterilization in the world.[5]

This campaign of sterilization stemmed from a growing concern in the United States about "inferior races" and the declining "purity" of Anglo-Saxon bloodlines. Throughout the 1920s and 1930s, Claude Fuess, a history teacher and headmaster of the prestigious Phillips Andover Academy, argued, "Our declining birth rate may perhaps indicate a step towards national deterioration. Among the so-called upper and leisure classes, noticeably among the university group, the present birth rate is strikingly low. On the other hand, among the Slavonic and Latin immigrants, it is relatively high. We seem thus to be letting the best blood thin out and disappear."[6] At its annual convention in 1934, the Eugenics Society of Canada (ESC) advertised the keynote speech by its president, Dr. William Lorne Hutton, as follows: "A Brief for Sterilization of the Feeble-Minded. Dr. Hutton and the ESC advocated the elimination of 'mental deficients,' and of races other than 'intelligent Anglo-Saxons.'"[7] In 1927, the US Supreme Court ruled that the state of Virginia could sterilize those it thought unfit, particularly when the mother was "feeble-minded" and "promiscuous."[8] Ten years later, US Public Law 136 legalized all sterilization in Puerto Rico, even for "non-medical" reasons.[9] In 1928, President Calvin Coolidge himself wrote, "We found the people of Porto Rico poor and distressed, without hope for the future, ignorant, poverty-stricken and diseased, not knowing what constitutes a free and democratic government."[10]

Within this context, Dr. Cornelius Rhoads arrived in Puerto Rico and made a brilliant career move. Born on June 20, 1898, the same year as the US invasion, and the son of an ophthalmologist, Rhoads attended Bowdoin College and Harvard Medical School, where he was class president and graduated cum laude in 1924. A somewhat ungainly man with a thick beard, short neck, and a Charlie Chaplin mustache, he had a brusque manner and spoke few words. After teaching pathology at Harvard, he eventually joined the newly formed Rockefeller Anemia

Commission to set up a "research laboratory" in San Juan Presbyterian Hospital. Shortly after his arrival in San Juan, on the night of November 10, 1931, Rhoads got drunk at a party. He emerged to find his car stripped and the tires flat. When he returned to his lab that night, in a foul mood and still drunk, he scrawled a note to a friend named Fred Stewart, who was a medical researcher in Boston:

> I can get a damn fine job here and I am tempted to take it. It would be ideal except for the Porto Ricans—they are beyond doubt the dirtiest, laziest, most degenerate and thievish race of men ever to inhabit this sphere. It makes you sick to inhabit the same island with them. They are even lower than the Italians. What the island needs is not public health work, but a tidal wave or something to totally exterminate the entire population. It might then be livable. I have done my best to further the process of their extermination by killing off eight and transplanting cancer into several more. . . . All physicians take delight in the abuse and torture of the unfortunate subjects.[11]

The letter was discovered and created an uproar throughout the hospital. An investigation by San Juan district attorney José Ramón Quiñones confirmed that of the thirteen recently deceased cancer patients at San Juan Presbyterian, eight had indeed been in Rhoads's care.

La Democracia and *El Mundo* published a photograph of Rhoads's letter. Copies were sent to the governor of Puerto Rico, the League of Nations, the Pan-American Union, the American Civil Liberties Union, newspapers, foreign embassies, and the Vatican. They were offered as evidence of systemic and lethal US racism toward Puerto Ricans.

Rhoads called his letter "a fantastic and playful composition, written entirely for my own diversion." His peers laughed along with him. Rhoads was never indicted and suffered no professional consequences for his actions. Throughout his long career, he supervised a staff of several hundred chemists, technicians, statisticians, librarians, and laboratory assistants. During World War II, he was commissioned as a colonel and assigned as chief of medicine in the Chemical Weapons Division of the US Army. He established US Army chemical weapons laboratories in Utah, Maryland, and Panama, for which he received the Legion of

Merit Award in 1945. After the war, Rhoads served as an adviser to the US Atomic Energy Commission, specializing in nuclear medicine. He directed the Sloan-Kettering Institute, where he supervised all research related to Department of Defense radiation experiments. In the early 1950s, his Sloan-Kettering team began a multiyear study of postirradiation syndrome in humans.[12] Many Puerto Ricans, to their astonishment, realized that "exterminating eight Puerto Ricans and transplanting cancer into several more" had been an excellent career move for Rhoads in the long run. It positioned him as a talented biological warrior and created a niche for him in US medical and military circles. In 1949, Rhoads was featured on the cover of the June 27 issue of *Time* magazine.

CHAPTER 6

Cadets of the Republic

Julio Feliciano Colón was not cutting sugar cane today. He was putting on a pair of white pants, black shirt, black tie, and white overseas cap with a Cross of Calatrava patch. He was going to march and drill today as a member of the Cadets of the Republic.

No one forced Julio to become a cadet. He joined because he was tired of cutting cane sixty hours a week for a salary of $4 and because four Yankee companies owned most of the farmland in Puerto Rico. He joined because he was trapped like a caged animal. He joined because a man who gets up at 4 a.m. every morning, climbs a mountain in rain or fog or killing heat, and sweats all day with mosquitoes in his mouth does not need an empire telling him how to live, which flag to wave, what language to speak, and what heroes to worship.

The Cadets of the Republic marched behind two flags: those of Puerto Rico and the Nationalist Party. The Nationalist flag contained a white Cross of Calatrava, used first during the Crusades and later by French revolutionaries. The black shirts were also symbolic, representing a *luto* (mourning) for the colonial condition of Puerto Rico.

Cadets of the Republic march in Lares, Puerto Rico
The Ruth M. Reynolds Papers, Archives of the Puerto Rican Diaspora,
Centro de Estudios Puertorriqueños, Hunter College, CUNY

Founded in 1922, the Nationalist Party of Puerto Rico quickly developed a clear and elegantly simple political platform: the complete and unconditional independence of Puerto Rico from the United States. The party rarely participated in the island's elections, and after 1932 it stopped altogether. Instead, the members devoted themselves to public education, international advocacy, and the development of the Ejército Libertador de Puerto Rico (Liberation Army of Puerto Rico), also known as the Cadets of the Republic.

The Cadet Corps was the official youth branch of the Nationalist Party, created in a public assembly on December 17, 1932, in the Victoria Theater in the town of Humacao.[1] The cadets underwent a full training program that included marching, field tactics, self-defense, and survival. Since they had no firearms, they trained and marched with wooden rifles.

The cadets set up recruiting stations in San Juan, Ponce, Arecibo, and a dozen other towns across the island. By 1936, over 10,000 cadets were marching and training in twenty-one towns.[2] They were divided into fifty companies of two hundred cadets, each with a command structure of sergeants, captains, colonels, and one commander in chief, Raimundo Díaz Pacheco. All of them reported to Pedro Albizu Campos, the president of the Nationalist Party.

The Cadets of the Republic and their mission were modeled on the six-day Easter Rising of 1916 in Ireland. Their objective was not outright military victory (impossible against the United States); rather, they aimed to focus international attention on the colonial status of Puerto Rico.[3] Cadets marched in parades, attended Nationalist, patriotic, and religious events, and drilled twice a week on private farms and in vacant lots. In Río Piedras they drilled on the property of the White Star Bus Company and behind an electric utility plant.[4] In Caguas they trained in the back yard of former Insular Police corporal Rafael Colón.[5] They even had an air force: one airplane owned by Horacio and Narciso Basso, Cadet colonels who hid the plane in plain sight: a Pan American airplane hangar in San Juan.[6] When four Nationalists were killed in Río Piedras on the orders of Police Chief E. Francis Riggs, the Bassos flew their plane over the funeral procession, dropping white lilies and a Puerto Rican flag.[7]

The Cadets of the Republic also had a female component, the Nurse Corps of the Liberating Army, also known as the Hijas de la Libertad (Daughters of Freedom). They dressed in white nurse's uniforms emblazoned with the Cross of Calatrava on the left shoulder. They did not drill or engage in military exercises but instead received instruction from registered nurses and participated in parades and other public events.

Nearly every cadet and nurse, except for the officers, was between fourteen and twenty-five years old. With their wooden guns, weekend drills, and one airplane hidden in a Pan Am hangar, the cadets posed no danger to the US regime. But they did represent a symbolic threat—and so, until the mid-twentieth century, many were shot and killed in police stations and at Palm Sunday parades, in town squares and dark alleys, in broad daylight and at dawn.[8]

SJ 100-3

SECRET

2. Origin

The following summary of facts concerning the origin of the Cadet Organization has been condensed from information provided by FAUSTINO DIAZ PACHECO, NPPR member from 1924 to 1939 and brother of RAIMUNDO DIAZ PACHECO (Commander-in-Chief of Nationalist Army in 1950); AGUEDO RAMOS MEDINA, described in sub-section one above, supplemented by reports from Insular Police and informants.

FBI document showing Faustino Díaz Pacheco to be an informant

The FBI followed them for twenty years and created hundreds of *carpetas* (surveillance files) sent directly to J. Edgar Hoover. The FBI also infiltrated the organization fiercely and with surgical precision, producing in July 1952 a thirty-page dossier covering its entire twenty-year history—including its origin, purpose, funding, command structure, membership, meeting venues, and activities. The dossier provided names, including those of six top leaders and twenty-six cadets, spread across eight municipalities. The in-depth report begins with a striking admission. In bold capital letters, it states that it contains information provided by two individuals: the first was Faustino Díaz Pacheco;[9] the second was Aguedo Ramos Medina.[10]

Faustino Díaz Pacheco was a fifteen-year member of the Puerto Rican Nationalist Party whose brother, Raimundo Díaz Pacheco, was commander in chief of the Nationalist Liberation Army in 1950. In addition, as of 1948, both Faustino and Raimundo Díaz Pacheco were members of the Río Piedras Municipal Board of the Nationalist Party.[11] Aguedo Ramos Medina had been the first commandant of instruction for the entire Cadets organization in 1933.

In other words, the report demonstrates that for twenty years, from its very inception, the Cadets of the Republic (and therefore the entire Nationalist Party) had been infiltrated at the highest levels. The FBI knew almost every decision, every plan, every move that the Nationalist leadership tried to make.

SJ 100-3

C. CADET ORGANIZATION

   1. Official names: "Cadets of the Republic"
                        "Liberating Army"

      According to AGUEDO RAMOS MEDINA, Commandant of
Instruction for the Cadet Organization in 1933, the first
title given to this organization by PEDRO ALBIZU CAMPOS, upon
its formation in 1930, was "Cadetes de la Republica" (Cadets
of the Republic). This title persevered and has been used
interchangeably with the name "Ejercito Libertador" (Liberating
Army). The latter name for the Cadet Organization has been
frequently used by ALBIZU CAMPOS and other NPPR leaders in
official references to the Organization.

FBI document showing Aguedo Ramos Medina to be an informant

☙

In Santa Isabel a young sugar cane cutter, barely in his teens, stepped into a cadet uniform and stood proudly in his one-room shack. Julio Feliciano Colón knew his position in life. He was a *jíbaro*, an honest and hard-working countryman. He was the property of the Green Pope, a man he had never met who controlled every aspect of his life.

But for one day a week, Julio was free: a cadet, a liberator, a man with a higher purpose. He was marching toward a glorious future—or at least one without mosquitoes in a sea of sugar cane. After a few years in the Cadet Corps, he was filled with hope on March 21, 1937—the day of the great cadet parade in Ponce, Puerto Rico. It was Palm Sunday, and families from all over the island were invited.

It turned into a massacre.

CHAPTER 7

The Ponce Massacre

For two years after the inception of the organization, while Julio and the Cadets of the Republic ran up and down hills, marched with wooden rifles, and shouted "Que viva Puerto Rico libre!" no one in the US government could have cared less. Then, in January 1934, the Nationalist Party led an agricultural strike that paralyzed the island's sugar economy for a full month and doubled workers' wages to an average of twelve cents per hour. From that moment forward, the party was under a severe microscope.[1] The FBI initiated round-the-clock surveillance of the Nationalist leadership. An additional 115 Insular Police were armed with carbines, submachine guns, and grenades. Nationalists were imprisoned for "incitement to riot" against the United States.[2]

On October 24, 1935, police shot and killed four Nationalists (including the party's treasurer, Ramón Pagán) in what became known as the Río Piedras Massacre. The incident occurred one block away from police headquarters, in broad daylight, before several witnesses. A stray police bullet also killed an old man named Juan Muñoz Jimenez, who was out buying a lottery ticket.[3] On February 23, 1936, the police executed two more Nationalists—Hiram Rosado and Elías Beauchamp—in the

San Juan General Police Headquarters.[4] Then on March 21, 1937, Palm Sunday, the entire island witnessed the bloodiest event in its history.

THIRTEEN MINUTES OF TERROR

It happened in the town of Ponce, on a pleasant corner of Calles Marina and Aurora, lined with trim two-story buildings and flowery poinciana trees. The Ponce town square, city hall, and several churches were just three blocks away.

The Nationalists had obtained parade permits, and many of them hurried with their families, from all parts of the island, to assemble outside the party's clubhouse in time. By 3 p.m. the street was full with nearly three hundred men, women, and children in their Sunday best, the men in straw hats and white linen suits, the ladies in flowery print dresses, and children playing all around. It looked like a festive after-noon in the park.

The crowd cheered when eighty Cadets of the Republic, twelve uni-formed nurses, and a five-piece marching band arrived in support of the Republic of Puerto Rico. As they approached, bystanders commented on the bright white dresses of the Hijas de Libertad and the cadets' neat white trousers, black shirts, and small caps. Everyone smiled and waved palm fronds, in recognition of the Palm Sunday holy day. Julio Feliciano Colón marched proudly and saluted his cadet leader, Tomás López de Victoria.

Suddenly, the mayor of Ponce, José Tormos Diego, and Insular Po-lice captain Guillermo Soldevilla jumped into the street and told every-one to go home; the parade was over. The permit had been revoked on the governor's orders. The governor had also instructed Police Chief En-rique de Orbeta to increase the police presence and prevent the demon-stration by any means necessary.[5] Two other police captains and over two hundred police officers stood behind Captain Soldevilla. They all wore jodhpurs, riding boots, and Sam Browne belts, as if dressed for a cavalry battle. They also carried Thompson submachine guns, rifles, pistols, and tear gas.

The mayor, the captain, and a few Nationalists argued for a min-ute—until López de Victoria ordered the band to play "La Borinqueña,"

the Puerto Rican national anthem,[6] and everyone started to march—
permit or no permit. The entire gathering sang along and proceeded
joyfully down the street, smiling at friends and family, waving their
palm fronds.

Then a shot rang out. Iván Rodriguez Figueras crumpled like a
rag doll, blood spurting from his throat with each dying heartbeat. It
sprayed a little girl next to him who started screaming. A second shot
cracked, and Juan Torres Gregory, an eighteen-year-old looking out a
window, fell down dead. A third shot dropped Obdulio Rosario, who
was carrying a palm-leaf crucifix. Obdulio's eyes widened, his mouth
flew open, and blood rolled down his chin onto his shirt. His gaze
ranged wildly over the crowd for a moment; then he fell on his face and
clawed outward with his fingers. Everyone stared unbelievingly at the
squirming figure on the ground, as Obdulio lifted himself up with his
arms, like a lizard, and then dropped for the last time. A thick stream of
blood ran down the crushed rock of the roadbed.

Panicked screams and curses erupted as people ran in all directions,
but they couldn't escape because Captains Guillermo Soldevilla, Pérez
Segarra, and Antonio Bernardi, along with two hundred men with rifles
and Tommy guns, were stationed all around them. They blocked every
route and created a killing zone. Then they started firing.

A boy was shot on a bicycle. A father tried to shield his dying son
and was shot in the back. An orange vendor hid behind a statue of Jesus
until a cop ran over and shot him in the head.

Clouds of smoke covered the street as twenty submachine gunners
set their feet and sprayed their ten-pound Tommy guns. An old man
flew upward, still clutching a palm leaf in his hand, his body split almost in two. Another man raised a bible and started to pray until the
shooters blasted off the back of his head in a bright red spray. The bible
went flying, and the dead man dropped like a sack of cornmeal.

The flag bearer of the Cadets was killed. Carmen Fernandez grabbed
the flag and was shot in the chest. Dominga Cruz Bacerríl, who was
visiting from another town, grabbed it and managed to run away.

In a contagion of panic and savagery, the police kept firing. They
shot into several corpses again and again. They fired over the corpses,
as if they didn't exist. Bullets flew everywhere. They hit the pavement,

The Ponce Massacre begins

© TopFoto/The Image Works; photographer Carlos (Aguilita) Torres Morales;
published in *El Imparcial*, April 2, 1937, 16–17

the buildings, the trees, and the telephone poles, filling the air with dust
and grit. One could hear the dense, vibratory *whap* as the bullets tore
into human flesh. The police climbed onto cars and running boards and
chased people down the side streets, shooting and clubbing anyone they
could find.

They shot a young girl in the back as she ran to a nearby church.
They shot a man on his way home, as he yelled, "But I am a National
Guardsman." They split a fruit vendor's head in two with a riot club.
They beat a man to death on his own doorstep. They clubbed fifty-
three-year-old Maria Hernández del Rosario on the head so hard that
her gray matter spilled out onto the street, and people kept slipping on
it. They shot men, women, and children in the back as they tried to
escape. They kicked several corpses to see if they were really dead and

Cadet Bolívar Márquez Telechea, shot dead

Photographer Ángel Lebrón Robles; published in *El Mundo*, March 22, 1937, 5

shot them again if they weren't.[7] A policeman named Ortiz Fuentes shot four men who pleaded for mercy with their hands raised.[8]

The Tommy gunners kept firing, spurting .45s at full cyclic rate from a range of fifty feet. The guns overheated and started to smoke as people fell by the dozen and blood filled the street and spattered the walls.

Cadet Bolivar Márquez Telechea dragged himself to a wall. Just before dying, with his own blood, he managed to write, "Long live the Republic, Down with the Murderers," and signed it with three crucifixes. A few moments later, he stopped moving forever.

The police kept shooting and clubbing for thirteen minutes. By the time they finished, nineteen men, one woman, and a seven-year-old girl lay dead; over two hundred more were gravely wounded—moaning, crawling, bleeding, and begging for mercy in the street. The air seethed with gun smoke. Everyone moved in a fog of disbelief as policemen swaggered about and blood ran in the gutter.[9]

Julio, the young sugar cane cutter, made it home that night of March 21. He had crawled over dead bodies, dragged wounded women and children away from the machine guns, and walked carefully along the back roads between Ponce and Santa Isabel. When he arrived home around midnight, his mother screamed at the sight of his uniform, which was saturated with blood. But Julio had been lucky—he'd only been grazed by one bullet and sustained a flesh wound on his right arm.

Many others were not as fortunate. As the smoke cleared over Calles Aurora and Marina, the following all lay dead:

- Iván G. Rodriguez Figueras
- Juan Torres Gregory
- Conrado Rivera Lopez
- Georgina Maldonado (seven-year-old girl)
- Jenaro Rodriguez Mendez
- Luis Jimenez Morales
- Juan Delgado Cotal Nieves
- Juan Santos Ortiz
- Ulpiano Perea
- Ceferino Loyola Pérez (Insular Police)
- Eusebio Sánchez Pérez (Insular Police)
- Juan Antonio Pietrantoni
- Juan Reyes Rivera
- Pedro Juan Rodriguez Rivera
- Obdulio Rosario
- Maria Hernández del Rosario
- Bolivar Márquez Telechea
- Ramon Ortiz Toro
- Teodoro Velez Torres

Ponce Massacre victims, killed on Palm Sunday

Photographer Carlos Torres Morales, March 21, 1937; published in *El Imparcial*, April 1, 1937, 1

The Cover-Up

After it was all over, Puerto Rico's chief of police, Colonel Enrique de Orbeta, arrived on the scene. He walked calmly through the carnage in a bright white suit, issuing commands. When there was no one left to shoot, Orbeta looked at the corpses in a sea of blood and did some quick thinking. Although he took his orders from Governor Blanton Winship, he and his men had just killed seventeen unarmed civilians and wounded two hundred more.

In order to explain all this, the colonel made a cruel decision. He saw a cameraman from *El Mundo*, Ángel Lebrón, running through the street, photographing everything. He also noticed a police officer, Eusebio Sánchez Pérez, a victim of friendly machine-gun fire. Orbeta called over the *El Mundo* photographer and several of his men, and they choreographed a series of "live action" photos to show that the police were somehow "returning fire" from Nationalists who were, at this point, already lying dead in the street.

The photos were cynical and obviously staged. One of them appeared on the front page of *El Mundo* on March 23, 1937, showing Colonel Orbeta and two of his men scanning the rooftops for Nationalist snipers. Everyone was neatly arranged around the corpse of Officer Eusebio Sánchez Pérez—who had already been killed in the policemen's own crossfire—to suggest that Nationalist snipers had been shooting down at the police and that Orbeta's officers had only engaged in self-defense.

The ruse did not work. Every island newspaper reported that there was no one to exchange fire with; that the cadets, the Nationalists, and everyone in the parade had been unarmed; that their only weapons had been Palm Sunday leaves. In the pages of *El Mundo*, a doctor from a local hospital, José A. Gándara, testified that many of the wounded he'd seen had been shot in the back.[10]

Six days after the massacre, *Florete* magazine ran an illustration by popular cartoonist Manuel de Catalán. It was an exact re-creation of the staged photo with Colonel Orbeta and his two hapless policemen, staring up at the rooftops, looking for nonexistent snipers.[11] The caption under the cartoon read, "Now we can say that they fired at us from the rooftops."

Police Chief Orbeta poses for a photo, "searching" for nonexistent snipers
Photographer Ángel Lebrón Robles, March 21, 1937;
published in *El Mundo*, March 23, 1937, 1

On April 2, 1937, the photographer who took the panoramic shot of the massacre, Carlos Torres Morales, published his own account of what he'd seen that day. He described the massacre as a "mass assassination."[12]

In addition to the still photographers taking photographs, a newsreel director named Juan Emilio Viguié had filmed the entire slaughter from a dark window.[13] Over the next twenty-five years, Viguié would show his thirteen-minute movie clip to private, very carefully selected audiences. It became, in effect, the Zapruder film of Puerto Rican history.

Immediately after the massacre, Governor Blanton Winship blamed it on "Nationalist terrorists," and his Insular Police followed the wounded to Tricoche Hospital in Ponce, arresting them in their stretchers and hospital beds. The Ponce district attorney, R. V. Pérez Marchand, resigned

" . . . y ahora podemos decir que nos dispararon desde las 'azoteas.'"

Caricature by Manuel de Catalán; published in
Florete magazine, March 27, 1937, 11

his post rather than carry out Governor Winship's order to indict the innocent survivors of the massacre, for "murdering" themselves.[14] But his successor, Pedro Rodriguez-Serra, pressured witnesses and family members to sign false affidavits regarding the events of that day.[15]

The island newspapers, especially *El Imparcial* and *El Mundo*, whose photographers had witnessed and filmed the entire massacre, were not so easily pressured. They ran photographs of the scene, showing the bullet holes from the machine guns.[16] Their front pages screamed about the Ponce Massacre and repeated the words of slain cadet Márquez Telechea, written in his own blood:

¡VIVA LA REPÚBLICA!
¡ABAJO LOS ASESINOS!

In El Norte, however, the US newspapers were telling a different story. The *New York Times* wrote that seven Puerto Ricans were killed in a "Nationalist riot" and that sixty-eight Nationalists had been arrested.[17] The *Washington Post* reported that "the battle started . . . when Nationalists fired on police."[18] The *Detroit News* headline read, "Puerto Ricans Riot."[19]

Of the fourteen articles that discussed the massacre in the *New York Times* in 1937, eleven used the word "riot" to describe the incident. Of the nine articles published in the *Washington Post* that year, seven used the same term.[20] Other frequent terms in the *Times* and *Post* were "outbreak,"[21] "battle,"[22] "disturbance,"[23] "political riot,"[24] "March uprising,"[25] "pandemonium,"[26] "liberty riots,"[27] and "lamentable affair."[28] None of the major newspapers—not one—called it a "massacre," "killing," "slaughter," or any of the other words used by the insular press. The largest and most authoritative US press organizations merely regurgitated an established narrative that Puerto Ricans had rioted on Palm Sunday and somehow shot, killed, maimed, and wounded themselves.

THE HAYS COMMISSION

In the weeks following the massacre, it appeared that dozens of Nationalists would be prosecuted, though no one could explain why—perhaps for the crime of getting shot. Governor Blanton Winship told the public that his policemen had acted "with great restraint" and "in self-defense" and that his police chief had shown "great patience, consideration and understanding, as did the officers and men under him." Accordingly no police officer was fired, demoted, suspended, convicted, jailed, or otherwise punished.[29]

The insular press refused to let the governor get away with this charade. They hammered at him and called for his impeachment. Article upon article appeared about the massacre and its aftermath.[30] A political cartoon in *El Imparcial* showed *la mano del pueblo* (the hand of the people) pointing squarely at the governor.[31]

Two months passed. Winship stuck to his story and issued no apology. Finally, the American Civil Liberties Union, led by Arthur Garfield

Ponce Massacre funeral procession
Photographer Carlos Torres Morales, March 28, 1937;
published in *El Imparcial*, March 29, 1937, 5

Hays, conducted a ten-day investigation in Ponce and San Juan. Finally, on May 22, 1937, a throng of more than 4,000 overran the Plaza Baldorioty in the capital, awaiting the declaration of the Hays Commission's conclusions.[32]

Just before sunset, as the electric lights turned on in the plaza, the commission announced three findings:

1. The facts showed that the affair of March 21 in Ponce was a "MASSACRE" (caps theirs).

2. Civil liberties had been repeatedly denied during the previous nine months by order of Governor Blanton Winship, who had failed to recognize the rights of free speech and assembly and threatened the use of force against those who would exercise those rights.

3. The Ponce Massacre arose out of the denial by the police of the civil right of citizens to parade and assemble, a denial ordered by the governor of Puerto Rico.[33]

In its formal summary, the Hays Commission wrote, "When we began our investigation we objected to naming our committee the 'Committee for the Investigation of the Ponce Massacre.' Now that we have heard all the proofs we agree that the people of Ponce had given this tragedy the only title it can possibly have: The Ponce Massacre."

The island newspapers reported the findings immediately. Blanton Winship ultimately lost his governorship in 1939, the Nationalists were all acquitted, and the matter was soon forgotten up north. But the full meaning of the Ponce Massacre was never lost on the people of Puerto Rico, over 20,000 of whom attended the funeral ceremonies in Ponce and Mayagüez.

Seventeen men, women, and children had perished on Palm Sunday, nineteen if you include the policemen caught in their own crossfire. Dozens more had been maimed for life. Hundreds had been wounded. A tragic awareness would soon spread throughout the island: the United States cared more about Nazi war crimes in Europe than murder in broad daylight in Puerto Rico.

The police riot in Ponce, under the orders of Governor Blanton Winship, was an instance of state-sponsored terror intended to cow an entire population into submission—particularly those who wanted independence—with a show of deadly brutality.[34]

CHAPTER 8

It's Only Chinatown

> When you consider, Mr. Speaker, that these gentlemen are sent there to make laws for a country they do not know, for a people whose laws, customs, and language they do not know . . . you may imagine, Mr. Speaker, the probability of their doing well.[1]
>
> —FEDERICO DEGATAU, the first resident commissioner from Puerto Rico, speaking to the US Congress in 1899

The film noir classic *Chinatown* is filled with rape, incest, murder, police assassins, and a massive land grab. It all ends with one of the great lines in American film—"Forget it, Jake; it's Chinatown"—five words that capture the seamy underside of the American dream.

The line also encapsulates America's view of Puerto Rico throughout the early twentieth century. The island was "down there" somewhere. Over 1,500 miles of ocean separated it from Washington, DC; over 1,000 miles lay between it and Miami. There were no televisions or computers, commercial flights were few, and boat travel from New York to San Juan took five days. Even the US Congress took thirty-four years to spell the island's name correctly—as "Puerto Rico" rather than "Porto Rico." Separated by an ocean, a language, and four hundred years of Spanish history, Puerto Rico and the United States existed on the same planet but in two different worlds. The concept of "what happens in Vegas stays in Vegas" was taken much further on the island. As far as the United States was concerned, what happened in Puerto Rico never happened at all.

This attitude was clear when the American press labeled the Ponce Massacre a "riot." It was clear when ownership of most of Puerto Rico's land was transferred to a few US banks. It was clear when a wave of carpetbaggers descended on the island like a plague of locusts.[2] For fifty years, Puerto Rico became the land of second chances: the place where poor relations, family embarrassments, Ivy League alcoholics, and political hacks could seek their fortunes with little or no oversight from up north. After all, it's only Chinatown.

This cavalier view of an entire people was most apparent in the choice of men sent to rule over them: the governors of Puerto Rico, appointed by the president of the United States.[3]

へっ

Charles Herbert Allen was the first civilian governor of Puerto Rico (1900–1901). Though he never served in the armed forces, he loved to dress in military regalia and have people address him as "colonel." He arrived like a Roman conqueror with a naval cannon salute, the Eleventh United States Infantry Band, and hundreds of armed men.[4] He marched through the heart of San Juan and into the governor's mansion.[5]

The mansion was gift-wrapped. Allen delivered his inaugural address behind the largest, most imperial flags that Puerto Ricans had ever seen.[6]

Allen had been a congressman, a US Navy bureaucrat, and commissioner of prisons for Massachusetts. During his one year as governor, he developed a passion for business. It started the moment he set foot in Puerto Rico on April 27, 1900.

Within a matter of weeks, and with little consultation or oversight, Allen created a budget for the entire island.[7] He raided the island treasury by raising property taxes, withholding municipal and agricultural loans, and freezing all building-repair and school-construction funds.

He redirected the insular budget to subsidize US-owned farm syndicates. He issued no-bid contracts for US businessmen and subsidized roads built by agents from his father's Massachusetts lumber business (at double the cost).[8]

Through his "dark room budget," Allen created new agencies, offices, and salary lines—all staffed by US bureaucrats. By the time he left in 1901, nearly all eleven members of the governor's Executive Council were US expatriates, and half the appointed offices in the government of Puerto Rico had gone to visiting Americans—626 of them at top salaries.[9]

But Allen had a larger plan. It was hidden in plain sight, like the purloined letter, within his first annual report to US President William McKinley. First, he wrote,

> Porto Rico is a beautiful island with its natural resources undeveloped, and its population . . . unfitted to assume . . . the management of their own affairs.[10]
>
> The soil of this island is remarkably productive . . . as rich as the delta of the Mississippi or the valley of the Nile.[11]
>
> With American capital and American energies, the labor of the natives can be utilized to the lasting benefit of all parties.[12]

Then Allen appealed to vanity and greed:

> The introduction of fresh blood is needed, and when the American capitalist realizes . . . that there is a supply of labor accustomed to the Tropics and . . . that the return to capital is exceedingly profitable . . . he will come here with his capital.[13]
>
> Porto Rico is really the 'rich gate' to future wealth . . . by that indomitable thrift and industry which have always marked the pathway of the Anglo-Saxon.[14]

Finally, the governor got down to business:

> The yield of sugar per acre is greater than in any other country in the world.[15]

A large acreage of lands, which are now devoted to pasturage, could be devoted to the culture of sugar cane.[16]

Molasses and rum, the incidental products of sugar cane, are themselves sufficient to pay all expenses of the sugar planters and leave the returns from his sugar as pure gain.[17]

The cost of sugar production is $10 per ton cheaper than in Java, $11 cheaper than in Hawaii, $12 cheaper than in Cuba, $17 cheaper than in Egypt, $19 cheaper than in the British West Indies, and $47 cheaper than in Louisiana and Texas.[18]

This was no mere first annual report to the president. It was a business plan for a sugar empire, and Allen quickly staked his claim. A few weeks after handing in this report, on September 15, 1901, Allen resigned as governor.[19] He then headed straight to Wall Street, where he joined the House of Morgan as vice president of both the Morgan Trust Company and the Guaranty Trust Company of New York.[20] He built the largest sugar syndicate in the world, and his hundreds of political appointees in Puerto Rico provided him with land grants, tax subsidies, water rights, railroad easements, foreclosure sales, and favorable tariffs.

Charles Herbert Allen became the Green Pope. By 1907 his syndicate, the American Sugar Refining Company, owned or controlled 98 percent of the sugar-processing capacity in the United States and was known as the Sugar Trust.[21] By 1910 Allen was treasurer of the American Sugar Refining Company, by 1913 he was its president, and by 1915 he sat on its board of directors.[22] Today his company is known as Domino Sugar.

As the first civilian governor of Puerto Rico, Charles Herbert Allen used his governorship to acquire an international sugar empire and a controlling interest in the entire Puerto Rican economy. No one stopped him. Why should they? It's only Chinatown.

෴

On November 20, 1921, the steamer *Tanamo* lurched into New York Harbor with several people screaming on board. A gangplank was hurried into place, and the governor of Puerto Rico ran out yelling, "There's a fire on the ship! They're trying to kill me!" According to the governor, the fire had been caused by "an infernal machine" secreted in the bowels of the vessel by a Puerto Rican patriot with the intention of sending his honor to the bottom of the sea. Some stevedores rushed aboard and, lo and behold, there was a fire in the ship's hold—she sank at the pier the very next day.

It was tremendous news, making the front page of the *New York Times*.[23] No one ever found the machine or the Puerto Rican, but in all fairness, the governor was not delusional. E. Montgomery Reily was the most hated man in Puerto Rico. In four short months, Reily had managed to insult virtually every politician, journalist, farmer, teacher, priest, and bootblack in Puerto Rico. Almost everyone wanted to eliminate him—if not from the world at least from the island. His arrogance and contempt for Puerto Ricans hastened his downfall.

On April 30, 1921, President Warren G. Harding appointed Reily, a former assistant postmaster in Kansas City, governor of Puerto Rico as a political payoff. Reily took his oath of office in Kansas City, then attended to "personal business" for another two and a half months before finally showing up for work on July 30.[24] By that time, he had already announced to the island press that (1) he was "the boss now," (2) the island must become a US state, (3) any Puerto Rican who opposed statehood was a professional agitator, (4) there were thousands of abandoned children in Puerto Rico, and (5) the governorship of Puerto Rico was "the best appointment that President Harding could award" because its salary and "perquisites" would total $54,000 a year.[25]

Just a few hours after disembarking, the assistant postmaster marched into San Juan's Municipal Theater and uncorked one of the most reviled inaugural speeches in Puerto Rican history. He announced that there was "no room on this island for any flag other than the Stars and Stripes. So long as Old Glory waves over the United States, it will continue to wave over Puerto Rico." He then pledged to fire anyone who lacked "Americanism." He promised to make "English, the language of Washington, Lincoln and Harding, the primary one in Puerto Rican schools" (it already was).[26] And he repeatedly referred to Puerto Rico as "these islands."[27]

Reactions to Reily were prompt. *La Democracia* portrayed the speech as "the ridiculous pose of a schoolteacher, of things he doesn't know about. He seems to think we're primitives."[28] *La Correspondencia* agreed that Reily showed "no knowledge of our manner or being."[29] *El Mundo* noted Reily's "hard and threatening tone."[30] *El Tiempo* wrote that Reily intended to "liquidate" the Union Party.[31] From that moment on, *La Correspondencia* lambasted Reily every week, in both English and Spanish. *La Democracia* carried a series of "open letters to Reily," some of them titled "Letter to the Emperor" and "Darling Caesar."[32]

Reily himself stated, "I received a number of letters threatening my life, others telling me to leave the island within 48 hours or else I would be killed, and that if I drove through the streets I would be murdered."[33] In long, rambling letters to President Harding, he wrote that "Porto Ricans are children,"[34] that they could not be trusted,[35] that "every Porto Rican professional politician carries a pistol,"[36] that his commissioner of immigration "is a half-blooded negro . . . the kind of man I cannot associate with,"[37] and that he had fired the treasurer of Puerto Rico because "he lived all the time with a negro woman."[38] In order to maintain law and order among all these children, half bloods, and Negroes, Reily reinstated the death penalty in Puerto Rico.[39]

The month after Reily's boat caught fire, things heated up again. A succession of Puerto Rican leaders steamed up to Washington, DC, demanding Reily's removal because he spent half his time outside Puerto Rico[40] and had recruited five carpetbaggers into the highest (and highest-paid) positions in his administration.[41] These included John R. Hull, the governor's own nephew and private secretary; George S. McClure of Kansas City, the chief of the Puerto Rican "Secret Service"; William Kessinger of Kansas City, auditor; Kessinger's son, an "inexperienced youth," assistant auditor; and a Mrs. Liggett of Kansas City, assistant commissioner of education. Reily had brought all of them down from Kansas City, and none of them had any knowledge of Spanish.[42] When the US Senate requested a record of Reily's appointments, he gave them an incomplete list showing none of these five individuals.[43] He then omitted the entire list of appointments in his annual governor's report for fiscal year 1920–1921.[44]

The fiasco continued when on April 7, 1922, a grand jury in San Juan brought formal charges of "misuse of public funds for private purposes" against Governor Reily, his secretary John Hull, and auditor William

Kessinger. The three men had used the fiction that "Puerto Rico owed the Governor $5,000" to withdraw this amount from the insular treasury. When Reily realized the investigation was serious, he sent a personal check for $1,449.03 to the auditor's office,[45] then fired San Juan district attorney Ramón Díaz Collazo to prevent him from filing the indictment. When the DA argued that he was being removed illegally, Reily had the police forcibly eject him.[46] Then, when the grand jury report was handed to Salvador Mestre, Puerto Rico's attorney general, Reily tried to get him fired as well.[47] The vice president of the Puerto Rico House of Representatives, Alfonso Lastra Charriez, wrote, "If revolution does not come soon, we shall die of nausea at contact with so much filth. . . . I accuse E. Mont Reily the Governor of Porto Rico, and J. R. Hull his private secretary, of obtaining money belonging to Porto Rico for their own benefit, using criminal means. I accuse them of being *thieves*."[48]

Congressman Horace Mann Towner, chairman of the House Committee on Insular Affairs, wrote to President Harding that the grand jury's report and Reily's subsequent actions were "most embarrassing."[49] US Secretary of War John W. Weeks forbade Reily from speaking publicly on political issues.[50] A *New York Times* reporter wrote of rumors of Reily's impending resignation.[51] Another reporter wrote, "The Governor chews gum. He is short, baldish, plump with a dimple. The boys who know him warn you to nail down the furniture."[52] The entire island joined in the fun and dubbed Reily "Moncho Reyes." Suckling pigs, called *moncho reyes*, were barbecued and devoured. Songs and plays about Moncho Reyes were performed throughout the island and caused great hilarity—because *moncho* is Caribbean slang for "congenital idiot."[53] When an entire island is laughing at its colonial governor, it is safe to say that he has outlived his usefulness. It is impossible to subjugate people who are laughing at you.[54]

Reily tendered his letter of resignation on February 16, 1923.[55] In less than two years' time, he'd gone from assistant postmaster to petty thief, caught with his hand in the till. This was the man the president of the United States had sent to govern Puerto Rico.

☙

The cigar, massive ring, waterproof "Oyster" Rolex watch, and colorful shirt and tie combo said it all. He landed in Puerto Rico with all the bluster and showmanship of P. T. Barnum and treated the island like a three-ring circus, and it all exploded in his face. He was forced to resign within six months.

Born dirt poor in the backwoods of Kentucky, Robert Hayes Gore Sr.'s early fortune was built on a gimmick. While working at the *Terra Haute Post*, he began to offer traveler's insurance for one cent a week to the newspaper's subscribers. Within one year, by January 1922, he was selling that same life insurance through 132 daily newspapers, and his 20 percent commission exceeded $100,000 per year (in 2014 dollars, that would be $1.4 million).[56] By 1930, Gore had purchased the *Fort Lauderdale Daily News* for $75,000, acquired newspapers in Daytona Beach and Deland, built a waterfront mansion (the old Angler's Club Hotel on Bontona Avenue), and was developing Florida real estate. In his spare time he wrote a children's fiction series called *Wampus Cat* and *Renfro Horn* young adult mysteries.[57] Life, for Gore, was good.

Then he entered politics. He gave $10,000 to Democratic Party leader James Farley and supported Franklin Delano Roosevelt's presidential bid through his newspapers.[58] In exchange, in August 1933, he received a convenient appointment. As governor of Puerto Rico he could shuttle back and forth to his Florida properties and develop further business around the Caribbean basin. It was a crude but workable political fix. There was only one problem: Gore was a brilliant businessman but one of the most inept governors in the history of Puerto Rico.

The *Nation* reported, "When he was appointed, Mr. Gore was not quite sure where Puerto Rico was. After a talk with him, it is clear that he is still confused on this point."[59] Before taking office he said to the president of Cuba, Gerardo Machado, of the anti-American sentiment and agitation there, "Unless you put an end to these outrageous goings-on here, the United States Government will send an army to do the job for you."[60] Machado telephoned President Roosevelt to inquire about this imminent invasion.

In 1933, Gore went to the Chicago World's Fair and told the press that Puerto Rico should become a US state.[61] The Department of War sent him a furious telegram, reminding him that "Puerto Rico is not even approximately prepared for statehood" and that statehood "is a policy matter for the War Department, the President, and Congress. The whole point of naming an American as Governor, not a Puerto Rican, was precisely to avoid this kind of political pitfall."[62]

FDR appointed Gore on April 29, 1933. Upon arriving in Puerto Rico on July 23, Gore announced his political program. He proposed an international cockfighting carnival in order to boost tourism.[63] He wanted all "disloyal" teachers removed from the school system on grounds of treason.[64] He wanted less Spanish in classrooms and preferably none.[65] He wanted Education Commissioner José Padín removed immediately because he was too "pro–Puerto Rican."[66] He wanted political appointees to provide him with an undated letter of resignation so that he could fire them at will.[67] He wanted Puerto Rican workers to relocate to Florida, especially to Fort Lauderdale.[68] He wanted Puerto Rico to produce large quantities of rum.[69] He wanted to train nightingales to sing the "Star Spangled Banner" and sell them in Texas for $50.[70]

The reaction to Gore's program was less than enthusiastic. Two thousand students paralyzed the University of Puerto Rico and marched to the governor's mansion carrying a casket, demanding his resignation. A bomb went off at the governor's summer home in Jajomé Alto. Four sticks of dynamite were found in the governor's mansion. *La Democracia* wrote, "Mr. Gore will disappear from Puerto Rico as a liar, for his incompetence, for his vindictiveness, for his fantasy, for being useless, for his ineptness, for his stupidity," and a Puerto Rican senator published an editorial titled "Governor Gore You Are a Damn Liar."[71]

When an agricultural strike broke out in November 1933, Gore was utterly incapable of slowing it down. By January 1934, it had spread throughout the entire island. Alarmed US corporations and sugar syndicates formed the Citizens Committee of One Thousand for the Preservation of Peace and Order and cabled President Roosevelt that "a state of actual anarchy exists. Towns in state of siege, police impotent, business paralyzed."[72]

Gore announced that someone was trying to poison his family and demanded that the FBI investigate all of his detractors, including senators, editors, students, labor leaders, sugar cane workers, and the chef in the governor's mansion. The request was declined, but the

War Department sent the president of Dartmouth University, Dr. Ernest Hopkins, to make sense of the situation. Hopkins's report sealed Gore's fate: "Robert Gore is probably the worst blunderer that ever came along. . . . He has the genius for doing things wrong and has a feeling of hostility or suspicion towards anybody not connected with the political group with which he is working."[73]

On January 12, 1934, President Roosevelt accepted Gore's resignation. He had lasted only six months and was physically and emotionally broken, but he did win one moral victory. Before he left the island, Gore uprooted the prized orchids from the inner patio of the governor's mansion, smuggled them back to Fort Lauderdale, and planted them around his house.[74]

☙

While ex-governor Gore was pulling out the orchids at the governor's mansion, President Roosevelt was pulling out his hair over Puerto Rico. A new labor union, the Asociación de Trabajadores de Puerto Rico (Workers Association of Puerto Rico) was demanding twelve cents an hour for its workers. The island-wide agricultural strike wasn't slowing down. The Citizens Committee of One Thousand for the Preservation of Peace and Order was in a panic, sending endless telegrams to Roosevelt about "paralyzed" business and exploding "anarchy." Despite his New Deal program of "relief, recovery, and reform," Roosevelt took a different approach to Puerto Rico.

Roosevelt listened to the Citizens Committee and the people clamoring for a "strong" governor, a military man who could "straighten things out in Porto Rico."[75] To restore law and order, he appointed General Blanton Winship, a retired army general from Macon, Georgia. Unfortunately, in the words of one Puerto Rican senator, Winship was "the most disastrous governor that Puerto Rico has had in this century."[76]

Winship's two primary legislative proposals were to plant gardens throughout Puerto Rico and to reinstate the death penalty. The latter went nowhere. Capital punishment was abolished in 1929 and never reinstated.[77]

From the moment he arrived, General Winship proceeded to militarize the entire island. He urged the building of a $4 million naval air

Governor Blanton Winship
Courtesy of the Library of Congress

base,[78] the cost of which ultimately ballooned to over $112.5 million.[79] He created new, vigorous police-training camps and spent his weekends touring them, along with every US military installation.[80] He also added hundreds of men to the insular police force, equipping every unit with machine guns, tear gas, and riot gear, and painted their cars a suggestive new color: blood red.[81] Winship also conveyed power and authority through the adroit use of police uniforms, which resembled those of World War II military officers.[82]

The man FDR sent to solve "the Puerto Rican problem" was uninformed about economics and legislative procedure, but he clearly understood power, force, and fear. The general's solution was similar to Jonathan Swift's in "A Modest Proposal": to cure the Irish problem, Englishmen should eat Irish children, preferably with succulent sauces as the tots were rather bony.

General Winship was not sent to Puerto Rico to negotiate. He was sent to crush labor strikes, subdue Nationalists, and kill them if necessary.[83] It didn't take long before he did just that.

THE RÍO PIEDRAS MASSACRE

On October 24, 1935, University of Puerto Rico students held a meeting to discuss their relationship with Pedro Albizu Campos and the Nationalist Party. To ensure a "peaceful" gathering, General Winship's police surrounded the campus in Río Piedras and stationed themselves on every street corner with carbines, tear gas, and machine guns.

At 10:30 a.m., before the meeting started, several police cars intercepted a Willis-77 sedan, license plate 6268, with four Nationalists inside. Two policemen jumped onto the running boards and ordered the driver to proceed slowly to a nearby police station. One block from the station, on Calle Arzuaga, several more police cars pulled up, a squad of officers surrounded the car, and all of them started shooting.

A Cadet of the Republic named José Santiago Barea ran toward the car and was killed instantly. Three Nationalists, Ramón S. Pagán, Pedro Quiñones, and Eduardo Rodríguez, were gunned down inside the vehicle. An old man named Juan Muñoz Jiménez was also shot and killed. Jiménez wasn't a Nationalist; he was out buying a lottery ticket.

The entire island was outraged.[84] Speaking to 8,000 mourners, Albizu Campos accused General Winship and his chief of police, Colonel E. Francis Riggs, of "deliberately murdering the Nationalist representatives of Puerto Rico."[85] Since Ramón S. Pagán had been treasurer of the Nationalist Party and had recently exposed a plot to assassinate Albizu Campos, this was no hyperbole.[86] Four days after the massacre, Police Chief Riggs stated in several major newspapers that he was ready to wage "war to the death against all Puerto Ricans."[87]

On the quiet Sunday morning of February 23, 1936, Riggs got his war. As a Yale-educated gentleman, member of the Scroll and Key, and heir to the Riggs National Bank fortune, perhaps he felt invulnerable. But after engineering the Río Piedras Massacre, he was ripe for retaliation. As he returned home to the El Escambrón luxury resort, two young men approached. Hiram Rosado shot and missed; Elías Beauchamp killed him instantly.[88] The police arrested Rosado and Beauchamp, took them to the San Juan District Station, and summarily executed them within an hour.[89]

**The newly militarized Insular Police,
armed and trained by Governor Blanton Winship**

The Erasmo Vando Papers, Archives of the Puerto Rican Diaspora,
Centro de Estudios Puertorriqueños, Hunter College, CUNY

General Winship took immediate personal command of all Insular Police. Later that evening two more Nationalists, Angel Mario Martinez and Pedro Crespo, were shot and killed by police in the town of Utuado.[90] Other Nationalists "disappeared" and were never heard from again; these became known as *los desaparecidos*. The next day, thousands of mourners from all over the island flocked to San Juan in a massive outpouring of grief and support. Winship tried to stop the marchers, but there were simply too many of them.[91] *El Imparcial* ran a story and the headline read "Go Ahead and Shoot. Then You'll See How a Man Dies.":

DISPAREN PARA QUE VEAN COMO
MUERE UN HOMBRE

At the funeral services for Rosado and Beauchamp, Albizu Campos declared, "The murder at Río Piedras was his work . . . General Blanton Winship, who occupies La Fortaleza. Cold-blooded murder, to perpetuate murder as a method of government, is being carried out by the entire Police Force."[92] General Winship countered with his own front-page funeral for Police Chief Riggs. One of the pallbearers, Police Captain Guillermo Soldevilla, would later lead the police slaughter at the Ponce Massacre.

POLICE RAIDS

After the assassination of Police Chief Riggs and the four Nationalists, General Winship unleashed a reign of terror across the island.[93] The day after the bodies were buried, on February 25, he repeated his call for capital punishment in Puerto Rico. He even convened a press conference to promote this demand, announcing, "I have recommended the passage of a death penalty to the legislature of Puerto Rico. This is absolutely necessary, in order to combat the wave of criminality on this island. . . . I will enforce law and order in Puerto Rico no matter what the cost."[94] The next day, on February 26, those same newspapers showed full-page photos of bloody clothes recovered from the corpse of Elías Beauchamp.[95]

As a lifetime military man, Winship moved forward in the only way he knew how. He hired more Insular Police and instructed them to raid Nationalist homes and offices and to arrest Nationalists throughout the island. Albizu Campos received death threats and relocated to the town of Aguas Buenas, where he posted a round-the-clock guard that repelled four assaults by police and FBI agents. Eventually, documents and recordings of Albizu's speeches were seized by the Insular Police and submitted to a federal grand jury.[96]

Winship's policemen, National Guardsmen, undercover detectives, FBI agents, military intelligence personnel, and several attack dogs packed the José Toledo Federal Building when Albizu and six Nationalists were convicted of conspiracy to overthrow the US government.[97] Officers with blackjacks, tear gas, rifles, and Thompson submachine guns barricaded entire sections of San Juan.[98] General Winship got what he wanted that day: the conviction of Albizu Campos and his removal from the island.

With the Nationalist leadership safely behind bars, Winship grew bolder. He prohibited all public demonstrations, including speeches at funerals.[99] At his discretion and without notice, Winship would declare martial law in random areas; the police would lay siege to those areas, conduct warrantless searches, break into people's homes, and prevent other residents from entering or leaving the zone.[100] Despite this police repression, or perhaps because of it, groups of students began to lower the American flag at public schools and to raise the Puerto Rican flag instead. At the Central High School in San Juan, the police arrested four students "standing guard" over their island's flag.[101]

President Roosevelt had gotten his expected result: the complete militarization of Puerto Rico and the establishment of a police state that could control the population. Then came the Ponce Massacre.

THE PONCE MASSACRE

The Ponce Massacre, the defining event in Blanton Winship's brutal administration, is described in Chapter 7—but it deserves one final review. When the Insular Police gunned down seventeen men, women, and children on Palm Sunday, they were acting under the orders of Police Chief Enrique de Orbeta, who reported directly to Governor Winship. By prearranged placement, Orbeta's policemen completely surrounded the unarmed civilians before the shooting began. This was not "riot control" or "crowd management"; rather, the officers had set up a killing zone—using lethal tactics, manpower, and weaponry—with hundreds of innocents forced into the crossfire. The man who led the operation, Captain Guillermo Soldevilla, had been a pallbearer at the funeral of E. Francis Riggs, the slain police chief of Puerto Rico.[102]

To add insult to injury, Winship then tried to frame the victims, forcing the Ponce district attorney to create false evidence and testimony so that the Nationalists could be imprisoned for murdering . . . themselves.[103] If it weren't for one photograph, which enabled the Hays Commission to see what had actually happened, Winship would have gotten away with it.

A Time to Celebrate

Even though the Hays Commission exposed the Palm Sunday murder of Puerto Rican civilians, FDR did not immediately evict Winship from the governor's mansion. President Roosevelt had fired the last governor; to fire two in a row would be a blatant admission that US colonial policy was failing in Puerto Rico. And so the General stayed on, chasing Nationalists around the island, building FBI files against them, and visiting his military installations.

One year after the Ponce Massacre, however, he pushed the island too far. The United States had first landed in Puerto Rico on July 25, 1898. General Winship decided to celebrate the fortieth anniversary with a massive military demonstration—but instead of doing it in Guánica, the town where the invasion occurred, he decided to celebrate it in Ponce, the town that had suffered the massacre.

The reviewing stand was in Plaza Degetau, just two blocks from the site of the massacre, where bullet holes still pockmarked the battered walls. Winship chose this celebration site to "send a message" to Puerto Ricans, regardless of the personal anguish it might cause.[104]

On July 25, 1938, US Navy cruisers steamed into the port of Ponce, filled with landing forces that marched into the town. Air force planes maneuvered over the town. US infantry paraded past the Plaza Degetau rotunda, where American military officers and police bodyguards stuffed the reviewing stand.

In the middle of the festivities, a Nationalist student, Angel Esteban Antongiorgi, ran up to the platform and fired on General Winship. A National Guardsman leapt in and took a direct hit; he died immediately but prevented the assassination. Antongiorgi was shot down, his body was hastily removed, and the corpse was never seen again.[105]

Despite the assassination attempt, General Winship clung to his governorship for nearly a year with President Roosevelt looking the other way. Finally, on May 11, 1939, Congressman Vito Marcantonio shouted a speech on the floor of the US House of Representatives, listing in great detail "the tyrannical acts of the Governor in depriving the people of Puerto Rico of their civil rights, the corruption and rackets that existed and were made possible only by the indulgence of the

Governor, and the extraordinary waste of the people's money."[106] The next day, FDR removed Winship from the governorship of Puerto Rico.

A PARTING GIFT TO THE ISLAND

Immediately after leaving the governor's mansion, Winship became a lobbyist for the US corporations and sugar syndicates that owned the economy of Puerto Rico. His job was to persuade the US Congress to exempt Puerto Rico from the 1938 Fair Labor Standards Act. He was performing brilliantly until Congressman Marcantonio fired another fusillade on the floor of the US House: "In keeping with his five years of terror in Puerto Rico, he acted the part of the slimy lobbyist, and fought by means fair and foul to have the wage-and-hour law amended so that the sugar companies could pay 12 1/2 cents instead of 25 cents an hour, and thereby gain $5,000,000 a year . . . so that the system of abysmal wage slavery could be perpetuated in Puerto Rico. Up to the very closing days of Congress this kicked-out Governor fought to have Puerto Rican workers removed from the protection of the wage-and-hour law."[107]

Winship was defeated. The workers got their twenty-five cents per hour. Because they worked under brutal conditions, this was eminently fair. It was additionally so because in the years that followed, 62,000 of these workers would serve in World War II, and another 43,000 would serve in the Korean War.[108] They fought in the front lines, with Winship safely in the rear.

The general was never indicted for his deadly actions in Puerto Rico. He was given a comfortable command during World War II and finished his career as the oldest active soldier in the US military. He even prosecuted Nazi war criminals at the Nuremberg Trials for their crimes against humanity.[109]

The hypocrisy of this final assignment was a fitting coda to the symphony of sleaze and slaughter that the United States bestowed on Puerto Rico in the name of good government. Winship was walking tall, waving documents, pointing fingers, trying others for their atrocities. His own crimes had been committed in Puerto Rico, and therefore they didn't count.

After all, it's only Chinatown.

CHAPTER 9

Carpetas

By the 1930s, after a generation of corrupt governors and absentee land-owners, Puerto Ricans started to question the motives of their northern benefactors. A 1929 article in the *American Mercury* stated it plainly:

> The American flag flies over a prosperous factory worked by slaves who have lost their land and may soon lose their guitars and their songs.
>
> Presto, the flag! The one and only. Puerto Rico is now a land of beggars and millionaires, of flattering statistics and distressing realities . . . a factory worked by peons, fought over by lawyers, bossed by absentee industrialists, and clerked by politicians. It is now Uncle Sam's second-largest sweatshop.[1]

This reexamination of American largesse prompted one of the largest police reprisals in modern history. The United States sent General Blanton Winship to "modernize" the Insular Police with machine guns, grenades, tear gas, and riot gear. According to *El Imparcial* and other newspapers, hundreds of FBI agents armed with Thompson submachine guns had deployed to Puerto Rico and fanned out across the island.[2]

Within one year of its opening in 1935, the FBI National Academy began to train hundreds of high-ranking police personnel from Puerto Rico. Five of these went on to become the island's chief of police,[3] who until 1956 was always an officer of the US armed forces with the rank of colonel.[4] On the island itself, Police Chief Colonel Enrique de Orbeta created a "military training program" in 1936 at Fort Buchanan for all Insular Police personnel. This program included "Tommy gun training" from FBI agents.[5] The Ponce Massacre followed on its heels.

The FBI and the Intelligence Division of the Insular Police also shared information. A confidential Intelligence Division document stipulated, "The Commander of the Intelligence Division shall maintain direct contact with the FBI offices in Puerto Rico. The Intelligence Division shall cooperate with all exchanges of information . . . and at all times, it shall cooperate fully with FBI agents in whatever actions these agents undertake."[6] This information was also shared with the US military: the Insular Police compiled 90 percent of the information sent by the FBI to US Army Intelligence.[7] The nature of this information was so invasive that it ultimately spawned a congressional investigation and thousands of lawsuits.

The information was organized into the infamous and universally reviled *carpetas*—secret police dossiers containing detailed personal data. A network of police officers, confidential informants, and FBI agents compiled them longitudinally, over years and decades. They contained a staggering amount of information on over 100,000 people.[8] Of these, 74,412 were under "political" police surveillance. An additional 60,776 *carpetas* were opened on vehicles, boats, organizations, and geographic areas.[9] Over 15,500 people had extensive police files for political reasons—a significant number on an island with a population of roughly 4 million. An equivalent level of political surveillance in the United States would require 10.5 million files for people, organizations, and property and over 1 million extensive files on "political subversives."[10]

The *carpeta* practice was so ubiquitous and widespread that it became a verb in Puerto Rico, as in *te arrestaron* (they arrested you), *te sentenciaron* (they sentenced you), and *te carpetearon* (they carpeted you).[11] A political cartoon from the era captures the public sentiment: A man is

"Yo se precisamente como cortar tu pelo . . .
lo veo aquí en tu carpeta."

Cotham/The New Yorker Collection/
www.cartoonbank.com

getting a haircut. His barber says, "I know exactly how to cut your hair. I see it right here in your *carpeta*."

Over time, the *carpetas* eventually totaled 1.8 million pages. The average file contained roughly 20 pages, but others were more extensive: the file on Albizu Campos filled two boxes with 4,700 pages.[12] The information in *carpetas* included school transcripts, employment history, religious practices, political affiliations, club memberships, bank accounts, property holdings, taxes paid, family and marital records, travel history, auto registrations and license plates, meetings attended, and publications written or received. They also included personal information: friends, business partners, sexual partners, mistresses, gigolos, debtors and creditors, personal letters (intercepted at the post office), recorded phone calls, photos, wedding lists, laundry tickets, and "miscellaneous items."

With regard to Nationalists, FBI director J. Edgar Hoover was typically blunt. In memo after memo, he instructed his agents to uncover anything "concerning their weaknesses, morals, criminal records, spouses, children, family life, educational qualifications and personal activities other than independence activities."[13] According to one memo, Hoover argued this would enhance "our efforts to disrupt their activities and compromise their effectiveness."[14]

This "disruption" was not a passive or abstract affair. Hoover launched a forceful FBI campaign "directed against organizations which seek independence for Puerto Rico through other than lawful means." The marching orders from Hoover were clear: "The bureau . . . is not interested in mere harassment."[15]

His agents responded aggressively. A subsequent memo to Hoover outlines an FBI program of sowing "disruption and discord," "causing defections from the independence movement," and "exploiting factionalism."[16]

This latter memo recommends "the use of handwritten, anonymous letters directed to one group [of Nationalists and *independentistas*] in which the seed of suspicion is planted regarding the real motivation and goal of the other group."[17]

The *carpetas* were used to imprison people, get them fired or ruin their careers, terminate their educations, and permanently discredit them—even if they weren't members of the Nationalist Party. This was especially true after the passage in 1948 of Public Law 53, otherwise known as La Ley de la Mordaza (the Law of the Muzzle or Gag Law), which outlawed any mention of independence, the whistling of "La Borinqueña," or ownership of a Puerto Rican flag.[18]

Even if you didn't whistle or own a flag, you could still appear on a list of "known Nationalists." One FBI list compiled in 1942 contained sixty-three people, all of whom had extensive *carpetas*.[19] At the whim of the governor or FBI director, any of them could be imprisoned merely for appearing "on the list." These individuals included ten school teachers, three professors, a school principal, a jail warden, a tax collector, a justice of the peace, a district attorney, four city councilmen, the chancellor of the University of Puerto Rico, the Speaker of the House of

Representatives, a senator and law professor, the mayor of Caguas, the treasurer and assistant treasurer of Puerto Rico, and a coffee inspector.

For several decades, Puerto Rico's first elected governor, Luis Muñoz Marín, and other members of his Popular Democratic Party used this and other FBI lists to prosecute not only Nationalists but creditors, romantic rivals, annoying journalists, and candidates from other parties.[20] In effect, the *carpetas* became instruments of political and social control. As the next two chapters show, a one-page FBI report from over seventy years ago, which found Muñoz Marín to be "a heavy drinker and narcotics addict," proved the power of these files.[21] The United States used the report to control Puerto Rican politics for nearly twenty-five years.

Eventually the US Supreme Court declared Public Law 53 unconstitutional and struck it down in 1957.[22] A government fund was established in 1999 to assist some of the victims of the *carpetas*.[23] In 2000, FBI director Louis J. Freeh admitted in a House Appropriations Subcommittee hearing that "the FBI did operate a program that did tremendous destruction to many people, to the country and certainly to the FBI." Freeh then vowed to "redress some of the egregious illegal action, maybe criminal action that occurred in the past."[24] Unfortunately, by that time, the damage was incalculable. It extended beyond any individual or group and even beyond the issue of independence.[25] As befits a sun-kissed island with wonderfully fertile soil, Puerto Ricans had been an open, gregarious, cheerful people—but sixty years of *carpetas* and police informants had burned fear, secrecy, mistrust, dishonesty, and betrayal into their collective psyche. The wound may never fully heal.[26]

People

CHAPTER 10

The Governor

Three days after Luis Muñoz Marín first opened his eyes in 1898, the USS *Maine* blew up in Havana Harbor; three months after that, the Americans invaded Puerto Rico. Twenty cannons blazed through the predawn haze, and the world exploded; walls crashed down, and women screamed as twelve warships pounded 1,300 shells into San Juan. The blasts shook the entire city, shattering windows and knocking out electrical lights.[1]

Luis was asleep, but the family cow was out to pasture in the open field of Fort San Felipe del Morro. When Luis's father, Don Luis Muñoz Rivera, ordered the Chinese servant to go out and get her, the servant refused.

"You should be ashamed of yourself," said Luis's mother, Amalia. "By not daring to go, you are denying this baby his milk!"

"If it's such a big honor, why don't you do it?" said the servant.

The cow was left in the field, and the family fled to Río Piedras until the bombing died down.[2]

A few months later, after the Americans took possession of Puerto Rico, Don Luis used his newspaper, *La Democracia*, to criticize José

Celso Barbosa, president of the Republican Party in Puerto Rico. Barbosa was friendly with the incoming Yankees, and his party advocated for eventual Puerto Rican statehood. For two years, strange people and whispered conversations filled Don Luis's house until 3 a.m. For two years, little Luis absorbed it all—until one night he ran to the balcony and yelled, "Death to Barbosa!"[3]

Barbosa was a reasonable man, but his followers were not. On September 18, 1900, one hundred Barbosa men crashed through the doors of *La Democracia* and attacked the printing press with machetes and hammers. With two friends and a few pistol shots fired into the air, Don Luis defended his newspaper—but the press, the galleys, and type fonts were all destroyed.[4] Moustache bristling, eyes glowering, muscles knotted in his neck, Don Luis wanted to kill someone. But he had a family to protect, so they moved to the neighboring town of Caguas. Then, in April 1901, Don Luis and his family boarded the USS *Philadelphia* and moved to New York City.

ᏋᎥ

Pier 9 teemed with horses, fruit salesmen, beggars, and rats. A scar-faced gentleman grabbed one of their suitcases until Don Luis beat him away; the smell of rotting vegetables followed them into the Battery Park trolley hut, from which they took the Ninth Avenue streetcar uptown.

As they rolled through a canyon of tenements, little Luis saw a bakery stuffed with provolone logs and prosciutto hams, women dressed in black, and children everywhere—leaning out the windows, running through the streets, throwing rocks at each other. Amalia held Luis tight and covered her nose. Every street was lined with garbage, horse manure, rotting vegetables, ash, broken furniture, and debris of all kinds.

Don Luis took the city by storm. He looked like a fighter, drank like a sailor, and, with his fierce moustache and fiery rhetoric, became a Don Juan–esque figure in the New York social scene. He leased an armory and started another newspaper, the *Puerto Rico Herald*. He published a book of poetry titled *Tropicales* and met other expatriates at the Café Martín. He found time for theater, boxing matches, and nightlong arguments about art, love, and politics. He became a regular at Koster and Bial's Music Hall and received (and honored) engraved invitations to the Seven Sisters brothel on West Twenty-Fifth Street.[5]

The don was a good businessman. Even as he roared like a lion, demanding the independence of Puerto Rico in his own newspaper, he accepted a job lobbying for Puerto Rico's largest plantation owners to convince Washington to expand their export quotas. When asked about this contradiction, he simply said, "I'm a patriot, not a Communist."[6]

⁂

Through her connection with the Daughters of the American Revolution, Amalia secured Luis's admission to the Collegiate, the oldest school in America—even older than Harvard—which had educated four centuries of the nation's elite, its senators, bankers, and industrialists. Students do as they're told at Collegiate—so when Luis Muñoz Marín forgot to bring his crayons to art class and was told to stand in a corner and keep quiet, he did just that. But Luis had to use the bathroom. Urine trickled down his leg and flowed in a long, hot rivulet, all the way to the art teacher. Every head in the classroom turned and stared. His face grew hot as the boys started to titter, then laugh, then shout at the skinny boy with the funny accent from an island called "Porto Rico" who had just peed on the floor.[7]

All the way home that afternoon, Luis cried and cursed his schoolmates. No one had ever treated him like this in San Juan. He missed the *jíbaros* of his island, the mountain peasants who wore straw hats, ate dried codfish, and acted funny. He missed the *flamboyán* trees and the multicolor sunsets. He missed the sound of the ocean. His family had traded one island for another, and the second one was much uglier. Worst of all, Luis always felt alone. He had with him no brothers, no sisters, and no friends. His life had no roots. It was filled with chaos.[8]

There was one consolation for Luis: the city itself. He could feel it breathing and growing, right under his feet. New York was dangerous, magical, shooting in every direction, even while he slept. Daimler motor cars prowled the streets. Telephones were everywhere, with hand-cranked magneto generators. Steam-powered elevators lifted him one hundred feet in the air, and his apartment building was twelve stories high.[9]

His mother bought him stunning outfits: suits with knee-length trousers, patent leather boots, tailored pea coats festooned with American military symbols—eagles, stripes, anchors, stars. So to all outward appearances, Luis was a budding member of the American bourgeoisie.

But his father had other plans. He rushed home from a meeting at the Café Martín one night and announced, "We're returning to Puerto Rico." They steamed back to the island, and within two weeks the don had started the Union Party, committed to Puerto Rican independence.[10] One month later, in November 1904, the Unionists defeated the Republicans (who favored eventual statehood for the island) by a margin of 89,713 to 54,092 and captured the Puerto Rican House of Delegates. With his newspapers and his new party, Don Luis was now the most powerful politician in Puerto Rico.[11]

Luis stood next to his father on the balcony of their home, overlooking the Plaza de Armas in Old San Juan. He had never seen such a crowd. Nearly everyone in San Juan was there, all crushed together on the cobblestone streets, on the plaza's dirt paths, over the grass, under the ceiba trees, past the town hall—a great mass of humanity over a quarter mile long, all the way out to the sea. Everyone waved at the balcony, laughing, singing, yelling, "¡Que viva Puerto Rico" and "¡Que viva Don Luis!"

It wasn't an inauguration, it was a massive party, and the crowd roared for a speech. Don Luis took one step forward, and the roar shook the entire town. Someone lit a firecracker, and for a moment Luisito thought they wanted to kill him—but when Don Luis raised his hands and called to the sweating crowd, his voice booming through the Plaza de Armas, past the battlements of El Morro, and out over the eternal sea, the little boy realized that somehow, in this chaos of a life, his father had become a hero.[12]

⁊

In 1905, when Luis began first grade in Santurce, every subject was taught in English. It didn't matter that most Puerto Ricans, including the teachers, didn't speak that language. The Official Language Act of 1902 banned Spanish in public schools because it was no longer the language of Puerto Rico. And so, six-year-old Luisito, who had spent three years in New York City, knew more English than every student (and half the teachers) in the William Penn Public School.

His classmates hated him for it. When he skipped to the third grade, they said *papi el politico* had pulled some strings for him and kept laughing behind his back. This was nothing new for Luisito. They had laughed at him in New York; they now laughed at him in Puerto Rico. He was an outsider everywhere he went, a stray leaf in the winds of his father's political career.[13]

His only friend was a place. They summered in Barranquitas, his father's hometown, where his grandfather had been the mayor. They had an old wooden house called Casa del Cielo and a splendid garden filled with avocado, almond, and lemon trees. The town nestled into the Cordillera mountain range, where the houses formed an enormous staircase, all the way up two mountains, and the roofs tumbled together like blocks, with flowers and grass growing right on them, blue feathers of smoke waving from their chimneys, and occasional palm trees sticking up between. The streets wound back and forth in picturesque patterns, climbing the mountains and the neighboring hills.

Every night, Luisito listened carefully to the night insects—the clamor of the coquí, the choir of crickets, the dirge of the toads, the rubbing of winged violins, the mooing of a great cow that sometimes lay in the moonlight, just beneath his window, breathing and chewing her cud.

He loved the lazy noises that floated up every morning: roosters crowing, pigs grunting, burros giving great racking sobs, old men playing dominos, women singing, the wail of babies. But most of all, he loved riding a little horse called Rocinante.[14] Every day, Luisito braved the thin mountain roads and the white dusty streets of the town. He even went where streets ended: along the burro paths between straw huts, where toothless barefoot women pounded their laundry and children stared at him with glassy eyes. Many of them were alarmingly skinny, and when they laughed, it seemed that their skin would crack open and expose their bones.

Luis stopped to hear the *jíbaros* tell their stories. They told him the secrets of the mountain, the trees, mysterious ghosts and fairies, and a mail carrier named Salto Padilla who fell down a waterfall. Luis felt at home among the *jíbaros* and their natural world. He spoke to the trees, and they answered him. He carried a little notebook, and one day he wrote,

> I understand and I smile
> I sing what you would sing
> If you were a poet.
> I know it.
> Because if I were a tree
> My branches would send out shoots like yours.[15]

One Sunday his father arrived from San Juan with a picnic on his back. They walked down the San Cristobal Valley and into the deep woods near the Río Hondo. Far away, Luisito heard the murmuring river and hundreds of little sounds—birds, lizards, the rustling of leaves—sounds full of mystery that he'd never heard. Then it started raining, and instead of running for shelter or back up the mountain, his father laughed and unpacked the picnic. "This is how you live," he said, handing Luisito a slice of ham. The tropical downpour came hard, hitting the leaves like bullets, and drenched Luis, his father, the food, and the valley. Don Luis made jokes, and they laughed, and only the trees heard them.

They were all alone in the world. Luis didn't have to share his father with anyone. The picnic was a rare moment, the finest day in his young life.[16]

After that day in the rain, Don Luis disappeared back into politics. He spent no time with Luisito or Amalia. The picnic was over, buried in the forest of the San Cristobal Valley. Feeling lost with no one to anchor him, Luisito became a horrible student. He failed all his third-grade tests, and a private tutor, Pedro Moczó, wrote, "Luis is bright but very undisciplined." Luis spent his time reading *The Three Musketeers* and *Robinson Crusoe* and daydreaming about becoming a war correspondent or a composer of romantic ballads.

In 1910, Don Luis was elected as Puerto Rico's resident commissioner in Washington, DC—the island's only (albeit nonvoting) member of Congress. The marriage between Luis's parents had deteriorated, so Don Luis moved to Washington, and Luis moved with his mother to a small apartment in New York, at 141st Street and Broadway. The boy's disorganized education continued—with a short stint in a public school, then another private tutor.[17]

In 1911, Don Luis put his foot down and brought Luisito to Washington. He enrolled the boy in the exclusive Georgetown Prep School, the oldest Jesuit school in the nation, known for "building character," demanding "precision," and, above all, instilling "discipline" in every student. It didn't work on Luis. He flunked every class except modern literature and had to repeat the entire tenth grade.[18] When his father returned to Puerto Rico to campaign for reelection in 1914, Luis dropped out of school and joined his mother in New York. He spent a year swimming in Coney Island, dancing in the Happy Hills Casino on 145th Street,[19] and sneaking into Nigger Mike's café in Chinatown, where Blind Tom played the piano and Irving Berlin, the singing waiter, made cameo appearances.[20]

One night he followed Blind Tom to a Hell's Kitchen opium den run by two crooks named Harry Hamburger and Sammy Goldstein and financed by a bank robber named Jim McNally. The house had heavy curtains, embroidered cushions, and deep bunks for the opium smokers, as well as many side rooms for VIP customers. Luis saw a lot of showgirls and businessmen and listened to Blind Tom play the house piano. Luis was fascinated by the showgirls smoking opium behind the closed doors. The multicolored opium lamps charmed him. He even loved the fragrance of the opium itself, its scent of crushed almonds.[21]

The party ended in 1915 when Don Luis won reelection and recalled his son to Washington. He forced Luis to take the high school equivalency exams and enrolled him in a Georgetown Law School night program. True to form, Luis passed only one course. A Georgetown classmate said, "Luis always behaved like a poet. In a restaurant, he would stop eating and stare into space. Sometimes he would get so absent-minded that he'd scratch his nose with his fork."[22] Years later, a roommate said that Luis's opium smoking caused him to itch and scratch incessantly, especially the tip of his nose.

Luis went to "the library" until 4:00 a.m., and his father would wait for him. Many nights, sitting in an old leather chair, he advised Luis to take life more seriously.[23] Don Luis tried to help by hiring him as his personal secretary in Washington. Luis typed and translated letters, helped Don Luis write and practice his speeches, and even corrected his pronunciation. On several occasions, Luis sat proudly in the gallery of the US Congress and heard his father's voice fill the chamber with words written by his son.[24]

On November 3, 1916, Don Luis left for Puerto Rico to discuss the terms of the Jones Act, which would soon give US citizenship to all Puerto Ricans. Two days later a family friend, Eduardo Georgetti, called Luis and his mother. They needed to rush to Puerto Rico right away; Don Luis's gallbladder had burst, and the infection had spread throughout his body. Georgetti paid for expensive treatments, but nothing could be done. Don Luis, only fifty-seven years old, was dying. He had one last wish: that Luis should become a lawyer. "The most important thing in life is your name," he said. "I'm leaving you a good one . . . and now it's your turn. Please become *el licensiado* Luis Muñoz Marín. You'll never regret it."[25]

On November 15, 1916, church bells tolled for the dead. A funeral procession passed through Barceloneta, Santurce, and finally Barranquitas, the town where Don Luis had been born. Hundreds of Unionists, all bearing flags and singing the party's battle song, rode on horseback before the funeral carriage. Two hundred automobiles followed. *Jíbaros* poured in from every town, from every road, from every mountain to pay their respects.

When the procession reached Barranquitas, young girls stood on both sides of the main street, dressed in white with black ribbons around their waists, holding flower bouquets. A chorus of Catholic priests began a solemn chant, pierced by the anguished cries of women and children. The band played "La Borinqueña," the island's national anthem. Then they buried Don Luis.

⁊

When Don Luis was alive, his son's life had been chaotic. When he died, it became even more so—a bottomless "rake's progress." Luis had spent ten of his first eighteen years on the US mainland. He had no brothers or sisters, no sense of home, and no sense of himself or what to do with his life. So he started to throw it away.

He broke down and cried when Eduardo Georgetti opened his father's briefcase. Inside he found meticulously packed items—razors, combs, black ties, a used collar, false cuffs, cuff links—and a checkbook with a balance of $600.[26] Don Luis had died poor, leaving his family in debt. Even his newspaper, *La Democracia*, was in arrears. Luckily Georgetti owned the second-largest pineapple plantation in all of Puerto Rico. He bought a house for the widow Doña Amalia and relocated the offices of *La Democracia* to the residence, insuring a small but steady income for Amalia and Luis.[27]

A few days after the burial, Luis published a grand poem in the literary magazine *Juan Bobo*:

> I would like to be a giant
> to embrace the mountains that he contemplated
> in his boyhood,
> the mountains for which he struggled from his youth onward
> the mountains that sheltered his countrymen, the *jíbaros*,
> and that today entomb his body.
> I would like to be a giant
> to hold close to my chest all these Puerto Ricans
> who keep forever in their noble hearts
> the sacred memory of my father.
> And I would like to be a giant
> to complete the work of Luis Muñoz Rivera,
> the giant of Borinquen.[28]

Two weeks later, "the giant" sailed back to New York with his mother. He didn't struggle for the mountains, the *jíbaros*, or anyone else. He ignored his father's last wish, sold his law books, and refused to return to Georgetown Law School. Instead he decided to become a surrealistic poet. The rake's progress had begun.

Over the next fifteen years, Luis started and abandoned three literary magazines—*Revista de Indias*, *Spartacus*, and *Quasimodo*—and wrote occasional news articles for H. L. Mencken. He used the printing facilities of *La Democracia* to self-publish a book of short stories called *Borrones* (*Ink Blots*). He wrote a play about a morphine addict named Julio Herrera y Reissig that ran for one night and sold only one ticket.[29] He married a writer named Muna Lee, had two children, and abandoned them repeatedly. He shuttled constantly between the United States and Puerto Rico and changed apartments twelve times, living in Manhattan and Staten Island; Washington, DC, and Philadelphia; West Englewood, New Jersey; and San Juan, Ponce, Santurce, Barranquitas, and Guayama.

Half the time he left his wife and children behind. For years, he did not contribute to their support. Muna had to work from the moment she married him.[30] One time he told her, "I'm going out to buy cigarettes; be back in a few minutes," and did not return for three months.[31]

Luis was especially drawn to Greenwich Village. He heard about Edgar Allan Poe starving and smoking opium in the attic of 84 West Third Street while writing "The Raven." He walked past Madame Blanchard's House of Genius at 61 Washington Square South, where the careers of Eugene O'Neill, Stephen Crane, Willa Cather, Theodore Dreiser, O. Henry, H. L. Mencken, and Walter Lippmann had blossomed. Luis had heard Blanchard's complaint that "art is grand and literature is wonderful, but it takes so many barrels of liquor to produce them. This is not a house, it's an aquarium."[32]

In fact, the Village was full of drunks: published drunks, dancing drunks, singing drunks, crying drunks, lying drunks, lurching drunks, running drunks, fighting drunks, important drunks, sneaky drunks, amorous drunks, mischievous drunks, sleepy drunks, and a drunk who flapped his wings and cawed like a seagull. It was the Latin Quarter, the Left Bank of New York, where free love, socialism, Freudianism, imagist poetry, flappers, fops, and fads ran wild on every street. It was a hotbed of nonconformity, where young people in dingy apartments hatched lofty plots to outwit a sordid world.

Luis couldn't get enough of it. For him it was the bohemian life he'd imagined while reading *Robinson Crusoe* and *The Three Musketeers*.[33] He loved the endless parade of poets, painters, prostitutes, pimps, gigolos, gangsters, financiers, frauds, hobos, heiresses, boxers, bank robbers, and the occasional Irish priest. He loved the attics, studios, bars, clubs, and restaurants. He loved the Fourth Ward Hotel, with trapdoors that dropped drunks and dead people directly into the East River. He loved the Hell Hole, where Eugene O'Neill drank with gangsters and the garbage disposal was a pig in the cellar. He loved Club A, the Brevoort, the Cripple's Home, the Dump on the Bowery, Harp House, and Romany Marie, the Moravian fortune-teller from Delancey Street. Luis visited all of them, and his attire—spats, a cape, and a Montana Peak hat—added to the mystique of the "revolutionary poet from Porto Rico."

After Luis's first child was born in 1920, his mother's allowance no longer covered his expenses, so he developed the "Greenwich Village Safari" for out-of-town explorers. The tour was a surrealistic masterpiece, Luis Muñoz Marín's greatest work of art. Years later, as governor of Puerto Rico, he would brag about it in La Fortaleza and offer it as further proof of American stupidity.

He conducted the tour every Saturday, starting with the Washington Square Arch, the House of Genius, the Provincetown Theater, and the Edgar Allan Poe garret on Third Street. Then, if the safari members were rich, he herded them into the Brevoort Café at 23 Fifth Avenue for an aperitif and caviar lunch. If they weren't, they visited a tearoom on Sixth Avenue. For a dab of culture they poked into Fifth Avenue and Tenth Street, where a lawyer named Charles L. Studin threw a "release party" for whatever book had been published that week. Hundreds of hungry Villagers, including Luis, jammed into four rooms for the free food and drinks and gossip. After the Studin party, the real safari began.

Luis led the group past the saloons, greasy spoons, flophouses, chophouses, smoke shops, rag vendors, barber colleges, bookie joints, and Democratic Clubs that bordered the Village and the Bowery. They visited the Palace of Illusions to see Jo-Jo the Dog-Faced Boy, Laloo the East Indian Enigma (who had a small head growing out of his side), and Lady Mephistopheles in a corset, red tights, horns, and tail. Every few minutes Lady M would chase the male patrons around with a bullwhip and lash them savagely when she caught them.

Next came Guido Bruno's Garret at 58 Washington Square South. A Village charlatan who created a layman's dream of the artist's life and crammed it into his loft, Bruno hired pretty girls and hot-eyed young men who declared themselves poets, writers, and painters and behaved like artistic freaks the moment anyone arrived. When Luis and his safari walked in, they saw poets reciting their poems, painters sketching nude models, and young people fighting, kissing, or crying in the bathrooms. "I fried eggs with Walt Whitman," Guido would say, then demand a twenty-five-cent donation to "Bruno's First Aid for Struggling Artists." He also sold a dozen literary magazines, such as *Bruno's Bohemia*, *Bruno's Chap Book*, and *Bruno's Weekly*.

Next on the safari, just a few doors from Guido's, came Romany Marie's Tea Room. Romany was a gypsy fortune-teller who dressed like a wild woman and told everyone that her father had raped her mother in a great forest in Moldavia. Actually, Romany Marie was born on Delancey Street, where her father owned a kosher pickle shop. But her "cold read" fortunes were uncannily accurate, and she split her fees with Luis, so he always stopped in.[34]

The high point of the entire night happened on the border of Chinatown. Luis led everyone to Mott and Bleecker Streets, through a dimly lit building, up some creaky stairs, and into a barely furnished tenement where a white woman named Lulu and a Chinese man named Georgie Yee ran an opium den. Luis would introduce Lulu as a great New England poet, "the next Emily Dickinson." Yee would bow formally, take a long pull on his bamboo pipe, twitch for a minute, then hop around the kitchen yodeling "T for Texas" like Jimmie Rodgers. At that point Lulu would burst into tears, and Yee would grab a knife. Then Luis would announce that Yee had become crazed from the opium and escort his people off the premises.

After this spectacle, Luis would simply walk the group back to the Washington Square Arch and say good-bye. The safari members would all look at each other, hug Luis, and jam a walloping tip into his hands for the most exciting day of their lives. After it was all over, Luis would head back to Chinatown. He'd pay Lulu and Georgie Yee, take a hit off Yee's opium pipe, and go home to the wife and kids. Sometimes he'd stay at Georgie Yee's, spend all the money, and go home broke.[35]

☙

In 1923, Luis left his wife and children (aged two and three) behind and headed for Puerto Rico to assemble his father's writings into a book titled *Political Campaigns*. He solicited $5,000 "donations" from his father's friends, spent all the money, and never published the collection.[36] The party lasted for two years while Muna raised the children by herself in New York.

After that, Papa was a rolling stone. He rolled to New York in 1925, to Puerto Rico later that year, to New York in 1926, to Puerto Rico later that year, and back to New York in 1927. This last time, he left Muna and the children behind in Puerto Rico. He spent the next four years without them in Greenwich Village.

He spent a lot of time at Georgie Yee's and repeatedly asked his wife and mother for money. After Luis burned through $600 in two months—the equivalent of over $8,300 in 2014 dollars—his mother wrote, "It is time for you to have a normal life." His wife added, "I can't help you in any financial way but I shall be utterly lost and undone if you cannot manage to help us immediately."[37] But Luis sent no money. Muna was on her own.

For a few weeks, he became a Washington lobbyist to get Congress to lower the tariffs on Argentinean grapes. The effort failed, and most of his meager income came from the "Greenwich Village Safari," which he now ran several times per week.

The business picked up when Luis met a Village character named Joe Gould, who added a real flair to the safari. Before the tour began, Gould would lecture everyone about spaghetti, false teeth, insanity, the jury system, Village lesbians, remorse, the size of Mandan Indian heads, and the emasculating effect of the typewriter on modern literature. Then he would sing an old Salvation Army song: "There Are Flies on Me, There Are Flies on You, but There Are no Flies on Jesus." During the safari, Gould would punch authors at Charles Studin's literary parties and tell Romany Marie, "You're no fortune-teller. You're an old Jewish fraud." In Georgie Yee's opium den, he complained about the prices and yelled, "I get better *chandoo* at Jimmy Foo's Laundromat!"

The tips nearly doubled with Joe Gould as a safari guide. But in December 1928, Gould ended the partnership because he felt that Luis was too irresponsible.

છે

Things were getting tight for Luis. He was spending more and more time at Georgie Yee's, averaging five pipes per visit, and he wasn't writing the way he'd planned—rather than poetry or plays, he turned out mercenary little articles at $25 a month for the *American Mercury* and *Smart Set*.[38] Luckily a fellow named Robert Clairmont arrived in Greenwich Village.

Clairmont stormed into New York as "the millionaire playboy" and a perpetual party source. His apartment at 143 West Fourth Street became the Grand Central Terminal of the Village as poets wrote on tables, artists drew on the walls, some guests recited, others discoursed on philosophy, most drank bootleg liquor, and everyone theorized about or practiced love. His parties lasted three days and usually ended with busted lamps, burned tables, and soiled chairs. After a few months, Clairmont grew tired of it all and started eating incognito at Hubert's Cafeteria.

Luis ate there too, before going to Georgie Yee's. He'd heard about Clairmont and devised an investment scheme: Luis and Clairmont were going to open the hottest nightclub in Puerto Rico. With Clairmont's money and notoriety, Luis's knowledge of the island, and constant promotion in *La Democracia*, the idea could not fail. The combination of gambling, beaches, Caribbean rum, music, and showgirls would turn San Juan into the tourism capital of America.[39]

For several months, Luis drew up plans and made inquiries into San Juan real estate. He negotiated with music composer Rafael Hernández and the Trío Borinquen band. He even had *La Democracia* dummy up a fake front page with a story headlined "Casino Clairmont el Nuevo Espectáculo" (Casino Clairmont the New Spectacle).[40]

The moment Clairmont saw the newspaper, he handed Luis $5,000 to continue developing the project. Unfortunately, two weeks later, on October 29, 1929, Black Tuesday rocked Wall Street and wiped Clairmont out. The playboy gave himself one last party, dropped out of sight, and never asked Luis for the $5,000.

Luis sent $500 to his wife, but he didn't return to the island. He wrote to Muna about another literary magazine he was starting with the balance of Clairmont's money. Muna wrote back, "Please stop lying to yourself. Your children need you."

Opium den in New York City's Chinatown, 1925
© Bettmann/Corbis

His wife was right, but Luis kept lounging at Georgie Yee's. Yee was a kindly old man and genial host who offered oolong tea and crackers to his clients. Luis enjoyed the camaraderie and humor of the place and the all-night mahjong games in a separate noisy room. After a few months, Luis just went for the opium. He would lie down on a bunk and rest his head on a blue porcelain pillow. Yee would warm and soften a pill of *chandoo* (he served the highest-quality Fook Yuen) and prepare the bamboo pipe; then Luis would lean over a coconut-oil opium lamp with silver dragons painted on the side and inhale slowly. As the *chandoo* bubbled and dissolved, a luscious magic would fill his lungs. The first few times Luis became thirsty, dizzy, and a little nauseous, but he slowly learned to enjoy opium's effects.

Within a few months, Luis had spent all his money at Georgie Yee's. The old man extended him credit for as long as he could, then in September 1931 finally gave him a jarful of seeds and explained how to plant a poppy field, harvest the opium sap, and distill it into *chandoo*. They parted as friends, and Luis visited him over the coming years. But for the moment, Luis was broke with nowhere to go except back to Puerto Rico.[41]

℘

By 1931, Puerto Rico bore a strong American footprint. All of the island's sugar farms belonged to forty-one syndicates.[42] The banks owned 60 percent of the sugar plantations, 80 percent of the tobacco farms, and 100 percent of the coastal railroads, shipping facilities, and maritime vessels.[43] AFL-CIO president Samuel Gompers reported, "I have never seen so many human beings showing so clearly the signs of malnutrition, nor . . . such an accumulation of misery in one people."[44]

Adding to the misery, Hurricane San Felipe blasted the island in 1928 with 160-mile-per-hour winds, killing over three hundred people, causing $50 million in agricultural losses, and leaving thousands homeless.[45] As if blown by this hurricane, a wave of *jíbaros* descended from the hills, begging for jobs, starving in the streets, and settling in the San Juan slums of La Perla and El Fanguito. In the evenings, fathers and children walked the streets calling, "Leftovers for our pigs!" but everyone knew the scraps were for their families to eat that night.[46]

This was the island to which Luis returned. He sent for Muna and the children, and they all moved into his mother's house, a two-story Spanish colonial on a quiet cobblestone street in Old San Juan. Luis planted his poppy seeds in the quarter-acre patio and garden and harvested them in January.

With $23 a week from *La Democracia* and the authority to publish whatever he wanted, Luis settled into his role.[47] His children were ten and eleven, and he'd spent only three years with them, so this was a great family opportunity. But Luis quickly grew bored, and a different idea took hold.

He saw the reverence across Puerto Rico for his father as one of the leading crusaders for the island's independence. He saw the starving *jíbaros*, the poverty in the streets, and the growing resentment against the United States. He studied the life of William Randolph Hearst, who used his newspapers to run for office and spark a war. He realized that, like Hearst, he had a platform on the little island of Puerto Rico. Luis decided to run for the Puerto Rican Senate.

The headline writers of the Puerto Rican press had a field day: the son of Muñoz Rivera—the failed poet, dilettante, high school drop-out, bohemian wise guy, bon vivant, erstwhile Socialist, heavy drinker, prodigal son, deadbeat dad, and miserable husband—had hijacked his daddy's newspaper to tell the island how to live and what to do. And if that wasn't enough, he wanted to be a senator too. Luis retaliated, calling Puerto Rico "a land of beggars and millionaires" and a factory "bossed by absent industrialists and clerked by politicians."[48]

At the Liberal Party convention on March 12, 1932, when a rumor circulated that Luis was a morphine addict, he mounted the stage and looked directly into the audience. "Throughout the island," he said, "someone has waged a campaign of defamation against me. They are claiming that I take morphine. I don't know who those persons are, but the poison has been spilled. Therefore I now accuse these persons of being ruffians, cowards and dogs. They are probably here right now, in this assembly. Look at them. You know who they are, even if I don't. I am going to stop now so that, if they dare, the ruffians will show their faces. Let the first ruffian rise, and walk up to this podium."[49] The hall went dead silent. The delegates all looked around to see who would move. No one stirred. One man coughed.

A few weeks later, Luis was elected to the Senate.[50]

❦

To Luis's delight, the Puerto Rican Senate was very similar to Georgie Yee's opium den. Con men, gamblers, and thieves paraded through every day, with new and ingenious schemes to raid the island treasury. Lobbyists and lawyers rushed in and out. Roads were built at triple the actual cost. Water companies received exclusive franchises. Week after week the senators got up and said nothing, nobody listened, then everybody disagreed—nineteen dogs barking idiotically through an endless night.[51]

Luis adjusted easily to this farce. He declaimed about "Wall Street vampires" on the Senate floor, denounced "Yankee sugar barons" in committee, and demanded independence for Puerto Rico in *La Democracia*.

Then he went home, spent time with his family, tended his opium plants, and smoked a few weekend pipes. He even wrote some verses in the style of the French symbolist poets.[52]

In 1940, Luis devised a plan: he created the Popular Democratic Party and campaigned feverishly through the Cordillera mountains and their surrounding small towns. He organized committees in all 786 rural barrios throughout the island and pursued the *jíbaro* vote—sometimes riding a donkey, sometimes wearing a straw hat. He came up with a catchy new slogan that updated the French revolutionary motto of "Liberté, Egalité, Fraternité" (Liberty, Equality, Fraternity) to "Pan, Tierra, Libertad" (Bread, Land, Liberty). He convinced the *jíbaros* that he would fill their bellies (bread), restore all farms stolen by the United States (land), and secure the independence of Puerto Rico (liberty).[53]

The promises did the trick. After the November 1940 elections, as president of the Puerto Rican Senate, president of the Popular Democratic Party, and publisher of *La Democracia*, Luis was the most powerful politician in Puerto Rico. He had stirred people's hopes and dreams all over the island. Cries of "Pan, Tierra, Libertad" and "¡Puerto Rico Libre!" resounded in every town, and Luis shouted the words loudly and often.

Then a strange thing happened. A US Senator named Millard Tydings finally introduced a bill that would give Puerto Ricans their independence. Every politician on the island supported it—except Luis. Throughout the 1940s, he repeatedly opposed the Tydings independence bill. He even traveled to Washington in 1943 and 1945 to lobby against it, saying that Puerto Rico "was not ready for self-government."[54]

This flip-flop troubled Puerto Ricans. Some said that Luis had developed a split personality, a clinical amnesia with regard to the central issue in Puerto Rican politics. His own father had fought for this cause throughout his entire life. How could he now turn around and oppose it? It would take almost sixty years to solve this mystery. The solution was quite tragic.

The US government had in its hands a one-page document that gave them complete and absolute control over Luis Muñoz Marín.

CHAPTER 11

How to Rule a Country with a One-Page Report

Luis Muñoz Marín was vulnerable. He had a weakness. The FBI found it, filed it, and fastened it around his neck.

Muñoz Marín was a narcotics addict. Multiple informants had reported the information, appearing at the end of the "synopsis of facts" in the document. Though dated April 1, 1943, and written by a ridiculously named "Nixon Butt," this report was no joke. It served as a leash on the first democratically elected governor of Puerto Rico.

Why did the FBI seek out this information? A series of related events suggest an answer: Attempts had been made on the lives of two US-appointed governors (Robert Gore and Blanton Winship). Police Chief E. Francis Riggs had been assassinated. The Insular Police had shot and killed four members of the Nationalist Party. An agricultural strike had paralyzed the island in 1934, and the Ponce Massacre had resulted in the deaths of nineteen people in 1937. A Citizens Committee had warned President Franklin Roosevelt that "a state of actual anarchy" existed in Puerto Rico and that towns were in "a state of siege." By the late 1930s,

FEDERAL BUREAU OF INVESTIGATION

Form No. 1
THIS CASE ORIGINATED AT San Juan, Puerto Rico   FILE NO. 100-302

REPORT MADE AT	DATE WHEN MADE	PERIOD FOR WHICH MADE	REPORT MADE BY
San Juan, Puerto Rico	4/1/43	1/15,20;2/9,12;3/23,29/43	NIXON BUTT, JR. rf

TITLE   CHARACTER OF CASE
JOSE LUIS MUNOZ MARIN; ET AL   INTERNAL SECURITY - C
                                           CUSTODIAL DETENTION

ALL INFORMATION CONTAINED
HEREIN IS UNCLASSIFIED
DATE 3-9-00 BY [illegible]

SYNOPSIS OF FACTS: JOSE LUIS MUNOZ MARIN, president of Puerto Rican Senate, alleged to have used Communist Party principles and leaders to gain political power during elections of 1940; since then, for practical reasons, has not aligned himself with Communists. Described by reliable informants to be intellectual with bad case of "Puerto Rican inferiority complex," which results in anti-American tendencies. He is not considered dangerous to point of acts against United States. Is known to be personally completely irresponsible; reported by reliable informants to be heavy drinker and narcotics addict.

                                    P

REFERENCE: 100-5745. Report of Special Agent JACK O. PARKER, San Juan, Puerto Rico, dated 8-16-41.

DETAILS: During the course of another internal security investigation the following information was volunteered by informant T-1, who is regarded by a large number ███████ his reliability being considered excellent insofar as his past record with the San Juan Field Division is concerned. It is not known how much of the following information ██████████ It is known that T-1's sources of information are many and according to T-1's own statement he was in ██████████ at which time he talked with ██████████

67C
67D

               T-1 stated ████████

APPROVED AND FORWARDED: [signature]   SPECIAL AGENT IN CHARGE   DO NOT WRITE IN THESE SPACES

COPIES DESTROYED 3/27/55   RECORDED
COPIES OF THIS REPORT   INDEXED
  5 Bureau cc State Dept
  2 San Juan   EX-25

FBI document identifying Luis Muñoz Marín as a narcotics addict

the colonial arrangement was deteriorating. The United States had to control this situation or risk losing the island forever.

The king of the *carpetas*, J. Edgar Hoover, rode in with his FBI cavalry. Barely three weeks after Luis Muñoz Marín's election as president of the Puerto Rican Senate in November 1940, Hoover commanded the San Juan FBI office to "obtain all information of a pertinent character concerning Luis Muñoz Marín and his associates."[1] He later issued a second demand for "a thorough and discreet investigation by the San Juan Office."[2]

The reports poured in immediately. Luis "has no profession." He is "absolutely irresponsible financially." He "never has any money in his pockets and never thinks of his responsibilities." He "never accepted the responsibility of marriage or of his family, and for years has not contributed to the support of Muna Lee [his wife] or his children."[3] In 1934 he "abandoned his home" and had since been "living with his mistress, Inéz Maria Mendoza."[4] Ruby Black, a prominent Washington journalist, was his "illegitimate half-sister." Her mother had been "the Washington, D.C. mistress" of his father.[5] In addition to being a deadbeat philanderer with a bastard half-breed sister, Muñoz Marín was "utterly unprincipled," had "no ideals whatsoever," and had been "a member of four different political parties during his political career."[6] Worse yet, he was "the Communist leader for Porto Rico and the entire Caribbean Sea area"[7] and the "ranking official of the Communist Party in the West Indies"[8] and had "appointed five professors to the University of Puerto Rico, all of whom [were] self-admitted Communists."[9]

The information kept coming. The day after his father died, twenty-four years before the FBI report, Muñoz Marín had been "seen in public in a drunken condition."[10] For several days after, he was seen "quite intoxicated in public places" and became "the talk of San Juan."[11] Two and a half decades later, Senator Muñoz Marín, president of the Puerto Rican Senate, was "a heavy drinker"[12] who "goes on protracted drunks which last from two or three days to two or three weeks"[13] and whose "bill for whiskey alone runs around $2,000 a year."[14] On one occasion he "got thoroughly drunk with Vicente Geigel-Polanco, the Majority Leader of the Senate, in the Normandie Hotel."[15] On another he arrived at El Escambrón Beach Club at 8 p.m., "ordered drinks" and then "more drinks," then "swore at his friends" and finally left at 1 a.m. "so intoxicated that he was hardly able to walk."[16] When El Escambrón told him that he owed $650, he offered the club "a $650 tax deduction."[17] He also had five-year-old outstanding bills for $300 at the Condado Hotel and $200 from "RCA."[18]

Hoover was an old hand at character assassination; he knew these antics were small potatoes. He needed something big and demanded that his overworked agents find it for nearly three years,[19] until they ran out of material and started sending him legislative summaries and press clippings.[20]

Then they struck gold. On April 1, 1943, Hoover received multiple reports from "reliable informants" that Luis Muñoz Marín was a narcotics addict.[21] In addition, a supplemental report showed that he was known as El Moto de Isla Verde (the Junkie of Isla Verde)[22] and that he'd been "involved in an important narcotics case, but nothing was done inasmuch as Muñoz Marín would fire all members of the Insular Government Narcotics Bureau if prosecution were even contemplated."[23] According to this report, "the Customs Service, U.S. Treasury Department, San Juan, Puerto Rico, had been informed of the existence of Muñoz Marín's participation in the narcotics case."[24]

Days after gathering this information, the FBI closed the case. Muñoz Marín's FBI file ended abruptly with the notation that "all background investigation has been completed in this case. . . . [T]his case is being placed in a closed status."[25]

Hoover finally had some real dirt and now had Muñoz Marín exactly where he wanted him. Muñoz Marín was an addict, he'd gotten caught in a narcotics deal, and he'd used his public office to bury the entire matter. The FBI had no desire to investigate further or to prosecute Muñoz Marín's narcotics case—because with this report and all it implied (addiction, drug sales, obstruction of justice), the FBI could end his career at any time. As the following sequence of events makes clear, this one-page report turned the political leader of Puerto Rico into a US sock puppet.

Through FBI back channels, Muñoz Marín was made aware of this report, which was filed on April 1, 1943. The very next day, April 2, Senator Millard Tydings (D-MD), chairman of the Senate Committee on Territories and Insular Affairs, introduced a bill in the US Congress that opened the door for Puerto Rican independence. It was modeled after the Tydings-McDuffie Bill of 1934, which had set the Philippines on the road to independence. The senator even sent a telegram to Muñoz Marín to enlist his support. To the shock and disbelief of the Puerto Rican people, Muñoz Marín opposed the independence bill.

The *El Imparcial* headline blared "Mr. Tydings Will Support Independence if Puerto Rico Desires It":

MR. TYDINGS PATROCINARÁ PROYECTO
INDEPENDENCIA SI PUERTO RICO LO QUIERE

A version of the Tydings Bill had been introduced in 1936 under entirely different circumstances. Senator Tydings had been a close personal friend of E. Francis Riggs and encouraged him to accept the post of police chief of Puerto Rico. On April 26, 1936, anguished by Riggs's assassination, he introduced an independence bill for Puerto Rico.[26] Under the terms of the 1936 bill, if Puerto Ricans voted yes in a referendum to be held in November 1937, the United States would grant the island independence after a four-year transitional period. During each of those four years, the tariffs on Puerto Rican commodities and products would increase by 25 percent. In the fourth year, when the tariff level on Puerto Rican goods had reached 100 percent (the same as that paid by any other country), Puerto Rico would become independent. Muñoz Marín and many others objected to the four-year provision (the Philippines had been given twenty years to phase in the tariffs), committees were formed, editorials were written, and in the end, Tydings simply withdrew his bill. In 1943, Tydings submitted a new independence bill, and Muñoz Marín opposed it again.[27]

Four factors distinguished the 1936 and 1943 Tydings bills: (1) The 1943 bill contained a twenty-year tariff phase-in structure, just like the Tydings-McDuffie Act for the Philippines. (2) In 1940 Muñoz Marín's campaign slogan had been "Pan, Tierra, Libertad" (Bread, Land, Liberty). The liberty component of the platform referred to Puerto Rican independence; he delivered it in person to hundreds of thousands of Puerto Ricans in 786 electoral districts between the months of August 1939 and November 1940. (3) On May 20, 1936, Muñoz Marín published in his own newspaper, *La Democracia*, that he would "continue to fight for independence." (4) In support of this fight, he created the *El Batey* newsletter, which advocated for liberty and was read widely, with 6 million copies in distribution.[28]

With the 1943 Tydings bill containing exactly the provision he had demanded (a twenty-year tariff transition) and his seven-year history of clamoring for Puerto Rican independence (from 1936 to 1943), Muñoz Marín had no conceivable basis for opposing the second Tydings bill. Yet he did so fiercely, even traveling to Washington, DC, to testify in opposition to the bill before a Senate committee. Tydings himself sent a telegram asking "Why? Why? Why?" he was opposing the bill.[29]

In 1945, the senator resubmitted his independence bill, and Muñoz Marín flew to Washington to oppose it again. This time he stated that if Congress approved the bill, "the Puerto Ricans [would] physically perish within five years." He gave this doomsday testimony despite the fact that eleven of nineteen senators, twenty-two of thirty-nine representatives, and forty-two of seventy-three mayors favored the bill. All told, 57 percent of Puerto Rico's democratically elected representatives officially supported independence. The unofficial percentage was probably higher, since many elected officials were hesitant to contradict their governor and party president, Muñoz Marín.[30]

On May 16, 1945, Tydings submitted yet another independence bill, the Tydings-Piñero Bill, which Muñoz Marín also opposed.[31] In 1946, Muñoz Marín abandoned the pretense of supporting any form of independence for Puerto Rico. In a two-day conclave of his Popular Democratic Party on July 3 and 4, 1946, he announced that he was no longer an *independentista*. After a ten-hour debate, the conclave adopted Muñoz Marín's position and dropped "independence" from its platform.[32]

By 1948, Muñoz Marín's transformation into US puppet was complete. He told reporters that "the only serious defect" in US–Puerto Rico relations was the law preventing the island from refining its own sugar.[33] Also in 1948, he convened an emergency legislative session to pass Public Law 53 (the Gag Law), which was almost identical to the US Smith Act. As previously discussed, the law made it a felony to own or display a Puerto Rican flag (even in one's home);[34] to speak in favor of Puerto Rican independence; to print, publish, sell, or exhibit any material that might undermine the insular government; and to organize any society, group, or assembly of people with a similar intent. Within two years, Muñoz Marín had used Law 53 to arrest over 3,000 people without evidence or due process and to imprison some of them for twenty years.

The island newspapers immediately protested against Law 53 as a threat to freedom of the press and of speech.[35] They even convened a protest assembly on May 25, 1948—sponsored by *El Imparcial, El Mundo, El Día*, and the president of the Press Circle and attended by hundreds of journalists, lawyers, union members, and teachers.[36] When newspapers started calling Luis a traitor, he responded, "This law is precisely to *prevent* anyone from gagging the Puerto Rican people through fascist threats of force. I have asked the FBI to enforce it."[37]

This was the same FBI that had records of Luis's own criminal narcotics activity—the same FBI that had him (and, through him, the entire island) on a tight leash.

Five months after the passage of the Gag Law, Luis captured the brass ring, the greatest prize of his life: he became the first elected governor of Puerto Rico. With the complete dominance of his Popular Democratic Party throughout the island and his lock on the vote of rural *jíbaros* more focused on food and survival than the nuances of First Amendment law, there was no stopping the Muñoz Marín juggernaut.

The inauguration at La Fortaleza, the governor's mansion in Old San Juan, was a glamorous international event covered by *Life*, the *New York Times*, CBS, and NBC. *Time* magazine put Muñoz Marín on its cover, rumpled hair and all. Guests included US senators and congressmen, David Rockefeller, and Beardsley Ruml, president of Macy's. Thousands of *jíbaros* poured down from the mountains in trucks and buses. Thousands more walked for hours, bearing fruits and sundry gifts for their new governor. The inauguration even had its own postage stamp, with a decidedly *jíbaro* theme.

For the first two years, Luis tinkered with the island bureaucracy and merged a few government agencies to control their spending—but the greatest changes occurred within his own mansion.

Luis divorced Muna Lee and remarried his mistress, a schoolteacher named Inéz Mendoza; she became the decorator in chief of La Fortaleza. Inéz knew the value of first impressions, particularly on visiting US dignitaries and business people. She purchased Queen Isabel II and King Alfonso XII antiques, coat-of-arms tapestries, European paintings

La Fortaleza, the governor's mansion
© Eric Fowke/Alamy

and mirrors, Italian marble tables, gilded bronze chandeliers, porcelain lamps, engraved silverware, and a golden console for the Throne Room.

It was a fine life, and Luis was proud of it. He had spun a high school GED, a bohemian youth, a famous father, and a drug habit into a governorship. President Harry S. Truman was a phone call away. WIPR radio broadcast his weekly show across the entire island. He owned a newspaper and a printing press. Viguié News filmed all his speeches and delivered "Muñoz Marín" newsreels to every island movie theater. He was no longer a Greenwich Village poet. He was the lead actor, writer, and stage director of a drama unfolding around an entire people.

Late at night, Luis wandered among the shadows of the great mansion. He walked through the Throne Room, Queen's Room, Governor's Room, Blue Room, Mirror Room, Music Room, Tea Room, and a dozen other rooms, then made himself a sandwich in the kitchen. He sat in the library where Puerto Rico's Carta de Autonomía (Charter of Autonomy) hung decoratively on a wall. He watched as US Navy ships passed under the Southern Tower and moonlight bathed the Mahogany Terrace.

Saturday nights were the most precious of all. After a long week of haggling with the legislature, dancing with the press, and reading FBI reports on the Nationalist Party, a little opium enabled Luis to regain some of the poetry of his youth. He would lock the door to his third floor study, which overlooked the immensity of San Juan Harbor. He'd read a few chapters of Harold Percival's *Thinking and Destiny* and listen to Mozart's string quartets and Lizst's *Années de Pèlerinae*. He would sit on a small, intricately carved mahogany bed with a low-hanging canopy of silk brocade—a womb-like space, enveloped by darkness and quiet.[38] He would set out a bamboo tray with a small knife, two knitting needles, several scrapers, and a sugar cane pipe, all neatly arranged around a coconut-oil lamp. He'd open a diplomatic pouch, cut off a chunk of black *chandoo*, and divide it into ten peanut-sized pellets. With the two knitting needles, he'd spin and knead the first pellet over the lamp's flame until it softened like taffy and turned brown, then tan, then burnished gold (Georgie Yee called it "cockroach wings"). He'd shape the gold into a little pyramid, pack it into the pipe bowl, and pierce a hole in it with a knitting needle. Then he'd lie on his hip, tilt the pipe over the lamp, and inhale slowly. Soon a bone-deep relaxation would spread through his body.

Inéz warned that people were noticing the dark circles under his eyes and commenting about his drinking and drug habits.[39] He countered that he was following the time-honored tradition of Samuel Coleridge, Ben Franklin, Charles Dickens, and Pablo Picasso, but the truth was probably more prosaic: no kiss had ever felt sweeter, suppler, or more enchanting than the mouthpiece of the opium pipe on Luis's lips. It provided the milk of paradise, and he would continue to drink.

Jean Cocteau said, "It is difficult to live without opium after having known it because it is difficult, after knowing opium, to take earth seriously."[40] But earth became very serious for Luis on October 30, 1950, when the revolution started and five Nationalists tried to murder him.

CHAPTER 12

The Nationalist

On July 28, 1898, General Nelson Appleton Miles, commander in chief of the American army, marched into Ponce. At that time, Puerto Rico was a province of Spain that had just secured its autonomy. Now another foreign power was invading again, passing the island from one owner to another.

There was no battle. The Spanish garrisons knew the Americans had already won in Cuba and the Philippines, and they had no intention of dying for the last island in their shrunken empire. They rigidly adhered to General Manuel Casado's order: "If there are many Americans, run; if there are a few, hide; if there are none, engage in battle."[1]

As Miles marched in and hoisted the American flag, a few reporters and local politicians clustered around him. Some townspeople listened to his speech, but most were uninterested. No one was more curious than a barefoot boy, seven years old and brown as a chestnut. His mouth and eyes formed three awestruck O's. He had never seen so many guns, such tall men, and such a big flag. Nor had he ever heard the strange language flowing from General Miles's mouth, which sounded like a dog with indigestion.

It was all so grand that when General Miles finished, the boy applauded and yelled, "¡Que viva Puerto Rico!" because he assumed it was the right thing to do. Everyone turned with a grave expression. The soldiers eyed the crowd. The boy kept smiling and yelled, "¡Que viva Puerto Rico!" again.[2] His name was Pedro Albizu Campos.[3]

∽

Albizu was born out of wedlock to a local mestizo named Juliana Campos. His father, Don Alejandro Albizu Romero, was a wealthy Basque merchant who refused to acknowledge his dark-skinned son, so Albizu ran barefoot through the Barrio Tenerías of Ponce.

Juliana spent most days wandering through the streets of Ponce, talking to herself, and, oddly, burning garbage in their family hut. She took Albizu several times to the nearby Río Bucaná in order to drown them both, but family and friends interceded. Neighbors started calling her La Llorona (the Weeping Woman). One day, when Albizu was four years old, she tried to walk across the river and was carried out to sea.

For a four-year-old orphan, Albizu was remarkably carefree. He didn't attend school until age twelve. His maternal aunt, Rosa Campos, adopted him, and for eight years he swam, fished, and threw mud balls in the same river that had carried his mother away. He stole coconut pies from La Panadería de Ponce and rigged the town bell to ring at 3 a.m. When he heard of a new sport called *beísbol* and that the Almendares Beísbol Club had trounced the US Infantry Regiment with a score of 32–18, Albizu learned everything he could about the game, cleared out a small field, and taught the local school kids to play. He made up half of the rules as he went along, but no one complained; this was his first lesson in leadership.

It was a lively, adventurous childhood, not unlike that of Tom Sawyer living with his Aunt Polly on the banks of the Mississippi River. Just like Polly, Aunt Rosa was a devout woman, and they walked several miles to the Catholic church every Sunday. She also made sure that even though Albizu's clothes were hand-me-downs and a size too small, they were always clean and pressed.

Every morning, rising sleepily from his warm bed, Albizu found Aunt Rosa boiling eggs by the early morning light, his clothes hanging over a kitchen chair. Home from school, he found Rosa sewing and ironing, tending great brown pots on a little stove. She moved in clouds of steam like a humble god, disappearing and reappearing, smelling of warm cotton, *sofrito* sauce, and simmering rice and beans.[4]

When Albizu entered the Percy Grammar School at the age of twelve, his classmates snickered at the overgrown first grader, but the tittering ended when he completed all eight grades in four and a half years. He graduated in two years from Ponce High School with a 96 percent average. He was the class valedictorian and captain of the debate team and received a scholarship to the University of Vermont.[5]

In Vermont, Albizu lived at 43 Middle Converse Hall and became known for "always wearing a black fedora hat" to ward off the cold, since Burlington was forty-five miles from the Canadian border and averaged eighty-one inches of snow annually. In 1913, Pedro Albizu Campos became the first Puerto Rican to be admitted to Harvard College.

Like the rest of America, Cambridge, Massachusetts, was a rowdy beast in the early 1900s. Noisy automobiles and belching delivery trucks clogged the streets. Carpenters, masons, and steel riveters were everywhere, as the campus exploded with a dozen construction projects: Harvard Stadium, the President's House, the Varsity Club, the Peabody Museum, the Germanic Museum, the Paine Music Building, the Gibbs Laboratory, Lars Andersen Bridge, Widener Library, two science buildings, three student dorms, and a twenty-six-acre medical school.[6]

From the moment Albizu arrived at Harvard, the giant kept swelling all around him, sprouting arms and legs, growing new muscles, declaring its manifest destiny all over Boston. The heirs to this destiny were clearly marked. They lived in a three-block strip on Mt. Auburn Street called "the Gold Coast." Apthorp House, one of the finer mansions in Cambridge, was large enough for impromptu football games, indoor rifle practice, and a house monkey. Randolph Hall had a swimming pool, squash courts, an interior courtyard, and a private phone system. Claverly Hall had a heated pool, high ceilings, crystal chandeliers, ash trim, marble fireplaces, building-wide steam heat, and servant's quarters in most suites.

The Gold Coast students came from established prep schools— Exeter, Andover, Groton, Deerfield, Taft, Choate, Hotchkiss, Milton

Academy, St. Paul's—and banded together in exclusive "final clubs," most notably the Porcellian and the AD. They were a select group defined by family, social class, and money. Theodore and Franklin Roosevelt, J. P. Morgan, T. S. Eliot, Oliver Wendell Holmes, William Randolph Hearst, and Owen Wister all belonged to a Harvard final club.

Albizu did not. He saw the Duesenbergs, Renaults, and Mercedes parked outside Claverly Hall, the liquor salesmen tromping through the Gold Coast, the students staggering out of their clubs, then throwing up on the cobblestone streets, and he wanted no part of it. He was thankful, though, for this intimate view of America's ruling class.[7]

Albizu enjoyed Thursday vespers in Appleton Chapel and watching the sun set over the Charles River. He enjoyed seeing the black eyes, nosebleeds, and shredded clothes of "Bloody Monday," the day when freshmen and sophomores beat each other silly for no apparent reason. He enjoyed the characters around campus: John the Orangeman, peddling fruits from a donkey-drawn cart; John Shea, who could locate any book in Widener Library and told students "don't be laxative in your work"; Adolphus Terry, Harvard's human encyclopedia, who memorized the names, faces, and course records of every student in the college. Albizu especially liked Adolphus because he was black.[8]

In addition to his Harvard studies, Albizu taught Spanish classes at Walpole High School and tutored other Harvard students in chemistry, French, and Spanish.[9] He wrote articles for the *Christian Science Monitor* and was voted president of the Cosmopolitan Club, which sponsored visits from foreign scholars and dignitaries. An exceptional student, he graduated with honors in 1916 and was admitted to Harvard Law School.[10]

Albizu became known around campus for his work ethic, good manners, and steadiness of character. His one impulsive act occurred when he met a Peruvian graduate student named Laura Meneses. He invited her to lunch at Union Hall. The next day they lunched again. The third day he asked her to marry him. She laughed in his face then, but eventually she agreed, and they remained partners for life.[11]

☙

When the United States entered World War I, Albizu volunteered and served as a first lieutenant in the US Army. He helped organize and train the Third Battalion Infantry of Puerto Rico and was the only "colored" officer at Camp Las Casas, the army training base on the island. Both in the army and during a military tour through the American South, Albizu encountered widespread racism: he saw it on buses and trains, at lunch counters, and in restrooms, stores, post offices, and even churches. He heard it when soldiers joked behind his back, not realizing that he understood every word.[12]

By the time he returned to law school in 1919, Albizu had made a decision. No matter how many degrees he earned or how many times the people at Harvard patted him on the head, he would never be one of "them." The United States would never take him, his people, or his homeland seriously. In fact, the Americans couldn't even spell or pronounce his island's name. And so, to give meaning and purpose to his own life, Albizu devoted himself to the cause of Puerto Rican independence.

He did this systematically. He studied the Magna Carta, the Declaration of Independence, the Articles of Confederation, the US Constitution, the *Congressional Record*, the Teller Amendment of 1898, the Platt Amendment of 1901, the Cuban-American Treaty of 1903, the parliamentary rules of the Spanish Cortes Generales, the admiralty rulings of the 1897 International Maritime Committee, and the Puerto Rican Carta de Autonomía (Charter of Autonomy). He confirmed that the Treaty of Paris was essentially a real estate closing and a violation of international law with regard to Puerto Rico.[13] He then reached out to other anticolonial movements, meeting with Éamon de Valera, president of the Irish Republic, and Mahadev Desai, a leader of the Indian anti-imperialists. He canvassed the factories of Cambridge and the Irish wards of Boston for donations to the Irish liberation movement.[14]

One night, he walked into a packed Sanders Theater where 1,400 students, faculty, and foreign diplomats were debating "the Irish Question." With references to the US Constitution, the Federalist Papers, the British Home Rule Act of 1914, and Jonathan Swift's *A Modest Proposal*, Albizu spoke in favor of the revolution and electrified the audience. Lord Miller, on diplomatic leave from the British parliament, interrupted the standing ovation to declare, "I am a British nobleman, so there is no need to inquire my opinion on the Irish question. But gentlemen I would not be a Britisher, I would not be a nobleman, if I failed to admit that Mr. Campos has just delivered the most complete, the most brilliant speech on this matter, that I have ever heard."[15]

In 1921, Albizu graduated from law school as class valedictorian and received multiple job offers: a clerkship with the US Supreme Court, a diplomatic post at the US embassy to Mexico, a judgeship in Yauco, Puerto Rico, and an executive position with a US corporation paying $15,000 per year. Albizu refused them all and returned to his hometown of Ponce to pursue his growing obsession: the independence of Puerto Rico.[16]

☙

Ponce's La Cantera section was one of the island's poorest districts, with cows in the village square, dusty brown streets, and hundreds of mud-floor shacks without plumbing or electricity. Alleys were piled high with mango pits, watermelon rinds, and chewed sugar cane stalks. A cloud of crane flies and mosquitoes descended on the garbage every morning, then migrated into the shacks.

Albizu rented a wooden house on a dirt road. From a hill behind his house, he could see the Central Constancia sugar cane plantation. The vista showed an infinity of cane: thousands of rows, multiplied in successive mirrors, all the way to the Atlantic Ocean.

Laura joined him in 1922, and they married and had three children: Pedro (1924), Rosa Emila (1925), and Laura (1927). It was a difficult time. Albizu was practicing poverty law, and his clients were simple people—mostly sugar cane workers and jíbaros—who paid with chickens, vegetables, and sometimes a simple thank-you. Albizu's children had to share clothing and often wrapped their ankles in vinegar-soaked rags to discourage lice from climbing on board.[17] Albizu had no savings or property, but he was building something more important: a reputation as a man of principle, a man who could be trusted.

This reputation grew when he started writing for *El Nacionalista de Ponce* and advocating for independence around the island. It continued to grow after a political rally in 1925, when he removed every miniature American flag from the podium and stuffed them in his pocket.

It grew from 1927 to 1930, when he traveled to Cuba, Panama, Mexico, Venezuela, Peru, the Dominican Republic, and Haiti, campaigning and networking for his revolution. When he spoke about US banks owning Puerto Ricans' land, the US Navy controlling their borders, the US Congress writing their laws, and US companies paying them starvation wages in the sugar cane fields, everyone knew what he was talking about. He reminded his audiences, "Everywhere you look, you see a Yankee army, Yankee navy, Yankee police and Yankee courts," and "According to the Yankees owning one person makes you a scoundrel, but owning a nation makes you a colonial benefactor."[18]

In 1930, Albizu became president of the Nationalist Party of Puerto Rico. Although the party did not have an island-wide electoral apparatus or any members in public office, it qualified for ballot status in the 1932 election cycle with the required 28,000 inscribed members.[19] The Nationalists were dedicated to one overwhelming cause: achieving independence for Puerto Rico as quickly and unconditionally as possible. This included the reclamation of all Puerto Rican lands, the nationalization of all banks, the reinstatement of Spanish as the primary language of public school instruction, and the elimination of tariff payments to the United States. This platform of unconditional independence became more compelling as the Great Depression swept through Puerto Rico, and hunger gripped the island.[20]

Also in 1930, Albizu used his legal skills to create a series of bonds registered on Wall Street. These bonds were an investment in the Republic of Puerto Rico, redeemable from the island's treasury on the day it became independent. The first bond offering was for $200,000 in increments of $10, $50, and $100.[21]

In 1931, Albizu defended a Nationalist named Luis Velasquez, who had slapped the chief justice of the Puerto Rican Supreme Court during a political dispute and been charged with assault.[22] The case went to the US Court of Appeals, and when Albizu won, it became known as "Velasquez's Slap in the Face." Throughout the early 1930s, Albizu continued to speak all over the island, and the crowds kept growing.

In 1932 Albizu ran for the Puerto Rican Senate. He lost, and the Nationalist Party did not win a single seat. In fact, a poet named Luis Muñoz Marín sailed in from Greenwich Village and took the very seat that Albizu had worked for. Despite all the speeches, conferences, debates, campaigns, editorial columns, and lawsuits, the United States was not taking Albizu or his Nationalist Party very seriously.

Everything changed with the sugar cane strike of 1934. From that moment on, the Americans wanted Albizu gone.

℘

As the Great Depression deepened, the US banks that controlled Puerto Rico's sugar plantations cut wages all over the island. Sugar cane workers who had gotten seventy-five cents for a twelve-hour day in 1929 were down to forty-five cents in 1933. Starvation was rampant, and during the last six months of 1933, eighty-five strikes and protests erupted in the tobacco, needlework, and transportation industries. The bitterest conflict, however, was in the cane fields.

On November 8, 1933, the mill workers of Central Plazuela in Barceloneta went on strike before the start of the harvest and stayed out of work until December 5. On December 6, cane fires erupted in Central Coloso, and 1,200 workers went on strike. By December 7, 8,000 more workers had joined the Coloso strike. On December 31, the largest sugar cane plantation on the island, Central Guánica, went on strike.

In early January 1934, the workers of Puerto Rico's entire sugar industry were striking—against not only their employers but their own labor leaders. Without consulting the rank and file, the Federación Libre del Trabajo (the Free Federation of Workers) had signed an island-wide labor agreement whose terms did little for laborers and left their wages virtually unchanged. The federation leaders, most of them comfortably ensconced in the Puerto Rican government, had sold out the workers.[23]

And so, on January 11, 1934, the sugar cane workers of Guayama reached out to a new leader. They asked Pedro Albizu Campos, as head of the Nationalist Party, to address an assembly of 6,000 people the next day.

℘

Albizu speaks to striking sugar cane workers
The Ruth M. Reynolds Papers, Archives of the Puerto Rican Diaspora,
Centro de Estudios Puertorriqueños, Hunter College, CUNY

It was a hot Friday night in the Plaza Pública Cristobal Colón. A breeze from the nearby Atlantic barely stirred the palm trees of the Guayama town square, as a man wearing a black jacket, white shirt, and black bow tie stepped up to the Nationalist Party platform. His eyes were dark and piercing, his cheekbones sharp. He was not tall, standing about five feet, four inches, but he spoke with an electric, almost religious fervor.

A murmur ran through the crowd: El Maestro (the Teacher) had arrived. And he was indeed a teacher, a great pianist of ideas, about to sit at his instrument and unleash a Wagnerian fury. He started slowly and built up a cadence. He cited history and religion, culture and tradition. It started to rain, but no one left the square. Albizu spoke to the people for two hours about their work, their land, and their island. He recited "Puerto Rico, Puerto Pobre," a poem by Pablo Neruda.[24] When he finished, the crowd of 6,000 applauded for over five minutes and asked him to lead the workers through the bitter sugar cane strike. The next business day, *El Imparcial* ran his entire speech on its front page.[25]

Albizu and the sugar cane workers formed the Asociación de Trabajadores de Puerto Rico (Workers Association of Puerto Rico), and he negotiated on their behalf with the sugar corporations and the government. Albizu and Nationalist organizers spoke personally in many towns, including Arecibo, Fajardo, Bayamón, Humacao, Río Piedras, Yabucoa, and Salinas. Alarmed US corporations formed the Citizens Committee of One Thousand for the Preservation of Peace and Order and cabled President Franklin Roosevelt in a panic about "anarchy" throughout the island.[26]

A few days after the speech, during a meeting with Guánica cane workers, Albizu received a phone call. It was Colonel E. Francis Riggs, the police chief of Puerto Rico, inviting Albizu Campos to lunch at the El Escambrón Beach Club.[27] Albizu agreed to meet, then quickly hung up. He had already heard about Riggs, the heir to the Riggs National Bank fortune.

The Riggs National Bank headquarters at 1503–1505 Pennsylvania Avenue NW was right across the street from the Treasury Department and a few hundred feet from the White House. The bank loaned the US government $16 million in 1847 for a war against Mexico and $7.2 million in 1868 for the purchase of Alaska. Fourteen US presidents or their families had banked at Riggs, including Abraham Lincoln and Ulysses S. Grant. As the largest bank in Washington, DC, with branches throughout the United States, England, Germany, and the Bahamas, Riggs specialized in "private international banking" for wealthy clients and "embassy banking" for 95 percent of the foreign ministries and embassies located in Washington.[28] Throughout Central America the Riggs National Bank was suspected of laundering money for right-wing dictators, bribing entire legislatures, destabilizing populist regimes, and financing military coups disguised as "revolutions" on behalf of the United Fruit Company.[29]

Now in 1934, within weeks of an island-wide labor strike, the president of this bank had sent a special envoy, his own son, as the chief of police of Puerto Rico. This "friendly neighborhood cop" with millions of dollars and thousands of armed men at his disposal had just invited Albizu for a sit-down.

☙

Riggs Bank headquarters in Washington, DC
Courtesy of the Library of Congress

El Escambrón Beach Club was Puerto Rico's most spectacular private resort. The restaurant sat on the water's edge with breathtaking views of El Morro, Fort San Cristobal, and the San Juan beachfront. A horseshoe-shaped boardwalk extended out over the water, right into the ocean, to create "the largest outdoor pool in the world."[30]

On January 18, 1934, as he walked into El Escambrón, Albizu noticed many US Navy officers, several local businessmen, two members of the Puerto Rican Senate, and Fay Wray, the Canadian American actress most famous for playing the female lead in 1933's *King Kong*.

Riggs sat at a corner table in military regalia: a white tunic with gold buttons, large epaulets, and a splash of medals on his chest. He shook Albizu's hand heartily. In a flurry of busboys, waiters, and sommeliers, they ate a splendid lunch and discussed the Golden Gate Bridge, the Spanish Civil War, Noel Coward's *Design for Living*, and Joe DiMaggio's hitting streak—everything but the sugar strike. Their waiter spoke English and listened attentively.[31]

Finally Riggs came to the point. He asked Albizu what he thought of Luis Muñoz Marín, to whom the Nationalist had recently lost the Senate election. Then he offered to donate $150,000 to the Nationalist Party, to ensure that Albizu won the Senate seat that year or in 1936, and to make Albizu governor of Puerto Rico within ten years' time. Millard Tydings, a good friend who owed Riggs a few favors, was about to chair the US Senate Committee on Territories and Insular Affairs. Tydings could sponsor a bill allowing Puerto Rico to elect her own governor, and Riggs could ensure that Albizu got the job. In exchange, Albizu would back down and let Riggs take care of the strike. If Albizu refused the deal, Riggs would take the offer to Muñoz Marín. Albizu rose slowly, thanked Riggs for lunch, and told him Puerto Rico was not for sale, at least not by him.[32]

⁂

Albizu knew a great deal about Riggs, but he didn't know that the new chief had worked in the Military Intelligence Department in Washington, DC. Nor did he know that Riggs had just come from Nicaragua, where he'd been advising a budding dictator named Anastasio Somoza, who, one month later, on February 21, 1934, would assassinate Augusto Sandino.

He also didn't know that Riggs would triple the size of the Insular Police force and arm its officers with grenade launchers, machine guns, carbines, and 12-gauge shotguns. In addition, he would recruit over a hundred FBI agents to follow Albizu all over the island and infiltrate the Nationalist Party.

On February 23, 1934, two days after the assassination of Augusto Sandino, the sugar strike was settled. The workers would receive $1.50 for a twelve-hour day, more than double the amount they'd gotten before. The island newspapers all reported Albizu's great triumph. As word of it spread through Washington and Wall Street, another word came back down: the Nationalist Party must be stopped by any means necessary.[33]

⁂

Albizu Campos speaks in his hometown of Ponce, Puerto Rico
Photographer Carlos Torres Morales; published in *El Imparcial*, December 22, 1930, 5

And so the violence began. After receiving several death threats, Albizu moved his family to a less exposed house in Aguas Buenas and posted a twenty-four-hour guard, which intercepted several FBI assaults and three fire-bombing attempts in 1934 and 1935.[34]

Albizu also created the Cadets of the Republic, the official youth branch of the Nationalist Party. By 1936, over 10,000 cadets were marching and training in twenty-one towns. Their commander in chief was Raimundo Díaz Pacheco, one of Albizu's most trusted friends. Vidal Santiago, Albizu's personal barber, was one of the captains.

Police Chief Riggs was not impressed. On October 24, 1935, an army of policemen raided a student rally, shooting and killing one cadet and three members of the Nationalist Party, in what became known as the Río Piedras Massacre.[35] The massacre was barely mentioned in the American press. Police Chief Riggs told *La Democracia* that if Albizu continued agitating for independence, there would be "war to the death against all Puerto Ricans."[36] Three months later, on February 23, 1936, Police Chief Riggs was assassinated on his way to El Escambrón. The two Nationalists who shot him, Hiram Rosado and Elías Beauchamp, were arrested, beaten for an hour, then executed in a San Juan police station.

Governor Blanton Winship moved quickly, prohibiting all public demonstrations throughout the island and ordering an investigation. The Insular Police raided several dozen offices and homes, seized documents and recordings of Albizu's speeches, and eleven days later arrested Albizu and eight other Nationalists. Lacking any evidence of murder or incitement to murder, the prosecution charged Albizu with conspiracy to overthrow the US government.[37]

The first jury of seven Puerto Ricans and five Americans failed to reach a verdict. Just before the retrial, at a cocktail party in the governor's mansion, US Attorney Cecil Snyder showed a list of handpicked jurors to a well-known artist named Rockwell Kent. According to Kent, the people on Snyder's list were precisely the ones later empanelled during voir dire, who then sat in judgment on Albizu. Kent went public with this information, but it had no effect on the case. He spoke directly to the press, stating, "Albizu Campos was denied the right to a fair and impartial trial by jury." He even submitted a letter to Senator Henry F. Ashurst, chairman of the US Senate Judiciary Committee—but no inquiry was ever made.[38] At the retrial, the clerk of the court declared fourteen potential jurors "unavailable" or "excused for cause," removed five others,[39] and controlled the entire voir dire selection process. When the smoke cleared, the new jury consisted of ten Americans and two Puerto Ricans.

On the first day of the trial, July 27, 1936, every room, hallway, elevator, and staircase in the federal courthouse was jammed with US soldiers and FBI agents. The surrounding streets were all blockaded. FBI agents mingled with the crowd. National Guardsmen roamed the halls. In the courtroom itself, over half the spectators were police and plainclothes detectives.[40] On July 31, 1936, the Insular Police arrived with Thompson submachine guns, rifles, and tear gas and cleared out the entire building. US military commanders from Camp Santiago and the new chief of police, Colonel Enrique de Orbeta, sat in the courtroom as the jury delivered its verdict: ten years' imprisonment for Albizu, six years for the other Nationalists.[41]

Elmer M. Ellsworth, a special assistant to Governor Winship, was a member of this hand-picked jury. In a fit of remorse, he sent a letter to President Roosevelt stating, "The jury was motivated by strong, if not violent, prejudice against the Nationalists and was prepared to convict them, regardless of the evidence. Ten of the jurors were American residents in Puerto Rico and even the two Puerto Ricans were closely associated with American business interests. It was evident from the composition of the jury that the Nationalists did not and could not get a fair trial."[42] The letter was ineffectual; Albizu was jailed in La Princesa prison in San Juan. A Palm Sunday march in support of Albizu resulted in the Ponce Massacre. Finally, after an unsuccessful appeal, Albizu was flown to the US penitentiary in Atlanta on June 7, 1937.

℘

Although the Atlanta penitentiary was a large facility with three hundred acres and 2,500 inmates, Albizu received special and constant attention. All his mail was opened. He could only correspond with an "approved list" of people (mostly a few family members) and could not send or receive any packages; nor could he receive any magazines or newspapers. He was allowed only one visit per month, and many people, such as Nobel Prize–winning poet Gabriela Mistral, were simply turned away.[43] His health deteriorated. Reports of anemia and extremely low hemoglobin received no attention until Congressman Vito Marcantonio threatened the warden. Marcantonio represented East Harlem, which at that time contained the largest Puerto Rican population on the US mainland.[44]

Despite all this, Albizu managed to write magazine articles on behalf of Puerto Rican independence and published them in Mexico (*Magazín Excelsior*) and Argentina (*Claridad*) under the witty pseudonym Pedro Gringoire (Pedro I'll Go Gringo). He also translated letters for other prisoners and worked in the prison library. One day in the library he encountered an unusual book, published by General Smedley Butler in 1935—*War Is a Racket*.

Butler had been a marine for thirty-three years and was the most decorated marine in US history. He had received sixteen medals, five for heroism, and was one of only nineteen men to receive the Congressional Medal of Honor twice. He retired as a major general and, for a brief period, was the highest-ranking commander in the US Marine Corps.

One section of the book reads:

War is just a racket. Only a small inside group knows what it is about. It is conducted for the benefit of the very few at the expense of the masses. I wouldn't go to war again as I have done, to protect some lousy investment of the bankers.

There isn't a trick in the racketeering bag that the military gang is blind to. It has its "finger men" to point out enemies, its "muscle men" to destroy enemies, its "brain men" to plan war preparations, and a "Big Boss" Super-Nationalistic-Capitalism.

I spent thirty-three years in active military service as a member of the Marine Corps. I served in all commissioned ranks from Second Lieutenant to Major-General. And during that period, I spent most of my time being a high class muscle-man for Big Business, for Wall Street and for the Bankers. In short, I was a racketeer, a gangster for capitalism.

I helped make Mexico, especially Tampico, safe for American oil interests in 1914. I helped make Haiti and Cuba a decent place for the National City Bank boys to collect revenues.

I helped in the raping of half a dozen Central American republics for the benefit of Wall Street. I helped purify Nicaragua for the international banking house of Brown Brothers in 1909–1912. I brought light to the Dominican Republic for American sugar interests in 1916. In China I helped to see to it that Standard Oil went its way unmolested.

Looking back on it, I feel that I could have given Al Capone a few hints. The best he could do was to operate his racket in three districts. I operated on three continents.[45]

Then Butler provides eleven pages of facts and figures, showing the profit margins of hundreds of US corporations during World War I. The table on page 125 shows six of the most egregious.

Butler's father had been a US congressman for thirty-one years and had chaired the House Naval Affairs Committee. By studying US Senate appropriation documents, Butler found that 49 steel plants, 340 coal producers, 122 meat packers, 153 cotton suppliers, and 299 garment makers had profited enormously from World War I. The war had cost $52 billion, and $16 billion of it (30 percent) had been pure profit for the war suppliers.[46]

Corporation	Prewar Annual Profits (millions US$)	Wartime Annual Profits (millions US$)	Percentage Profit Increase
DuPont Chemical	6.0	58.0	966
Bethlehem Steel	6.0	49.0	816
Anaconda Copper	10.0	34.0	340
Central Leather	1.167	15.0	1,320
General Chemical	0.8	12.0	1,400
International Nickel	4.0	73.0	1,830

War Is a Racket confirmed everything Albizu had seen in Puerto Rico. When he tried to do something about it by leading labor strikes and advocating for independence, the United States had rigged a jury and thrown him in jail. Around this time, on June 3, 1943, Albizu was released on probation in New York City. He had been in prison for over seven years.

Within three days, on June 6, 1943, Albizu was admitted into Columbus Hospital with a diagnosis of arteriosclerosis, coronary sclerosis, brachial neuritis, and anemia. FBI director J. Edgar Hoover didn't believe the diagnosis and sent a memo to the US State Department: "Albizu Campos is reported to be using his private room in the Columbus Hospital as the headquarters of the Nationalist Party of Puerto Rico in New York City. He receives many notable visitors and holds meetings in this room. Campos continues to be hospitalized on his own volition in order to elicit sympathy and appear as a martyr."[47]

Hoover bugged the hospital room and listened in until a nun discovered a microphone in a wall lamp. That same day, Congressman Vito Marcantonio rushed down from East Harlem. He yanked the wiring out of the walls, cursed Hoover through the microphone, and threatened to produce the wire on the floor of the US House of Representatives.[48]

Albizu stayed in Columbus Hospital until November 9, 1945, and lived in the Bronx until December 11, 1947. On that day, he went to the Brooklyn Navy Yard, boarded the SS *Kathryn*, and returned to Puerto Rico.[49]

From the moment Albizu set foot in San Juan, Hoover became obsessed with following and recording his every movement, essentially becoming his Boswell. In a memo to US Secretary of the Interior Julius Krug, he wrote,

> Pedro Albizu Campos, the President of the Nationalist Party, arrived in San Juan, Puerto Rico, December 15, 1947, from New York. He was greeted upon arrival by the leaders of the Nationalist, Communist and Independence Parties of Puerto Rico.
>
> A crowd of several thousand met him at the dock, the crowd including an honor guard of forty black-shirted "Cadets of the Liberating Army" under the command of "Colonel" Raimundo Díaz Pacheco.
>
> Later at a mass rally of the Nationalists, Communists and *independentistas*, Albizu condemned (1) United States Navy expropriation of Vieques, Puerto Rico, and warned of further expropriation by the United States; (2) teaching of English in Puerto Rican public schools; (3) application of the Selective Service Act to Puerto Rico, and claimed that now is the hour of decision and action, not words.[50]

The anti-Communist hysteria aside, Hoover's description is accurate. Thousands of Puerto Ricans and dozens of FBI agents met Albizu at the dock. They packed into San Juan Cathedral and followed him in a heaving mass to Sixto Escobar Stadium, where he would address a standing-room-only crowd of 14,000. The Puerto Rican flags flew everywhere—from cars, storefronts, houses, trees, and even the stadium rafters, and WPRP broadcast Albizu's speech island-wide. The FBI agents added a curious glamour, as they openly filmed and taped the event and noted the identity and license plate of every Nationalist leader in attendance.[51]

A youth choir sang "La Borinqueña," and then Albizu began his speech: "My name is Pedro Albizu Campos. You are my people. And this is our island." A roar filled the stadium. For over an hour, he thundered about independence. The stadium shook as the crowd members stomped and chanted and cheered and pumped their fists in the air. El Maestro was back.

Every newspaper on the island reported Albizu's dramatic return. After a brief stay in the Hotel Normandie, he gathered his family and settled into a second-floor apartment in Old San Juan, on the corner of Calles Sol and Cruz. The stream of visitors seemed endless, and on the first floor below them, the Bar Borinqueña became a hot spot for journalists and university students.

For the first few weeks, Albizu felt the joy of family he hadn't seen in ten years and the warmth of many holidays: Christmas Day, New Year's Eve, Three Kings Day, the eight days of Octavitas.[52] But soon he noticed some changes across the island. The newspapers weren't clamoring for independence anymore. No labor movement had developed. Nationalist Party funds were scarce. Enrollment in the Cadets of the Republic had dropped by 80 percent, to less than 1,000.[53] And the US military was everywhere. The navy had occupied Vieques and was using it for artillery practice, exploding 5 million pounds of ordnance per year. Camp Santiago occupied 12,789 acres in the town of Salinas. Ramey Air Force Base covered 3,796 acres in Aguadilla. Fort Buchanan had 4,500 acres in metropolitan San Juan, with its own pier facilities, ammunition storage areas, and massive railroad network into San Juan Bay. Every July 4 the US flexed its muscles with a military brass band, three infantry battalions, a tank company, a bombardment squadron, three aerial fighter squadrons, the 504th Field Artillery Battalion, the 18th Mechanized Cavalry Squadron, and 4,000 soldiers—the entire 65th Infantry Regiment—marching down Calle Fortaleza (just three blocks from Albizu's house) to remind everyone who was boss.[54] And then there was Roosevelt Roads—the largest naval station in the world. Spread out over Vieques Island and the Puerto Rican mainland, it encompassed 32,000 acres, 3 harbors, 9 piers, 1,340 buildings, 110 miles of road, 42 miles of oceanfront, and an 11,000-foot runway. It housed 17,000 people and serviced up to 1,000 ships annually.[55]

The island's politics were also beginning to change. Luis Muñoz Marín controlled the Puerto Rican Senate and had shifted the dialogue from "independence" to "economic development" with a program known as "Operation Bootstrap." In 1947, Puerto Rico passed its first tax-exemption law to excuse all new businesses from insular and local taxes. That same year the government legalized gambling, constructed an enormous textile mill, and contracted with Conrad Hilton to build a superluxury hotel, the Caribe Hilton.[56] But most importantly, on May 2, 1947, the US Congress authorized Puerto Ricans to choose their own governor, with the first election slated for 1948.[57]

In the editorial pages and on radio shows, in the barbershops and beauty parlors, in living rooms and dining rooms and at domino tables, the talk had shifted from "Will Puerto Rico become independent?" to "Who will be the first governor?" Albizu's goals had become marginalized. He had been rendered irrelevant. To make his Nationalist dream come true, Albizu would have to do something dramatic, theatrical, and desperate—something that could reach beyond the borders of Puerto Rico and explode onto the world stage.

The FBI knew this and so kept his house at 156 Calle Sol under siege, stationing a police car outside day and night and photographing and interrogating every person who entered the building. If Albizu stepped onto the street, the news was transmitted to the central radio station of the Insular Police. If he or his family members went for a walk, police agents followed them. They also broke the traffic lights around the house, which gave them a legal excuse to detain any motorists in the vicinity and to question, ticket, harass, or arrest them. His mail was intercepted, and he had to sell his car because it was constantly stopped and searched on the streets and highways. The transcripts of all this surveillance—of Albizu, the Nationalist Party, and other "subversive" individuals—eventually totaled nearly 2 million pages.[58]

On March 29, 1948, J. Edgar Hoover placed the Nationalist Party on the FBI list of organizations working to "subvert" the US government. This entitled him to more funds, more electronic surveillance equipment, and more agents in Puerto Rico.

A few months later, the leash tightened further. On June 10, 1948, Luis Muñoz Marín engineered the passage of Public Law 53 (the Gag Law). This law was nearly a word-for-word translation of Section 2 of the anti-Communist US Smith Act, and it authorized the police and FBI to stop anyone on the street and to invade any Puerto Rican home. If the police found a Puerto Rican flag, the residents could all be arrested and jailed.[59]

On October 19, 1949, on the floor of US Congress, Representative Vito Marcantonio gave the following report on Albizu Campos:

> Today he lives in San Juan under the type of police surveillance and intimidation that could only have been duplicated in Hitler Germany. . . . When the leader of the Nationalist Party leaves San Juan to attend a meeting or to make a speech, his car is trailed through the countryside by an armed column of police cars and jeeps. Every hotel or home in which he stays is immediately surrounded by a cordon of police. Every meeting of the Nationalist Party takes place behind police lines. Campos is an American citizen, yet he and his party are harassed and intimidated at every turn.[60]

❧

Business had tripled at the Salón Boricua over the past two years; the little barbershop had become a hothouse of gossip, arguments, and unlicensed liquor. The loudest arguments occurred when a tipsy barber nicked a customer during a shave.

Ever since the passage of the Gag Law, Albizu went there every two weeks and received a hero's welcome. When he entered, he'd be asked, "How's it going, *viejo?*"

"The same as always," he would reply. "I've got 40 FBI agents on my tail."

Everyone would laugh, and Albizu would sit down for his haircut, trade jokes with shop owner talk with the customers, and buy a lottery ticket or two. When he paid for his haircut, he would pass a handwritten note to Vidal along with the dollar. Sometimes he'd leave another dollar under the statue of Santa Barbara. Then he would go to the bathroom, where he had a five-minute window of opportunity.[61]

Albizu would remove a false panel, climb over some plaster, and crawl into the next-door apartment at 353 Calle Colton. He would talk for three minutes to Raimundo Díaz Pacheco, Blanca Canales, and other top lieutenants of the Nationalist Party. Then he would scramble back into the Salón Boricua's bathroom and flush the toilet.

"Did an agent follow you in?" Vidal would ask.[62]

"He tried to, but I wouldn't let him," Albizu would say. Then everyone would laugh uproariously.

This crude exchange was actually a signal that the meeting had occurred, and everything had been discussed. For nearly two years, until the revolution of October 1950, the Salón Boricua was a lifeline for Albizu, providing the only secure way for him to communicate with his Nationalist Party leaders.

On October 7, 1950, he heard that Faustino Díaz Pacheco and Vidal Santiago had joined *los desaparecidos* (the ones who have disappeared). Faustino was the brother of Raimundo Díaz Pacheco, Albizu's commander in chief. With Vidal gone, Albizu could no longer visit Salón Boricua and slip into the apartment next door. In fact, the disappearance of these two could mean the entire party had been infiltrated. The walls were closing in on Albizu, and he decided to go for a walk.

Two FBI men followed as he strolled past the Cine Luna theater with its *Sands of Iwo Jima* posters, circled around Fort San Cristobal, and walked along the ocean's edge. To his left was La Perla, the poorest district in San Juan, a tin-roof shantytown just a few hundred feet from the governor's mansion. He walked past the battlements of El Moro with its ancient Ordoñez cannons, which had failed to hold off the American invasion in 1898. Out in the bay a battleship cruised toward Fort Buchanan and then Vieques. He followed the shoreline till he reached El Escambrón, with its tennis courts, cabana boys, white-gloved waiters, and the restaurant where Police Chief Riggs had offered him $150,000.

Albizu sat on an embankment and looked across the harbor. The Caribe Hilton, Hotel Normandie, Condado Lagoon, and a dozen other luxury hotels dotted the shoreline. Thousands of tourists splashed in the water and basked in the sun. Coca-Cola signs sprouted up from nearly every street. His island was becoming difficult to recognize. The landscape of his childhood was being erased bit by bit.

And now, after working and studying so hard, he had gone to prison and lost his law license. He had no real livelihood, his phone was tapped, his family was being followed, FBI agents analyzed his garbage, and most of his friends were in jail or had disappeared. Meanwhile, Luis

Muñoz Marín had cut a deal with the United States and was sitting in the governor's mansion smoking opium.[63]

Albizu sighed and shook his head. Perhaps he was fighting for an island long gone and simply needed to wake up. Others had given up and were now building tourist traps all over the island.[64]

A cheer erupted from the FBI men some fifty feet away. They were huddled over their short wave radio, listening to Game Four of the World Series. Albizu looked over, and they waved at him.

"The Yankees won!," they said.[65] Albizu smiled and waved back.

CHAPTER 13

The Artist

Juan Emilio Viguié loved to tell stories. He entered the world a sponge and heard a million of them, the sum of which became his life. Stories had great power, and he knew it. They were the only things that mattered to him.

Just like Pedro Albizu Campos, he was born in 1891 in the town of Ponce and orphaned at an early age. Unlike Albizu, he was adopted by Don Caballer, a municipal judge who treated him like a son and supported all his efforts. Juan loved to draw, so the judge enrolled him in the Michael Pou Academy, where he studied painting and visual arts and learned to view the world differently—in terms of light, form, symmetry, and color.

At age ten he walked into the Teatro La Perla, an enormous 1,000-seat theater, and saw three silent films—*Christmas Eve*, *The Butterfly*, and *Little Red Riding Hood*—that he could not stop talking about. The next year, in San Juan's Cine Luna, he saw a print of Georges Méliès's *A Trip to the Moon* and knew, at age eleven, that this would be his life's work. Two years later, during a trip to Paris, he saw ten Lumiere Brothers shorts at Le Salon Indien du Grand Café. His favorite was

Baby's Breakfast because it showed the power of this medium: the simple image of a baby spilling food on his chin held everyone in the theater spellbound.

Juan got his first job at age fifteen as a projectionist in Ponce's Teatro Habana. The house manager was French, and Juan loved it when the *jíbaros* became impatient between reels, yelling, "Apaga, misu!" (Hit the lights, monsieur). By 1911 Juan was an expert on the pioneers of early film, including Edwin S. Porter, Robert W. Paul, and Ferdinand Zecca. He bought a Pathe camera, two used movie projectors, and opened his own movie house in the town of Adjuntas.[1]

His first documentary, *Escenas de Ponce* (*Scenes of Ponce*), consisted of various street and landscape scenes and was screened in various theaters throughout the island. His movie house broke even, but a little arithmetic told the larger story: thirteen theaters in San Juan were charging ten cents admission and collectively pulled in $1,500 per day, about $500,000 per year. Each theater made a profit of at least $10,000 per year, but the market was saturated, and Juan didn't have the capital to compete with them. Besides, he wanted to make movies, not show them—so when he heard about a new movie studio in Florida, he packed a bag and headed north.

❧

According to *Moving Picture World*, the Lubin South Studio in Jacksonville, Florida, had "the best outdoor facilities this side of Los Angeles." Director Arthur Hotaling rented a large boathouse on Riverside Avenue and built an enormous open-air studio with movable sunscreens, prismatic glass filters, and a private dock on the St. John River. Four directors worked on five stages, employing fifty full-time personnel and up to three hundred local residents as extras. When Juan arrived in 1913, Lubin South was producing 4,000 feet of film a week, and Oliver Newell Hardy (of Laurel and Hardy fame) was debuting in his first film, *Outwitting Dad*.[2]

Juan introduced himself to Hotaling, screened *Escenas de Ponce* for him, and was hired on the spot as a snake wrangler. Over the next few months he moved on to painter, carpenter, script clerk, assistant cameraman, assistant director, and Spanish translator for the title cards. But something was bothering him.

Many of Hotaling's comedies depended heavily on vicious ethnic stereotypes. They depicted Italians, Irish, Germans, Jews, Mexicans, and blacks in cruel and racist terms. The Irish were drunks with baboon faces always spoiling for a fight; Italians were sneaky and sex-crazed; Germans were beer-bloated dummkopfs. Most insulting of all were the "colored comedies." *Coontown Suffragettes* demeaned all women and blacks and marked the first cinematic appearance of a black mammy with big lips. In *He Wanted Work*, a black man disguised as an Irish bricklayer is nearly beaten to death when his makeup washes off under a hose. Juan didn't find this funny, but the colored comedies were so popular in the South that in 1913 Hotaling built a separate "colored" studio, with its own dining facilities, six blocks from the main studio. When Hotaling asked Juan to be its production manager, Juan quit in disgust and headed west.

ↄ

In 1914, he arrived in Presidio, Texas, with $10 in his pocket. As he stepped off the train, a middle-aged man stepped forward and introduced himself as Lieutenant Manuel Ortega. He was wearing the biggest sombrero Juan had ever seen and looked like a Mexican chandelier.

He led Juan to a waiting car and sped off across the border, until they reached a military camp at the edge of Chihuahua City. There were no tents. Un-uniformed soldiers stretched out on blankets and serapes, each wearing just a big sombrero, a dirty cotton shirt and trousers, a bandolier of bullets, and a gun. The smell of tobacco and *aguardiente* (a strong, sweet liquor) wafted in from somewhere, probably their clothes. A few women sang as they mashed corn on large stones. An old man walked around the camp, waving a fistful of printed sheets over his head. "Two cents for a prayer to the Crucified Christ. Two cents . . . "

Two other men walked up. A handsome, confident young man, obviously American, shook Juan's hand and said, "I'm Raoul Walsh." The other man, built like a bear, with a fierce mustache, big head, wide shoulders, thick body, and eyes that reminded Juan of a wild panther, said, "I'm Pancho Villa." They wasted little time on pleasantries, because Villa was waging war against the government of Mexico.

For the next month, Juan served as the (uncredited) assistant director of *The Life of General Villa*, Raoul Walsh's first film, the first biopic ever made, and the first feature-length film in American history. The producer was D. W. Griffith, who would direct *Birth of a Nation* the following year.

The concept of the film was spectacular: Pancho Villa would star in the movie. Walsh would follow Villa, film his battles as they actually happened, and incorporate them into the film. In exchange, Villa received a $25,000 advance that he used to buy cannons, rifles, horses, coal, dynamite, and ammunition. In this way, to get footage for their epic film, D. W. Griffith and his Mutual Film Corporation helped finance the Mexican Revolution. You could say that Griffith financed the first reality show.[3]

To prepare everyone for the project Walsh took Pancho Villa, Lieutenant Ortega, General Tomas Urbína, a one-eyed bodyguard named Cholo Martinez, and a few other officers to a movie theater in Juárez that was showing a film about Jesse James. The problems started at the ticket stand, when Cholo Martinez insisted he should only pay half price because he had only one eye. The ticket seller countered that if everybody in Juárez wore an eye patch, then his theater would go broke. "In that case," said Cholo, "just make everybody with an eye patch show you what's underneath it." He pulled up his patch and thrust the raw empty socket toward the ticket seller, who vomited and let everyone in for free.

The movie screen was just a white sheet tacked to the wall, and when the movie started, mayhem erupted. As the James gang rode onto the screen, shooting in all directions, many of the spectators dove for cover under the benches. A moment later a posse of lawmen pursued the bandits, and in the spirit of outlaw brotherhood, somebody in the theater joined Jesse in shooting at them. In the next instant the whole movie house was engaged in a gunfight, and four men were killed. When the smoke cleared, everyone still wanted to see the film, but the projectionist was dead too, and he'd kicked over the projector as he fell. The audience would have shot the house manager in protest if he hadn't already

Pancho Villa attacks *Los Federales* . . . again
Courtesy of the Library of Congress

been taken away with a bullet in his leg. On the way back to camp, Pancho Villa summed it all up: "One thing about movies," he shouted from his horse, "only people with strong nerves should be permitted to watch them."

On January 26, 1914, Villa and 10,000 men assaulted the city of Durango. He sent his cavalry to encircle the garrison and cut off any retreat. Then his infantry formed three long battle lines that attacked in wave after wave. The battle lasted a few hours, but once the men swarmed over the walls and battered their way through the front gate, it all ended too quickly for Raoul Walsh and his cameraman, Hennie Aussenberg, to capture on film.

There were dead men on the ground, many wounded, lots of blood, and two horses with their heads split open. Inside the city, Villa's men were shooting Federal officers and hanging them from trees. A mob of peasants used rocks to knock the teeth out of Federal corpses in order to harvest their gold fillings. But Walsh still wanted "more drama," and it was Juan's job to persuade Pancho Villa to reenact some of the battle while the corpses were still lying on the ground.

After much diplomacy and flattery, Juan managed to convince Villa that, for the glory of the revolution, a few extra shots wouldn't hurt.

They shot Villa riding into Durango, firing his pistol over the cameraman's head. They shot Villa trapped behind a boulder, shooting back at four Federales. They shot Villa leaping off the boulder. They stripped the clothes, caps, and boots off dozens of dead Federales and told Villa's men to put them on in order to stage a mock battle. At that point, Villa, growing irritated, threatened to shoot Walsh, and tensions mounted until Juan had a stroke of genius: since the Federales were a bunch of alcoholics, the actors should get drunk in order to portray them.[4]

The idea was an instant hit, and nearly two hundred men volunteered for the scene. The mock battle was a great success but had to be reshot several times because Villa's men kept laughing during the scene. When Villa attacked the towns of Ojinaga and Torreón, Walsh again insisted on reshooting some of the battle savagery.[5]

The movie was delayed a few days when Villa kidnapped a Spanish rancher in León and ransomed him for $5,000 and two hundred cows. It was delayed another day when Villa stole a train from the Mexican Central Railroad and filled it with the rancher's cows.

By the time Villa captured Mexico City on February 17, his entire army was fed up with the *pinche* film crew, but Walsh had enough footage and returned to Hollywood. The movie opened in New York on May 14, 1914, to favorable reviews, nationwide distribution, and box office success. Juan worked with Walsh for a while (on *Regeneration*, *Carmen*, and *Peer Gynt*) and was hired in 1916 by the Tropical Film Company to help shoot *Following the Flag in Mexico*.

The moment he arrived in Columbus, New Mexico, Juan realized the Tropical Film Company was a US Army propaganda unit. Every crew member wore a military uniform, and *Following the Flag in Mexico* consisted of interviews with Generals John Pershing and Frederick Funston and the president of Mexico, combined with leftover footage from *The Life of General Villa*. Since Villa had just attacked a US garrison in Columbus, Juan was not shocked. In fact, he was intrigued. The US Army was juxtaposing and manipulating the footage from *The*

Life of General Villa to tell a completely different story. It felt like he'd discovered an entirely new art form: that of lying to millions of people, all at once, all over the world.

ᕦᕤ

On March 2, 1917, the US Congress passed the Jones-Shafroth Act, which authorized a Puerto Rican bill of rights and bicameral legislature, an elected resident commissioner to the US Congress, and immediate US citizenship for Puerto Ricans.[6] Critics of the bill—including the Puerto Rican House of Representatives, insular historians, and Albizu Campos himself—pointed out the profound flaws in the Jones-Shafroth Act: (1) the US Congress could ignore any Puerto Rican bill of rights, (2) it could override any "laws" passed by the Puerto Rican legislature, (3) the resident commissioner had no vote in the US Congress, and (4) US "citizenship" was a vehicle for drafting Puerto Rican men into the US military.[7]

Exactly one month after passage of the Jones-Shafroth Act, President Woodrow Wilson presented his declaration of war against Germany before the US Congress. Then on June 27, 1917, Wilson ordered the registration and recruitment of the male inhabitants of Puerto Rico between the ages of twenty-one and thirty-one.[8]

Before anyone could stick Juan Emilio Viguié in a European trench, he called some of his *Following the Flag* contacts and volunteered for the film division of the Committee on Public Information (CPI). He served out the war editing a weekly newsreel called *Official War Review*, which appeared in theaters nationwide. He also wrote the Spanish titles for Charlie Chaplin's *Shoulder Arms* and Goldwyn Pictures' *The Service Star*.

The CPI also staged some "reality newsreels" of German soldiers throwing babies out windows and raping nurses and schoolteachers. Juan managed to stay away from them, but they confirmed what he'd seen in *Following the Flag*: this medium was powerful and easily abused. Then, in 1918, he saw the results of an audience experiment by Russian film director Lev Kuleshov.

The experiment was quite simple. Kuleshov intercut one shot of an actor with three other images: a dead girl, a bowl of soup, and a sexy woman. The film clip was shown to several audiences, who believed that the expression on the actor's face changed depending on whether he was "looking at" the girl in the coffin, the bowl of soup, or the reclining woman—that he showed grief, hunger, or desire, respectively. The audiences even raved about the actor and the depth of his emotions. Yet in all three cases, Kuleshov had used the exact same shot of the actor.[9]

For Kuleshov, this proved the importance of montage in filmmaking. For Juan it proved what he already knew: that film was the most powerful, and the most dangerous, art form in the world. As if to confirm this, within one week of the Kuleshov announcement, an internal memo circulated through the CPI, titled "How to Harness the Kuleshov Effect for our War Effort."

Returning to Puerto Rico after the war, Juan saw how the art of filmmaking had developed on the island. One- and two-reel "travelogues" were all the rage, showing pictures of "our new possessions" and footage of "Porto Rico scenery." In San Juan, the Farándula, the Cine Lido, and other venues had installed dozens of *traganickels* (coin-operated kinetoscopes) with sexually suggestive themes, all scripted and shot by American film crews. Many of those early films showing a tawdry, immoral Puerto Rico were actually shot in the United States using burlesque dancing girls.[10]

The only active film company on the island was Porto Rico Photoplays, which hired Juan as a cameraman for a Paramount production of *Tropical Love* starring Reginald Denny and Ruth Clifford. The film was set in the Loíza Aldea township, poorly planned, and doomed from the start. Juan was the only Puerto Rican on the entire crew, and every character was played by an American actor who spoke no Spanish and used a ridiculous accent. To darken their skin, the actors used Max Factor Color Harmony makeup, which kept melting under the klieg lights and in the tropical heat, until scene after scene came to a grinding halt.

To make matters worse, leading man Denny and director Ralph Ince argued and threatened each other throughout the entire production. Denny would call Ince a fool, Ince would say, "I've directed 110 films, how many have you directed?" and Denny would challenge him to a fight.[11] The arguing suited the film crew just fine because it increased

Poster announcing "Our New Possessions"
Courtesy of the Library of Congress

their overtime pay in Prohibition-free Puerto Rico. The film finally wrapped when a gaffer was almost electrocuted and a rumor circulated that Eusebio, the most powerful witch doctor in Loíza Aldea, had cursed the production.[12]

Predictably, *Tropical Love* bombed in 1921. Porto Rico Photoplays was dissolved, and Juan purchased its equipment. The following year Radio Mundo (WKAQ) became the first radio station in Puerto Rico, and Juan announced the formation of Noticiero Viguié (Viguié News), which, for the next thirty years, became the principal historian of Puerto Rico. Until the first TV station arrived in 1954, it provided the only permanent record of hurricanes, political events, military parades, celebrity interviews, baseball games, human-interest stories, and the changing physical landscape of the island itself.

Juan still wanted to be a film director, and in 1926 he directed the location scenes for Paramount's *Aloma of the Seas*. His documentaries of Charles Lindbergh's visit to Puerto Rico and the devastation caused by Hurricane San Felipe won global recognition, and he signed international distribution contracts with both MGM and Fox News.[13] With a $10,000 investment from a San Juan lawyer, he finally directed *Romance Tropical*—an ambitious project with large production numbers, original music, and underwater photography.

The film was a hit in 1934, with extended runs in New York, Los Angeles, and Puerto Rico; it broke house records in Spain's Teatro Campoamor. MGM was so impressed that it offered Juan a four-picture deal, and Frank L. Clemente, MGM's director of Latin productions, planned to establish his central offices in Puerto Rico.[14] Unfortunately a copyright dispute erupted between Juan and his *Romance Tropical* investor, and MGM canceled its contract with Viguié Productions. Embittered and disillusioned, Juan swore he'd never make a commercial film again—until he saw a German masterpiece.

☙

Juan knew a thug when he saw one. He'd seen hundreds of them in his adoptive father's courtroom and hundreds more in the film business. But that was the disturbing brilliance of *Triumph of the Will*. It turned a demented little man like Adolf Hitler into a Nietzschean demigod.

There were no actors in the film besides Hitler—yet, through camera placement, traveling and low-angle shots, wide-angle lenses, aerial photography, multiple setups, backlighting, scenic dissolves, and symphonic music, Leni Riefenstahl created the greatest propaganda film ever made, intercutting massive crowds with flags, eagles, and swastikas and weaving visual symbolism and emotional stimuli into every shot. The music was subtly evocative. It was the most manipulative yet riveting film he had ever seen.[15]

But *Triumph* had another impact on Juan. As he walked out of the Cine Luna with images of the Nuremberg rally marching through his head, his own feet took him to San Juan Harbor. He heard the gentle song of the coquí and three men laughing around a domino table. He saw an old woman walking down the steps of a sixteenth-century church and two lovers under a scarlet *flamboyán* tree, watching the stars come to life. As he neared the ocean and felt its dark power, Juan realized he didn't have sixteen camera crews, 700,000 extras, and a psychotic dictator, like Leni Riefenstahl did, but he had the same film knowledge, a beautiful island, and a people whose story had never been told.[16]

☙

Over the years, Juan built the greatest documentary newsreel company on the entire island. He shot political and sporting events, instructional shorts, and Spanish-language newsreels. News agencies from all over the world used his Noticiero Viguié footage, particularly of hurricanes. As his business grew, Juan created his own film lab—using phenidone, acetic acid, and ammonium thiosulfate for developer, stop bath, and fixer—and built his own drying cabinets. For sound effects he hired the most incredible Foley man he had ever encountered, El Blablazo.

The invisible man of Puerto Rican radio, El Blablazo went from station to station like a wandering Jew—in fact, he was a Jew and rumored to own three houses in Aguadilla. A fat, bald, coffee-colored man, he dressed like a beggar and carried his work tools with him: a sheet of tinfoil, a wooden plank, a fan, a water pail, a kazoo, a Jew's harp, a bar of soap, a bag of sand, a staple gun, two coconut shells, four high-heeled shoes, a head of lettuce, and half a door. El Blablazo was a genius of sound. Hired mostly for baseball games, weather reports, and radio soap operas, he put on quite a show.

During the 1930s, Puerto Ricans thought they were listening to live New York Yankees games—but they were really hearing El Blablazo. Three hours after a batter hit a home run in New York, El Blablazo would read from a ticker tape in a San Juan radio station, bang two sticks together, play an FX record, and yell, "Hon run! Babe Roo, he do it again!"

For Juan's Noticiero Viguié newsreels, El Blablazo would study the script and lay out his equipment. Then, at a signal from Juan, he would recreate a busy street, a car crash, a barroom brawl, a ladies' tea party, a hurricane, or even a zoo. He walked on all fours to create simultaneous footsteps. By clacking his tongue, gurgling, uttering, and whispering, he generated the scattered chatter, shouts, echoes, and laughter of a busy town square. With his fan and tinfoil he unleashed rain and wind and even a hurricane. He created horses with his coconuts and broken bones with lettuce. Roaring, croaking, grunting, and screaming, he incarnated the entire Mayagüez Zoo. By the end of every recording session, El Blablazo—panting, with big dark circles under his eyes, and sweating like a horse—looked as though he'd run a marathon.

⌘

The Noticiero Viguié newsreels had unparalleled sound effects, and in 1937, to upgrade their image quality, Juan purchased an Arri 35 camera. In March of that year, he heard about a Palm Sunday parade in support of Albizu Campos. It was happening in Ponce, Juan's hometown, so he was happy to go. It would be the first test of his Arri 35. On Sunday, March 21, Juan found a perfect camera angle from an abandoned warehouse window that overlooked the parade ground. His father's old courthouse was just around the corner. The Ponce town square, city hall, and several churches were just three blocks away.

Then the massacre happened. Seventeen people were killed in broad daylight. Up in a dark window, Juan filmed it all.

He rushed to his lab and developed the three four-hundred-foot rolls he'd shot and viewed the footage through his movieola. The advance of the police, the relentless shooting, the terror in every face, the bodies, the blood . . . all the images evoked scenes from *Battleship Potemkin*. But the Odessa Steps massacre had never happened, and this was all too real. Maria Hernández del Rosario, the fifty-three-year-old woman with her brains spilled into the street, had been Juan's babysitter.

Juan studied every frame. In those thirteen minutes he learned a lifetime's worth of history, philosophy, psychology, political science, sociology, anthropology, and economics. They told him everything he needed to know about what men were capable of and what men in "America" thought of him and his people. Those thirteen minutes made clear that, to those from the north, Puerto Ricans were not equals, or citizens, or even fully human. They were animals. And so they could be shot on Palm Sunday like rabid dogs in the street.[17]

If Juan wasn't careful, someone might come and shoot him. So he developed a second print and placed the prints and the negative in three waterproof tins. That very night he buried them all in his backyard.

Over the next few days, Juan kept his mouth shut and his ears open. The police had followed the wounded to Tricoche Hospital and arrested them in their stretchers and hospital beds. Pedro Rodriguez-Serra, the Ponce assistant district attorney, was pressuring witnesses and family members to sign false affidavits regarding the day's events. The island newspapers screamed about the Ponce Massacre, and dozens of Nationalists would be prosecuted.

☙

Juan never forgot what he'd seen on that Palm Sunday, and the memory gave his life direction. One day he would tell this story, all of it, even if he had to bury pieces of it in his backyard. He would save every piece until the story was complete. Then he'd splice it all together and show the world what men were capable of.

From that day forward, Juan became the relentless documentarian of the Nationalist movement in Puerto Rico. He shot footage of the Cadets of the Republic and Nationalist events throughout the island. He shot funerals, meetings, and speeches. When Albizu Campos returned to Puerto Rico in 1947 after ten years of imprisonment and exile, Juan was ready to film him. Albizu would be the central character, the driving force in Juan's epic documentary film about Puerto Rico.[18]

Juan filmed Albizu's return on the SS *Kathryn*, the tumultuous crowds, the march down Calle San Augustín, the flags, the motorcades, and the speech to 14,000 supporters at Sixto Escobar Stadium. He made a short newsreel of it, *Recibemiento a Don Pedro* (Reception of Don Pedro), and gave a copy to the Nationalists.[19] He filmed Albizu all over the island as he spoke in Ponce, Lares, Río Piedras, Fajardo, Mayagüez, Aguada, Utuado, Jayuya, Manatí, and Arecibo. He contacted friends at the WENA, WPBP, and WPRP radio stations and got transcripts of Albizu's radio speeches.

El Maestro had returned to his island, and revolution was in the air. Because of him, someday soon, Juan would outdo Leni Riefenstahl. Where D. W. Griffith had manufactured lies, Juan would preserve the truth.[20]

CHAPTER 14

The OSS Agent

In the town of Santurce there is a small cemetery, about 1.5 acres in size, called Villa Palmeras. Grave 285 there differs from most—it is dedicated not to a person but to Club Nosotros, which "died" on January 7, 1942. Of the several stories surrounding the death of the club, one involves Waller Booth, a man known as the smoothest and most popular Office of Strategic Services (OSS) agent in Latin American history. Some Puerto Ricans likened him to James Bond. Others compared him to Humphrey Bogart's character in *Casablanca*.

Booth was born in 1904 in Owensboro, Kentucky. Since 1791 his family had worked, farmed, saved, and accumulated a series of landholdings along the Ohio River that passed from one generation to the next. They were honest, hard-working people, and their family papers reveal a century of cotillions, church matters, land grants, and promissory notes, all paid in full and on time. Owensboro even has a Booth Avenue and a Booth Field Road.

Booth attended Greenbrier Military, Phillips Andover, and Princeton, graduating with the Class of 1926. His senior year as a Tiger was the best of his entire life. He lived in F. Scott Fitzgerald's old dorm

(12 University Place), ate at Ivy, played on the varsity football team, and was voted president of his class and president of the Triangle Club. He starred in four Triangle productions and played the title role in *Fortuno*, a comic opera about love and betrayal in Renaissance Italy, which went on a fourteen-city tour.[1] The *New York Times* said Booth "made a good-looking hero."[2]

Then reality set in. Booth's old-money family reminded him that acting was a disreputable profession, particularly for a southern actor named "Booth." He graduated and became a cruise director for the Raymond & Whitcomb Company, arranging "exceptional tours to South America."[3] The company brochures assured, "South America is still a land of fascinating crudeness, barbaric color and movement. It will make you feel you are an adventurer—a discoverer of romance and mystery." The company arranged travel parties for "the best class of North Americans" to the West Indies, Cuba, Panama, Ecuador, and every country in South America. It did the same in Africa and China. The serious traveler could take a one-year cruise through most of the Third World and "see the zoo in its home."

Booth arranged steamship, railway, and hotel accommodations; automobile and horse carriage rides; restaurant reservations and sightseeing tours; guides, messengers, interpreters; and any "extra" services his travelers might require. The job had its benefits: Booth learned flawless Spanish and respectable French. He arranged trips for numerous Princeton pals and was paid to host them.

After fourteen years of this, Booth received a call from yet another Princetonian named Allen Dulles. As secretary of the Council on Foreign Relations, Dulles was organizing a new foreign intelligence service and looking for a few lads with "the right stuff."[4] As president of his 1926 Princeton class, a varsity football player, and a world traveler who spoke three languages, Booth clearly filled the bill. They had a lively conversation, and a few days later Waller Booth volunteered for the foreign intelligence service.[5]

§

"Keep your head down . . . keep it down!"

Booth didn't have to be told twice. Two Browning M1919 machine guns were shooting live .30-caliber rounds over his head as he crawled under a field of barbed wire. For three months he was shot at, punched, slapped, thrown, drowned, frozen, starved, interrogated, lied to, pumped with drugs, thrown out of airplanes, and shoved off cliffs. It was called Camp X by some, the School of Mayhem and Murder by others, and it taught Booth his new trade: spy craft.[6]

He learned the mechanics and firing of a rifle, carbine, Colt .45 automatic pistol, Browning automatic rifle, Bren light machine gun, British Sten gun, Thompson submachine gun, M1 bazooka, M2 mortar, and 6-pounder antitank gun. He studied the use of various explosives and timing devices to destroy railroad tracks, bridges, tunnels, radio towers, supply depots, and industrial facilities. He practiced how to inflict and resist a brutal interrogation, install bugging devices, and create false documents, certificates, and passports. He ran five miles a day, swam in the freezing waters of Lake Ontario, and learned to disable or kill an enemy with his hands, feet, a knife, or any instrument at hand. As a graduation exercise, Booth infiltrated a Canadian gun factory and stole its financial records, then night-parachuted into the boreal forest with no water or compass and made it fifty miles back to camp.

In 1942 he became an OSS commander.

გ~

With his fluent Spanish and traveler's knowledge of Latin America, Booth was assigned to "keep an eye on things" in Puerto Rico. The US Army was especially concerned about two things: first, that Nationalists were buying weapons from Puerto Rican soldiers known as the "Borinqueneers," who were stationed at Camp Las Casas in Santurce;[7] second, that Nationalists were planning to murder all the American managers and overseers at the major sugar plantations.[8]

Sent to monitor the Borinqueneers and the Nationalists, Booth devised an excellent cover. He didn't travel in uniform or refer to himself as a military man. Instead, he entered Puerto Rico as the head of Booth, Carroll Bottling Company—a phony bottling and import firm specializing in *aguardiente* and sugar cane rum—which enabled him to

Members of the 65th Infantry Regiment, known as the "Borinqueneers"

perform security sweeps of all the plantations under the guise of making a "marketing and sales" visit.

In early 1942 he opened an after-hours dive bar called Club Nosotros off the corner of Avenida Eduardo Conde and Calle Martino. It was right across the street from the Villa Palmeras Cemetery and, more importantly, just half a mile away from Camp Las Casas. With its half-priced drinks and 78-rpm jukebox, every soldier and señorita in Santurce knew about Club Nosotros.

When the United States declared war on Japan, Commander Booth was called to active duty. He closed the bar, and exactly one month after Pearl Harbor, on January 7, 1942, grave 285 was created in the Villa Palmeras Cemetery. Apparently someone really missed Booth's club.

☙

The Borinqueneers fought in Panama, France, Italy, and Germany and suffered a total of forty-seven battle casualties.[9] But for many of them, the most memorable deployment was to Casablanca in November 1942. Two weeks after the army arrived, on November 26, 1942, *Casablanca* was released and an advance print was screened in the city of Casablanca itself. Thousands of GIs poured into the theater, night after night, to hoot and yell at the screen. The Borinqueneers were there. So was Waller Booth.

He was an undercover agent throughout North Africa and Spain,[10] and his most memorable exploit occurred in 1944, when he parachuted into Vichy France as commander of "Mission Marcel Proust" to gather intelligence and develop tactical support teams behind enemy lines. One week before the D-Day invasion of Normandy, Proust scored its greatest intelligence coup: operatives stole the papers of Colonel Klaus von Strobel, the opposing German commander.[11]

After the war ended, Booth returned to Puerto Rico using his old Booth, Carroll cover. The barracks at Camp Las Casas were shut down permanently in 1946, but Booth wanted to keep an eye on Puerto Rican soldiers and veterans. Remembering the wild *Casablanca* screenings in Morocco, he converted a two-story house in Hato Rey (not far from the old club) into a theme bar. Upstairs, a screening room played only one movie: *Casablanca*. Downstairs, Rodney Rabassa, a piano player from Caguas who looked like Dooley Wilson, led a little house band.

A rotund little fellow, Rodney would sit at the piano like a tiny king and sing,

Yo soy negro social (I am a society Negro)
Soy intellectual y chic (I am intellectual and chic)

Booth tamed Rodney's flamboyancy, and the band rehearsed a more "classical" repertoire of "Lamento Borincano," "Preciosa," "Bésame Mucho," and the inevitable "As Time Goes By."

When it opened in late 1947 the club was unmarked and didn't even have a name, but Booth must have been very persuasive because the CIA put some real money into it. On opening night he greeted everyone warmly, and at 9 p.m. the *Fantasia Caribeña* floor show began. The lead-in act featured frolicking señoritas, conga drums, and a bikini-clad dancer with a four-foot stack of sombreros on her head. Next, a *bomba y plena* dance troupe performed, followed by Rodney's rendition of "As Time Goes By."

Then came a spectacular number called "Sun Sun Babae."[12] Six Taíno warriors danced furiously to a set of *batá* drums, then jumped offstage into the audience. They stopped before a small, frightened woman nursing a banana daiquiri at a corner table. A spotlight shined on the sweating half-naked men, as they lifted the poor woman out of her seat and carried her onstage. She tried to run away, but the men, chanting "Sun Sun Babae," stopped her.

Then a strange thing began to happen. The terrified woman seemed to grow curious and then intoxicated by the drums and chanting, which grew louder and more intense. The audience became mesmerized and confused, not sure whether this was real or part of the show. Without warning, the little woman suddenly ripped off her black cocktail dress and began dancing in black lace underwear and a garter belt. The audience now suspected this was part of the act—but the woman still appeared hypnotized, dancing feverishly under the spell of the Orisha spirits as the men tossed her around in their arms. Then, amid the heightening music and movement, the woman suddenly snapped out of her trance. She looked at the men, the drummers, and the audience— then let out a blood-curdling scream, grabbed her clothes, and ran out of Booth's club.

After a few seconds of silence, the entire club jumped up and gave a stomping, table-rattling ovation. Audience members shouted "Bravo!" and applauded for several minutes—stunned, amused, and aroused all at the same time. As the band launched into "Mambo at the Ritz," the whole club was laughing, dancing, and drinking, and the opening night of Booth's Club with No Name was a smashing success. As the night wore on, Booth settled into a dark corner of the piano bar, where he could smoke and watch everyone who came in the door. After all, that's what the CIA had paid for. When they counted the money at 6 a.m., the club had taken in almost $800—the equivalent of $7,900 in 2014.

❧

The *Casablanca* screenings on the second floor developed a cult following. Every night dozens of Puerto Ricans yelled out their favorite Humphrey Bogart lines; those who didn't speak English simply yelled. The film played continuously till 4 a.m.—unless a fight broke out during the singing of "La Marseillaise." Booth started attending the screenings himself, since a lot of Nationalists and malcontents were showing up. It was easy to spot them: they yelled their own dialogue at the screen.

"Do me again, Sam!"

"We'll always have the FBI!"

"Round up the usual Nationalists!"

By late 1948 a social division had developed in the club that Booth didn't like. American soldiers hobnobbed with a few rich islanders downstairs, while the poorer, darker Puerto Ricans sat upstairs yelling at Humphrey Bogart. It was great fun though, and some of the ad-libs were inspired.

"As leader of all illegal activity in San Juan, I am an influential and respected man."

"J. Edgar Hoover has been shot. Here's looking at you, kid."

"There are certain sections of Ponce that I wouldn't advise you to invade."

The club grew even more popular, and Booth became something of a local hero when an FBI man barged in and tried to arrest a suspected Nationalist. Booth stepped out from his dark corner, stood between them, and asked the agent his business. Unintimidated when the agent flashed his badge, Booth put his hands on his hips, briefly revealing a snub-nosed .38 special holstered under his left shoulder. The band stopped playing, and Rodney started creeping around his piano, getting ready to duck. Everyone's eyes were on Booth and the FBI man. The agent finally muttered that Booth would be hearing about this, then turned and left.

A cheer erupted. "Que viva Waller!" "Que viva Humphrey Bogart!" The band broke into "La Borinqueña," and half the club started singing the Puerto Rican national anthem. The other half mobbed around Booth, trying to buy him a drink.[13]

☙

A few days later, a ruckus erupted in the *Casablanca* room, and Booth hurried upstairs. A drunken Nationalist was yelling at the Germans on-screen, and everyone was yelling at him. When the Nationalist would not shut up, they started throwing peanuts at him. Then the Germans started singing "Die Wacht am Rhein," and the French started singing "La Marseillaise," and someone pelted the Nationalist with an orange. It was all in good fun until two men flashed their badges and tried to arrest the Nationalist.

When Booth ran over, the first FBI man took a swing, but Booth chopped him in the throat and he went down. The second agent tackled

Booth, and suddenly another pair of agents charged into the room. Chairs flew, bottles broke, and women screamed, as Booth exchanged blows with the FBI men. "La Marseillaise" was still playing, and Booth's white dinner jacket was streaked with blood, when he pulled out his .38 and shot once in the air.

The world stood still.

Booth and the agents stared at each other. Even the music downstairs stopped, as the five men breathed heavily in the silence. Then Booth told the FBI men that the next time he saw them at his club, he would kill them. As the agents started to leave, Booth noticed a badge on the floor and threw it at their backs. Then he wiped the blood off his mouth as the room exploded with applause.[14]

Unbeknownst to those present, Booth and the FBI men had staged these fights. They were calculated to build affection for Booth and trust in his club. The plan worked: night after night the profits rolled in, and Booth just sat in his dark corner, beside a cozy little lamp, watching. He was always gracious and helpful, and if anyone dragged him into a "political" discussion, he'd calmly say, "Excuse me, gentlemen. Your business is politics. Mine is running a saloon." But all the time he was listening.

After the passage of the Gag Law, Booth's club became even more popular. Between the mojitos, the daiquiris, the Cuba Libres and all the screaming in the Casablanca room, nobody noticed or cared about a few Nationalists cursing their lot in life. They came and went freely, argued openly, and added to the general ambiance. The Club with No Name was the only place on the island where the First Amendment still applied—so long as you paid your bar tab. But Booth was still listening.

∽

It all came to an end with the Korean War.

As of 1941, the United States had occupied Vieques Island—an eighty-four-square-mile island eight miles east of the Puerto Rican mainland—for military exercises, as a firing range, and as ground for testing new bombs and missiles. Every year the army detonated an average of 5 million pounds of ordnance on the island, particularly on its beaches.

On March 8, 1950, the United States "attacked" Vieques with all of its armed forces—army, navy, air force, marines. The 80,000 men involved included infantry, airborne paratroopers, frogmen, undercover agents, and guerillas. The three-day assault required two months of planning. It was the largest war game in US history, a dress rehearsal for the Korean War, known as Operation Portrex.

Booth was called to lead all espionage and guerilla activities for the 65th Infantry, the Puerto Rican Borinqueneers, who were assigned to defend the island. This would burn his cover as a civilian saloonkeeper, but it didn't matter. As soon as the war started, he was shipping to Korea, so he didn't care anymore.

Actually, he was in his element. With fewer than two hundred men, he organized a guerilla unit that donned US military uniforms and infiltrated the enemy's ranks, disrupted communications, reported troop and artillery movements, and penetrated the radio network to misdirect cannon fire. Booth's men even "killed" the enemy corps and division commanders by simply knocking on their tent poles, handing each a musette bag, saluting, and disappearing. The bags held simulated bombs that exploded when opened and spilled red ink all over their uniforms.[15] Booth's unorthodox, devastatingly effective tactics were later recreated in a movie called *The Dirty Dozen*.

Thanks to Portrex, Booth became a hero to the Borinqueneers, every one of whom was Puerto Rican. Hundreds of soldiers told their families about the great Colonel Waller Booth, who helped defend Vieques from 80,000 marauding Yankees. The news swept through Puerto Rico, and people from as far as Cabo Rojo, Mayagüez, and Guánica made a pilgrimage to the *Casablanca* screenings. Booth handled all the attention gracefully but demanded reassignment as soon as possible. With his cover burned, it was only a matter of time before the Nationalists bombed his bar as a matter of pride and general principle.

In 1950 the club closed down, and Booth left the island. He went on to command a native guerrilla unit in North Korea during the Korean War, then joined the first Military Assistance Advisory Group in Vietnam, taught at the infamous School of the Americas in Fort Benning, Georgia, and consulted on guerilla warfare, counterinsurgency, and clandestine activities throughout the Third World.[16] All that remains physically of his time in Puerto Rico is the grave marked "Club No-sotros—January 7, 1942" in the Villa Palmeras Cemetery.

But Waller Booth left a trail of legend and rumor.

Some say he was a brilliant showman, a Caribbean Flo Ziegfeld, who stole the "Sun Sun Babae" number from the Sans Souci club in Havana and a *Casablanca* print from the Warner Brothers vaults.

Some say he was an Ivy League dilettante, a member of the "Oh-So-Social" club (the OSS) who treated war and peace as a personal adventure.

Some say he was an old-money overseer whose stints at Raymond & Whitcomb, the OSS, and the CIA were covers for "seeing the zoo in its own home" and making sure it stayed there.

Some say he was a lifelong agent for the Riggs National Bank, a personal friend of Police Chief E. Francis Riggs, and that both men assisted Anastasio Somoza in Nicaragua, Jorge Ubico in Guatemala, and other right-wing dictators throughout Latin America.

Some say he coordinated the interrogation, torture, and disappearance of Nationalist and Communist prisoners at various safe houses throughout the island—particularly the one near Ramey Air Force Base in Aguadilla.

But in all fairness to Booth, these are only rumors. In the blurred edges of history, in the twilight zone of truth, the record shows that Waller Booth was an officer and a gentleman who never watered his drinks and brought a touch of class to colonial espionage.[17]

CHAPTER 15

The Barber

Vidal Santiago Díaz was the most famous barber in Puerto Rico. A graduate of the Arecibo Barber Academy and author of *El Texto de Barbería Practica y Científica* (*The Textbook of Practical and Scientific Barbering*), he owned the Salón Boricua, a four-chair barbershop stuffed with customers and thieves. The action was nonstop. Every day, someone got thrown out of the *salón*. Every week, three unlicensed barbers climbed out the back window when San Juan's health inspectors raided the establishment. Every month, San Juan's top second-class citizens filled the shop with fierce debates about women, horses, politics, baseball, sugar cane, and how the Yankee bastards were keeping Puerto Ricans down.

People went to the *salón* for a haircut, a loan, a drink, or a used refrigerator. They could do more business in the *salón* than in most banks. They would learn more there than from any newspaper. And they certainly had fun. During Vidal Santiago's trial for treason, Governor Luis Muñoz Marín said, "Just open the door to this barbershop, and the lies pour out onto the street."[1]

Vidal loved his *salón*, with its manly scent of pomades and neck powders and the pungent smells of witch hazel, Bay rum, and Lucky

Tiger hair tonic. He loved the beveled-edge mirrors, the Polaroids on the wall, the Oster electric clippers, and the Campbell latherizing machines. He loved his Koken barber chair, a monstrous three-hundred-pound throne carved from oak and walnut with a plush leather seat, ash trays in the arm rests, and hydraulic side levers. He loved dancing around the chair, playing mambos on the radio, and keeping time with the Machito Orchestra with his scissors.

Most of all, he loved what his barbershop stood for. It had been there, on the corner of Calles Colton and Barbosa, since the beginning of Calvin Coolidge's second term. It had survived two hurricanes and the Great Depression. The Koken chair cost $400 and was entirely paid for—everything in the shop was. The men in Salón Boricua weren't digging ditches or rolling cigars or cutting sugar cane for somebody else. They were working for themselves. And one of them owned the place.

಄

For thirty years Vidal Santiago's grandfather, one of the most respected men in the town of Aguas Buenas, used his big, booming voice as a *lectór*, reading to the cigar workers all day, every day, while they rolled cigars. There were no television or radio sets, and many workers were illiterate—so the *lectór* provided a vital link between them and the outside world.[2]

Every morning the *lectóres* climbed up a short, narrow staircase to a *tribuna* (a chair on a platform with a thin railing around it) and looked out over a sea of wooden desks covered with tobacco leaves. They always arrived a few minutes early to savor some strong Puerto Rican coffee and greet the workers as they came in. Then, at 9 a.m., they'd read the morning newspapers, which contained local and international news, sports columns, editorials, even some comic strips. In the afternoon they read novels by Zola, Cervantes, or Tolstoy, books by Kropotkin or Unamuno, and speeches by José Martí and Simón Bolívar. For the women, they read *Marianela* or *Madame Bovary*. Sometimes they read poetry written by the workers themselves. They might even read a marriage proposal from one worker to another.

The work was harder than it sounds. *Lectóres* purchased their own books and newspapers, developed different accents and character voices,

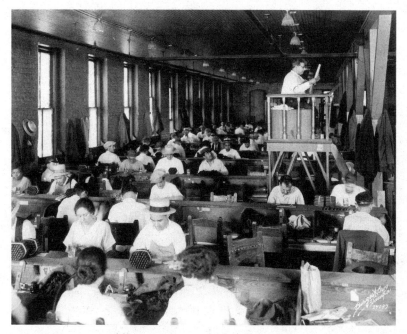

El lectór reads to cigar factory workers
Courtesy of the State Archives of Florida

and had to project and enunciate. They frequently endured bouts of laryngitis, sore throats, and swollen vocal chords. But the rewards were great. Like an opera singer or Shakespearean actor, the better *lectóres* got hired by the bigger "houses." By the end of his career, Vidal's father was reading to five hundred workers, who all paid him fifteen cents per week. He was taking home $300 monthly and becoming one of the more prosperous men in the town of Aguas Buenas. He was also a visiting *lectór* in Ybor City, Florida.[3]

A *lectór* was also a leader, and people asked Vidal's grandfather for advice on almost every subject. He gave it freely and was proud to hear cigar makers, who could hardly read and write, discussing books like Zola's *Germinal* or Kropotkin's *Fields, Factories and Workshops* during their evening walks in the town square. He was also proud that his family admired him and knew they could depend on him.

Stay in school, he'd admonish Vidal, telling him that education made all the difference between becoming the man rolling cigars or the one standing on the *lector*'s platform. Vidal followed his grandfather's advice, but by the time he graduated from high school, Puerto Rico had changed forever.

Starting in 1926, the United Porto Rico Sugar Company bought every tobacco plantation in Aguas Buenas and built the second-largest sugar mill on the island, with a 205-foot chimney and boilers that processed 9 million pounds of cane per day. The National City Bank bought another 54,000 acres of farmland, plus warehouses, port facilities, and 133 miles of railroad. The American Colonial Bank, the House of Morgan, and Bankers Trust controlled another 100,000 acres. All of them turned Puerto Rico into a one-crop economy.[4]

Vidal's father lost his job, and within a few years, there wasn't a single *lector* left on the island. By the time Vidal graduated from high school, his father was cutting sugar cane in the Santa Juana Central, and Vidal was cutting right next to him. There was no more *lector*, no platform, no Cervantes, just a sea of cane in every direction.

From far away, the sugar cane plantations seemed picturesque—an arched bridge, stone buildings, tin huts, and deep woods—as though painted by some medieval artist. But up close it was a gluttony of green geometric lines, logical and direct, like a balance sheet or bank statement. Thousands of green walls multiplied on all sides in endless succession to the horizon.[5]

It was a degrading and exhausting life. Vidal's grandfather was over sixty years old. The other cane workers extended every courtesy and kindness they could to the former *lector*, but his spirit was broken, and his body would soon succumb. During his second harvest season, in May 1929, he had a heart attack while cutting cane. He toppled over and died with a machete in his hand and Vidal standing beside him.

A month after the funeral, Vidal visited his grandfather with a report card in his hand. He had graduated with honors from the Josefa Pastrana High School. Vidal buried the report card over the grave. By the time he got home, he'd vowed that he would never work in the cane fields again. He called some of his grandfather's friends and heard about a barber named José Maldonado who might be hiring. The shop was in

El Barrio Obrero (the Worker's District) of Santurce, just east of Old San Juan. It was called Salón Boricua.

എ

El Barrio Obrero, sandwiched between the Camp Las Casas military base and the Condado Beach hotels, was the most densely populated district in Puerto Rico—more crowded than New York City—with 11,000 people per square kilometer. The streets were crammed with children, horses, dogs, fruit peddlers, ice vendors, stevedores, socialites, and soldiers. Weekends were a free-for-all, with soldiers chasing *las rubias* (blondes) until the chapel bells pealed from Nuestra Señora de Lourdes on Sunday afternoon. The armistice would last until the following Friday.

Santurce was the crossroads of Puerto Rico. On the border of Old San Juan, it was only 1,500 feet from the capitol building and contained the island's main international airport. It had sixteen shipping piers and three miles of beachfront; surrounded by six bodies of water—the Atlantic Ocean, San Juan Bay, the Martin Peña Channel, and three lagoons—it was a haven for swimmers by day and smugglers by night. If anyone wanted to sneak something on or off the island, the place to go was Santurce.

With his high school diploma in his pocket, Vidal Santiago walked the fifteen miles from Aguas Buenas to El Barrio Obrero. He saw the sign at 351 Calle Colton and walked in to find eleven men in the shop but no hair being cut. Three barbers stood beside their chairs, eight men sat on pine benches, everyone was shouting, and a little boy ran around serving *aguardiente* to everyone. They were arguing about Mussolinia, the new land-distribution program in Italy, and about the merits of allowing women to vote. Vidal looked around: dozens of black and white photos signed by local celebrities adorned the mirrors on every wall.

Vidal introduced himself to José Maldonado and produced his high school diploma. José looked him over: the boy was a bit short with a curious face that seemed designed by committee. His ears stuck out like holstered pistols; his hair curled in odd directions.

José, who had known Vidal's grandfather, hired him on the spot. Vidal cleaned the bathroom, scrubbed windows, and whisked the customers off after every haircut. Within a few days, the regulars were nodding at José—he'd found a good employee. Soon José entrusted Vidal with a grave responsibility—he was the only one allowed to fiddle with *la maquina* (the machine), a General Electric Octagon radio whose dials no one could figure out. Some believed the FBI had installed an "evil eye" on the top panel to spy on them.

Vidal grew to love his job. The place had a dramatic flair: one of the barbers was nearly blind, another one was so short he had to stand on an apple box, and both jumped out the back window whenever the health inspectors arrived. The customers were even more colorful: Santo was missing an eye and claimed to be a priest. Tato sold insurance. Sergio sold stolen chickens. Filadelfo played the fiddle and claimed that Xavier Cugat owed him $10,000. Chicharra had a domineering wife and sighed a lot. Diógenes drank too much, until his wife stormed into the shop and slapped him so hard his chair spun.

One customer never gave his name or got a haircut. He'd just walk in and sit in the farthest chair, reading the same magazines over and over. Every few minutes a different man would enter and head for the bathroom, with the mystery man behind him. Eventually Vidal figured it out: he was a *bolitero*, the local numbers man.

The *salón* was not just a theater; it was also a powerful broadcast medium. Anyone wanting to share news would either go to church or Salón Boricua, and the news would travel through the entire town within twenty-four hours. People called it Radio Bemba (Radio Lip) because it was more effective than a radio station.

After three months, José let Vidal give his first haircut. The man had long hair, which afforded some margin of error, but when Vidal finished, the man cried, "¡Ea rayo! You messed up my hair." The whole barbershop went quiet as the one-eyed barber walked over and straightened out the cut. Vidal took a long walk, came back, and botched a second haircut. Then he clipped off half of a man's mustache. It turned out that Vidal had astigmatism, but José stuck with him, and within one year he was a first-class barber who could handle any style of cut or shave any man in fourteen perfect strokes.

Vidal bought new eyeglasses every year. He read some barber books and movie magazines to develop a full repertoire of styles, which he advertised on flyers throughout the neighborhood and a big sign outside the shop. By 1930, business was good at Salón Boricua. But there was another side to the establishment.

José Maldonado had many friends, including two mess sergeants and a procurement officer, who called himself Captain Astro, attached to the 65th Infantry Regiment (the Borinqueneers). They purchased all the food for 4,000 men and were stationed less than a mile from the barbershop at Camp Las Casas. For Captain Astro, who procured 360,000 meals per month for the soldiers, it was an easy matter to divert 5,000 meals and sell them at a steep discount to his friend.[6]

Every month José received a truckload of eggs, rice, beans, cheese, corn, salted meats, and canned ravioli. He rented the house next to Salón Boricua and "sold" the food from there. He actually gave it away to poor local families but attached a nominal price of two cents for a dozen eggs or five cents for a slab of beef in order to preserve his customers' self-respect. As time went on, Vidal realized that this was the true purpose of Salón Boricua. José had found a way to feed nearly fifty families with a little help from the US government.

☙

In May 1930 a quiet man in a bow tie, white shirt, and black jacket entered the *salón*. José introduced him to Vidal: it was Pedro Albizu Campos, just returned from a three-year journey to Mexico, Cuba, Venezuela, and several other South American countries, drumming up support for Puerto Rican independence. Just a few days earlier, on May 11, 1930, he had become the president of the Nationalist Party.

José enthroned Albizu in the big Koken chair, where he got a haircut and running commentary from everyone in the barbershop. They all seemed to know and respect him. After about an hour, José led Albizu into the other apartment, where they talked privately for most of the afternoon. Then José gave Albizu a carload of food, and he left.

The day after Albizu's visit, José called Vidal into the next-door apartment, with the shades drawn and everything in shadow. The place was filled with canned peaches and corned beef, sacks of rice and kidney beans, and a wall of potato crates. He fished out a picture frame with a yellowing portrait. It showed José on a white horse, waving a machete and leading the Intentona de Yauco, a revolt against Spain in 1897. The revolt had failed, but José's role had earned him an island-wide reputation as El Águila Blanca.[7]

Now that Albizu Campos was back, José told Vidal, he was going to help him obtain some guns from Camp Las Casas. He peered out the drapes, then added that he was sharing this information for a reason, that someday he wouldn't be there to do this important work, and when that day came, he hoped Vidal would carry on in his stead. Someone had to.[8]

౭౩

The day came sooner than anyone had expected. In September 1930, José went to San Juan Presbyterian for anemia and was given "iron injections" by a new doctor named Cornelius Rhoads. Two weeks later he had trouble swallowing hard food, and by November he could barely swallow soft food, then liquids, then finally his own saliva. He lost twenty pounds, even though he was a slim man to begin with.

Dr. Rhoads gave José a new set of injections and assured him that his body would adjust to the medication, but it never did. He developed a lump in his throat, and in January 1931 Rhoads announced that José had throat cancer.

On advice from Albizu Campos, José asked for his medical records but the hospital refused on the grounds that all medical records were confidential. Albizu was preparing to sue the doctor and the hospital when, in late February, José started vomiting blood and died in the Salón Boricua bathroom.

Hundreds of people—farmers, soldiers, sugar cane workers, prison buddies, barbershop customers, and every person José had been feeding for the past ten years—attended the funeral. The mourners told many stories about El Águila Blanca and shed many tears, all agreeing that the world had lost a good man. When everyone had gone home, Albizu showed Vidal the last will and testament of José Maldonado. It left Salón Boricua, with all its joys and headaches, to Vidal Santiago.

A few months later Albizu discovered that the doctor who gave José the "iron injections" had been Rhoads—the same man who had written, "The Porto Ricans are the dirtiest, laziest, most degenerate and thievish race of men ever to inhabit this sphere. . . . I have done my best to further the process of extermination by killing off eight and transplanting cancer into several more. . . . All physicians take delight in the abuse and torture of the unfortunate subjects."

Albizu sent copies of Rhoads's letter to newspapers, embassies, the League of Nations, and even the Vatican. No one did anything about it, and Vidal never forgot how El Águila had been killed.[9]

⁂

Salón Boricua survived the Great Depression. The business grew with senior discounts, half-price haircuts for balding men, and Cesar Romero specials on Saturdays. Vidal built a "wall of fame" with photos of Italian singers—Frank Sinatra, Tony Bennett, Perry Como, Dean Martin, Mario Lanza—all autographed as if they had visited the shop. He also built enormous goodwill during the sugar cane strike of 1934 by giving free haircuts to unemployed cane workers. They need only bring a machete, show their calluses, or say that Albizu had sent them. The *salón* also gave free haircuts to any member of Albizu's Cadets of the Republic.

In a corner of the shop, right behind the shoe-shine stand, Vidal created a little shrine. Over it, he hung a photo of his father, the *lectór*, and the photo of El Águila Blanca leading a few brave men in the revolt against Spain. Underneath them he arranged a bible, a rosary, and a statue of Santa Barbara that his father had left him—the only legacy he could afford.

There were three turning points in Vidal's life: the day his father died, the day El Águila Blanca died, and the day he witnessed the Ponce Massacre of 1937. He was there for the Nationalist parade, one of the lucky few to escape unharmed. He watched as the Insular Police machine-gunned innocent men, women, and children and clubbed a woman in the head until her brains spilled into the street.

A few days later he joined the funeral procession. Over 20,000 people escorted the dead through the streets of Ponce. There were no speeches as the coffins were lowered into graves at the Cementerio La Piedad, just the quiet grief of an entire town. That very day, Vidal became a Nationalist.

The Nationalist Party was starting to suffer in 1937. Albizu Campos had been shipped off for a ten-year prison sentence. The FBI was arresting party members, breaking into their homes, and getting them fired from their jobs. Some had simply disappeared.

When news of the Ponce Massacre ripped through the island, many began to fear that if they revealed nationalistic sentiments or shouted, "Que viva Puerto Rico!" at the wrong time, they would be killed. Within a few months, Cadets of the Republic enrollment had dropped from 10,000 to fewer than 500 recruits, and Nationalist Party meetings were held in secret. But this didn't stop Vidal.

He called Captain Astro at Camp Las Casas and haggled furiously with him for a larger shipment of "special items" in addition to the food. By late 1937, weapons or ammunition accompanied every monthly delivery to Salón Boricua. Over the next ten years, until Albizu returned from prison, Vidal accumulated an arsenal for the Nationalist revolution. This included firearms (24 revolvers, 17 pistols, 6 rifles, 3 shotguns, 1 submachine gun), munitions (2,200 bullets, 600 cartridges, 270 thirty-round magazines, 20 pistol caps), explosives (72 percussion caps, 56 Molotov cocktails, 23 dynamite sticks, 22 grenades, 19 explosive bombs, 1 detonator), and knives (5 machetes, 5 daggers, 5 knives, 1 saber).[10]

He stored the weapons in a hidden basement next door, right under all the food. He also built an entrance to the apartment from the Salón Boricua, through a concealed panel in the bathroom. For $200 Captain Astro showed him how to load, fire, and maintain the weapons and even snuck him onto a firing range in Las Casas.

Vidal did all this quietly and patiently. He could never match the bravery of El Águila Blanca or his own father, but his lack of courage could be an asset. It helped him operate in the shadows, where decisive battles could still be won.

By 1946, Vidal saw that the Nationalists were losing heart. Party members were being arrested, and rumors of torture and execution were circulating. There were less than one hundred Cadets of the Republic, and morale was low everywhere. Vidal decided to create a Cadet internship program. Any cadet could get a free haircut and free barber training at Salón Boricua. At first no one came. But then the first cadet dropped by in early December, two more followed the next week, and five more showed up by Christmas for a grand total of eight.

On January 6, 1947, during the annual Three Kings Day party, Vidal turned on the radio, Filadelfo played the fiddle, and Santos told the story of his missing eye. Then Vidal broke out some 120 proof *aguardiente* and gave a long, impassioned toast to El Águila Blanca, the Robin Hood of Puerto Rico and spiritual leader of all barbers. The words were a bit slurred, but it was a great speech, and everyone was in tears when the door opened and eight Cadets of the Republic walked in with perfect haircuts.

Raimundo Díaz Pacheco, the cadets' commander in chief, was with them, and he wanted Vidal to become a captain. Vidal accepted and became a part of the chain of command, which was headed by Albizu as president and included Tomás López de Victoria as subcommander. As Captain of Santurce, Vidal became responsible for recruiting and training young men in Albizu's army of liberation.

☙

Vidal drilled his troops without mercy. They performed calisthenics and marching exercises and ran up the Monte de Hatillo for weeks on end. Captain Astro provided him with the *US Infantry Field Regulations Manual*, and his cadets followed it religiously, learning all the coordinated platoon movements and hand signals. Every Saturday they practiced one of five battle drills: squad attacking, reacting to contact, breaking contact, reacting to far and near ambush, and knocking out a bunker. They had no weapons or ammunition—just wooden rifles, hand signals, and war whoops—but they made up for it with enthusiasm. Occasionally, the commander in chief came by with his brother, Faustino.

During one particularly strenuous assault on Monte de Hatillo, filmmaker Juan Emilio Viguié showed up and introduced himself. He invited Vidal to dinner at La Casita Blanca on Calle Tapia, where they discovered that they had a lot in common. Most importantly, both had witnessed the Ponce Massacre, and it had changed their lives. The very next day, Viguié took Vidal to his film lab and showed him several hours of newsreel, including the thirteen minutes from the Ponce Massacre. They watched those thirteen minutes several times in absolute silence. By the end of the night, Vidal agreed to let Viguié film his cadets.

༒

Viguié called, "Action," and the Cadets of the Republic charged up Monte de Hatillo with renewed energy and vigor. One of them crawled through mud. Another dove behind a tree, rolled left, and came up firing. All of them screamed like banshees as they captured a flag atop the miniature mountain 266 feet above sea level.

"Cut!" yelled Viguié, and they moved on to the next shot. The cadets all cheered, clapped each other on the back, and ridiculed each other's acting.

Over the past week the Santurce Cadet Corps had nearly tripled in size. Once word got out that a movie was being filmed, everyone wanted to liberate the island from its evil oppressors.

As they charged the mountain for the twentieth time, Raimundo and Faustino Díaz Pacheco arrived. They'd heard about this "Hollywood" production and wanted to have a few words with Vidal.

After a short argument, Vidal returned with bad news: there would be no more filming of Cadets of the Republic. The commander had even recommended the destruction of all film negatives. They packed up the camera equipment. To express sympathy, Vidal took Viguié to the barbershop and told him the story of El Águila Blanca. He said that the ghost of El Águila still visited the *salón* and was planning another revolution.

༒

On December 15, 1947, when Albizu Campos returned from prison, Vidal was there with his Santurce cadets and 15,000 cheering islanders as they followed Albizu through the streets of San Juan. Over the next few months, Vidal and his cadets accompanied Albizu to dozens of towns and radio stations, where he spoke passionately about Yankee imperialism and Puerto Rican independence.

When the Gag Law passed in June 1948, people in the barbershop suspected that the government was trying to arrest Albizu Campos again and that Governor Luis Muñoz Marín had become an American lapdog—a traitor of the first order. Vidal also knew (though he didn't tell anyone at the time) that the Gag Law would force Albizu's hand. Unable to communicate, motivate, or inspire, Albizu would have to take action. Sure enough, in August 1948, the *salón* door opened, and Albizu walked in.

After a few minutes, Vidal whispered in Albizu's ear about the hidden bathroom panel and the weapons in the basement next door. Albizu waited a bit, then headed over. When he returned, he squeezed Vidal's arm and asked quietly who knew about the arsenal. Vidal assured him that he had told no one, and Albizu told him to keep it that way. There was a leak in the party, and he did not know whom to trust.

Over the next two years Albizu visited the Salón Boricua every month, and each time Commander Raimundo Díaz Pacheco and other top Nationalists were waiting for him in the next-door apartment, behind the loose panels in the Salón Boricua bathroom. The night before each visit, Vidal carefully laid out three or four weapons, under the same pile of rice sacks, for them to take away with them; then he covered the basement entrance again. No one but Albizu and Vidal knew about that basement and the cache of arms it held.

After his brief trips to the bathroom, Albizu would say his good-byes and leave the *salón* with a sharp Cesar Romero haircut. He would climb into a black 1941 Chrysler sedan with license number 910 and drive home, tailed by two FBI cars. If it wasn't too hot and he really wanted to torture the agents, Albizu would walk the five miles home and let everyone see his haircut.

௸

Vidal was happy with this arrangement and with his place in the world. He wasn't a rich man, but he was doing something important with his life. He owned his own business and fed fifty families each month, just like El Águila Blanca had done. He was quietly helping the Nationalist cause as one of Albizu Campos's most trusted men. Once in a while he headed over to the Club with No Name and yelled at Humphrey Bogart in the *Casablanca* room. He even bought some new glasses so he could see the screen better.

Things changed for Vidal in August 1950. The 65th Infantry Regiment shipped out for Korea, and Captain Astro's food shipments stopped. In late September, the FBI, as part of its intense scrutiny of all Nationalists, started circling Vidal's shop several times a day, and Albizu Campos had to stop visiting.

On October 6, at 7 a.m., the streets were empty around the Salón Boricua except for one drunk across the street, who appeared to be asleep.[11] Vidal yawned and rubbed his hands together, then flicked on the old Marvy pole. The red, white, and blue lines started their endless race.

As Vidal entered the shop, the drunk started coughing, and a black Buick sped up. Four FBI agents jumped out and ran into the *salón* with their guns drawn. When Vidal identified himself, an agent punched him in the face. The other three handcuffed and shoved him in the car. It all happened in less than one minute, and the drunk had disappeared.

Inauguration of Charles Herbert Allen Courtesy of the author

Tydings "Independence Bill" for Puerto Rico
Courtesy of the author

Under Public Law 53, ownership of a Puerto Rican flag was a felony
Courtesy of the author

**US military celebrates its annual July 4 "Independence Day"
parade in Old San Juan** Courtesy of the author

"Air Force bombards Utuado"

Courtesy of the author

Police and National Guard surround the Salón Boricua
Courtesy of the author

Vidal Santiago Díaz (the barber) hauled out of Salón Boricua
Courtesy of the author

CHAPTER 16

The Academy of Truth

The Ramey Air Force Base covered 3,796 beautiful oceanfront acres in the northwest corner of Puerto Rico near the town of Aguadilla. As a Strategic Air Command bomber base, it housed the 55th Strategic Reconnaissance Wing and was rumored to contain underground missile silos for the "Truman atomic bomb."[1] The base had a two-mile runway, seventeen airplane hangars, barracks, and its own elementary and high schools, hospital, officer's club, swimming pool, and golf course.[2]

The drive to Ramey was a little over two hours from the barbershop, but Vidal wasn't able to see any of the scenery; the FBI men had placed a hood over his head. By the time they stopped at an unmarked building about a mile from the base, Vidal had no idea where they were beyond their proximity to the ocean because he could smell it. Two attendants ushered Vidal in through the basement, then finally removed the hood.

The building was an unfinished US Air Force barracks. Many bars in the reinforced concrete stuck out of the masonry; the staircases had no railing; tubing and electrical wires hung down from the ceilings. As they headed up the stairs, Vidal saw a constant movement of prisoners dressed in rags with several-day-old beards. Most of them appeared

Puerto Rican, or at least Latino. Amid a racket of stomping boots, laughter, and ridicule, US soldiers pushed them from one floor to another.[3] Conversations on every floor echoed throughout the building.

A sickening odor, like the stench of rotting meat, hit Vidal on the third floor. He glanced over quickly and saw a row of metal-gated rooms arranged like a prison corridor. In one room, a pair of bloody skid marks led to the door.

On the fourth floor, Vidal was shoved into the large living room of an unfinished apartment. It contained only a collapsible table, some blurred photographs of wanted individuals on the wall, and an old field telephone. A military captain sat behind the table. Vidal couldn't tell his rank, but he wore an enormous beret much too large for his face, which was small, triangular, and long like a desert fox. His voice was sharp and pointed, with the undertone of a spoiled choirboy, and it resounded throughout the floor.[4]

The officer introduced himself as Mr. Rolf, explained that he was responsible for the *carpeta* based on which Vidal had been arrested, and encouraged Vidal to speak candidly with him. When Vidal asked what the charges against him were, Rolf started asking about guns. Nearly an hour later, Vidal still didn't know what he'd been arrested for, when Rolf leaned over and grabbed the field phone. He instructed the party on the other end to get ready for "a session" and asked that someone named Moncho come up.[5]

Within moments a short, olive-skinned young man in an Insular Police uniform with pomaded hair and a small forehead walked in, smiling, and greeted Vidal as his "new customer." He led Vidal to the kitchen of yet another unfinished apartment on the third floor. It held a sink, an earthenware stove, and a pile of wooden crates that blocked the window. The room was dark.

Moncho instructed Vidal to remove his clothes and glasses. He then pushed Vidal toward another unfinished room—a bedroom. The only piece of furniture was a copper bed frame with no mattress; it smelled of feces and vomit. Vidal saw several drops of dried blood underneath it.

Moncho instructed him to lie down, and when Vidal hesitated, four more soldiers walked in and shoved him onto the bed frame. They secured his arms and legs with thick iron chains, while Moncho stood at the foot of the bed with his legs spread and arms folded. He looked down at Vidal and frowned.

In heavily accented English, Mondo informed him that Mr. Rolf was giving him time to think, but that afterward he would talk. Everybody did. And he would tell them everything.

Vidal heard a faint scream in a distant room. Then he thought he heard an airplane, as a current of cold air blew in from underneath the window. Naked on the bare copper bed, he started to tremble. Moncho, interpreting this as fear, asked him if he already wanted to talk. Vidal answered that he was not afraid; he was cold. Moncho replied snidely that in fifteen minutes he'd be talking freely.

Rolf walked in smoking a cigarette. The four soldiers snapped to attention, but he waved them down and walked straight to Vidal. His voice boomed. He wanted the other prisoners to hear him.

He asked for a paper and something to write on, and the soldiers brought him a box to sit on. Then Moncho wheeled in a magneto and connected it to the bed with two alligator clips. Rolf grabbed one of the remaining clips, brought it close to Vidal's face, and asked him if he knew what it was.

To show that he was not intimidated, Vidal demanded that he be handed over to the appropriate authorities within twenty-four hours as prescribed by law. When he requested that he be addressed as *usted*, the polite form for "you," rather than as *tu*, the form reserved for children and friends and family, the soldiers burst into laughter.

Then Rolf gave them the go-ahead. One soldier sat on Vidal's chest, smiling like a schoolboy about to pull a prank. The other three stood on either side of the bed, and several more walked in to watch the fun.

❧

At 9 a.m. that same day, Santo walked along Calle Colton and saw the door to the Salón Boricua standing wide open. He looked in with his one good eye and saw no one there. This had never happened before. Vidal was always in the shop by this hour, with his newspaper and morning coffee, wearing a tie, ready for business. Santo entered slowly, carefully, in case a thief was inside.

His call of hello received no answer. There were signs of a struggle. A few pomade jars had been knocked over and the portrait of El Águila Blanca lay on the floor—torn right down the middle. Something was definitely wrong. Santo rushed to the phone and dialed.

❧

Vidal's body bounced on the bed as Rolf administered electric charges.[6] The barber struggled, screamed, and strained until the chains cut into his flesh. Rolf launched one shock after another and repeated the same question: Where are the guns?[7]

Moncho threw cold water on Vidal's chest to increase the intensity of the current, as Rolf fastened the clips to Vidal's chest, abdomen, and nasal septum. The barber gnawed on his sock to relieve the cramps that contorted his body. But he didn't talk.

❧

A group had formed at the Salón Boricua: Santo, Sergio, Diógenes, and nearly a dozen other customers, even the *bolita* numbers man, were there. One of the Santurce cadets quietly swept and mopped the floor, but he was not in uniform. No Nationalists had been called because an FBI Buick Roadmaster was parked right across the street with two agents itching for an arrest. The men searched for a note or some other clue from Vidal. They looked in the bathroom, around the shoe-shine stand, and even under the statue of Santa Barbara. Nothing. Vidal had simply vanished, and an FBI car was parked across the street.

❧

In the office, Rolf ordered two soldiers to fetch a man named Lázaro. When two soldiers dragged him in, Vidal recognized him as an old Nationalist whose hair he had cut many times. Now he shuffled into the room, a pale emaciated man who could barely stand up. He looked as if he'd lost a hundred pounds. Gazing at Vidal from a place of infinite sadness, Lázaro simply told him that "it was hard." When he started crying, the soldiers took him away. Lázaro was clearly a broken man.

For the umpteenth time, Rolf asked where the guns were. When Vidal again answered that he didn't know, Rolf signaled to his men. Within minutes they had strapped Vidal to a wooden plank in an empty kitchen. Moncho affixed a rubber tube to the sink tap, as a soldier propped Vidal's head up against the sink. They wrapped his head in a rag, jammed a piece of wood between his lips, and told him that when he wanted to talk, he need only wiggle his fingers.

They turned on the tap. The rag soaked rapidly and water flowed into Vidal's mouth, up his nose, and all over his face. He took small gulps of air and tried to contract his throat. He kept the air in his lungs for as long as he could—but he couldn't hold on for more than a few moments.[8]

His fingers shook. His muscles struggled uselessly. He was dizzy from lack of air. Vidal was drowning. When his body started to slacken, the soldiers would stop—long enough to let him throw up water and get his breath back. They did this again and again, until the barber lost consciousness. But he didn't talk.

❧

When Vidal came to, he was in a pitch-black cell. He searched for a crack of light along every inch of the door and the walls, but the darkness was absolute. It was a sea of black ink.[9]

After many hours, a soldier banged some keys against a wall, and Vidal heard a mechanism creak. He crawled over, feeling his way through the dark, so as not to bang his head. When he reached the mechanism, he felt a cup of soup and a biscuit on a little platform, which someone had pushed through a retractable wall panel. Vidal ate and returned the cup to the platform. Then he heard a hand-operated crank, as the platform slowly retracted into the wall again.

They fed him one cup of the same stale pea soup every day. Vidal counted the days by the number of cups he'd been given. Twice he didn't eat because someone had urinated in the food. They were slowly starving him.

He tried not to move too much. He started to become dizzy every time he stood up, and dust rose to his nostrils every time he stirred on the floor. When he lay down, insects crawled over his blanket and under his clothes.

On the sixth day, after eating his cup of pea soup, Vidal crawled over to the sink for some water. With his left hand, he felt for the tap and turned it. He heard the trickle of water and held his cup underneath the faucet, until it felt nearly full. Then he raised the cup carefully to his lips and tilted it back to drink.

Vidal felt the legs and bodies of many insects run up his face, over his eyes, and into his hair. He flung down the cup and brought his hands to his face. He heard someone screaming from far away, and it was him. He fell against a wall and catapulted across the cell to the opposite wall. He bounced back and forth, from one wall to another, screaming, his mind gone.

❧

In late October, Raimundo Díaz Pacheco went to Pedro Albizu Campos's apartment on Calle Sol. Vidal's disappearance had both men worried. If someone had kidnapped him and he should talk, then Albizu and the Nationalist leadership would be going back to jail—probably for life. Through his cadets in San Juan and nineteen other towns, the commander spread word of Vidal's disappearance. If anyone had seen him or had any knowledge of his whereabouts, he needed to know immediately.

Raimundo also sent word to those Nationalists who had received any of Vidal's guns. They were stored all over the island in nine private homes, on three farms, in a cane field and a cave, and at an Esso gas station. If anyone knew about those weapons—even a family member—then they had to be moved immediately.

❧

After Vidal had been allowed to leave the "black room" and to shower and shave, Rolf asked if he was ready to disclose where the guns were and whom he'd given them to. The barber had lost ten pounds in two weeks. Breathing was becoming difficult. He barely had enough energy to hold up his head defiantly and tell Rolf he had nothing to say.

Rolf then asked about Albizu Campos. When Vidal responded that he merely cut Albizu's hair and that they talked about the Yankees, Rolf slapped him so hard that he fell out of his chair. Another soldier kicked him in the ribs and yanked him back into his seat.

Then Rolf shouted, loudly and clearly, so every prisoner could hear him, that he could afford to be very patient because he always won in the end. Vidal was at the Academy of Truth. Some people left; others didn't. But all of them talked in the end. And all of them told the truth.

Vidal just stared at him and wiped the blood from his mouth. Then Rolf said he was going to give Vidal another chance.

૯૦

Rolf brought in a 16-mm projector, soldiers jammed into the room, and they all watched a newsreel projected onto a wall. The soldiers laughed as Vidal's Santurce cadets ran up and down the Monte de Hatillo. Way in the background, almost offscreen, Vidal barked orders from the *US Infantry Field Regulations Manual.* The scene lasted only a few seconds, and he was nearly impossible to recognize, so Vidal admitted to nothing.[10]

They walked him through the third floor, lined with cells that held clusters of naked men, then forced him down a long staircase. The sharp odor of vomit, excrement, and burned flesh filled the cellar. They tore off his trousers, shirt, underwear, shoes, and socks. When he was naked, they handcuffed him again. The soles of his feet felt wet with a sticky substance that covered the rough concrete floor. They shoved him into an even darker room and sat him down on a chair lined with metal plates, with straps and metal rings for his hands and feet.

Nothing happened for a few minutes, and Vidal began to pray. Then one of the soldiers began to spray the air, and he recognized the scent of English Leather perfume. By now Vidal's eyes had adjusted, and he could make out the faces of the people crowded around him. He recognized Rolf with his pointy little face. Another officer stood beside him: he had a flabby face, double chin, and a prominent belly.

Vidal was about to tell them they looked like Laurel and Hardy when the electrical current flattened him against the straps and rings that held him down. He felt needles in his pores, his head exploded into little fireballs, and he vomited. A bucket of water revived him—and then, to his surprise, Lázaro and another Nationalist prisoner were ushered into the room. Evidently Rolf wanted to terrify them, as well.

When Rolf demanded that Vidal tell him about guns and ammunition, Vidal denied having anything to say.

A second charge rocketed him against his bonds. Vidal felt his eyes popping out of their sockets—like a frog's—and he lost consciousness. The soldiers threw buckets of water on him, and Rolf shocked him a third time.

The current soldered Vidal's jaw shut. He could not unclench his teeth, no matter how hard he tried. His eyelids twitched open and shut. His head started banging, uncontrollably, against the back of the chair. Then he passed out again. The buckets of water would not revive him.

They sprayed the air with English Leather again to hide the stink of vomit and burned flesh. Old Lázaro started to weep, and they dragged him away. Then they brought a doctor over to see if Vidal was dead.

ઝ

Vidal wasn't the only prisoner being electrocuted. From his cell he could see part of the corridor, the landing, and some of the stairs. The thin walls of the partition allowed him to hear snatches of conversation from the other cells. There was no privacy anywhere. Vidal didn't mind. It enabled him to observe how the Academy of Truth—this torture factory—actually worked.

During the day there was an incessant coming and going in the corridor and on the stairs as soldiers shoved prisoners from one room to another. On each floor—except the third—they kept five to ten people in rooms converted into dungeons. The prisoners slept on the cement, or two or three shared a mattress. They existed in constant darkness because the blinds were always closed so that nobody could see in from the outside. They waited days or weeks to be questioned, or transferred to a prison, or shot in the back during "an attempted escape."

Twice a day, around 10 a.m. and 2 p.m. (if the soldiers didn't forget), prisoners received army biscuits and water. At 8 p.m. they got bread and a cup of soup made from all the soldiers' leftovers. One time Vidal found a broken tooth, another time a used Band-Aid, another time a maggot.

A Puerto Rican named Chicharín was in charge of this distribution. He was five feet tall and wore a ridiculous outfit of riding breeches and an army tunic, like a miniature General Patton or a military lawn jockey. He sported a blue beret and carried a rubber truncheon, which he used on occasion to please his masters. Everyone despised this lackey, the soldiers as well as the prisoners.

Every few nights, more "suspects," mostly young men, were hauled in. Many had not been allowed to dress when arrested: some were still in shorts or slippers. Women went to a separate wing. The process of breaking these new prisoners began immediately. Within an hour of their arrival, the building was filled with shouts, insults, and loud, brutal laughter. Then the first piercing scream would cut through the night. Someone had met the electric bed.

One night Vidal heard them torture a man on the floor above him: he was quite old, to judge by the sound of his voice. Between the horrible cries exacted by the torture, he said, exhausted, "¡Que viva los Estados Unidos. . . . Que viva los Estados Unidos!" But the soldiers laughed as they continued to torture him.

Around midnight, the door of a prison cell would open suddenly. A soldier would call a man's name, then yell, "Get up, you maggot!" Everyone knew what this meant. There was always a long silence, and the soldier would have to yank the man onto his feet, then kick and push him out of the cell. A few minutes later the man's screams would echo through every hall.

During a quiet moment, a prisoner in the adjoining cell told Vidal two horrific stories. The first was that Governor Luis Muñoz Marín had become an opium addict in New York and that the US government not only knew about it but was using it to control his every move. The second was the cruelest story Vidal had ever heard. An old Nationalist from Jayuya had shot a cop, so they starved him for two weeks. One night, instead of the usual army biscuit, they brought him a heaping plate of meat, but without a knife or fork. The man gulped it down with both hands until it was all gone and the juice dripped down his face. A few minutes later an officer walked in and asked him if he enjoyed eating his son. The old man asked him what he was talking about. Then another soldier walked in with a big smile on his face, holding a boy's severed head by the hair. "Did your son taste good?" asked the officer. "We cooked him special for you." The old man vomited his son back onto the floor. Then he went into shock and died of a heart attack.[11]

Vidal could not sleep that night. He had fallen into some sort of hell—and his tormentors would someday be feted as heroes, promoted in rank, and decorated with the highest military and civilian honors. Their torture was based on racial hatred. They would never do this to one of their own. The barbarities in this hidden building were the clearest expression of how these men from El Norte viewed Vidal's people.

ᘯ

The next evening, just after sunset, Vidal was taken to the infirmary, a large windowless room with several camp beds and a table overflowing with medical supplies in complete disorder. One wall had an enormous poster on it.[12]

Vidal also saw several forceps on the medical table. He thought they were going to pull his teeth until a doctor he had never seen before walked in, wearing a guayabera and a friendly smile. He introduced himself as Dr. Hebb.

The doctor smiled, took his pulse, and listened to his chest through a stethoscope. An assistant plunged a needle into Vidal's right arm. Within seconds, he was falling in and out of consciousness, and the doctor began plying him with questions about his family, the barbershop, Albizu Campos, and where the guns were.[13] It was a "soft" interrogation. As the night wore on, the doctor was friendly but relentless. For a brief moment, he even claimed to be Albizu Campos—and repeated the questions about guns. But the barber revealed nothing.

A second injection from the medical assistant sent Vidal into a deep sleep.[14] When he awoke, a skinny, ferret-faced man was peering down at him. Vidal recognized Faustino, the brother of Raimundo Díaz Pacheco, commander in chief of the Cadets of the Republic.

Faustino told him that Raimundo needed another gun and demanded to know where he'd hidden his arsenal. He implored Vidal for the name of this contact. A long round of bluffing and trickery ensued,

Margaret Bourke-White's *The American Way*, seen by Vidal Santiago Díaz in (of all places) the medical interrogation room in Aguadilla

© Margaret Bourke-White/Time Life Pictures/Getty Images

with Faustino trying to milk the information from a confused Vidal. But the barber grew tired and fell back to sleep. Everyone got up and filed out of the room.

For just a moment, Vidal snapped back into consciousness. He saw Faustino at the door and screamed that they could bring back their electric bed, that he wasn't afraid of them, that he wasn't a traitor!

Events

CHAPTER 17

Last Days

The news of Vidal Santiago's kidnapping spread rapidly through the Nationalist Party. As of October 23, Vidal and Faustino Díaz Pacheco had been missing for nearly three weeks. The tension grew throughout the island as Insular Police forces broke into more and more people's homes, searching for guns, Puerto Rican flags, and other subversive material. Several prisoners in La Princesa claimed they'd been tortured in Aguadilla somewhere near an airport. Maybe Vidal was there.

It was clear to everyone that the Nationalist Party had been infiltrated. Whether due to bribery, trickery, or torture, someone at a very high level had betrayed them. There were too many arrests, and the police and FBI were too precise; they knew exactly where to look and whom to follow. On top of everything, Pedro Albizu Campos received word that someone—from the FBI or CIA or a highly paid professional—was preparing to assassinate him.[1]

In order to justify all this, Governor Luis Muñoz Marín was accusing Albizu and the Nationalists of being Communists,[2] fascists,[3] subversives,[4] and political gangsters.[5]

J. Edgar Hoover was fuming. As FBI director, he was supposed to control the spread of communism in the United States, but Governor Luis Muñoz Marín was complaining about it in Puerto Rico. This meant that Hoover, with over two hundred FBI agents throughout the island, was failing at his job.

The more he thought about it, the more he blamed Muñoz Marín. The man was a mess, smoking opium and drinking rum while Nationalists were buying guns, waving flags, and holding rallies all over the island. What use was a governor who couldn't keep his own people in line? "This drug addict wants to have a banana republic with U.S. air conditioning," he told Clyde Tolson, his handsome assistant; then he burned up the phone lines.[6] "Arrest somebody, you son of a bitch!" he told Jack West,[7] the unfortunate agent who had picked up the phone at San Juan's FBI headquarters.

Within twenty-four hours the surveillance detail on Albizu Campos was doubled, and a zero-tolerance order was sent to all FBI and Insular Police personnel. The Nationalists were to be followed, hounded, and arrested as never before. Hoover also made a phone call to Ramey Air Force Base with instructions regarding a prisoner named Vidal Santiago, known to be Albizu's personal barber and a member of the Santurce chapter of the Nationalist Party.[8]

❧

Vidal was waiting for the end. It might come that evening or the next day at dawn; in any case, it would be soon. Ever since the sodium pentothal injections, he'd been left alone, but Vidal knew it was only a matter of time. They hadn't been able to break him. Now they had to kill him.

Sure enough, that night at around 10 p.m., Rolf opened the cell and told him to get ready. Vidal put on his soiled pants and filthy, torn undershirt and said nothing. At least a dozen times he'd prepared himself for the last moments of life. He thought of his father, of Albizu, of all those he had loved, and he was thankful to be dying true to a belief and to his companions in battle.

Soldiers hooded and handcuffed Vidal, then stuffed him into a large black car with tinted windows. Rolf sat in front; Vidal was sandwiched between two soldiers in the rear. He closed his eyes in the cramped space and tried to talk to God as he had many times before, but he couldn't concentrate on the prayer; his anxiety was too great. God would understand.

After nearly an hour, somewhere in the Cordillera mountain range, the car came to a stop. A great many soldiers had cordoned off the road, blocking traffic in both directions. This had to be the site of the assassination. But no, they switched Vidal into another identical car and drove on.

As they passed Vega Alta on PR-22 and came within twenty miles of San Juan, Vidal thought of another possibility: they weren't going to shoot him; they were going to throw him in jail for life. They'd found the guns in the basement next door to his shop, or maybe Faustino Díaz Pacheco had informed on him, but they didn't want to make a martyr of him. They would first discredit him in a messy public trial—paint him as a black-hearted terrorist, a psychotic antichrist—and then they'd lock him up and throw away the key—just as they had with Albizu Campos.

Despite the hood, Vidal knew when they passed La Peña and the Vergaras mountain peaks. These were the bumpiest, most winding roads in the Bayamón township. There was no mistaking them. The car was less than ten miles from San Juan.

Vidal wasn't sure if Rolf was still with them. No one had spoken for the past hour. They rode in silence as the car twisted and dipped. Then they came to a hard stop, Vidal had no idea where. The hood was snatched off his head, and the car door opened. A soldier told him to get out and shoved him onto the street.

As he looked up from the ground, Vidal saw Rolf's boot an inch from his face. He cringed immediately, but the blow never came. Instead, Rolf yanked him to his feet and pointed to four black Buick Roadmasters, parked fifty feet apart on each street corner. It was an FBI spider's web.

Rolf told Vidal that the cars were there for him. If he wanted to go anywhere, even to church, he had to ask the FBI for permission—otherwise he would be shot.

For a moment, about a block away, Vidal, still disoriented, saw a familiar face—one of his old Santurce cadets. Without thinking, he

**Student meeting at the University of Puerto Rico;
under Gag law 53, everyone in this room could be arrested and
imprisoned for ten years, due to the presence of Puerto Rican flags**

The Ruth M. Reynolds Papers, Archives of the Puerto Rican Diaspora,
Centro de Estudios Puertorriqueños, Hunter College, CUNY

yelled, "Faustino es la chota!" (Faustino is the traitor!). The words re-sounded through the street. Rolf slapped Vidal and shoved him through a doorway into a large room.[9] Then Rolf and the soldiers drove off.

Vidal was alone. He looked all around. He was back in his old bar-bershop, the Salón Boricua.

છ/ગ

That same day, October 26, Albizu Campos and other Nationalists drove to the town of Fajardo to commemorate the birth of General Antonio Valero de Bernabé, a nineteenth-century hero of Puerto Rican independence. They visited his grave with enormous Puerto Rican flags—each measuring over two hundred square feet—in open violation of the Gag Law.

The FBI and Insular Police surrounded the cemetery, but they did not arrest Albizu for the flags. Faustino Díaz Pacheco had already informed them of greater, more rewarding violations by the Nationalists. The police only needed to wait. At 8:30 p.m., Albizu broadcast a speech on WMDD about General de Bernabé and his dream of Puerto Rican independence.

During the dinner that followed, a Nationalist walked into the restaurant and told Albizu that Vidal Santiago was back in the Salón Boricua surrounded by a horde of FBI agents. Then he leaned in and whispered what Vidal had shouted: "Faustino es la chota."[10]

Albizu nodded quietly; he'd already suspected as much. Faustino had disappeared completely. Only three people on the whole island knew the locations of the weapons, the schedule and strategy for the entire revolution, and the identities of its leaders: Albizu, Cadets commander Raimundo Díaz Pacheco, and his brother Faustino.

Albizu gazed through a window at three parked Insular Police cars. He remarked that the policemen would kill them right then, if they could get away with it. It was brother against brother on this island.

∽

After dinner, around midnight, they all drove back to San Juan in a six-car caravan: Albizu's own car, two Nationalist cars, and three police cars.

After a few minutes, once they were clear of the town, the police cars repeatedly attempted to force Albizu's car to the side of the road, but the other Nationalist cars kept blocking them. Finally, after much maneuvering, Albizu's car—driven by another Nationalist, not Albizu—got home safely.

The other two cars, however, encountered a serious problem. At 3:10 a.m., Sergeant Astol Calero cornered one of the Nationalist escort cars on Avenida Juan Ponce de León, near the Martín Peña channel.[11] He opened the trunk and found two .37-caliber guns, five Molotov cocktails, and a Thompson submachine gun.

At 3:15 a.m., Officers Elmo Caban and Vicente Colón received a radio call at the Santurce Police Station. "Bring a bus, quick!" yelled Sergeant Calero.

At 3:30 a.m., the bus arrived, and Antonio Moya Vélez was arrested.

By 4 a.m. the second Nationalist car had been detained near Calle Guayama in Santurce. Officers found Molotov cocktails in the trunk.

Rafael Burgos Fuentes, Eduardo López Vásquez, and José Mejías Flores were arrested.[12]

And so it began.

When he awoke the next morning, Albizu heard about the arrests. Unless he acted immediately, he would be arrested too—within a matter of days, if not hours. They'd rig another jury, ambush him with the Gag Law, and imprison everybody for another ten years. And that would be the end of the revolution.

He also heard from journalist Ruth Reynolds that US Secretary of Defense Louis Johnson had ordered Governor Luis Muñoz Marín to liquidate the Nationalist Party and arrest its leadership. Should the arrests prove difficult, then the leadership should be assassinated.

But no, not this time. This time they would not be victims. This time they would fight back with whatever weapons they had. On October 27, 1950, Albizu Campos said, "No mas." On that day he contacted his top leaders, and the Puerto Rican Revolution got under way.[13]

The very next day, the same newspaper reported two stories:

OCUPAN BOMBAS, PISTOLAS A LÍDERES NACIONALISTAS
DUPONT HACE UNA BOMBA DE HIDROGENO
SUPERPODEROSA

The first described the weapons found in a Nationalist car: three pistols and five Molotov cocktails. The second described the new US hydrogen bomb: a 10.4 megaton beast, hundreds of times stronger than those dropped on Japan, whose mushroom cloud would bloom 120,000 feet into the stratosphere. Many on the island called it "the Truman atomic bomb." In addition, during World War II the United States had produced 22 aircraft carriers, 8 battleships, 48 cruisers, 349 destroyers, 420 convoy escorts, 203 submarines, 99,000 fighter aircraft, 97,000 bomber planes, 57,000 training aircraft, 23,000 transport aircraft, 92,000 tanks, 105,000 mortars, 257,000 artillery pieces, 2.3 million military trucks, and 2.6 million machine guns.[14]

In a twentieth-century version of David versus Goliath, Albizu Campos and the Nationalists were waging a revolution against the most powerful nation in history.

CHAPTER 18

Revolution

On October 28, 1950, the Puerto Rican Revolution started with a prison break planned by a prisoner named Pedro Benejám Alvares, and executed by a notorious murderer named Correa Cotto.[1]

Cotto started an argument during a morning baseball game in the exercise yard of El Oso Blanco (the White Bear) penitentiary in Río Piedras. He made sure that the argument spilled over into the lunchroom, with both teams fighting and throwing plates at each other. Cotto used the chaos to slit a guard's throat, grab his gun and keys, and lead a raid into the prison arsenal. A dozen armed prisoners followed Cotto out to the main gate, where they killed a second guard, wounded four others, and shot their way to freedom.[2]

Within twenty minutes the prisoners were running down Calles Bori and Cavalieri, Avenida José de Diego, and a dozen other streets. Over 500 prisoners rioted, and 110 managed to escape to all corners of the island.[3] As *El Imparcial* noted on the front page:

MOTIN EN EL PRESIDIO
110 SE FUGAN TRAS MATAR GUARDIAS

It was a bold, unorthodox move. Instead of chasing Nationalists, the Insular Police now had to chase 110 fugitives all over Puerto Rico. Also, since Correa Cotto was a career criminal with no interest in politics,[4] no one could blame the Nationalists for the prison break. Finally, from a public relations standpoint, it would look patently absurd—and outright colonialist—for the authorities to arrest Albizu Campos while 110 murderers, rapists, and thieves were on the loose.

The chess game had begun.

The government made the next move. The same night as the prison break, acting on information from confidential informants, the Insular Police raided the house of Melitón Muñiz Santos, president of the Ponce chapter of the Nationalist Party. Within minutes they found pistols and ammunition, twenty-two Molotov cocktails, sixty-nine Puerto Rican flags, and a portrait of Pedro Albizu Campos—all in violation of Public Law 53.[5]

The next morning, on October 29, while the Insular Police pursued the fugitives, J. Edgar Hoover flew sixty more FBI agents to Puerto Rico. He demanded that Governor Luis Muñoz Marín declare a state of martial law in order to facilitate the mass arrests that Hoover insisted were "long overdue." But Hoover didn't have to stand for reelection; the governor did. No martial law was declared.[6]

Within a few hours, the bullets started flying in eight towns.

Peñuelas

Melitón Muñiz Santos was not home when the FBI raided his house in Ponce, but according to his mother, the agents knew exactly where to look for his weapons. They went directly to them. Someone had evidently informed the bureau.[7]

Melitón Muñiz Santos immediately rushed to various safe houses in the Ponce area and relocated over fifty crates of submachine guns, pistols, ammunition, and grenades. He hid them on a farm in Barrio Macaná in the town of Peñuelas.[8] It didn't help. The police knew about this location too. At 3 a.m. on October 30, three dozen Insular Police surrounded the farm and attacked the main house. When greeted by a hail of Nationalist bullets, they retreated to their vehicles and strafed the house for nearly an hour.

At one point, a young Nationalist named Guillermo González Ubides horrified the combatants on both sides of the gunfight. He opened a door and walked slowly, as if in a trance, toward the police. Everyone stopped shooting. He didn't say a word; he simply looked straight ahead and kept walking. Then, when he was twenty feet from the police, he raised a pistol. Every gun fired, hitting Guillermo from all sides. Over a dozen bullets tore into his face and body, but somehow Guillermo kept walking.

When he was ten feet from the police cars, he raised his pistol again, and another fusillade ripped him apart. Then no one moved.[9] A silence descended. The coquís sang in a distant field. A frightened cow mooed in a barn. The smoke from the police rifles curled up into the sky.

The fight didn't last much longer after that. Six policemen were wounded; three Nationalists were killed, and the rest were arrested. The leader of the raid, Insular Police lieutenant Ismael Lugo Torres, received a special departmental commendation. Two days later, several farmers said they saw Guillermo's ghost walking around in circles with a gun in his hand, as if patrolling the fields.[10]

Jayuya

Eight hours after the Peñuelas shootout, in the home of Blanca Canales, eighteen Nationalists stood before a Puerto Rican flag and bowed their heads as Canales led them through a solemn oath: "I pledge my life to the liberty of Puerto Rico."[11] The group then jammed into three vehicles and left Canales's home in the Barrio Coabey section of Jayuya. By noon, two vehicles had reached the Jayuya police station, and fourteen Nationalists had surrounded the building.[12]

"Surrender your arms, and there will be no bloodshed today," yelled their leader, Carlos Irizarry Rivera. Carlos was a respected man in Jayuya—a World War II veteran and a law student at the University of Puerto Rico—but the Insular Police ignored him and started firing.[13] The first man they hit was Carlos.[14] Shots rang out through Calles

Figueras and Mattei as the police barricaded themselves behind piles of steel drums, blocking every entrance to the building.

An Insular Police car rolled up from Barrio Mameyes and took a position on Calle Torrado. Within an hour, the policemen jumped off a rear balcony, ran into the rectory of Our Lady of Monserrat, and asked the priests for asylum.

By 12:45 the police station was on fire.[15] The post office was in flames at 2 p.m. The US Selective Service Office was overrun at 4 p.m. The Nationalists removed all the draft cards, paperwork, machines, and equipment and set them on fire in the middle of the street.

By 5 p.m. Blanca Canales had cut all telephone lines to the town.[16] A crowd formed in the town square at 6 p.m. The smoke was still rising from the police station as Canales announced the start of the revolution. Her hands trembled as she unfurled a Puerto Rican flag.[17]

"¡Que viva Puerto Rico Libre!" she shouted, then raised the banner. After a brief, impassioned speech, a young boy arrived to tell her that Carlos Irizarry Rivera had been seriously wounded. He later bled to death.

Blanca Canales was arrested on the outskirts of Jayuya that night while trying to find a doctor for Carlos. The Insular Police didn't dare reenter the town and told reporters that "hundreds of Nationalists with machine guns" had attacked the police station. Their story was so convincing that on November 1, the United States scrambled ten P-47 Thunderbolt fighter planes out of Ramey Air Force Base and bombed the town.[18]

The planes dropped 500-pound (227-kilogram) bombs and strafed the town with .50-caliber armor-piercing machine guns, each Thunderbolt releasing up to 1,200 rounds per minute. It was the only time in history that the United States bombed its own citizens.[19]

After bombing Jayuya, the planes machine-gunned the farms, sugar cane fields, and mountains surrounding the town. Anyone who staggered out, wounded or not, was arrested immediately.[20] People were arrested on public roads and in their homes.

The day after the bombing, the 296th Regiment of the US National Guard occupied Jayuya, arriving in hundreds of army trucks. Guardsmen stormed every neighborhood and shut down all the avenues. Nearly 4,000 troops marched through a town with only 12,000 residents. They

The 296th Regiment of the US National Guard arrives to occupy Jayuya and Utuado
© Bettmann/Corbis

The US National Guard surrounds the home of Blanca Canales
© Bettmann/Corbis

established positions on every intersection and bus stop, raided several schools, and arrested people at random. They also attacked Blanca Canales's house, even though no one was home.

In Barrio Coabey and Barrio Mameyes, on Calle San Felipe and Avenida Vicens, the troops created firing lines with machine guns, mortars, carbines, and Garand semiautomatic rifles. They fired over 1,000 rounds of .30-caliber bullets into one mountain alone and hid within the rubble of bombed-out houses in order to fire on those still standing.

On November 3, the adjutant general of the National Guard, Luis R. Estevez, reported to the governor that Jayuya had been pacified.[21]

UTUADO

Utuado was a strategically vital town. Located near the center of Puerto Rico, it was the island's third-largest municipality, and whoever held it would control troop movements into the western half of the island. The Río Abajo forest on the border of Utuado and Arecibo provided nine square miles of uncharted hiding spaces. Utuado also had strong local agriculture and several livestock haciendas, whose owners sympathized with Albizu's cause.

With all these natural advantages in mind, Albizu developed a two-step plan for a revolution with Utuado as its centerpiece. First, the Nationalists would organize simultaneous revolts at 12 p.m. in San Juan, Jayuya, Peñuelas, Arecibo, Mayagüez, Naranjito, Ponce, and Utuado. Second, after the initial wave of revolts, all the rebels would head into Utuado, where they could hold out for a month or more.

Utuado was thus crucial to the revolution. The Nationalists did not need to win a war against America, which was impossible. They only needed to get the world's attention so that the United Nations and other international organizations would pressure the United States to give up its colony.

The plan's only flaw was that the Americans had already heard about it from Faustino Díaz Pacheco.[22] And so, on October 30, 1950, a tragedy unfolded in Utuado.

৩

In the early morning, thirty-two Nationalists gathered at the home of Heriberto Castro Ríos and split into two groups. The first attacked the federal post office just before noon and set it on fire.[23] The second attacked the Insular Police station, but the officers were ready and waiting for them with snipers and street barricades all along Avenida Estevez. They shot several Nationalists, so the rebels retreated to the house of Damian Torres, president of the Utuado chapter of the Nationalist Party.[24]

"¡Ea rayo!" said Antonio González, as gunshots followed them into the house and continued for two hours. The Nationalists returned fire from Damian's balcony, and hundreds of shell casings piled up on the floor. After the first hour, seventeen-year-old Antonio started to break down. Tears ran down his face and he whimpered as he reloaded his gun, aimed, fired, and rammed home another cartridge. But he never stopped firing.

At sunset the Nationalists turned off every light and looked out from a darkened house. In the distance, a plume rose from the burnt post office. In the shadows, the police crept closer. They stormed a rear door, but the Nationalists stopped them.

At 8 p.m. 1,000 National Guardsmen stormed into Utuado. They concentrated their troops around Damian's house, and one unit set up a M2 Browning .50-caliber machine gun at a gas station 120 yards away. At 11 p.m. they fired six hundred bullets per minute for nearly five minutes into Damian's house. At 11:30 p.m. they did it again. Every resident of Utuado heard the machine gun as it blasted over five thousand bullets into one wooden structure.[25]

The Nationalists lay on the floor while the house exploded around them. The staircase shattered, and part of the second floor crashed into the living room. Several of the Nationalists began to pray; others had to be pulled out from under the rubble.

"¡Ai santo!" shouted a Nationalist, and all the others rushed over. Their leader, Heriberto Castro, was dead, shot in the neck and chest. They lowered him onto a shot-up mattress, wrapped him in a large Puerto Rican flag,[26] and said a few quick prayers.

Suddenly a booming voice announced, "Come out with your hands up, and no one will be hurt. We guarantee your safety if you surrender. If you don't surrender, we will grenade your house within five minutes."[27]

The nine surviving Nationalists argued fiercely among themselves. None of them trusted the National Guard, but within five minutes they filed out of the house. They were immediately surrounded by guns and bayonets, thrown onto the ground, and searched. Then the National Guard prodded them with bayonets down Calle Dr. Cueto and ordered them to remove their shoes, belts, and personal belongings.

US National Guard troops occupy the towns of Jayuya and Utuado

The Ruth M. Reynolds Papers, Archives of the Puerto Rican Diaspora,
Centro de Estudios Puertorriqueños, Hunter College, CUNY

They marched down the street nearly naked, holding their pants up, with the National Guard laughing behind them.

At 1 a.m. they neared the police station, but they never made it to the front door. The Guardsmen shoved them into a side street, on the corner of Washington Street and Betances Avenue, where a M1919A4 Browning machine gun had been set up.

"You won't be killing policemen any more," said an officer, and the machine gun opened fire.[28]

Every Nationalist was shot. Antonio Ramos died instantly, shot through the head and chest. Augustín Quiñones Mercado's legs were shredded like ground beef; his left leg was almost completely severed from his body, remaining connected only by two tendons. Antonio González asked for water while bleeding to death. "You want water?" said a Guardsman, then stabbed him in the chest with a bayonet.[29] Julio Feliciano Colón died while writing "Asesinos" on the pavement with his own blood. The soldiers later erased it.[30]

The machine gun fired nonstop at the men for several minutes. A few doors and windows opened along the Cumbre Alta, and several civilians started yelling, "Murderers! Criminals! We see what you're doing!" The Guardsmen fired over their heads and told them to close their doors and mind their own business.[31]

The Insular Police precinct was less than two hundred feet away, but no one—not the police, not the National Guard—called for medical attention. They just stood there and watched the men bleed to death, listening to them beg for water as they slowly dehydrated.

Four hours later the first sugar cane workers left home for work. They saw the bodies of nine men lying in a pool of blood. When a doctor finally arrived at 5 a.m., five Nationalists were gravely wounded. Four were dead. The corpses were left on display, for the entire town to see, for five more hours until 10 a.m. Blood ran in the gutter. Stray dogs roamed over the dead, licking their faces and eating their intestines, which had spilled out onto the street.[32]

Later that day, the Guardsmen retreated temporarily from Utuado, while four P-47 Thunderbolt planes bombed the town more thoroughly than they had Jayuya. Each plane carried a payload capacity of 2,500 pounds. By the time they were finished, the town lay in ruins.[33] *El Imparcial* ran a huge, full-page headline that said "Air Force Bombs Utuado":

AVIACION BOMBARDEA EN UTUADO

The priest at the Church of San Miguel, Father Barandiarán, had fled from Spain during the Spanish Civil War. "This whole town has gone crazy," he said. "If I had known this, I would have stayed in Navarro."[34]

ARECIBO, MAYAGÜEZ, PONCE, AND NARANJITO

The October 30 uprisings in Arecibo, Mayagüez, Ponce, and Naranjito were a disorganized mess. With the hurried order to start the revolution, everything happened too early or too late. Decisions were made on the fly. There was no coordination or communication between the towns. Once the National Guard shut down the major roads, it was every town for itself.

Arecibo started too early. It was the only town that enjoyed the element of surprise when it attacked the police station at 11:00 a.m. The Nationalists killed Lieutenant Ramón Villanueva and three other Insular Police officers but did not capture the station. They hurried away, and one of them, Hipólito Miranda Díaz, was shot and killed while covering their retreat.[35]

Mayagüez started too late. By the time the Nationalists approached the Insular Police station at 2 p.m., the policemen had been waiting for them for nearly two hours. The Nationalists backed off.[36] The next day, October 31, in Barrio La Quinta, police attacked the home of José Cruzado Ortíz,[37] and the Nationalists retreated into the mountains.[38]

In Ponce, a Nationalist tried to burn a building on Calle Victoria del Barrio Segundo and was arrested.[39] Another group was stopped in front of the Ponce cement factory.[40] A gunfight ensued, and police officer Aurelio Miranda was killed.[41]

The police were also ready and waiting in Naranjito. The Nationalists failed to take the police station and retreated into the surrounding mountains. A World War II veteran named José Antonio Negrón, however, managed to put up a remarkable fight, staging raids and gunfights for over a week.[42] Negrón did not drink, gamble, or owe anyone any money. He was "a man of respect" and held in great local esteem, which enabled him to wage a one-man guerrilla war against the police and National Guard until November 10, with no one ratting him out.[43] When Negrón was finally arrested in the Barrio Palos Altos de Corozal, a reporter asked him why he'd held out for so long. Negrón responded, "Because giving up was not our mission. We were trying to bring international attention to the reality of Puerto Rico."[44]

SAN JUAN

A blue 1949 Plymouth made its way to the governor's mansion. It was 11:55 a.m. and unusually hot on October 30, as the Nationalists drove west on Calle La Fortaleza. Everywhere they looked—on every rooftop and street corner, on balconies and in parked cars—they saw the evidence of Faustino Díaz Pacheco's betrayal. Soldiers and snipers lined their path.[45]

For the last four days, the FBI and Insular Police had arrested Nationalists all over the island. They knew exactly where the weapons were stashed and who had buried them.[46]

The world fell apart for the Nationalist Party the moment Vidal Santiago yelled, "Faustino es la chota!" With great regret, Pedro Albizu Campos realized that Vidal was right, and he removed Raimundo as his commander in chief. The military head of the revolution was now Tomás López de Victoria,[47] and Raimundo was completely shut out of all planning and decision making. Faustino, of course, was nowhere to be found.

Raimundo could not bear the shame. His own brother had turned the revolution into one great, island-wide martyrdom. Now there remained one last suicide mission, and Raimundo had to lead it.

No one spoke in the car; everyone knew what was coming. If by some miracle they penetrated the mansion, they would rush the second-floor offices, find the governor, and threaten to kill him. Then they'd call every news agency and demand Puerto Rico's independence. Killing the governor was not a priority, but they were prepared to do it.

The mansion was 1,500 feet away; a police car followed about 200 feet behind them. Insular Police, National Guardsmen, and roof-top snipers packed every cross street—Calle O'Donnell, Calle Cruz, Calle McArthur, Calle del Cristo, Calle Clara Lair—yet none of them stopped the car. With each passing block they were driving deeper and deeper into a seeming trap.[48]

Two men rode in front, three in back, all of them lost in their own thoughts—saying good-bye to their families, friends, and loved ones, praying. They had all worn their Sunday best—best suit, best shirt, best tie. They were all prepared to die.[49]

Raimundo told them to get ready, and they all fingered their weapons. Raimundo had a submachine gun on the floor of the car. As they approached the main entrance to La Fortaleza, the first shot hit the driver, Domingo Hiraldo Resto, in the temple. He spilled out of the car, with his head nearly underneath it.[50]

Raimundo was the first one out. He leaped from the front passenger seat, firing his submachine gun and wounding two guards. Then he shot into the second-floor windows and ran for cover behind a palm tree.

Roberto Acevedo Quiñones jumped out of the right rear door, shooting in all directions, and made it about twenty feet. He was hit and fell facedown with a dust-raising thud. Manuel Torres Medina jumped out of the left, circled right, and was killed as quickly as Quiñones less than ten feet from the car.

From the roof of the mansion, Detective Carmelo Dávila took careful aim with his carbine and fired once. Raimundo dropped dead in the hot sun beside a splendid palm tree.[51] The driver, Domingo Hiraldo, though hit in the temple, crawled to the mansion and leaned against a wall. The police thought he was dead, but they approached him with their guns drawn to make sure. "I'm already dead. Please don't shoot me anymore," Hiraldo pleaded. They shot him again.[52]

The only survivor, twenty-three-year-old Gregorio Hernández, crawled under the car and traded gunfire for an hour, losing blood the whole time. When he finally passed out, they dragged him into the open by his feet. He had nineteen bullet wounds and five bullets still inside him.[53]

Governor Luis Muñoz Marín watched from the mansion. When a bullet crashed through the blinds and buried itself in his office wall, he shoved past his attorney general, crawled into an inner room, and urgently called US Brigadier General Edwin L. Sibert, demanding a battalion of National Guardsmen to fight the five Nationalists.[54] When Sibert said that he thought the governor didn't want to declare martial law, Muñoz Marín shot back that he was declaring it now.[55]

Later that afternoon, a photographer captured the scene in a high-angle panoramic photo: Two men lie dead in the hot sun. No one pays any attention to them. Police and FBI agents stand around taking notes, exchanging views, smoking cigarettes, killing time. The dead men lie in their own blood, arms and legs akimbo, devoid of dignity, like broken toys in the hot sun.

The revolution was ending in San Juan.

❦

Less than six blocks away, at 156 Calle Sol, dozens of police and National Guardsmen had surrounded Albizu Campos's apartment. They took positions on all corners, behind cars, and on the rooftops. Two Browning

Courtyard of *La Fortaleza*, after the Nationalist attack of October 30
© Bettmann/Corbis

.50-caliber machine guns set up forty yards away, on opposite ends of the street, placed Albizu's balcony in a deadly crossfire. Efraín López Corchado tried to enter Albizu's apartment and was killed on the spot.[56] Soldiers carried him away like last night's garbage.

A little after 5 p.m., Albizu peered through the window blinds and saw the mounting firepower. He and three supporters—José Muñoz Matos, Doris Torresola, and Carmen María Pérez—began to build a wall of books behind the window. When it had reached almost four feet, a police captain shouted through a megaphone, "Pedro Albizu Campos, you are under arrest. Will you surrender peacefully." It was an order, not a question, and Albizu ignored it. They built the wall higher until, without warning, a machine-gun volley ripped into the apartment.[57]

The window shades shattered, and the room's occupants threw themselves to the ground as bullets smashed into the stucco wall, destroying everything they hit. Books flew, and a table split in two. When the barrage finally ended, Doris lay on the floor, shot in the throat.[58] Albizu pressed a towel against the wound, but the bleeding didn't stop. At Albizu's request, José and Carmen carried Doris down to the street, and all three of them were arrested immediately.

In all the confusion, by some fluke, a Nationalist named Alvaro Rivera Walker managed to run upstairs. He had been a cadet and visited Albizu several times; the old man trusted him. He invited Alvaro to come in and grab a gun. For the next few hours they guarded the window, watched the door, and traded shots with the police. By nightfall Albizu understood the situation. He told Alvaro that their attackers would love to kill him but couldn't; they needed a prisoner, not a martyr.[59]

The lights and water had been cut off, but Albizu had two gallons of water and some canned sardines. They slept fitfully that night; every few minutes a desultory shot would hit the vicinity of their window.

The next morning, Chief of Police Salvador T. Roig sat inside a bulletproof car and, through a bullhorn, called for a parley. Albizu and Alvaro crept slowly to the balcony, from which they saw dozens of men rushing in all directions. Despite this, through his bullhorn, Roig assured them that they'd be safe.

Albizu demanded to know who had been shooting at his window all night. No one responded. Then he asked whether the newsmen had reported the death of Efraín López the previous day. Still no response. Next he asked where Doris Torresola was. Again, no answer.[60]

Albizu noticed that a city garbage truck was blocking Calle Sol. He looked to his right—another garbage truck. Police buses blocked both ends of the cross street Calle Cruz. Albizu was totally cut off.

The enclosure was a killing zone. Military and police vehicles were everywhere; soldiers, policemen, and detectives crouched behind them; searchlights had been brought in; machine guns had been mounted and bazookas assembled; snipers lay on the rooftops; two armored jeeps drove around the perimeter. It was a full-scale assault, a scene out of World War II.[61]

Albizu shook his head in disgust and walked off the balcony. For the rest of the day, he watched the windows, and Alvaro watched the stairs, while Chief Roig waited. Time was his friend. At one point he generously tossed up a pile of newspapers listing all the arrests made and Nationalists killed over the past two days.

Albizu read them all carefully without saying a word. He noticed a comment from President Harry Truman dismissing the entire revolution as "an incident between Puerto Ricans."[62] That night Albizu rambled on for a while. He talked about Vidal, the barbershop, and the rumor that the barber had been kidnapped. He talked about religion and the difficulty of changing one's fate, both for people and for entire nations.

Then he asked a strange question: "Alvaro, are we invisible?" He said it seemed that they only existed to each other on their island, that nobody heard them or even saw them. Alvaro responded that God saw them.[63]

The next day, on November 1, 1950, two men tried to assassinate President Harry Truman to prove that the revolution was not "an incident between Puerto Ricans" but rather a war between two countries. They went that far and risked that much to be seen and heard.

A few hours after the assassination attempt, the US National Guard tear-gassed Albizu's apartment, the FBI rushed in, and the Insular Police arrested him.[64]

WASHINGTON, DC

At 2:20 p.m. on November 1, President Harry S. Truman was napping in his underwear. It was an unusually hot day, and the Trumans were staying in Blair House at 1651 Pennsylvania Avenue while the White House was undergoing renovations.[65] Awakened by a sudden thundering, the president padded to the second-floor window, peered down, and saw a vicious gunfight in the street.[66]

Griselio Torresola and Oscar Collazo had come to assassinate him. Oscar was also a president—of the New York chapter of the Puerto Rican Nationalist Party. Griselio was the brother of Doris Torresola, the woman shot in Albizu's apartment, and cousin of Blanca Canales, leader of the Jayuya uprising.

The two had planned their attack carefully. They had scouted Blair House twice, mapped out all the defenses, choreographed and rehearsed the assault, prepared and oiled their weapons, and walked around like

Albizu Campos arrested in San Juan
© AP Photo

tourists all morning. Once they penetrated the house and killed the president, they knew they would never escape. It was a suicide mission, just like the attack on La Fortaleza in San Juan. But they had the element of surprise. And whether they succeeded or not, the world would know that the revolution was real. It was not a Caribbean clown show or a mere "incident between Puerto Ricans."

After getting out of a cab at 2:12 p.m. on the corner of Fifteenth Street and Pennsylvania Avenue in front of the cathedral-like Riggs National Bank, they took one last stroll past Blair House. Nothing had changed. Only the usual four men stood guard.

Just like Raimundo Díaz Pacheco and the Nationalists who attacked La Fortaleza, the two men wore their Sunday best. Griselio wore a gray suit, black shoes, and a brown hat. Oscar chose a striped banker's suit, brown Crusader shoes, and a pocket handkerchief.

Oscar Collazo after the Truman assassination attempt
© AP Photo/Harvey Georges

The men approached from separate directions on the sidewalk, carrying a Walther P38 pistol, a Luger, and sixty-nine bullets. Oscar was supposed to shoot first, but his pistol jammed. He pounded it against his chest and finally managed to fire. Griselio shot a guard and ran toward the Blair House entrance. No one had time to think. Over a hundred shots rang out. At one point Truman opened his second-floor window and looked out. Griselio was only thirty-one feet away and looking in Truman's direction as he reloaded his Luger. In three or four seconds he'd have a clear shot at the president.

But Griselio never took that shot. A bullet passed clear through his head, spraying pieces of brain, as he staggered through a low hedge and died instantly. A guard named Leslie Coffelt was killed. Oscar took multiple hits and fell to the sidewalk with three tracks of blood running down his face.[67]

The next day, nearly every paper in America wrote about the assassination attempt.[68] They showed diagrams of the gun battle.[69] Some called it "the biggest Secret Service gunfight in U.S. history" and "the first conspiracy to kill a president since Booth shot Lincoln." Many called Oscar and Griselio "terrorists"[70] and "desperados."[71] The *Washington Post's* headline blared:

ASSASSIN SLAIN, ANOTHER SHOT AT TRUMAN'S DOOR;
PUERTO RICAN TERRORISTS KILL GUARD, WOUND 2;
PRESIDENT GLIMPSES BATTLE'S END FROM WINDOW

In a clever red-baiting trick, Governor Luis Muñoz Marín claimed that Communists were behind the Truman assassination attempt and the entire Nationalist revolution.[72] The *New Republic* wrote, "The Puerto Ricans who tried to kill Truman were as stupid as they were fanatical."[73] *Life* reported, "The acts of violence made no sense—except to Communists who thrive on disruption in the Caribbean and elsewhere."[74] *Time* branded it "a weird assassination plot" involving "irrational, unpredictable behavior."[75]

The papers reported what Oscar and Griselio had done. Not one paper examined why they had done it. No newspaper mentioned that within the last twenty-four hours, Griselio's sister Doris had been shot in the throat, his brother Elio had been arrested, his cousin Blanca's house had been invaded by US troops, and all three of them now faced life imprisonment.

No writer noticed that Oscar's socks were orange and green, the colors of the flag of Jayuya.[76]

Most importantly, no newspaper mentioned that just twenty-four hours earlier, the US Air Force was bombing Jayuya, the town where both these men were born and raised, and where their families still lived.

CHAPTER 19

Salón Boricua

It was October 30. The black Buick Roadmasters sat parked outside the barbershop. The FBI had assigned seventeen agents to watch Vidal around the clock, and today was day five. On day one, two longtime customers, Filadelfo and Santo, were promptly arrested when they walked out of the shop. No one visited Vidal after that, and the FBI wouldn't let him leave. They even broke the green light in front of the *salón* to control the traffic around him.[1] The broken light didn't bother him much. It was a useless old signal, granting permission that no one had asked for and nobody needed—certainly no one in the Salón Boricua.

The FBI agents brought him food, water, and newspapers. The telephone worked but was obviously bugged, and anyone he called would be arrested as fast as Filadelfo. A tragedy was unfolding, and Vidal was powerless to stop it. He could merely turn on the radio and listen, just like everyone else.[2]

⌘

Vidal rubbed some Aceite Rabassa coconut oil on the burns on his chest and right leg where Rolf had put out a few cigarettes. For the last four days he'd listened to the radio and read *El Imparcial*. He heard about the prison break at El Oso Blanco, the shootout at La Fortaleza, the burned police stations, the governor's declaration of martial law, the deployment of 5,000 National Guardsmen, the siege of Pedro Albizu Campos's home. And there was nothing he could do.

He made a quick trip to the bathroom and discovered the secret panel was still there. The hidden basement next door contained dozens of loaded weapons and over 6,000 rounds of ammunition. *Ea rayo!* he must have thought. Those weapons belonged where the battle was being waged, where they could do some good!

Vidal paced around the barbershop, talking to himself and yelling at the radio as an *Amos 'n' Andy* rerun played on CBS. As the sun went down, out of sheer frustration, Vidal snatched a bottle of Bacardi from under the shoe-shine stand.

ᘒ

He awoke the next morning with a hangover. The FBI had already tossed *El Imparcial* against his door. He read it from cover to cover, paying special attention to the arrests occurring all over the island. In San Juan, Ponce, and Peñuelas, 400 suspected Nationalists had already been detained; nearly 1,000 more arrests were expected. Governor Luis Muñoz Marín had demanded even more US troops (beyond the 5,000 National Guardsmen) and the use of Fort Buchanan as a prisoner detention center.[3]

The most disturbing story was about Albizu Campos. They'd cut off his water and electricity and barricaded the streets. Hundreds of snipers, police, and National Guardsmen had him surrounded, and they'd already shot Doris Torresola in the throat. Anything could happen to Albizu.

And then the idea hit him—a way to get himself out from under house arrest and enable him to tell Albizu that they still had weapons. Lots of them. Even after Albizu's inevitable arrest, the revolution could continue.

Vidal talked to the FBI agents out front, and they sent a telegram to Vicente Géigel Polanco, the attorney general of Puerto Rico. Vidal had offered to broker Albizu's surrender.[4] Then Vidal called *El Imparcial* and told the paper to send a reporter because Albizu's barber was ready to talk.[5]

&

Three hours had passed. Vidal called the attorney general's office twice and left messages. It was now past noon, but no one had come or called. Instead, Vidal noticed a few more cars parked outside the barbershop, most of them belonging to police.

Vidal squinted as another car drove up from the Santurce Insular Police station. WIAC radio—the best news station on the island—was repeating everything he'd read in *El Imparcial,* so he tuned into NBC and listened in irritation to several commercials for Lucky Strike Cigarettes, Ex-Lax, Ipana Toothpaste Bucky Beaver, and the Roy Rogers Quick Shooter Hat. Men who rose at 4 a.m. every morning, climbed a mountain in rain or fog or killing heat, and cut sugar cane with mosquitoes flying into their mouths didn't need an empire telling them what to do, what language to speak, what flag to salute, what heroes to worship, or what products to buy.[6] Vidal took a swig of Bacardi to calm his nerves. Unfortunately there wasn't much left. He walked over to the shoe-shine stand with the little shrine behind it and prayed, a rarity for him. He leafed through a Bible and touched the pages gently, with the tips of his fingers. He picked up a statue of Santa Barbara and asked her to guide him. Then something caught his attention, and he rushed to a window.

A US Army truck had just rolled up, and a dozen National Guardsmen jumped out. They didn't look like an escort for the attorney general. They had rifles and grenades and were taking positions outside the Salón Boricua.

Vidal looked quickly around the barbershop, peered out at the soldiers, and came up with a new plan. He turned the radio up loud, ran into the bathroom, and slammed the door. Then he opened the hidden panel, plunged into the next-door basement, and grabbed a boxful of weapons. Within five minutes he'd scooped up two more boxes and brought them all into the barbershop. He peeked out a window: the soldiers were still in position, awaiting further orders. They weren't even looking at him and chatted amiably among themselves, as if on a field trip or training exercise.

Vidal strolled casually around the shop, singing "All By Yourself in the Moonlight" along with the Champion Barbershop Quartet. By the time the song ended, Vidal had placed three shotguns and five revolvers around the shop, concentrating them near two windows and the main door. He stacked six Molotov cocktails on a staircase that led to a second-floor apartment. He tucked a Colt M1911 pistol into his waistband. Near the shoe-shine stand, behind a three-foot-thick concrete column, he hid another shotgun, two Molotov cocktails, an M3A1 submachine gun, and forty magazines, each with thirty rounds of .45-caliber ACP bullets.

A commercial for Aunt Jemima pancake flour played as the door opened to the shop and an Insular Policeman walked in with his gun drawn. Vidal asked if he could help him, then shot in his general direction. The cop's cap flew off, and he ran out of the shop.[7] Vidal ducked behind the shoe-shine stand, and a few seconds later, a hail of bullets tore into the wall behind him. Two mirrors shattered onto the Koken barber chair.

Vidal took a deep breath, then stood up with the M3A1 submachine gun and blasted twenty rounds through two windows and the front door. He also shot out the light bulbs over the four barber's chairs, throwing the shop into dappled shadow.

The soldiers ducked for cover. They hadn't expected return fire, let alone from a submachine gun.

Reporter Imperio Rodriguez ran into El Machango, a local bar at 379 Calle Colton and phoned *El Imparcial*, telling the paper to send a photographer immediately.

Soldiers surrounded the building on the corner of Calles Colton and Barbosa, as Insular Police snipers took positions atop the buildings on the adjacent corners. With a colorful stucco exterior and pleasant upstairs terrace, the Salón Boricua looked like a harmless senior citizen's home—until a Molotov cocktail sailed down from the second floor. It landed like an angry comet on a police car, scattering cops and soldiers in every direction.

The soldiers blasted the terrace with rifle fire, but then a bronze face with ivory teeth appeared in a second-floor window, and another Molotov cocktail exploded near a National Guard jeep.

With everyone scrambling for cover, a spray of .45-caliber ACP bullets from a third window hit the surrounding rooftops, and the snipers ducked. Then everyone started shooting in all directions, as NBC Radio took a friendly commercial break.

Hit in the leg, Vidal wrapped a towel around his thigh and ducked the fusillade crashing in through two windows as the *Bell Telephone Hour* began and Eve Young started to sing, "If I Knew You Were Comin' I'd've Baked a Cake."

Vidal started to laugh. Under the circumstances, it was the funniest thing he'd ever heard. He started singing along and firing a shotgun out one window, then another.[8]

El Imparcial's photographer had arrived. She'd already shot two rolls and was calculating the raise she would demand that very afternoon. These photos were priceless and she knew it. *El Imparcial, El Mundo*, and *El Nuevo Día* had all sent their best metro reporters. Over a dozen radio stations had sent mobile units, including WIAC, WNEL, WITA, and WKAQ (San Juan); WPRB (Ponce); WCMN and WEMB (Arecibo); WSWL (Santurce); WMDD (Fajardo); WENA (Yauco/Bayamón), and WVJP (Caguas). Even Mayagüez had sent a WECW radio unit, from the opposite end of the island. A live shoot-out between thirty Nationalists and the US National Guard was not to be missed.

As the reporters, photographers, and radio announcers set up, more National Guardsmen arrived with machine guns, rifles, carbines, and a bazooka and cemented a line of fire along Calle Barbosa.[9]

WIAC's Luis Enrique "El Bibí" Marrero and Miguel Ángel Álvarez were on the scene. Bibí had been born and raised in the Chícharo section of Santurce and knew Vidal personally.[10]

When he asked a platoon lieutenant how many Nationalists were in the barbershop, he was told twenty or thirty. The lieutenant had no reason to exaggerate, but Bibí was not convinced. He hadn't seen twenty Nationalists who could agree on anything, let alone coordinate a military defense. Maybe things had changed. Maybe this revolution had a chance after all.

Then Bibí saw two M1919A4 Browning machine guns setting up and a bazooka team unpacking M6A3 rockets. He forgot he was an uninvolved reporter and tried to inject some reason into the situation. He called up and asked Vidal how he was doing. When Vidal called down that he was "all fucked up," Bibí replied that he was famous, that every radio station on the island was there. Vidal told him he'd been listening to the radio as well but was only getting "American crap." When Bibí asked if he needed anything, he said he could use a ticket to Cuba. Bibí said that maybe that could be arranged and was about to ask how many were with him when a dozen soldiers opened fire all around him.[11]

Bibí ducked for cover. No one was going anywhere that day. He counted fifteen police and twenty-five soldiers, and they concentrated their fire on the front door and windows. The machine guns blew a window off its hinges and bottles exploded in the shop.

A lieutenant called for a cease-fire. The world went still. The front door had blasted into toothpicks; a wisp of smoke curled off a machine gun. Vidal the barber couldn't possibly be alive. A few Guardsmen poked out their heads, a police detective crept toward the front door, and the reporters looked at each other. Some of them felt bad for the Mayagüez radio crew; they'd come a long way for nothing.

Then suddenly a madman appeared at the door and sprayed everyone with hot .45-caliber ACP rounds, then disappeared. Bullets flew, a bazooka shell hit the barbershop, and the reporters screamed.

Everyone dashed behind a car, truck, or lamppost, and the radio men went wild. Every town in Puerto Rico was hearing the gunfight. For the first time in history, the entire island was listening to the same live event. The reporters shouted into their microphones, their eyes popping, the bullets snapping over their heads even as they described the scene.[12]

Inside the *salón*, Vidal saw the reporters chattering away, so he crawled over to his General Electric Octagon radio, which had been shot in more places than Vidal, yet miraculously still worked. He lay underneath it, raised an arm, and flipped from one station to the next: WIAC, WPRB, WSWL, WENA, WVJP, WECW. All were reporting that twenty or thirty Nationalists were involved in a shootout with the US government at the Salón Boricua. Vidal shook his head. All this technology was supposed to unite people and create a better understanding. Instead it kept them apart and confused the simplest things. Maybe that was the idea all along.[13]

Police and National Guard take cover from the barber's gunfire
The Ruth M. Reynolds Papers, Archives of the Puerto Rican Diaspora, Centro de Estudios
Puertorriqueños, Hunter College, CUNY

Through a bullhorn, the lieutenant called out to Vidal that he and his men did not want to harm him; Vidal shouted down that they should tell that to his leg, which they'd shot pretty badly. The lieutenant yelled for Vidal and his associates to come out with their hands up, and Vidal shouted back that he didn't have any friends. The lieutenant rejoined that what he did have was one minute; after that they were coming in.[14]

Vidal didn't need a minute. He snuck up the back stairs and flung down three Molotov cocktails, but only one of them exploded, and two machine gun volleys ripped into the building. The .30-caliber bullets knocked off almost every door and window, blew louvers off their hinges, pockmarked the stucco facade, and pierced and splintered the wooden balcony in a hundred places.[15]

Vidal ran back downstairs and hid behind the only protected spot: the three-foot-thick concrete column near the shoe-shine stand at the base of the old staircase. He dragged the radio to safety with him behind the column. Another machine gun salvo blasted in. Mirrors shattered;

bottles exploded; everything was vaporized, atomized, and liquefied in all directions.

Vidal reloaded his submachine gun and several shotguns. He had lots of bullets left, and from behind the concrete column, he could shoot through three separate windows and two doors. He was an army of one, at least for today.

He flipped through several stations on his radio until he found something useful. WAJH was airing an old Albizu Campos speech. Vidal played it at full volume; the reporters could hear it outside.[16]

Why do we even vote for these people? This year on election day, just stay in bed with your wife. By next year Governor Luis Muñoz Marín will make staying in bed on election day a felonious act punishable by ten years imprisonment.[17]

Vidal shot a .45-caliber ACP clip through the windows, firing thirty bullets in three bursts at full cyclic rate. Everyone outside ducked for cover. Then he hid behind the cement column and reloaded his submachine gun.

If independence could be obtained with a cigarette in the mouth, a bottle of champagne, or walking with a good-looking girl, I would be the first to lie down here on the plaza and wait for independence drinking champagne. But independence is won with a gun.[18]

Sniper shots bounced off the floor and ricocheted off the walls. The machine guns blasted chunks of cement, glass, and jagged wood through the air; something sliced Vidal's cheek like a razor. He threw himself down, rolled across the floor, grabbed a shotgun by the center window, and fired straight at a police car as a photographer snapped a picture from across the street.

For the past fifty years, the United States has been at war with Puerto Rico. They steal our land, sterilize our women, inject us with cancer and tuberculosis, they find traitors to rule over us, parasites who live by robbing their own people . . . hiding in castles where they drug themselves with morphine and drink rum continuously.[19]

A hail of bullets split a wall as a cloud of concrete dust engulfed the shop.

Empires are devils disguised as guardian angels. The American flag is a skull and crossbones over two bunches of bananas. Democracy is a lady who presents herself with a machine gun between her legs, tear gas at her breast and her hat adorned with pistols and .45 revolvers.[20]

The Salón Boricua was crumbling. Shrapnel flew everywhere. Flying glass and concrete hit Vidal again and again.

Our country is past speeches. Puerto Ricans have to fight for their liberty with all arms at their disposal. We must fight for our own sanity . . . because their propaganda is so complete, that the only reality anymore is the one we create for ourselves.[21]

The battle raged for another hour. Vidal was shot four times and lost three fingers on his left hand, but like a man possessed, he fired ceaselessly from behind the cement column, the three main windows, and even the front door of the Salón Boricua.

According to the Yankees owning one person makes you a scoundrel, but owning a nation makes you a colonial benefactor. Forty detectives follow me around, even to the toilet. Everywhere you look you see a Yankee army, navy, police and Yankee courts. But one day our patience will end . . . because man is essentially free, and freedom is a force stronger than any empire on earth.[22]

A crowd gathered a block away on Callejón La Esperanza, and neighbors peeked cautiously through their window shades. A betting pool grew in El Machango regarding how many Nationalists were in the *salón* and how long they'd be able to hold out. A few veteran journalists were already filing their stories and knocking back their Cuba Libres, when a scruffy kid ran in to announce that Vidal was singing.

Everyone rushed out to hear this latest development. Vidal was singing all right—a traditional Christmas *aguinaldo* with a few new couplets thrown in. He punctuated each verse with a shot from his Colt pistol.

Yo tengo una pistola	(I have a pistol)
Con manago de marfil	(With a marble handle)
Para matar to' los Yankees	(To kill all the Yankees)
Que vienen por ferrocarril	(Who come by railroad)

The reporters started to laugh, especially when the National Guard lieutenant asked for a translation. His eyes widened considerably upon receiving it.[23]

When the reporters started cheering for Vidal, the soldiers decided they'd had enough. The lieutenant marched over to a field radio, spoke for a minute, and returned with his orders. It was time.

They lit up the universe with hundreds of rounds; they blasted the building relentlessly. Bullets snapped all around Vidal's head, and he hit the floor repeatedly, cutting and abrading himself each time, his clothes torn to bits. He took a bullet in the ribs and saw his thumb vanish from his left hand; a chunk of cheekbone flew off in a splatter of red bone. And still he fought back, firing from behind the cement column, spraying .45-caliber ACP bullets all over the sidewalk—until the staircase collapsed and buried him in the rubble.

Vidal heard a bell toll in La Iglesia del Espíritu Santo. He saw his father reading to the tobacco workers again, and his father waved. He saw the room where he was born, spotless with a little sewing machine in the corner. Then he was gone.[24]

The soldiers didn't know this. They launched three canisters of tear gas, waited two or three minutes, then edged carefully toward the barbershop. Bibí and the other reporters craned their heads to see what was going on inside. Everyone expected twenty or thirty Nationalists to come staggering out, but none appeared.

The lieutenant ordered his soldiers to gas the upstairs, and three more canisters sailed up to the second floor—two made it through the windows, one landed on the balcony. Still no one came out.

At a signal from the lieutenant, five Guardsmen in gas masks rushed in through the front door; six others covered them from either side of the three windows. The soldiers darted all around, ready to shoot anything that moved, but they found no Nationalists, just four walls spattered with blood and a foot-high pile of rubble covering the entire floor.

They searched for a rear exit or trap door but found nothing. It was as if they'd been fighting a ghost. Then suddenly, from behind a concrete column, a soldier told them to come look.

Vidal was covered in blood and broken glass, not moving, apparently dead, but just to be sure, a soldier cleared the rubble off Vidal's head and shot him at point-blank range. The bullet exploded through Vidal's forehead and lodged in his brain. "Que viva Porto Rica," the soldier said in a southern accent, and then dragged him out by the feet.[25]

The soldiers completed their reconnaissance and looked at each other in disbelief. It was a highly embarrassing scene: this tiny barber from Salón Boricua had held forty armed men at bay. But then, as they hauled the corpse of Vidal Santiago into the street, things got even worse. The corpse opened its eyes.

The soldiers gave a start and dropped Vidal on the sidewalk. One of them yelled "Oh, Jesus!" Another yelled, "I thought you shot him." A third ducked behind a car and started praying. The reporters started running in all directions, taking photos, grabbing their microphones, telling 2 million Puerto Ricans that Vidal Santiago was still alive.

The Insular Police grabbed Vidal off the ground and smiled for a photo, as if they had caught a big fish. Then they threw him into an ambulance.

It was 6 p.m. The battle had lasted three hours. People heard it in their homes, at work, and in their cars. They heard it in every town, hospital, and school, in every pawnshop, barbershop, beauty salon, and bodega. The governor heard it. The attorney general heard it. The prisoners in El Oso Blanco and La Princesa heard it. In just three hours, next to Albizu Campos, Vidal Santiago Díaz had become the most famous Nationalist in Puerto Rican history.

He was the barber who stood up to an empire with a bullet in his brain.[26]

❧

Later that night, the soldiers cordoned off the area and searched for Nationalist fliers, Puerto Rican flags, and other subversive material. They didn't speak much to the press; there had been enough embarrassment for one day.

They found a few weapons, a broken radio, and dozens of celebrity headshots. The statue of Santa Barbara was still behind the shoe-shine stand. The portraits of Vidal's father and El Águila Blanca had been placed carefully underneath her. The soldiers didn't find the panel in the bathroom or the hidden basement next door. They gutted the entire barbershop and searched through the debris for clues—but by midnight they still couldn't understand how one man, all alone, could have waged such a savage battle. It didn't seem human. The rubble hid a great mystery.

A hundred yards away a man watched from a rooftop, hidden from view, recording every movement of the soldiers and police. He knew what they were seeking and understood everything that had occurred, but what he knew and understood didn't matter. The world wasn't ready to hear it: Vidal, a hero today, would be gone tomorrow. He was doomed to die a cipher in some vast statistical operation; the coroner would count his teeth, and the family might save some hair, but otherwise his death would be unknown, unhonored, and unremarked.

He knew that Vidal existed—a man of substance, flesh and bone, fiber and liquids, and a strong mind—but he was still invisible to El Norte because they refused to see him. They saw only his surroundings, or themselves, or figments of their own imagination; anything and everything except Vidal.

He knew some races were condemned to solitude, and Vidal's story would never get off the island.

He knew the green light in front of the Salón Boricua had been broken on purpose.[27]

He knew that people were imprisoned by other people's habits, attitudes, defeats, boredom, quiet desperation, and muted, icy, self-destroying rage—and that this applied to nations as well.

He knew the Ponce Massacre was not an isolated incident.

He knew people were being interrogated, tortured, bombed, and killed.

He knew his job was clear: to keep quiet and document it all, to keep the record intact, to pass it on to the next generation, until someday the story could be told.

That was good enough for him. The best an artist could hope for was to leave an honest account of himself—even if it was nothing more than a hanged man's right to the last word. And so with a long zoom lens, Juan Emilio Viguié filmed the soldiers as they swarmed over the street, fiddled with the dead green light, and picked over the bones of Salón Boricua.

CHAPTER 20

La Caja de Chinchas

Immediately after the revolt, Governor Luis Muñoz Marín declared martial law throughout Puerto Rico.[1] US military personnel locked down entire towns, blocked roads, and searched cars. FBI agents, Insular Police, and National Guardsmen raided thousands of homes, searching for "subversive" materials in violation of Public Law 53 (the Gag Law), including patriotic leaflets and Puerto Rican flags. And then came the arrests. Insular Police officers arrested Nationalists, Nationalist sympathizers, and people who played dominoes with Nationalists or simply knew them. They arrested escaped convicts and accused them of being Nationalists.

The press blamed one Nationalist, Juan Esteban Nuñez Laracuente, for half the mayhem in Utuado—including burning down the post office, the telephone building, and the San Miguel Medical Clinic. *El Imparcial* noted in two different headlines:

ARRESTOS EN MASA
CAPTURAN 32 DE LOS PROFUGOS

Jayuya farmers arrested by the US National Guard
©Bettmann/Corbis

Further inspection proved the reports wrong: none of those buildings had caught fire.[2]

The governor and the Associated Press (AP) further alleged that the Nationalists, as part of a Communist conspiracy, had destroyed the town of Jajuya. In an article filed on October 31, 1950, James Fowler, the AP correspondent in Puerto Rico, quotes the governor calling the revolution "a conspiracy against democracy, aided by the Communists." It then states that the town of Jayuya was "virtually destroyed by fire" and implies that the Nationalists were responsible. The article contains no mention of the US Thunderbolt airplanes that bombed and machine-gunned the town for several hours, leaving it in ruins.[3]

With martial law firmly in place, the wave of arrests grew. Soldiers arrested farmers and schoolteachers, men, women, and children. They dragged *jíbaros* down from their mountain shacks. In the town of Jayuya, they yanked farmers off their plows and paraded them through the town streets. They arrested women alongside the farmers. A journalist named Ruth Reynolds, a schoolteacher named Olga Viscal, and a housewife named Carmen Pérez were indicted for treason, attempted assassination, and conspiracy to overthrow the US government.[4] The table below lists a number of women arrested and the sentences they received.[5] After the first two hundred arrests in Jayuya, the National Guard commandeered several schools to hold all the prisoners. Some of them were children, imprisoned in their own schools.

Women and children arrested as "suspected Nationalists"
The Ruth M. Reynolds Papers, Archives of the Puerto Rican Diaspora,
Centro de Estudios Puertorriqueños, Hunter College, CUNY

Name: **Blanca Canales**
Charges: Burning the Jayuya post office
Sentence: Life imprisonment
Prison: Alderson, West Virginia; in 1956, back to Vega Alta; served seventeen years

Name: **Olga Viscal**
Charges: Violation of Public Law 53; thirty-seven cases of contempt of court
Sentence: One to ten years; thirty-one months
Prison: La Princesa (San Juan) and Arecibo District Jail

Name: **Rosa Collazo**
Charges: Arrested (no charges)
Sentence: Two months
Prison: Women's Federal House of Detention, New York City

Name: **Leonides Díaz**
Charges: Violation of Public Law 53; four charges of first-degree murder; six charges of intent to commit murder
Sentence: Life without parole (496 years); 7 years forced labor
Prison: Women's prison in Vega Alta

Name:	**Juanita Ojeda**
Charges:	Violation of Public Law 53
Sentence:	Eight to thirteen months
Prison:	Arecibo District Jail

Name:	**Carmen Perez**
Charges:	Attempted assassination
Sentence:	Twenty-two months
Prison:	La Princesa (San Juan) and Arecibo District Jail

Name:	**Ruth Reynolds**
Charges:	Violation of Public Law 53
Sentence:	Two to six years
Prison:	La Princesa (San Juan) and Arecibo District Jail

Name:	**Isabel Rosado**
Charges:	Violation of Public Law 53
Sentence:	One year, three months
Prison:	Humacao District Jail

Name:	**Carmen Torresola**
Charges:	Arrested (no charges)
Sentence:	Two months
Prison:	New York City Women's Federal House of Detention, New York City

Name:	**Doris Torresola**
Charges:	Violation of Public Law 53
Sentence:	Ten years
Prison:	La Princesa (San Juan) District Jail

The Insular Police, the National Guard, and the FBI traveled together through dozens of towns. At the University of Puerto Rico campus in Río Piedras, they arrested students on their way to class. Across the island, they arrested people on mere suspicion or accusation. They did not need warrants, evidence, or probable cause—they simply used a "list" of Nationalists and "tips" to police. An informant who disliked someone, or owed him some money, or was interested in his wife could simply denounce him as a Nationalist and have him arrested.[6] The "list" was so old and inaccurate that it included the attorney general of Puerto Rico, the mayor of Caguas, the Speaker of the House of Representatives,

Roadside arrest of "suspected Nationalists"
© Bettmann/Corbis

four city councilmen, and Governor Muñoz Marín's wife, Inez.[7] No matter. The "list" became the governor's excuse for arresting whomever he wanted.

Terror coursed through every town. Anyone could be arrested at any time, day or night. Many were dragged from their beds. Some prisoners arrived in pajamas. The National Guard and Insular Police held them in custody without due process and without bail.[8] In the San Juan area, the arrests continued around the clock. Citizens were lined up against concrete walls; US troops pointed submachine guns and rifles at their heads.

Still smarting from the assault on his own mansion, Governor Muñoz Marín demanded additional US troops in Puerto Rico and the use of Fort Buchanan to hold more prisoners. He salted this demand with a call to US Secretary of the Interior Oscar L. Chapman to discuss "the Nationalist tie-in with a few Communists on the island."[9]

Within a matter of days, over 3,000 people had been arrested throughout the island.[10] In La Princesa alone, 350 inmates were moved to accommodate the tidal wave of Nationalist prisoners, another 300 were jammed into the Arecibo prison, and over 500 went to El Oso Blanco (the White Bear) penitentiary in Río Piedras.[11]

After several long months (during which evidence and affidavits were created), the trials finally occurred, and they were severe. Here is one firsthand account:

> They took us to court. It was a clown show. We all knew the verdict beforehand: a prejudiced judge, a handpicked jury, prosecutors with strict orders to send everyone to jail. We entered the room in hand-cuffs, and my father tried to hug me, but a policeman shoved him away. My father said, "God bless you, son."

The trial lasted several weeks. The prosecutors presented even the bones of the policeman who had died in Jayuya. They called us traitors, assassins, subversives, every epithet they could think of. They threw the

**Mass arrest of "suspected Nationalists,"
with people being held at gunpoint in San Juan**
© Bettmann/Corbis

Puerto Rican flag around like a dishrag, with no respect whatsoever. It was clear to everyone: the verdict had been decided from the start.

We were all exhausted from this clown show. Finally the jury came back, they told us to stand up, and Judge Padró Parés read the verdict with great ceremony: "Guilty." We were all guilty of every charge: murder, arson, assault, possession of arms.

When he sentenced me, the judge looked me in the eye. He seemed angry at me. "Heriberto Marín Torres, this honorable court sentences you to life imprisonment with hard labor, plus an additional forty-five years, to be served consecutively." I heard a commotion behind me. Someone had fainted. It was my mother. A marshal ran over, grabbed my arm, and ordered me not to move.

The judge cleared everyone out of the courtroom. He did not appreciate my mother fainting. After everyone was sentenced, the judge smiled, and the prosecutors congratulated each other. They shook hands and looked at us with great contempt.[12]

After their sentencing and remand to La Princesa, El Oso Blanco, and other large penitentiaries, the Nationalists received harsh treatment. Bright light bulbs shined in their cells twenty-four hours a day. They were given no sheets, towels, or toilet paper; no showers were allowed for three weeks; visitors and correspondence were prohibited. The leaders were all placed in solitary confinement.

At night, National Guardsmen would fire their weapons outside the Nationalist cells. During the day, prisoners would have to ask these same men for permission to go to the bathroom. Their meals were often half-cooked rice, old bread, and wormy pig's feet. As time went on, out of sheer hunger, the Nationalists would simply remove the worms.

The case histories of these men and women read like chapters from *The Gulag Archipelago*. Their experiences—strip searches, cavity searches, sleep deprivation, starvation, isolation, and humiliation—were engineered to destroy their dignity and break their spirits.

One room in La Princesa, known as *la caja de chinchas* (the bedbug box), contained hundreds, perhaps thousands of bedbugs that had been allowed to multiply. The guards would remove a Nationalist's shirt and throw him into *la caja*. Immediately the hungry bedbugs would assault

**More mass arrests of
"suspected Nationalists" in San Juan**

Photographer Juan Hernandez, November 5, 1950;
published in *El Imparcial*, November 6, 1950

him, crawling onto him from the walls or dropping off the ceiling. At first the Nationalist would wage war, crushing them on his body and against the walls, suffocated by their stink. But after several hours, he would weaken and let them drink his blood without a murmur.

The psychological warfare was equally relentless. Two months after his arrest, with no charges yet filed against him, Heriberto Marín Torres had received great news: he was being set free from La Princesa. He distributed his meager possessions, said his tearful good-byes, and headed for the warden's office, where several FBI men were waiting for him. They told him his mother's health was shaky but that his release would probably revive her—and if he told the FBI everything he knew (i.e., informed on all his cell mates), he could go free immediately. Marín Torres said nothing.[13]

Justo Guzmán Serrano's mother died. The US Department of Justice prohibited him from attending her burial. The funeral procession passed right by the prison, and the pallbearers knew that Justo was there, so everyone kept quiet—and in that silence, Justo shouted, "Good-bye, mom!" Then he buried his face in his hands.[14]

Gregorio Hernández Rivera (Goyito) was the only surviving Nationalist from the attack on La Fortaleza. He'd lost several fingers, and a dozen bullets had pockmarked his body; once the wounds healed, he was thrown in solitary. Over a year later, he was finally allowed his first visit. He hugged and kissed his wife and asked about their two-year-old daughter. Hadn't he gotten her telegram? she asked. The girl had died a few months before. The prison had thrown away the telegram.[15]

Deusdedit Marrero, a social worker, had played no part in the revolt. He was arrested for being a Socialist—not exactly a Nationalist, but close enough—and convicted of attempting to overthrow the US government, even though he was at work during the entirety of the revolt and was leaving behind a pregnant wife. The brutality of these charges ultimately drove him insane. When he discovered that his wife had committed suicide,[16] Deusdedit killed himself.[17]

Ricardo Díaz was arrested "for being a member of a revolutionary family." The guards ridiculed him mercilessly, trying to goad him into violence or suicide. Unable to contrive any evidence against him, they released him after seven months.[18]

Francisco Matos Paoli was arrested for having a Puerto Rican flag in his house and sentenced to twenty years. The warden knew that Paoli was the secretary general of the Nationalist Party and a prolific poet, so he inflicted an evil punishment: he deprived Paoli of paper and writing utensils. To the warden's chagrin, Paoli always found a pencil or two and covered his prison walls with poems. He even managed to write on the ceiling. Years later, in 1977, Matos Paoli was nominated for the Nobel Prize in literature.[19]

US Army doctors conducted medical experiments at La Princesa. Two or three times a week, they visited the *hospitalito* (the medical clinic) and persuaded healthy prisoners to take "new, experimental drugs for tropical diseases." They paid these prisoners with cartons of cigarettes. The "treatments" would last several months, and when prisoners died, the cause of death would be listed as "atrial fibrillation" or "myocardial infarction" (heart attack); the experimental drugs were never mentioned.[20]

The army doctors persuaded Hector, an orderly in the *hospitalito*, to take some "new pills" for bilharzia, even though he was not afflicted with this. Within a few days Hector started to vomit, his stool became bloody, and his liver became inflamed; the pain was excruciating. Governor Muñoz Marín commuted his sentence and he went home. One week later, his mother found him dead.[21]

The most extreme medical experiment of all was revealed on the floor of the United Nations and reported around the world. A great cloud of mystery still surrounds it.

CHAPTER 21

Atomic Lynching

At 3 a.m. on November 1, 1950, while everyone slept, Pedro Albizu Campos, president of the Puerto Rican Nationalist Party and leader of the 1950 revolt against the United States, was transferred to La Princesa. A dozen Insular Police surrounded the van as it glided quietly up to the *hospitalito*, while another dozen police officers lined the path to the door, all armed with rifles. In absolute silence, the officers slipped the man through a side door, and the van drove away with its lights off—so quickly and quietly that the only sounds were coquí (tree frogs) and the ocean waves of San Juan Harbor.[1]

The officers led Albizu to a specially outfitted cell in solitary, then calmly resumed their rounds. The cell, backed by a bolted, unmarked room that everyone assumed to be a storage closet, was close to the *hospitalito*; it had four walls with no window, no ventilation, and an overflowing pail that served as his latrine. The stench was heavy and pervasive. He remained in isolation there for six months, with no visitors or access to lawyers, a telephone, or writing instruments.[2]

A couple of months after his arrival, in early 1951, strange rumors began to circulate around the prison. A "death machine" designed and installed by a mad scientist—a US Army doctor or, worse, Josef Mengele himself, up from Argentina—could send "death rays" through the walls of La Princesa and kill prisoners while they slept. It was a ridiculous idea, but the warden would interrogate anyone who asked the guards about it, then send them off to solitary.[3]

Albizu's trial started in August 1951. He was convicted on August 15 and sentenced to life on August 29.[4] But before his trial, before he'd seen a lawyer, while he was still trapped in that airless cement block, strange things began to happen.

On February 18, six months before his trial, odd lights somehow penetrated the concrete walls of his cell. He saw "ribbons of light on all the walls, in all colors, brilliant as the aurora borealis. Sometimes it looked like a cascade of melted gold."[5] Then, for the first time in his life, he passed out.

When he regained consciousness, he had a splitting headache and what felt like a full-body sunburn. The next day the lights returned, and so did his headache. The lights never stopped after that; only their intensity varied. Even when there was no visible light, he could still feel the rays. After a week he noticed that each wave of radiation swelled his legs, his hands, his head, and whatever other part of the body it hit after only four minutes.[6]

Since Albizu was in complete isolation, he was unable to communicate this to anyone. Three months later, when he was finally allowed to write, Albizu sent a letter to the warden of La Princesa, Juan S. Bravo, on May 10, 1951.[7] It went unanswered. By May 29, he had written four more letters, still receiving no response from the warden.[8] Instead, on May 12, 16, 19, 21, and 22, a succession of five doctors and two psychiatrists examined him. Although they saw the burn marks and found arterial hypertension (high blood pressure), they ignored these and reported that Albizu suffered from "an interpretative psychosis of injury and danger," "overtones of paranoia,"[9] and "hallucinations of all his five senses."[10] In short, they deemed him insane.

In a memo fired off to US Attorney General J. Howard McGrath, Secretary of the Interior Oscar L. Chapman, Chief of the Secret Service U. E. Baugham, the Pentagon, the Treasury Department, and the Office of Naval Intelligence, FBI director J. Edgar Hoover gloated that Albizu "complains of North Americans shooting cosmic rays into his head," of "being attacked by certain luminous rays which he alleged were part of an electronic experiment being conducted by the U.S. Army," of "feeling lame due to the rays," and of "suffer[ing] from continuous severe headaches."[11] Later, in June 1951, Hoover sent out another memo containing the medical report of Dr. Troyano de los Ríos, the psychiatrist of the Insular Department of Prisons, in whose assessment "the cause of his paranoia is . . . an intense urge to be something which he is not, an inferiority complex."[12]

Hoover neglected to mention in these memos that other prisoners in La Princesa were reporting the same radiation as Albizu. At the doctor's suggestion, two prisoners named Robert Díaz and Juan Jaca Hernández were temporarily moved into Albizu's cell—and almost immediately they started complaining of headaches and radiation burns.[13] Warden Bravo switched a second group of prisoners into Albizu's cell, and they wrote a letter on June 7, 1951, complaining of "electronic rays," "black rays," and "white emanations" that were causing burns to the chest, stomach, and ankles.[14] Three women in La Princesa—Ruth Reynolds, Doris Torresola, and Carmen Pérez—also reported humming motors, vibrations, and electric shocks directed at their heads while they slept.[15]

As of October 1951, Albizu was allowed an extremely limited visitation: one visit every two weeks for half an hour. The visitors were usually his sister, Ana Maria Campos, his lawyer, Juan Hernández Valle, or a family friend. A few months later, despite Warden Bravo's efforts to keep the story quiet, it exploded throughout Latin America.

An *El Mundo* article headlined "Albizu Campos Alleges That They Are Directing Light Rays at Him" reported that his blood pressure had risen to 220/120,[16] that he could scarcely walk,[17] and that he had suffered "atomic torture."[18] *El Imparcial* reported that Albizu's feet, chest, and stomach were severely inflamed, and the muscles in his neck were infected.[19]

In Argentina, the magazine *Verdad* (*Truth*) put Albizu on its front cover and ran an article headlined "The Atomic Lynching of a Martyr for Liberty," which stated that the "Apostle of Puerto Rican liberty is slowly being murdered in jail by means of electronic rays."[20] In Mexico, the

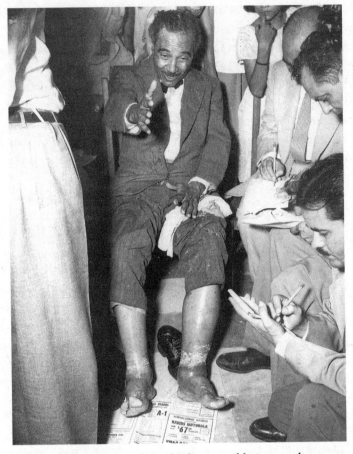

Pedro Albizu Campos shows his burns and lesions to the press

The Ruth M. Reynolds Papers, Archives of the Puerto Rican Diaspora,
Centro de Estudios Puertorriqueños, Hunter College, CUNY

magazine *Correo Indoamericano* charged, "Fatal rays are being used against Albizu Campos."[21] The daily newspaper *Tiempo en Cuba* (*Time in Cuba*) reported that Albizu was the victim of a scientific plan to induce cerebral hemorrhage, cardiac collapse, or both, and that these attacks were producing visible burns on his extremities, swelling of his face, and a severe choking around the neck. The article concluded dramatically, "God knows that this is a lynching at the height of the atomic age."[22]

The journalist Teofilo Maldonado was allowed to visit Albizu on September 23, 1953.[23] On another occasion, Cuban journalist Vicente Cubillas received permission to visit; he wrote a detailed eyewitness account:

> His head is covered by two wet towels, his neck rests on a bag of ice, and around his neck he has another bag with cold water; over his heart are two handkerchiefs soaked in ice water and his belly and legs are under wet blankets. The sheets and mattress are also soaked with water. His body is smothered with cold cream and Pomedero Pomade.
>
> The electronic attack is blinding and burning, and protection can be obtained only by the use of towels and sheets wetted in ice water.[24]

Due to the mounting concern throughout Latin America, the Cuban government requested that Albizu be transferred out of La Princesa. On May 28, 1951, the Cuban House of Representatives passed a resolution stating, "The House of Representatives of Cuba, taking into consideration the very grave state of the Puerto Rican patriot Dr. Pedro Albizu Campos . . . DECLARES . . . [that] the conditional liberty of DR. PEDRO ALBIZU CAMPOS can be obtained, and [he can be transferred] to the Republic of Cuba to attend to his cure."[25]

On December 19, 1952, a petition filed on behalf of Albizu in the General Assembly of the United Nations denounced his torture in La Princesa and demanded his extradition to a territory outside the United States.[26] The petition was supported by the personal testimony of Dr. Frédéric Joliot-Curie, a winner of the Nobel Prize in Chemistry for his discovery of "artificial radioactivity," that the technology for "total body irradiation" was in existence and that such attacks were possible.[27] After review by the FBI, the secretary of the interior, the Department of Justice, the Secret Service, and the intelligence agencies of the US armed forces, the petition was denied.[28]

In 1953 the International Writer's Congress of José Martí sent a letter to President Dwight D. Eisenhower on behalf of Albizu and the Nationalist prisoners. Twenty-eight prominent writers, journalists, and intellectuals from eleven countries signed it. The letter was ignored.[29] Later that year, Dr. Orlando Daumy, president of the Cuban Cancer Association and an expert on radiation, examined Albizu. Dr. Daumy found that (1) the sores on Albizu Campos were produced by radiation burns, (2) his symptoms corresponded to those of a person who had received intense radiation, and (3) wrapping himself in wet towels had been the best way to diminish the intensity of the radiation.[30]

Due to all this international pressure, Albizu Campos received a brief release from La Princesa on September 30, 1953, until March 6, 1954.[31] In November 1953, Carmín Pérez, Doris Torresola, and Isabel Rosado Morales came to Albizu's house at 156 Calle Sol (the same house where he'd been arrested in 1950) and witnessed an alarming physical phenomenon. They approached Albizu with a Geiger counter that registered four to nine clicks per minute upon entering his room and fourteen clicks when close to the man himself. When they placed the probe near Albizu's body, the needle jumped wildly, and the entire apparatus broke.[32]

The FBI reports sent directly to J. Edgar Hoover acknowledged that Albizu was "physically incapacitated with body swellings," that he had "more bluish marks appearing on his body," "fever and pain," "high blood pressure," "headaches and swellings on his legs," that he was "in such bad health that he can scarcely walk," that he was "very ill and sinking fast," and that "he might not recover from his present illness."[33]

Despite all this, for five years (1951–1956) nothing was done about Albizu Campos's medical condition. The United States kept sending teams of psychiatrists to his cell, all of whom declared him insane.[34] Albizu repeatedly requested that a radiologist or nuclear physicist examine him, to no avail.[35] Over and over, he stated that the radiation was intended to induce either a stroke or a heart attack.[36] In December 1952, he reported to the Organization of American States that he expected to suffer "heart failure or cerebral hemorrhage."[37]

And that is precisely what happened. In a stunning admission, an internal FBI report states that Albizu suffered a cerebral thrombosis in prison on March 27, 1956, and was moved to Presbyterian Hospital on March 29. In other words, after suffering a major stroke, Albizu did not receive proper medical attention for two full days.[38] The result was predictable: for the rest of his life, the right side of Albizu's body was paralyzed. He was never able to speak again.[39]

Albizu Campos had been silenced forever.

CHAPTER 22

Weird Science in Puerto Rico

There is a great deal at stake in determining whether the US government "irradiated" Pedro Albizu Campos. If it did not, then one might conclude that he was insane, which would substantiate the logic of the US government: that no one in his or her right mind would wish for Puerto Rican independence. If, on the other hand, Albizu was irradiated, then the US government acted with scientific savagery, using physics and mathematics for the purpose of assassination, burning defenseless prisoners alive in their cells.

A conclusive, irrefutable determination of Albizu's radiation claim is impossible since the US government maintained complete dominion over Albizu's body and controlled all access to it, and FBI reports contain the only written records about that body. Despite these limitations, a reasonable analysis is still possible—especially given facts that began to surface in the mid-1980s.

In November 1986, Congressman Edward Markey delivered a report to the House Committee on Energy and Commerce. Titled "American Nuclear Guinea Pigs: Three Decades of Radiation Experiments on U.S. Citizens," it covered 695 people exposed to radiation in thirty-one experiments sponsored by the US Army and the US Atomic Energy Commission, some in the 1940s and 1950s. In many instances, the government covered up the nature of the experiments after the subjects died.[1]

These victims included 131 prisoners at Oregon and Washington state prisons whose testicles were irradiated with X-rays during a ten-year study between 1963 and 1973. The levels reached six hundred roentgens per exposure, at two-week intervals, though the "safe" level of testicular exposure is only five roentgens per year. In other medical studies during 1943 and 1944, people underwent total body irradiation (TBI) with no prior disclosure about the dangers of X-rays.[2] This was only the start.

In August 1995, the US Department of Energy dropped a bombshell, announcing that federally supported radiation experiments had used up to 20,000 men, women, and children between World War II and the mid-1970s.[3] Some 435 confirmed experiments used children, mental patients, mentally disabled people, and prison inmates. In many cases these individuals were exposed to lethal beams of radiation and then died.[4] In twelve secret "Cold War" experiments, atomic weapons researchers released thousands of times the radiation that would be considered safe today.[5] In the worst cases, the experiments were kept secret from the public and the victims themselves in order to "avoid liability or embarrassment to the Government."[6] In one cynical study, mentally disabled children at the Walter E. Fernald State School in Waltham, Massachusetts, were told they were joining a "science club" and fed radioactive materials in their cereals for ten years (1946–1956).[7]

All this exposure, combined with aggressive journalism, forced the US Department of Energy to pay $4.8 million to bereaved family members in "an effort to make amends for the many unethical Government-sponsored radiation experiments carried out by Government doctors, scientists and military officials from 1944 to 1974 on as many as 20,000 people."[8]

THE CASE FOR ALBIZU

It is not certain, but it is possible, that Albizu Campos was one of the 20,000 people subjected to radiation experimentation. It is not certain, but it is possible, that Albizu endured TBI for five years. FBI reports repeatedly mentioned visually apparent physical signs. There is no dispute that he exhibited

- Swollen legs
- Sores on his legs, arms, and torso
- Bluish marks on his skin
- Facial and neck swelling
- Raw, peeling skin on his hands and feet
- High blood pressure (220/110)

These conditions persisted throughout his incarceration from 1951 until his stroke in March 1956.[9] In addition, Albizu complained of continuous severe headaches that were most intense after the alleged radiation attacks.[10]

A January 21, 1954, an FBI radiogram sent directly to FBI director J. Edgar Hoover stated, "A Cuban doctor visited Albizu in November 1953 and upon returning to Cuba has declarations about Albizu's case that he will place before the next international congress of doctors . . . identity of Cuban doctor unknown." This same radiogram continues, "A sample of matter from a blister on subject's [Albizu's] leg was shown or sent to a Mexican doctor, who stated there was no doubt it was caused by some sort of electronic or radioactive emanation." It concludes, "New York and Chicago are requested to obtain from informants any information assisting identification of Cuban or Mexican physicians who are alleged contacts of subject."[11] The bottom of the radiogram contained an instruction from Hoover: "If the intelligence contained in the above message is to be distributed outside the Bureau, it is suggested that it be suitably paraphrased."

Another FBI radiogram instructed the New York and Chicago offices to "furnish any available information re identity of alleged 'group of experts' and furnish plans of any doctors or experts to visit Albizu in Puerto Rico."[12] Thus, rather than attempting to identify the organic causes of Albizu's illness, the US government was conducting clandestine surveillance of any doctors who independently tried to diagnose his condition. This surveillance reached epic proportions with regard to Dr. Nacine Hanoka.

An FBI memo to J. Edgar Hoover stated, "Subject [Albizu] is seeking medical attention from physicians, who are alleged authorities on radiation." The memo indicated that mail intercepted at Albizu's home showed a letter from a Dr. Hanoka in Miami Beach, Florida. The memo ended with an instruction: "The Miami office is requested to identify Dr. HANOKA, determine whether he made a trip to Puerto Rico since 9/30/53, and furnish any subversive information concerning him."[13]

The FBI then unleashed a spectacular investigation into Dr. Hanoka. A search through records at the Miami Beach Police Department, the Miami Police Department, the Dade County Sheriff's Office, and the Miami Municipal Court found no criminal history for him. A Credit Bureau search showed that he had an income in excess of $8,000 ($71,000 in current dollars) per year. A "pretext inquiry" showed that Hanoka was living in 12 Dongan Place in New York City (the Washington Heights section) and had a winter address at 42 Collins Avenue in Miami.

A file search in Kansas City and Chicago showed that a Dr. N. Hanoka had resided at 215 South Kedzie Avenue in Chicago, then 300 West Forty-Second Street in New York, before moving to 12 Dongan Place. A search of Immigration and Naturalization Service records showed that pursuant to Petition #148314, Nacine Samuel Hanoka had also lived at 65 West 117th Street and was born in Turkey on Three King's Day (January 6) in 1886.[14] Another Credit Bureau search revealed that Dr. Hanoka had resided not at 300 but at 340 West Forty-Second Street. A letter from the Inspector in Charge, Law Division, US Department of Labor, Immigration Service, Office of the Commissioner of Immigration at Ellis Island requested information concerning one Dr. Nacine Hanoka, an alleged Communist.[15] A profile of the doctor ultimately revealed that he was white, slender, and balding with a dark complexion, brown eyes, and greying black hair. He stood five feet, nine inches tall, weighed 150 pounds, and wore glasses part-time. He was an intelligent talker, indicating extensive travel, and a retired dentist who claimed to have performed dental work for Pandit Nehru. His one peculiarity: he was a vegetarian.[16]

This manic investigation of Dr. Hanoka was more than a waste of energy and taxpayer dollars. It clearly indicates government efforts to prevent access to Albizu Campos, particularly by doctors trying to diagnose his illness.

In early 1951, another doctor entered the picture: in February and March Dr. Marshall Brucer, director of the medical division of the Oak Ridge Institute for Nuclear Studies (ORINS), visited Puerto Rico. He met with several farmers and University of Puerto Rico administrators to create a radioactive fertilizer study on Puerto Rican coffee plantations.[17] The declassified FBI records for Albizu Campos omit the period of Dr. Brucer's visit to the island—which coincides exactly with Albizu's first report of radiation in his cell.

ORINS was the primary US facility for the construction and operation of TBI chambers. It built the first state-of-the-art Medium Exposure Rate Total Body Irradiator (METBI) and the first Low Exposure Rate Total Body Irradiation Chamber (LETBI) and used them to irradiate nearly two hundred people over almost fifteen years.[18] The US Army and National Aeronautics and Space Administration both provided extensive funding for ORINS to study the effects of single, repeated, and protracted doses of radiation on human subjects. These studies used both the METBI and LETBI chambers.[19] ORINS also conducted the first three field tests in radiological warfare for the US Department of Defense.[20]

In this murk of coincidence, missing FBI documents, and TBI chambers, another coincidence developed. In the early 1950s, the Special Weapons Agency of the US Department of Defense awarded the Sloan-Kettering Institute in New York a multi-million-dollar contract to study postirradiation syndrome in humans.[21] From 1945 until 1959, the director of the Sloan-Kettering Institute was Dr. Cornelius P. Rhoads, who was also a consultant to the US Atomic Energy Commission.[22] Rhoads's name even appears in the contract documents for this postirradiation syndrome study.[23] As discussed earlier in this book, Albizu had hounded Rhoads out of Puerto Rico, after Rhoads wrote an infamous letter about "killing eight Puerto Ricans" and "transplanting cancer into several more."

Finally, in terms of doctors and medical care, the fact that Albizu had a severe stroke but was denied medical attention for at least two full days speaks volumes about the hostile environment in which he was imprisoned. A great deal of evidence, both direct and circumstantial, supports Albizu Campos's claim that he was subjected to TBI. Let us now consider the US government's argument against it.

The Case Against Albizu

Albizu Campos claims he is being "irradiated." Therefore he is crazy.

That's the entirety of the federal government's position.

The United States neither investigated the matter nor provided a radiologist or nuclear physicist to examine Albizu. To the contrary, it unleashed the FBI on any doctor who dared to inquire about his health or even to send him a letter. For five years, a caravan of paid psychiatrists conducted the only US medical inquiry. They conducted no tests and provided no answers with respect to the burns and lesions all over Albizu's body, which journalists throughout the Western Hemisphere had repeatedly witnessed, photographed, and reported. The US government simply denied the physical evidence and declared Albizu Campos insane.

∾

In 1994 *Albuquerque Tribune* reporter Eileen Welsome won the Pulitzer Prize for National Reporting for her three-part exposé on the government-sponsored radiation experiments from 1944 to 1974. She later published a book titled *The Plutonium Files*, in which she concluded the following:

- The US federal government conducted hundreds of secret radiation experiments on its own people.
- Thousands of Americans were used as laboratory animals in these radiation experiments, funded by the federal government.
- The radiation experiments revealed a deliberate intent, a willingness to inflict harm.
- The TBI procedures caused intense suffering and premature death.
- A web of deception and denial enabled the experiments to continue for decades.[24]

Thirty-five years after Albizu Campos's death, his FBI files were declassified, finally lifting a veil of secrecy. The physical evidence overwhelmingly indicates that Albizu was trapped in this web of deception and denial and irradiated over an extended period. No physical evidence to the contrary has been found—not in the FBI files or the medical records or anywhere else. It is difficult to escape the conclusion that Albizu was one of 20,000 US citizens treated as little more than lab rats. In Albizu's case, it finally killed him.[25] As one newspaper headline blared:

PIDEN INVESTIGAR LA MUERTE DE ALBIZU CAMPOS

CHAPTER 23

The King of the Towels

By June 1951, La Princesa was overflowing again. A second wave of Nationalists flooded in as their trials and sentencings were completed. Pedro Albizu Campos and over fifty patriots were given life imprisonment.[1] Some received 400-year sentences;[2] the sentences handed down across the island totaled over 16,000 years.[3] A headline appeared in the *Daily Worker*: "Albizu Campos Jailed on Wall Street's Order."[4]

As political prisoners, the Nationalists were treated severely. Whenever a large group arrived, over a hundred escort guards and National Guardsmen would encircle the transport van and create an armed gauntlet into the prison. The Nationalists were surrounded by machine guns and rifles pointed in their faces and dozens of snarling dogs. They were ushered into a rectangular stone building and taken to a large room, where the floor was covered with filthy water a few inches deep, and ordered to undress.

As the Nationalists removed each item of clothing, the guards would grab it, search it, and throw it in the water. Then the guards commanded the prisoners to put on the filthy, wet clothes. In this condition they were processed, "played the piano" (had their fingerprints taken), and were assigned to their *galerías* (galleries).

Built for one hundred prisoners, the *galerías* were packed with over four times that many. There were no exercise periods. There was no bedding or privacy. No prisoner was left alone for a single moment, not even to sleep. Spiked cuffs cut into their skin until their hands became swollen and numb. They ate rice and beans every day. At night, a legion of ants and bedbugs bit their flesh. Watches and timepieces were all confiscated. They were allowed no letters, newspapers, or contact with the outside world. Anyone who asked to see a lawyer was thrown into solitary confinement.

The Nationalist leaders were all in solitary until the warden decreed that they were no longer a threat. Albizu Campos was in a special dungeon at the far end of the *calabozos* (solitary cells). The prisoners in adjacent cells kept changing every week; they all behaved very strangely; he was sure they were spying on him, goading him to insanity, or both.[5]

To his left, Cano was tattooed with a close pattern of African flora and fauna—elephants and lions, baboons and strange birds with enormous beaks. A magnificent human eye was etched at the base of his throat. Cano called it the "eye of the police."

To his right, Eliezer scratched on the wall day and night, thinking his mother was next door (in Albizu's cell), dying. His fingers bled, literally worn to the bone.

A tooth fell out of Albizu's mouth. He was developing scurvy; his gums were bleeding; his legs were purple and black. In the absence of ventilation or a window, his own body heat and breathing raised the temperature in his tiny cell to 95 degrees Fahrenheit. He covered himself with wet towels and walked the length of the cell—five steps back and forth. Life had turned him into a pendulum. It had all been mathematically worked out.

～

One, two, three, four, five, and turn . . .

He had to keep moving—to keep his blood flowing, his lungs full, his joints hydrated—to keep his body from shutting down.

One, two, three, four, five, and turn . . .

He might never leave this room. He recalled the sunsets over Ponce, the smiles of old Aunt Rosa, the gaslit streets with the *sereno* (town crier) proclaiming that it was 11 p.m. and all was well. He remembered so many faces, voices, cries, and whispers—and said good-bye to them all.

One, two, three, four, five, and turn . . .

He remembered a tiny green light on the far side of the Río Bucaná. He gazed at it often during his childhood, in the vast obscurity beyond the city. The twinkling light had given him hope—a feeling that if he ran faster or stretched his arms further, there was still a dream some-where, so close he could hardly fail to grasp it.

One, two, three, four, five, and turn . . .

He heard a sudden cry, an anguished wail of despair inside his cell. What was it, the death of a dream? Had it come from him? It sounded like a man being tortured or going mad—it was so easy in these cells, where nothing ever happened.

One, two, three, four, five, and turn . . .

His face grew dark, and his skin began to peel. His head was bloat-ing. Ulcers grew on his legs. Blue-black warts covered his arms, his thighs, even his scrotum. Albizu was rotting alive.

One, two, three, four, five, and turn . . .

He knew what they were doing to other Nationalists: feeding them worms, burying them in bedbugs, keeping them on their feet, sleepless, for three days, interrogating them in a room with a bloody carpet, ar-resting their friends, and threatening their families, all in the name of freedom and democracy.

One, two, three, four, five, and turn . . .

La Princesa was killing them all, bit by bit, dissolving their spirit to feces and ash. The highest levels of science and lowest levels of govern-ment had joined to create a monster. It stole your youth, health, and humanity. It claimed your house and land and body and finally even your mind. It was a malignant cancer.

One, two, three, four, five, and turn . . .

The cancer threw a hidden leash on your neck and cheated you from birth until the overcharge on your coffin. The cancer needed wealth—created by other men, poor men, landless men, sweaty men, greasy men, men soaked with fever, men blinded by physical misery, men who'd fallen out of the present, whose past was surrounded by barbed wire, whose future was owned and operated by the cancer.

One, two, three, four, five, and turn . . .

They'd turned him into a dead man, a lonely ghost uttering a truth that nobody would ever hear. Albizu had learned to accept it. He knew that people died every day; they'd been squeezed empty, left hollow, then filled with the cancer.

One, two, three, four, five, and turn . . .

He had no property, no position, no future, nothing except the few cubic centimeters inside his skull—but the cancer and its operatives wanted that too. If they couldn't own it, they would destroy it with surgical precision and scientific savagery.

One, two, three, four, five, and turn . . .

It seemed that owning one man made you a scoundrel, but owning an entire nation made you a colonial benefactor. The air thickened. It started to rain. If it rained forty days and forty nights, he wondered, would it be enough to wash humanity's sins away?

One, two, three, four, five, and turn . . .

A storm raged outside. Mosquitoes swarmed in and bit Albizu's neck, as if blaming him for it. A rat scuttled up the wall and out of the cell, carrying some urgent message, no doubt. Yes, Albizu would never leave this room. It had been conceived the moment he was born, engineered specifically for him, and he could only leave it in pieces, bit by bit, in the mouths of the rats that bit him and the insects that sucked his blood.

One, two, three, four, five, and turn . . .

He walked through life with a revolution inside his head, a vision of man and woman, an island left in peace, a Garden of Eden without the cancer. But the vision was dying in a holocaust of strange science. It was burning in a man-made inferno.

One, two, three, four, five, and turn . . .

It was impossible to found a civilization on fear and hatred and cruelty. It would never endure; it would have no vitality; it would disintegrate. It would commit suicide.

In killing Albizu they were ultimately killing themselves, but they were too young to know this. The lesson would have to age and mature, like a fine wine in a forgotten cellar.

One, two, three, four, five, and turn . . .

Each baby step brought him closer to an appointed end. In the last days, in those final moments, he never once betrayed his dream. He carried it with dignity, proclaimed it with his heart, and protected it with wet towels.

The government called him a terrorist. The doctors declared him insane. The guards laughed in his face and called him the King of the Towels.

One, two, three, four, five, and turn . . .

The government got it wrong. Pedro Albizu Campos was the conscience of his people. They killed his body but forgot his voice—and it echoes across all borders, from one century to the next. Albizu was a champion of freedom.

A prophet.

A piercing light.

A fallen soldier in the war against all Puerto Ricans.

EPILOGUE

On December 11, 1964, shortly before Pedro Albizu Campos's death, Ernesto "Che" Guevara spoke before the United Nations General Assembly on his behalf. He said, "Albizu Campos is a symbol of the as yet unfree but indomitable Latin America. Years and years of prison, almost unbearable pressures in jail, mental torture, solitude, total isolation from his people and his family, the insolence of the conqueror and its lackeys in the land of his birth—nothing broke his will."[1]

Albizu Campos died on April 21, 1965. His family received hundreds of telegrams, cables, and letters from around the world. Both the Senate and House of Representatives of Puerto Rico commemorated him, and the Venezuelan parliament observed five minutes of silence in his memory. Government officials, journalists, and friends from every country in Latin America arrived to attend the funeral services. For three days before Albizu's burial on April 25, over 100,000 people passed his open casket, and 75,000 black mourning ribbons were distributed throughout the island.[2]

❧

The life, torture, and death of Albizu Campos were the direct, nearly inevitable result of American foreign policy and an ongoing flaw in the American character. The broken body of Albizu throws a spotlight on the fault lines that run through our national psyche.

These fault lines had long been apparent. Centuries of slavery and Native American genocide contradicted the bromide "All men are created equal." After the annexation of most of Mexico's territory, President Theodore Roosevelt baldly declared, "It was inevitable and in the highest degree desirable, for the good of humanity at large, that Americans ultimately crowd out the Mexicans. It was out of the question to expect Texans to submit to the mastery of the weaker race."[3] Applying this "weaker race" philosophy to Latin America, Roosevelt added, "It is Manifest Destiny for a nation to own the islands which border its shores. . . . [I]f any South American country misbehaves it should be spanked."[4]

Much like the British imperial doctrine of the white man's burden, the American notion of a Manifest Destiny rested on a belief in the superiority of the Anglo-Saxon race and its right to rule the Western Hemisphere. President William Howard Taft candidly proclaimed this right in 1912: "The whole hemisphere will be ours in fact as, by virtue of our superiority of race, it already is ours morally."[5] This theme of racial superiority reached ludicrous heights on the floor of the US Senate, in April 1900, when a legislator warned that Puerto Ricans were savages "hostile to Christianity," "incapable of self-government," and "addicted to head-hunting and cannibalism."[6] As late as 1940, *Scribner's Commentator* stated, "All Puerto Ricans are totally lacking in moral values, which is why none of them seem to mind wallowing in the most abject moral degradation." Naturally, this US moral superiority served as a prelude to plunder.

In 1912 the Cayumel Banana Company (a US corporation) orchestrated the military invasion of Honduras to obtain hundreds of thousands of acres of Honduran land and tax-free export of its entire banana crop. By 1928 the United Fruit Company (also a US corporation) owned over 200,000 acres of prime Colombian farmland. In December of that year, its officials savagely ended a labor strike in what became known as the Banana Massacre, resulting in the deaths of 1,000 men, women, and children. By 1930 United Fruit owned over 1 million acres of land in Guatemala, Honduras, Colombia, Panama, Nicaragua, Costa Rica, Mexico, and Cuba. By 1940, United Fruit owned 50 percent of all private land in Honduras. By 1942, it owned 75 percent of all private land in Guatemala, plus most of Guatemala's roads, power stations, and phone lines, the only Pacific seaport, and every mile of railroad. By 1950, US banks owned over half the arable land in Puerto Rico, plus the insular postal system, the entire coastal railroad, and San Juan's international seaport. The Pentagon controlled another 13 percent of the island.

⋙

Throughout the twentieth century, the US installed authoritarian regimes devoted to US interests and supported by local armed forces. Being a "good neighbor," in fact, meant supporting dictators: Rafael Léonidas Trujillo in the Dominican Republic, Juan Vicente Gómez in Venezuela, Jorge Ubico in Guatemala, Tiburcio Carias in Honduras, Fulgencio Batista in Cuba, Augusto Pinochet in Chile, and the Somoza dynasty in Nicaragua. The US government financed all these regimes, providing military support whenever necessary. Any dissent or discussion of national sovereignty was viewed as "rebellion" and crushed bloodily—not for "democracy" or "civilization" but for the benefit of vested interests.

General Smedley Butler confirmed this with shocking clarity and detail in his 1935 article "I Was a Gangster for Capitalism": "I helped in the raping of half a dozen Central American republics for the benefit of Wall Street. I helped purify Nicaragua for the international banking house of Brown Brothers in 1909–1912. I helped make Mexico safe for American oil interests in 1914. I brought light to the Dominican Republic for American sugar interests in 1916."[7]

American exceptionalism—the sense of racial superiority and national destiny—psychically undergirded this international plunder. In the case of Puerto Rico, the very first civilian governor, Charles Herbert Allen, saw the opportunities for immediate exploitation: "With American capital and American energies, the labor of the natives can be utilized to the lasting benefit of all parties. . . . [T]he introduction of fresh blood is needed."[8] With justification granted by Manifest Destiny, Allen resigned his governorship and assumed control over the entire Puerto Rican economy through a company that eventually became known as Domino Sugar.

Exceptionalism worked well for Allen, US investment bankers, and other members of the American elite. Ironically, though the vested interests remain to this day, the exceptionalism proved a myth. In 2007, China became the world's top exporter. As of 2010 it is the world's leading manufacturer and the greatest producer of patents. In 2012 it unveiled the world's most powerful computer and also became the world's primary source of global trade. Also in 2012, for the second time in a row, Chinese school children led the world in the Program for International Student Assessment scores for reading, math, and science. South Korea and Japan ranked second and third. The United States came in thirty-sixth, behind Vietnam, Taiwan, New Zealand, the Slovak Republic, and nearly every country in eastern and western Europe. The American Century had ended—with a whimper rather than a bang.

Albizu Campos understood the fraudulence of American exceptionalism. As the first Puerto Rican to attend Harvard College and Harvard Law School, he witnessed power and privilege in its nascent stages and willingly forewent its suasions—rejecting judgeships, corporate sinecures, and outright bribes and devoting himself obsessively and single-mindedly to the cause of Puerto Rican independence.

He was rewarded with twenty-five years in prison. His family received constant death threats. His homes were attacked in Ponce, Aguas Buenas, and San Juan. His law license was revoked. His neighbors were investigated. His phone was tapped. His mail was intercepted. FBI vehicles parked outside his house, and dozens of FBI agents followed him seven days a week all over the island. Public Law 53 (the Gag Law) was passed specifically to thwart him—to eliminate his freedom of speech. Finally, strong evidence indicates that after being condemned to life imprisonment, Albizu was irradiated until a stroke paralyzed half of his body and left him unable to speak. His only crime was to remind the American republic of its own founding principles: that every man is created equal and that government requires the consent of the governed.

The story of Albizu Campos is the story of Puerto Rico. It is also the story of empire. It starts a hundred years ago, when America was a rising power, and continues to this day. The theologian Reinhold Niebuhr once wrote, "One of the most pathetic aspects of human history is that every civilization expresses itself most pretentiously, compounds its partial and universal values most convincingly, and claims immortality for its finite existence, at the very moment when the decay which leads to death has already begun."[9] Albizu Campos understood this. He tried to warn the world and to save a tiny island from the ensuing chaos.

FIFTY YEARS OF CHAOS

Following Albizu's death, the next fifty years saw a descent into the maelstrom—a downward spiral of chaos and corruption that turned the island into a punch-drunk fighter, unsure of its whereabouts, wobbling on its feet, pawing at empty air. Even its leadership is seeing triple and trying to "hit the one in the middle." A corporate red carpet stretches from San Juan to Wall Street. Every year, a new wave of entrepreneurs (aka carpetbaggers) rolls in from El Norte with fast-money schemes disguised as "economic development projects." For fifty years, this charade has drained the island's economy and, more tragically, its spirit.

The Caribe Hilton Hotel provides an early example of this predatory capitalism, disguised as "economic aid" to Puerto Rico. Through the Puerto Rico Industrial Development Company (PRIDCO), Governor Luis Muñoz Marín built the three-hundred-room complex at a cost of $7 million ($69 million in current dollars), then handed the entire resort—the building, casino and swimming pools—to Conrad Hilton on a twenty-year lease.[10] One year after the hotel opened, in 1950, the people of Puerto Rico and even Congressman Vito Marcantonio (D-NY) were still waiting for the governor to disclose the terms of that lease. The congressman called it a part of the governor's "Operation Booby Trap" economic plan for the island.[11]

Everything used in the hotel, including the furniture and even the sugar, was purchased and flown in from the United States. Nearly every management employee was from the American mainland. PRIDCO paid half of the hotel's advertising costs ($150,000 in 1950), but all the hotel profits (except a slush fund for local politicians) were repatriated to the Hilton International Corporation. Nothing was reinvested in the island.[12] Puerto Ricans have a phrase for this: "Monda la china pa'quel otro la chupe" (Peel the orange so that someone else can suck it).

This glaring abuse of Puerto Rican land, taxes, and labor was repeated throughout the entire island during "Operation Bootstrap." By 1965 over 1,000 "bootstrap" factories dotted the island, lured by cheap labor and ten-year corporate tax exemptions. Instead of growing fruit, coffee, and sugar cane, Puerto Ricans now manufactured bras and razors behind concrete walls. Unfortunately, once Playtex and Schick found cheaper labor in Asia, the factories all disappeared. In the end, rather than providing a real economic base and self-sustaining growth, Operation Bootstrap produced only more dependency on the United States and more unemployment.[13]

In 1965, Congress created special tax exemptions for the petrochemical industry, and Phillips Petroleum, Union Carbide, and Sun Oil rushed down to build facilities on the island. When the OPEC oil embargo hit in 1973, they canceled all plans and shut down their Puerto Rican operations.[14]

In 1976, Congress passed 26 US Code § 936, a tax credit for businesses operating in Puerto Rico, commonly known on the island as "La 936." As a result, a pharmaceutical industry exploded on the island: Johnson & Johnson saved $1 billion in federal taxes between 1980 and 1990; Smith-Kline Beecham saved $987 million; Merck & Co., $749 million; Bristol-Myers Squibb, $627 million. Puerto Rico became the offshore tax haven for the entire US drug industry and the world's largest producer of pharmaceuticals, accounting for nearly 25 percent of total shipments. All of this ended in 2006 when Congress eliminated the tax credit, and 100,000 Puerto Ricans were rapidly unemployed.[15]

A 6 percent economic growth rate in the 1950s slowed to 5 percent in the 1960s, 4 percent in the 1970s, and 0 percent in the 1980s. From 1972 to 1986, the number of Puerto Ricans employed in manufacturing dropped by 2,000, and the government payroll rose by 49,000. In 2015, the unemployment rate is over 15 percent, and the government is teetering on bankruptcy.[16] Operation Bootstrap, with its corporate giveaways and trickle-down economics, was a complete failure in Puerto Rico.[17]

In all of this chaos, there clearly is no "economic development plan" for Puerto Rico—just a series of tax shelters for well-connected corporations. As noted by historian and journalist Eduardo Galeano, this pattern is common throughout Latin America: "There are always politicians and technocrats ready to show that the invasion of 'industrializing' foreign capital benefits the area invaded. In this version, the new-model imperialism comes on a genuinely civilizing mission, as a blessing to the dominated countries . . . [but] it spreads poverty even more widely and concentrates wealth even more narrowly. . . . [I]t assumes proprietary rights." With great wisdom, Galeano concluded, "'Aid' works like the philanthropist who put a wooden leg on his piglet because he was eating it bit by bit."[18]

For several decades the piglet fought back. In 1954, Lolita Lebrón and two Nationalists opened fire on the US House floor, wounding five congressmen. In 1971 the Hilton Hotel, a Selective Services center, and a GE office building were all bombed in San Juan. A revolutionary group called Los Macheteros stole $7.1 million from a West Hartford, Connecticut, branch of Wells Fargo on September 12, 1983, the anniversary of Pedro Albizu Campos's birthdate.[19]

Chaos Theory

Today, fifty years after Albizu's death, the piglet is tired, and the chaos is full-blown. Unemployment (15.4 percent) is higher than anywhere in the United States,[20] and the poverty rate (45 percent) is nearly twice that of Mississippi, the poorest state in the Union.[21] The per capita income of $15,200 is barely over one-third (36 percent) of US per capita income.[22]

In 2006, the government shut down for two weeks because it lacked the cash to meet expenses. Since 2010, the island has eliminated 33,000 government jobs, rolled back pensions, raised the retirement age, hiked university tuitions, and increased sales and business taxes. Utility rates are now 300 percent higher than the US average. Throughout San Juan and in smaller cities, shuttered houses and empty storefronts line the streets.[23]

Puerto Rico owes $70 billion in public debt and $13 billion in unfunded pension liabilities, totaling over $22,000 for every man, woman, and child on the island. This debt is more than that of New York City and nearly four times that of Detroit. On February 4, 2014, Standard & Poor's (S&P) lowered Puerto Rico's credit rating to junk bond status, and Moody's Investor Service lowered it to "Ba2," one step lower than the S&P score.[24]

The turmoil doesn't end there. The crime rate has soared, with a per capita murder rate six times (600 percent) higher than that of the

United States. In 2011, Puerto Rico broke its own record, with 1,136 homicides—putting it on par with civil war zones like Congo and Sudan. Of these murders, 70 percent are drug-related, and 80 percent of those drugs flow into the US mainland.[25] Just as in El Norte, the most accessible career for many young Puerto Ricans is to sell drugs, get shot, go to jail, and become a *reggaetón* rap artist. The entire island has become that cynical.

The police aren't helping much. In 2001, one of the largest police corruption cases in US history saw twenty-eight police officers arrested for drug dealing, protecting cocaine dealers, and transporting drugs through and off the island.[26] Between 2005 and 2010, over 1,700 Puerto Rico Police Department (PRPD) officers were arrested on charges ranging from theft and assault to drug trafficking and murder.[27] In 2011 the Department of Justice issued a report citing "the staggering level of crime and corruption involving PRPD officers," including drug dealing, gun running, and murder.[28] A 2012 American Civil Liberties Union investigation determined that the PRPD is "a dysfunctional and recalcitrant police department that has run amok for years."[29]

People are fleeing the island. In 2011 alone, it lost a net 54,000 residents, or nearly 1.5 percent of its population. In both 2012 and 2013, it lost another 1 percent. Puerto Ricans are pouring into Florida, New York, and Texas to escape the gunfire tearing through their homeland. More than 5 million now live in the mainland United States—over 2 million of them in New York and Florida alone. Puerto Rico is on pace to lose 40 percent of its population by 2050.[30] They're leaving because the Puerto Rico they once knew is gone.

Is there a solution to all this? Of course. But the complicated ones rarely work. Those that have been tried include corporate tax subsidies to giant pharmaceutical companies, a fraudulent war on drugs, government subsidies, austerity programs, and real estate speculation. These "solutions" breed government fraud, police corruption, absentee ownership, junk bonds, media spin, and rampant hotels, shopping malls, and parking lots.

The answer may be much simpler. It starts with an honest self-appraisal. It acknowledges the eviction of an entire people—literally and systematically—from their own land. It recognizes that predatory economics is a raging parasite that will destroy its host. It sees that Puerto Rico is a harbinger of cultural and political consequences that are imminent, global, and unavoidable.

Too many people have been converted into debtors, renters, consumers, gullible voters, abused taxpayers, ill-paid laborers, and passive audiences, all for the benefit of a privileged few. The notion of floating an American way of life at the expense of the entire planet is no longer sustainable—particularly when that life consists of little more than Black Fridays, widescreen TVs, Internet chat rooms, comic book films, and corporate and political fraud.

A positive future for Puerto Rico and other comparable republics will require less greed and more humility. Across the social order, from the 1 percent to the 99 percent, we might listen a little more to our artists and less to our corporations. Here is a good place to start:

They paved paradise
And put up a parking lot
With a pink hotel, a boutique
And a swinging hot spot

Don't it always seem to go
That you don't know what you've got
'Til it's gone

They paved paradise
And put up a parking lot
They paved paradise
And put up a parking lot

APPENDIX

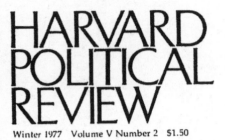

HARVARD POLITICAL REVIEW

Winter 1977   Volume V Number 2 $1.50

THE CURIOUS CONSTITUTION OF PUERTO RICO

THE CURIOUS CONSTITUTION OF PUERTO RICO

A history of "friendly paternalism" has made a sham of this island's autonomy.

by Nelson A. Denis

Citizens of San Juan awakened one morning in February 1971 to find that their Selective Service office, the local branch of General Electric and a portion of the San Juan Hilton Hotel had all been bombed. An extreme expression of the widespread dissatisfaction with its political relationship to the United States, such attacks have become a daily fact of life in Puerto Rico. Coincident with the growing Puerto Rican independence movement of the 1970's have been an approximate 100 annual bombings, the majority aimed at American corporate offices. The underlying target of these assaults has been the popular image of Puerto Rico as the "happy commonwealth" — a sultry playground for American tourists and the showcase of U.S.-guided progress in the Caribbean. While the dust from the first pro-independence explosions was settling more and more Puerto Ricans, especially the young, were beginning to see how tourbook rhetoric concealed the bitter fact that their island has been and continues to be the only classic colony in the American experience.

As a people under the rule of one country or another for the past 500 years, colonial status is nothing new for the Puerto Ricans. Coming close to achieving independence in 1897 through an autonomous constitution from Spain, Puerto Rico lost it one year later when the island was "ceded" to the U.S. as part of the spoils of victory in the Spanish-American War. Ruled first by the U.S. military, later by presidential appointees, and only recently by an elected governor, Puerto Ricans have had little power over the fate of their island; they were even declared U.S. "citizens" in time for World War I, over the objection of their one elected body. U.S. federal agencies today control Puerto Rico's foreign relations, customs, immigration, postal system, communications, radio, television, commerce, transportation, social security, military service, maritime laws, banks,

NELSON A. DENIS is a member of the Editorial Staff. He is a senior, with a special interest in the domestic politics of Puerto Rico.

currency and defense — all of this without the people of Puerto Rico having a vote in U.S. elections.

The extent of military control over the island is particularly striking. One cannot drive five miles in any direction without running into an army base, nuclear site, or tracking station. In 1969 a detachment of Green Berets was discovered in the famed El Yunque rain forest, presumably using the island as a training ground. The Pentagon controls 13 percent of Puerto Rico's land and has five atomic missile bases, including Ramey Air Base. A major base for the Strategic Air Command, Ramey includes in its confines everything from guided missiles to radio jamming stations which prevent Radio Havana reaching Puerto Rico and Santo Domingo. In addition to the major bases, there are about 100 medium and small military installations, training camps, and radar and radio stations.

It is within this context that the island's major political document — its constitution — must be studied. Designed as the international legitimator of U.S. — Puerto Rican relations, the construction, substance, and implementation of this constitution all reflect the paternalistic arrangement over which it presides. Although the advent of the United Nations necessitated a change in U.S. Congressional and State Department vocabulary from the realpolitik of "Caribbean possession" and "Panama Canal protectorate" to "the self-governing territory" and "the commonwealth of Puerto Rico," American policy from the Cold War to the present represents no departure from the priorities under which control of Puerto Rico was originally assumed.

Early on, the United Nations had proclaimed its own authority in the matter of determining whether territories had or had not attained a measure of self-government. On January 11, 1952 the General Assembly issued Resolution 567 (VI), appointing an Ad Hoc Committee to establish the criteria by which to evaluate a condition of "self-government." The Ad Hoc Committee submitted a preliminary list of criteria which was provisionally approved by the General Assembly in its seventh session on December 10, 1952. As long as a territory did not meet the requirements approved by the General Assembly, the conclusion would be that colonial or dependant status still existed.

According to the United Nations Charter, Article 73e, the United States was obliged to periodically submit information regarding economic, social, and educational conditions in its non-self governing territories. Since 1946, the United States had done so for Puerto Rico. However, in March 1953, the United States announced during the eighth session of the General Assembly that its reports were no longer necessary because Puerto Rico's new political status, that of "commonwealth," removed it from the non-self-governing category. Henry Cabot Lodge asserted "Congress has agreed that Puerto Rico shall have . . . freedom from control or interference . . . in respect to internal government." The overall impression conveyed was that Puerto Ricans had chosen "by an overwhelming vote to associate themselves with their larger neighbor."

Even Puerto Rican Governor Luis Muñoz Marín and Resident Commissioner Dr. Fernos-Isern appeared before the U.N. on behalf of the United States, claiming their representation of a "free people with a voluntary government." During the hearings held by the 4th Committee on Trusteeships, Fernos-Isern defended "Public Law 600" as a basic status change, asserting that Puerto Rico was locally governed by a Constitution and that she was related to the mainland by a compact which could not be amended unilaterally. With the two-thirds rule waived in November

1953, the U.S. petition for acceptance of Puerto Rico's "new status" was approved over the opposition of Socialist states, recently liberated countries, and the Latin American nations of Mexico, Uruguay, and Guatemala.

Let us examine the grounds on which the U.S. was able to exempt itself from submitting reports on Puerto Rico to the United Nations. Public Law 600, passed in the U.S. Congress on July 3, 1950, provided for "the organization of a constitutional government by the people of Puerto Rico." If the people voted "yes" then "the legislature of Puerto Rico would be authorized to convoke a Constituent Convention that would work out a Constitution for the island of Puerto Rico. Said Constitution would provide a republican form of government, and include a declaration of rights." In late 1951, the "Constituent Convention" was in fact organized to draw up the Puerto Rican Constitution. A large number of outside "experts" in constitutional and international law were contracted — and highly salaried by the U.S. government — to conduct hearings and arrive at some type of resolution between federal control and the creation of a "new," "Free Associated State" (Estado Libre Asociado, ELA).

As soon as the bill for P.L. 600 was introduced in the 81st U.S. Congress, the State Department began lobbying in favor of its passage. A letter for example, from Asst. Secretary of State Jack K. McFall to Sen. Joseph C. O'Mahoney, the relatively progressive Chairman of the Senate Committee on Interior and Insular Affairs, urged passage "in order that formal consent of the Puerto Ricans may be given to their *present* relationship to the United States" and cited the pending constitution's "great value as a symbol of the basic freedom enjoyed by Puerto Rico, *within the larger framework of the United States of America* (author's emphasis)." Secretary of the Interior Oscar L. Chapman also sent the Chairman the written reminder that "the bill under consideration would not change Puerto Rico's political, social, and economic relationship to the United States."

Thus before even considering the content of the subsequent constitution, P.L. 600 was intended as a political legitimization of Puerto Rico's relationship with the U.S., with a minimum of either bilateral American obligation towards the Puerto Rican government or regard for the constitutional demands of the Puerto Rican people.

On June 4, 1951, the Puerto Rican electorate voted in favor of a constitutional convention. Of the 777,391 total registered voters, 387,016 voted for and 119,169 against P.L. 600. Turnout was thus 65%, with 75% of the recorded vote favoring P.L. 600. March 3, 1952 saw the constitution itself accepted by significantly fewer numbers: of 783,610 eligible voters, only 457,562 voted — 374,649 in favor and 82,923 against.

In brief, these elections demonstrate the repeated mismanagement of democratic process. The June '51 election occurred under an undeclared state of martial law. A nationalist uprising on October 30, 1950 in eight major towns which included attempts on Governor Muñoz Marín's (Oct. 30) and President Truman's (New York City, Oct. 31) lives incurred   reinforcement of Public Law 53, a translation of Section 2 of the U.S. Smith Act which made it a felony to "promote, advocate, advise, or preach . . . paralyzing or subverting the insular government or any of its political divisions, by means of force and violence," or to "print, publish, edit, circulate, sell, distribute or exhibit publicly any writing or publication where the above mentioned acts were advocated, as well as any attempt to or-

ganize an association, group, or assembly of persons to carry out these acts." The colonial government made mass arrests of all the leaders of the Nationalist Party and held the entire country under police and military control. While this may have represented an understandable military response to armed rebellion, it clearly created a condition of political uneasiness and coercion unsuitable for free exercise of the

No major increases in political sovereignty or even in protection of individuals' rights accrued from the 1952 constitution.

franchise. It is certainly possible that thousands of citizens eager to vote for the rejection of P.L. 600, whether Nationalist and Independence Party sympathizers or not, abstained from registering on November 3rd and 4th, 1950. In its Sept. 1, 1953 memorandum to the U.N., the Puerto Rican Independence Party also cited instances where "government agents prohibited the registration of new voters at the date prescribed by law, used public property for political campaigning, controlled the radio, the press and all means of communication with the people."

As a possible consequence of this, though also because the acceptance of P.L. 600 and not the specific provisions of the Puerto Rican constitution were crucial in the U.S. presentation to the U.N., the island electorate refrained from, or was not prodded into, voting heavily on the "constitutional referendum" of March 3, 1952. Turnout failed to reach 60% and, as on June 4, 1951, the question was settled by less than half of the total eligible electorate.

The best way to evaluate the substance and impact of the constitutional arrangement "chosen" by the Puerto Rican people in 1952 is in light of the U.S. claims made in the U.N. in its behalf. The general thesis behind the U.S. documents transmitted to the U.N. was that the people of Puerto Rico had "acquired a new constitutional status." Yet no major increases in political sovereignty or even in protection of individual rights accrued from the 1952 constitution. The congressional committee hearings of 1950-1952 amply demonstrated, as Gordon K. Lewis notes, that "at no time . . . did any group conceive of seriously abrogating the Congressional review power; or that Congress was binding itself permanently not to intervene in local affairs under certain circumstances; or indeed that it was doing anything more radical than merely engineering an enlargement of the local self-governing power, as it had done previously in 1917 . . . even the most liberal of Senators, Senator O'Mahoney, for example did not want to go beyond the stance of 'friendly paternalism.' "

U.S. documents submitted to the U.N. indicated that with the July 25, 1953 enactment of the constitution of Puerto Rico, the "Commonwealth of Puerto Rico" (Free Associated State, in the Spanish version voted on by the Puerto Rican people) had been created. Yet under the political and constitutional structure of the United States there are no "Commonwealths," no "Free Associated States." There are States and territories: the *States*, as component units of the Federal Union; the *territories* — as possessions, either incorporated as was the case for Hawaii and Alaska in 1952, or unincorporated as it was for Puerto Rico. The latter do not form part of the United States, but simply belong to it. Under the Law of Federal Relations, these are subject to the plenary powers of the U.S. Congress. Certainly the "free association" of Puerto Rico is compromised and circumscribed by such federal edicts — notably by Section 9 of P.L. 600 itself, which asserts that "the statutory laws of the United States which are not locally inapplicable, excepting what has already been provided in this respect and what in the future may be provided, will have the same force and effect in Puerto Rico as in the United States, except for the internal revenue laws."

To rename a body politic as "Commonwealth" or "Free Associated State," then, means nothing if essentially the same political structure imposed since 1898 is maintained. Such names — especially the Spanish version of "Free Associated State" — are misnomers of greatest utility in the realm of public relations.

The U.S. went on to inform the U.N. that the people of Puerto Rico had freely expressed their will through democratic processes. In addition to the irregularity of the conditions during the June 4, 1951 and the March 3, 1952 elections, however, was the surprising dismissal *without a hearing* of election infraction charges brought before the Puerto Rican Elections Board by the Independence Party. Thereafter, local law routed appeals not to a court of justice, but to the same individual who had personally presided over the referanda themselves — Governor Luis Muñoz Marín.

U.S. documents further indicated that a free association had been agreed upon by the territory of Puerto Rico and the United States. This reference to "agreement" implies the important dimension of joint action, a compact of sorts, entered into by two consenting and mutually independent parties. Given the wording of the aforementioned Puerto Rico Federal Relations Act regarding "Puerto Rico and adjacent islands *belonging* to the United States", (author's emphasis) however, it is implausible that the United States expected a *territorial possession* to enter into free and equal agreements with its administering power. With no acknowledged legal status from which to negotiate, both the Puerto Rican "constitution" and the notion of "compact" with the U.S. assume a transparent and offensive air.

Not having been incorporated into the community of sovereign nations of the globe, Puerto Rico must always have her international relations sifted through the U.S. State Department.

Finally, the "Constitution of the Commonwealth of Puerto Rico" presented to the U.N. stated that the Puerto Rican people had attained internal autonomy. Yet when the constitution stated that political power "emanates from the people and shall be exercised in accordance with their will," it was directly contradicted by the entire Puerto Rican Federal Relations Act; by Joint Resolution 151 of the 82nd Congress, 2nd Session; and by Article IV, Section III, paragraph 2 of the Constitution of the United States. The precedent behind these laws, as applied to Puerto Rico, was simply that the Congress of the U.S. would exercise concurrent jurisdiction in all affairs of local character and exclusive jurisdiction in all external matters. As in the cases of the Rent Control Law, the Fair Labor Standards Act, the Bankruptcy Law, and various other federal statutes, whenever Congress legislated on purely local Puerto Rican affairs all Puerto Rican laws on such affairs became automatically inoperative. Before and after the Puerto Rican "constitution," U.S. Congressional legislation immediately

EL SALVADOR DE PUERTO RICO,
TIO SAM

Excuse me, Señor,
but you're standing
on my foot !

Omar

terminated Puerto Rican "autonomy" over the subjects related thereto, as clearly shown by the long list of U.S.-controlled Puerto Rican affairs.

This perogative of congressional decree was exercised over the determination of the final form of the Puerto Rican Constitution itself. After lengthy debates on whether Congress would be legally bound to "consult with the people of Puerto Rico on future changes in U.S.-Puerto Rican relations, the U.S. Senate itself changed parts of, and then passed, the Puerto Rican Constitution. They deleted Article II, Section 20 on basic human rights, Article II, Section 5 on compulsory school attendance, and objected to the use of the word "democracy" when the United States Constitution required a "republican form of government" from each of the states. Even more serious changes were proposed by South Carolina Senator Olin Johnston, whose business friend Leonard Long had suffered a financial disappointment in San Juan. These did not emerge from committee, but the other changes concerning human rights and school attendance were accepted. On July 3, 1952 President Truman approved the new constitution by signing Public Law 947. Congress then finished its revisionary cycle with the

---

In brief, these elections demonstrate the repeated mismanagement of democratic process.

---

decision that the amended constitution would not take effect until another "Constitutional Convention" passed a new resolution accepting the changes — at which point the Puerto Rican people were to relegitimize the entire procedure through yet another "referendum." This referendum occurred on July 10, 1953.

Thus the apparent motivations, the highly structured constitutional conventions and elections yielding low turnouts, and the casualness with which the U.S. received the constitution's strictures, combine to form a legal pattern, of almost fraudulent overtones. The Puerto Rican people *did* yield a plurality in favor of their "constitution," although the numbers were not convincing and the conditions surrounding such elections were clearly not conducive to clear choice. A document providing for ostensible "self-government" *was* drawn up, but its range of jurisdiction was humiliatingly minute. The newspaper *El Mundo* had told Puerto Ricans that "once the compact is formalized, the Constitution of Puerto Rico may not be ammended except in the manner provided for in the Constitution itself" and had assured them that "Public Law 600 would solve the status problem of Puerto Rico." Apologists on the mainland composed predictable accounts, such as Earl Parker Hanson's noble but untrue assertion in *Puerto Rico: Ally for Progress* that when the island voted to accept their Constitution, "Congress voluntarily relinquished the powers to legislate specifically for Puerto Rico." And even on the island, Governor Munoz Marín would tell his own people that "the principle of compact and consent is really the fundamental feature of the act." That statement was a sad deception.

The facts are clear for assessing the quality of Puerto Rico's highly opportune "autonomy." Events subsequent to the adoption of a "constitution" such as the shelving in committee of the 1959 Fernos-Murray Bill (HR 9234) to clarify Puerto Rico's commonwealth status and to determine her debt-incurring capacity, and the 1967 "status plebiscite" which repeated the irregularities and utilized the same malapropisms as the 1952 referenda, indicate the limits to how far Puerto Rico will be permitted to travel towards self-determination while in its present economic and political relationship to the U.S. At present, the island serves as America's "showcase" to the world — and especially to Latin America — of "democratic politics" and "free market" economics. Not having been incorporated into the community of sovereign nations of the globe, Puerto Rico must always have her international relations sifted through the U.S. State Department.

That this is an arrangement suitable to U.S. interests is demonstrated by its determined refusal to permit the Committee on Decolonization of the United Nations to include Puerto Rico on the list of territories which "have still not obtained their independence" under the provisions of Resolution 1514 (XV), passed by the General Assembly of the

United Nations in December 1960. Using to good advantage the control which she had over this international body, the United States has maintained — like Portugal in the case of Angola — that the matter of Puerto Rico is an "internal affair" which only concerns her and not the United Nations. The U.S. delegate even threatened in the Committee on Decolonization to abandon the session if the case of Puerto Rico was brought up — a threat in violation of provisions of the Charter of the United Nations.

The greatest native opposition to colonial status lies with the Partido Independentista de Puerto Rico (PIP). Led by Oxford- and Yale Law School-educated Ruben Barrios, the PIP has acquired strength in numbers and respectability. Numbering four former Puerto Rican Bar Association presidents and other comparable situated members of the Puerto Rican establishment among its membership, the movement is centered around the intellectual community of the University of Puerto Rico, and its growing "segundo nivel" (second level) membership among individuals in government, the major political parties, and the press provide it with inside intelligence.

The Independence movement leaders can arouse some sympathy and support by pointing to the sad state of the Puerto Rican economy: a 30 per cent unemployment rate (about 300,000 workers), a per capita income of approximately $1600 ($450 less than that for Mississippi, the lowest of the 50 states), and a cost of living 20 to 25 per cent higher than that of New York City. But the movement still confronts a juggernaut, and must struggle against the fear of direct economic retribution against any nationalistic tendencies which Puerto Rico might exhibit. Such accession and resignation to the present arrangement by the Puerto Ricans at once represents both the perseverance and the greatest obstacle to mobilization of effective opposition to American domination. The recent Nov. 2, 1976 election yielded a familiar

---

With no acknowledged legal status from which to negotiate, both the Puerto Rican "constitution" and the notion of "compact" with the U.S. assume a transparent and offensive air.

---

outcome: Carlos Romero Barcelo won the island governorship heading the ticket of the insurgent New Progressive Party (Partido Nuevo Progresivo), whose avowed aims include eventual statehood of Puerto Rico. While radical independentistas are hard pressed to interpret this as electoral victory for their movement, dissatisfaction with the present political arrangement is clearly widespread.

Today, through the simultaneous profession of the island's "self-governing" status and maintenance of laws such as the Puerto Rico Federal Relations Act, the United States perpetuates its failure to fulfill its legal and moral obligation to place in the hands of the Puerto Rican people all those powers that are concomitant with the existence of a sovereign nation. Self-determination is the indispensable key to Puerto Rico's future and until it occurs every plebiscite, every election held in that country, will but further legitimate or appear to legitimate the present order, further postponing the resolution of colonial status. Not until Puerto Rico is given or is able to procure that choice, will it emerge from the margin of historical development.

ACKNOWLEDGMENTS

"A heterogenous mass of mongrels."
"Savages addicted to head-hunting and cannibalism."

This was the early view of Puerto Ricans, as expressed on the floor of the US Senate. It has been a long road from that perception to the publication of this book.

I am deeply indebted to the Nationalists who risked their lives and livelihood in defense of a human principle called freedom. They took further risks by confiding in me. This book would have been impossible without them.

Ed Vega Yunqué, a brilliant writer, focused my historical understanding and taught me to ask the right questions. Ed left too soon, but his heart lives in this book.

At the Centro de Estudios Puertorriqueños, senior archivist Pedro Juan Hernández and archivist/librarian Yosenex Orengo provided invaluable help in archival research, compiling statistical data, and locating documents and photographs.

Tony "the Marine" Santiago, creator of over six hundred Wikipedia articles on Puerto Rican history and biography, was a key inspiration and advisor.

Thanks to Bertil Nelson for his intellectual rigor, sound advice, and for reading my work over the past thirty years. Thanks to Alex Rodriguez, Jr., for devoting many days and nights to researching hundreds of photographs, both in New York City and at the University of Puerto Rico in Rio Piedras, Puerto Rico.

Thanks to Remy, Georgie, and Lombardo for believing in me, and Roberto for defending me.

Thanks to Migdalia Bernal for reading this book, loving me, living with both of us, and showing us an infinite patience.

Thanks to Richard Realmuto for his insightful reading and advice from the earliest stages of the project, and to Wendy Realmuto for her research assistance in the Rare Book and Manuscript Library of the Columbia University library system. Thanks also to the entire staff of the Manuscripts, Archives, and Rare Books Division, and the Photographs and Prints Division, of the New York Public Library.

The National Association of Hispanic Journalists, the New York State Council on the Arts, and the New York Foundation for the Arts have supported my writing over the years. The Teachers and Writers Collaborative, Grosvenor Neighborhood House, Poets in the Public Service, and the Shaman Repertory Theatre have allowed me to teach it. I am deeply grateful to all of them.

El Diario/La Prensa enabled me to publish over three hundred editorials in their newspaper. The research for those editorials informed some key aspects of this book, and I greatly appreciate it.

Harvard Political Review and its president, Daniel Backman, provided great support and enthusiasm for the book.

Thanks to my agent Ronald Goldfarb, my publisher Clive Priddle, and my editor at Nation Books, Daniel LoPreto, for bringing this book into the world. Thanks to managing editor Melissa Raymond and copyeditor Jen Kelland, for teaching it some manners.

Thanks to Howard Zinn and Dee Brown for kicking open the doors of historical inquiry, and to Oliver Stone for following in that fine tradition.

Finally I thank Harvard, Yale, and the New York State Legislature for teaching me, through many painful lessons, that established truths are often a convenient narrative and nothing more.

SOURCES AND METHODOLOGY

The voices in this book remained unheard for a hundred years. The events were hidden, misrepresented, or ignored. The major participants are dead. This book has a responsibility to represent people and events fairly and accurately, for the first time, after a century of official suppression and neglect.

I used over 6,000 public records, many of them obtained under the US Freedom of Information Act (FOIA), from agencies including the FBI, the CIA, the Puerto Rico Insular Police, the Puerto Rico Department of Public Instruction, the Puerto Rico Department of Labor, the US Department of Justice, the US Department of Defense, the Office of Naval Intelligence, federal courts, public hospitals, morgues, and police precincts. These documents served two critical roles. They confirmed, in great detail, the events related to me by dozens of Puerto Rican Nationalists. They also revealed the means by which government corruption and indifference can erase from the public record the experiences of a colonized people.

Throughout the book, the thoughts of individuals were not divined—they were ascertained through diaries, personal correspondence, autobiographies, monographs, and interviews. The interviewees included the direct participants themselves, as well as observers, family members, friends, and on-the-scene reporters. In several key areas those interviews were longitudinal: I repeated them for years and, in some cases, over several decades. Whenever I sought to grasp, retrospectively, a person's thinking at a given moment, or when I sought to retrace the complexity of someone's views, the interviewing, document review, and fact-checking intensified before any paraphrase was employed.

The prison conversations were relayed by several Nationalists, by inmates from La Princesa and El Oso Blanco prisons, and by survivors from the Aguadilla safe house (near Ramey Air Force Base). One medical assistant from the Aguadilla safe house was especially specific with regard to Captain Rolf, Dr. Hebb, and their sessions with Vidal Santiago Díaz.

Customers, barbers, and several members of the 65th Infantry Regiment (the Borinqueneers) who frequented the shop reported the conversations in Salón Boricua. WIAC journalists Miguel Ángel Álvarez and Luis "El Bibí" Marrero described to me events and discussions at the battle of Salón Boricua; both men were present at the scene throughout the entire battle and reported it live via radio.

Borinqueneers and other customers confirmed the events in the Club with No Name. Three Borinqueneers who served under Waller Booth in Operation Portrex heard the details about his Camp X training and World War II experiences behind enemy lines. They were kind enough to share these details with me.

The information about Luis Muñoz Marín's early years in New York (about Collegiate, Georgie Yee's, Greenwich Village, and Joe Gould) stems from several Cuban Socialists who lived with Muñoz Marín on Thirty-Ninth Street and Broadway, knew Joe Gould, lent money to both of them, and grew tired of buying them drinks.

My mother, Sarah Rabassa, and my maternal grandmother, Salome Rodriguez, both attended Central Grammar School and reported to me the conditions and classroom events at the school. Chief Justice José Trías Monge confirmed island-wide conditions in *Puerto Rico: The Trials of the Oldest Colony in the World*.

Julio Feliciano Colón was a sugarcane cutter (*machetero*) in Santa Isabel for forty years. He supported his mother and younger brother, then his own wife and children, with two worn hands and a crooked spine. I met him in Santa Isabel, where he recounted a lifetime of struggle, dreams, and despair. As a Cadet of the Republic he was present at the Ponce Massacre on Palm Sunday, March 21, 1937.

Juan Emilio Viguié related to me his experiences and conversations after a screening of his film *Vecinos* (*Neighbors*), a propaganda film sponsored by the Puerto Rico Department of Education. In a private home before a small, invited audience, of which I was member, Viguié screened both versions of that film (Governor Muñoz Marín had censored the original, deeming it "Communistic"), as well as his Ponce Massacre film and footage from the battle of Salón Boricua. Viguié also discussed the repressive climate in the aftermath of the Ponce Massacre, the prevailing sense of terror throughout the island, the visit of Pedro Rodriguez-Serra from the district attorney's office, and the making of *The Life of General Villa*. A subsequent interview with his son, Juan Emilio Viguié Jr., confirmed all of these events. A meeting with actor Juano Hernández additionally confirmed the discussions and events relating to *The Life of General Villa*.

Interviews with dozens of Nationalists over a period of forty years have substantiated the research in this book. These individuals had all lived in a world where selfishness was a great asset, a world owned by strangers and governed by corruption, a world so threatening and capricious that to tell the truth was to risk one's livelihood, one's freedom, and sometimes one's life. It took a long time (in some cases years) to earn their trust, but it was worth every moment. I extend to them my deepest appreciation and respect. Their testimony was consistent with the historical record—yet subtler, more granular, more detailed. Their personal recollections—with respect to the Ponce Massacre, the Río Piedras Massacre, the trial of Albizu Campos, the Gag Law arrests, the 1934 sugar cane strike, the police terror of Governor Blanton Winship, the haplessness of Moncho Reyes, and the conditions at La Princesa and El Oso Blanco prisons—all closely parallel the newspaper accounts, congressional testimony, and FBI files from 1930 to 1965.

In addition, the sheer volume of people who disappeared (*los desaparecidos*) throughout the island, the murder of seventeen unarmed Puerto Ricans in broad daylight during the Ponce Massacre of 1937, the bombing of Jayuya and Utuado by the US Air Force, the machine-gun execution of four men in Utuado, the mass arrest of 3,000 US citizens without evidence or probable cause, and the 100,000 secret and illegal *carpetas* all affirm the experiences related by these brave men and women, who fought a lonely battle against the most powerful empire in history.

During every interview, I saw a melancholy in the eyes of these Nationalists. They reminded me of something my grandmother once told me: "Puerto Rican eyes are all dark, with lots of yesterdays in them."

NOTES

Chapter 1: La Princesa

1. The personal sources for this chapter were five Nationalist prisoners from La Princesa. These five were tried, convicted, and incarcerated at the same time as Albizu Campos. Nearly 400 more Nationalist prisoners accompanied them to La Princesa, and 350 inmates had to be moved in order to accommodate this tidal wave of Nationalists.

The five Nationalists provided testimony during repeated interviews conducted longitudinally over the course of forty years, from 1974 to 2014. The same interview pattern was followed with Nationalist prisoners from El Oso Blanco penitentiary and from a safe house near the Ramey Air Force Base in Aguadilla.

Some of these prisoners lived into the twenty-first century; few lived until 2014. I compared and cross-referenced all of the interview information from every Nationalist for chronology, consistency, and accuracy. As the years progressed their testimony held up: no vagueness and very few inconsistencies emerged. In addition, their testimony correlated strongly with the press accounts of the era and with the many boxes of FBI reports.

2. Eventually, an official record of the conditions at La Princesa was finally written. On February 18, 1976, the US District Court for the District of Puerto Rico found that La Princesa was operating in violation of the US Constitution. After a hearing on the merits and an inspection of the prison, the district court entered a twenty-paragraph order concerning the administration of La Princesa and ordered that the defendants cease using the jail as a correctional institution as of August 1, 1976. *Martinez Rodriguez v. Jimenez*, 409 F.Supp. 582 (1976).

Specifically, the court found that La Princesa was operating at 240 to 347 percent of capacity (par. 17), that at least 22 inmates were without beds, and that 130 to 163 inmates were sleeping on the floor. Prisoners were not issued a toothbrush, soap, towel, comb, brush, or underwear (par. 12, 28). The court found that "the quality of incarceration at La Princesa is punishment of such a nature and degree that it cannot be justified by the Commonwealth's interest in holding defendants for trial, and therefore it violates the due process clause of the Fifth or the Fourteenth Amendment" (par. 7).

The conditions faced by Albizu Campos and the Nationalist prisoners had been much worse. La Princesa operated twice as many dungeons in 1950. It conducted medical experiments on the inmates and subjected the Nationalists to physical and psychological torture that will be discussed (and documented) throughout this book.

3. The Insular Police, as it was called in the first half of the twentieth century, is the island-wide Puerto Rico Police Department, known today as the PRPD.

4. For additional information regarding the Nationalist prisoners at La Princesa and the brutal treatment they received, see Heriberto Marín Torres, *Eran Ellos* (Río Piedras, PR: Ediciones Ciba, 2000). See also Letter to David Helfeld, Esq., Counsel to Human Rights Commission, "Information on Discrimination and Persecution for Political Purposes," 1989, 49, as cited in Marisa Rosado, *Pedro Albizu Campos: Las Llamas de la Aurora*, 5th ed. (San Juan: Ediciones Puerto, 2008), 364.

For information regarding the treatment of female prisoners in La Princesa, the Arecibo presidio, and the Alderson Federal Prison Camp in West Virginia, see Margaret Pour, "Puerto Rican Women Nationalists vs. US Colonialism: An Exploration of Their Conditions and Struggles in Jail and Court," *Chicago-Kent Law Review* 87, no. 2 (2012): 463–479. The article includes reports of radiation experienced by the women at La Princesa, which is also discussed in a memoir written by the wife of Albizu Campos. See Laura Meneses de Albizu Campos, *Albizu Campos y la Independencia de Puerto Rico* (Hato Rey, PR: Publicaciones Puertorriqueñas, 2007), 126–128.

For information regarding the arrest and imprisonment of Puerto Rican university students, see Ruth Mary Reynolds, *Campus in Bondage* (New York: Research Foundation of the City of New York, 1989). See also the Ruth Reynolds Papers in the Archives of the Puerto Rican Diaspora, Centro de Estudios Puertorriqueños, Hunter College, CUNY.

5. Albizu Campos was consulted to draft what would ultimately become the constitution of the Irish Free State. See Aoife Rivera Serrano, *Ireland and Puerto Rico: The Untold Story* (New York: Ausubo Press, 2012). In an interview, Ms. Rivera Serrano stated that Albizu's battle against US colonialism was "entirely modeled on the Irish struggle against Britain." See William Cadiz, "Ausubo Press Will Publish Ireland and Puerto Rico: The Untold Story," PR Web, September 23, 2009. See also Federico Ribes Tovar, *Albizu Campos: Puerto Rican Revolutionary* (New York: Plus Ultra Publishers, 1971), 22–23; Rosado, *Pedro Albizu Campos*, 70–72.

Chapter 2: Four Hundred Years of Solitude

1. El Yunque National Forest, US Forest Service, US Department of Agriculture, site maintained at http://www.fs.usda.gov/elyunque. See also Victor Manuel Nieves, *El Yunque* (Guaynabo, PR: Impressive Publications, 2010); Alan Mowbray Jr., *The*

Animals of El Yunque (Charleston, SC: Create Space, 2012); Zain Deane, *San Juan, Vieques and Culebra* (Woodstock, VT: Countryman Press, 2011), 154.

2. Kassim Bacchus, *Utilization, Misuse and Development of Human Resources in the Early West Indian Colonies* (Waterloo, Ontario: Wilfred Laurier University Press, 2000), 6–7. See also Kari Lydersen, "Dental Studies Give Clues About Christopher Columbus's Crew," *Washington Post*, May 18, 2009.

3. Irving Rouse, *The Taínos: The Rise and Decline of the People Who Greeted Columbus* (New Haven, CT: Yale University Press, 1992), 150–161.

4. Ibid.

5. Olga Jimenez de Wagenheim, *Puerto Rico's Revolt for Independence: El Grito de Lares* (Princeton, NJ: Markus Wiener Publications, 1993).

6. Manuel Maldonado-Denis, *Puerto Rico: A Socio-historic Interpretation* (New York: Random House, 1972), 48–49. See also Pedro Albizu Campos, *La Conciencia Nacional Puertorriqueña*, ed. Manuel Maldonado-Denis (Cerro del Agua, Mexico: Siglo Veintiuno Editores, 1972), 14, 59.

7. Declared by US Congress on April 25, 1898, the Spanish-American War lasted until August 12 of that same year. When the Treaty of Paris was signed on December 10, 1898, it formalized Cuban independence from Spain and ceded the Spanish territories of Puerto Rico, Guam, and the Philippine Islands to the United States. Héctor Andrés Negroni, *Historia Militar de Puerto Rico* (Madrid: Sociedad Estatal Quinto Centenaria, 1992). See also Ángel Rivero Méndez, *Crónica de la Guerra Hispanoamericana en Puerto Rico* (Ann Arbor: University of Michigan, 1922), 59–106; "Chronology of Puerto Rico in the Spanish-American War," in *The World of 1898: The Spanish-American War*, Hispanic Division, US Library of Congress, http://www.loc.gov/rr/hispanic/1898/chronpr.html; Edwin J. Emerson Jr., "Alone in Porto Rico," *Century Magazine* 56, no. 5 (September 1898): 668–669 (an extremely vivid account of the aftermath of the bombardment of San Juan).

8. "Our Flag Raised in Puerto Rico," *New York Times*, July 27, 1898.

9. Maldonado-Denis, *Puerto Rico*, 57–58. See also Thomas Aitken Jr., *Poet in the Fortress* (New York: New American Library, 1993), 35.

10. Charles F. Redmond, *Selections from the Correspondence of Theodore Roosevelt and Henry Cabot Lodge, 1884–1918* (New York: Scribner's, 1925), 1:299.

11. Ibid.

12. *New York Journal of Commerce*, May 11, 1898.

13. Amos K. Fiske, *New York Times*, July 11, 1898, 6.

14. Carl Sandburg, *Always the Young Strangers* (New York: Harcourt, Brace, 1953), 403.

15. *New York Times*, July 4, 1898, 4.

16. Ibid.

17. Maldonado-Denis, *Puerto Rico*, 56.

18. "Diary of the War," *Harper's Weekly*, July 30, 1898, 754.

19. *Speech of Hon. J. B. Foraker of Ohio in the Senate of the United States* (Washington, DC: Government Printing Office, 1900), 6.

20. Howard Zinn, *A People's History of the United States* (New York: HarperCollins, 2005), 297–301. See also Howard K. Beale, *Theodore Roosevelt and the Rise of America to World Power* (Baltimore: Johns Hopkins Press, 1984).

21. Maldonado-Denis, *Puerto Rico*, 67–70. See also Walter La Feber, *The New Empire: An Interpretation of American Expansion, 1860–1898* (Ithaca, NY: Cornell University Press, 1963), viii, 91, 110.

22. Maldonado-Denis, *Puerto Rico*, 61.

23. Méndez, *Crónica de la Guerra Hispanoamericana en Puerto Rico*, 16.

24. S. S. Harvey, "Americanizing Puerto Rico," *New York Times*, February 22, 1899.

25. Charles E. Hewitt Jr., "Welcome Paupers and Crime: Puerto Rico's Shocking Gift to the US," *Scribner's Commentator* 7–8 (March 1940): 11.

26. Jack Lait and Lee Mortimer, *New York Confidential: The Low-Down on the Big Town* (Chicago: Ziff Davis, 1948), 126.

27. *Congressional Record*, 56th Cong., 1st Sess., April 2, 1900, 3612.

28. Journalist Juan Gonzalez provides an eclectic review of the "incompetent Latino" stereotype: "Whenever conflict erupted with a recalcitrant nationalist leader, the foreign companies simply called on Washington to intervene. The pretext was usually to save U.S. citizens or to prevent anarchy near our borders. To justify those interventions, our diplomats told people back home the Latin Americans were incapable of responsible government.

"Journalists, novelists, and film producers reinforced that message. They fashioned and perpetuated the image of El Jefe, the swarthy, ruthless dictator with slick black hair, broken-English accent, dark sunglasses, and sadistic personality, who ruled by fiat over a banana republic. Yet even as they propagated that image, our bankers and politicians kept peddling unsound loans at usurious rates to those very dictators." Juan Gonzalez, *Harvest of Empire: A History of Latinos in America* (New York: Penguin Books, 2000), 59.

Chapter 3: Our Children Speak English and Spanish

1. A recollection of Central Grammar School appears in Jesus Colón's *A Puerto Rican in New York and Other Sketches* (New York: International Publishers, 1982). Chief Justice José Trías Monge detailed island-wide educational conditions in his book *Puerto Rico: The Trials of the Oldest Colony in the World* (New Haven, CT: Yale University Press, 1997) and in his Spanish-language memoir *Como Fue: Memorias* (San Juan: Editorial Universidad de Puerto Rico, 2005).

2. The school conditions, classroom events, English and math lessons, and classroom discussions in this chapter were reported by my mother, Sarah Rabassa, and maternal grandmother, Salome Rodriguez, both of whom attended the Central Grammar School. My traditional research supports their testimony.

3. *American Progress*, painted by John Gast in 1872, captured the prevailing view of Americans at the time. Dubbed "Spirit of the Frontier" and widely sold, the painting portrayed settlers moving west—guided and protected by the goddess-like figure of

Columbia and aided by technology (railways, telegraphs), driving bison and Native Americans into obscurity. Note that the angel is bringing "light" to the continent. It emanates from the eastern side of the painting as she travels toward the "darkened" west.

4. M. Annette Jaimes and Ward Churchill, "Behind the Rhetoric: English-Only as Counterinsurgency Warfare," *Issues in Radical Therapy: New Studies on the Left* 13, nos. 1–2 (spring–summer 1989). See also Paulo Freire, *Pedagogy of the Oppressed* (New York: Penguin Books, 1996).

5. Manuel Maldonado-Denis, *Puerto Rico: A Socio-historic Interpretation* (New York: Random House, 1972), 60–61.

6. Cayetano Coll y Cuchí's article "Ireland in America?" first appeared in Spanish in *Repertorio Americano*, a Costa Rican political weekly, on March 27 and April 3, 1922; it later appeared in English translation under the title "American Rule in Puerto Rico," in *Living Age* 27 (1922): 262–266.

7. Pedro Salinas, *Aprecio y Defensa del Lenguaje* (San Juan: Editorial Universitaria, 1974), 40–78. See also Solsiree de Moral, *Negotiating Empire: The Culture and Politics of Schools in Puerto Rico, 1898–1952* (Madison: University of Wisconsin Press, 2013).

8. James Crawford, ed., *Language Loyalties* (Chicago: University of Chicago Press, 1992).

9. Cayetano Coll y Cuchí, "American Rule in Puerto Rico," 262–266.

10. The imposition of English did not end in 1915. As stated by José Trías Monge, a former attorney general and chief justice of the Supreme Court of Puerto Rico,

> The policy of Americanizing Puerto Rico (began) as fast as possible. . . . [T]he Commissioners of Educations ordered all schoolchildren to start the school day by saluting the American flag, declaiming the Pledge of Allegiance, and singing the national anthem and other patriotic songs. The teachers, often in broken English, would lead the exercise while the children mouthed words that most did not understand.
>
> The teaching in English of the whole public school curriculum started as soon as the teachers became available. The situation was deeply resented by most segments of the population. (*Puerto Rico*, 55)

11. Over thirty years later, the battle was still raging on the island, in Washington, DC, and in New York publishing circles with a vested interest in textbook sales. The following letter to President Harry Truman from Representative Vito Marcantonio (D-NY), dated May 22, 1946, discusses a bill favoring the classroom use of Spanish:

Hon. Harry S. Truman
President of the United States
The White House, Washington, D.C.

Dear Mr. President:
I hereby respectfully urge the approval of Senate Bill 51 passed by the Legislature of Puerto Rico at its last session, over the veto of the Governor of the Island, providing

for the use of the Spanish language as the means of instruction in the public schools of Puerto Rico.

Spanish is the vernacular language of the 2,100,000 inhabitants of Puerto Rico. They possess a rich literature of their own, and Spanish is their intellectual vehicle of expression. They have made substantial contributions to the literature of Spain and Spanish-America. In Puerto Rico, Spanish is the language of the home, the courts, the legislature, the churches, the government offices, and everyday life. Nevertheless, and contrary to established pedagogical principles, teaching is conducted in English in the public schools of the island.

By so doing, the fundamental educational principle that instruction should be transmitted in the vernacular language of the students has been violated.

The language question has been a burning issue in Puerto Rico ever since the occupation of the island by the United States forces in 1898. At the time of the invasion, our soldiers found in Puerto Rico a Spanish-speaking community of nearly 1,000,000 people, endowed with a common Spanish heritage and homogeneous in character as far as language, customs, and traditions are concerned, more so than a large number of the old Spanish provinces. Spanish was, of course, at that time the means of instruction in all levels of education. Foreign languages were taught as special subjects at the Provincial Institute and in some of the then existing private secondary schools.

Let me say right now that the situation was quite different from the one prevailing in the Philippine Islands. These had 87 dialects, none of which was spoken by even one-tenth of the population. On the other hand, as I have heretofore said, Puerto Ricans had a common language, spoken by 100 percent of the population, perfectly suitable as a means of social intercourse, not only among the inhabitants of the island but between these and the inhabitants of Spain and all the Latin-American Republics, with the exception of Brazil and Haiti. Puerto Rico had its own literature and also the rich heritage of the literature of all Spanish-speaking countries.

Since 1898 to date, Puerto Rico has unfortunately been taken as a field of experimentation in the language realm. The result has been confusion, misuse of the monies appropriated for education, suffering on the part of the student, excessive time given to language study, and inability to master either Spanish or the English language.

But these policies of confusion have not been pursued without the utmost protest on the part of the Puerto Rican people. Every civic association, including the powerful and influential Puerto Rico Teachers' Association, have repudiated these language policies and have advocated the teaching in Spanish in all levels of education.

May I add that the problem here involved is a pedagogical, and not a political one, and that it should be solved according to the historic experience of all peoples throughout the world, that is, by the use of the vernacular. There are very few exceptions the world over to the established practice of teaching in the vernacular. The only exceptions known to me are to be found in Egypt and in the African French Colonies. In Egypt, an effort is being made to popularize the classical Arabic language, and it is used in place of the vernacular. France insists on the use of French in her colonial schools, yet this policy is now being changed.

The use of a foreign language as the means of instruction is justified only in cases like that of the Philippines, or when the vernacular cannot be used as an effective means of social communication.

Law 51 passed by the Legislature of Puerto Rico over the veto of the Governor, and which provides for the use of Spanish as the means of instruction in the public schools of the island, is now before you for consideration.

In the name of the children of Puerto Rico who are being tortured by the prevailing system; in the name of the people of Puerto Rico, who have spoken through their elected representatives and their civic and professional organizations, and in the name of an enlightened educational policy at a time when we are trying to fight cultural chauvinism and to correct past errors, I respectfully urge you, Mr. President, to sign the above-mentioned bill of the Puerto Rican Legislature.

Respectfully yours,
Vito Marcantonio

Chapter 4: The Green Pope

1. Sidney W. Mintz, *Worker in the Cane: A Puerto Rican Life History* (New York: W. W. Norton & Co., 1974), 256. See also César J. Ayala, *American Sugar Kingdom* (Chapel Hill: University of North Carolina Press, 1999); Gillian McGillivray, *Blazing Cane* (Durham, NC: Duke University Press, 2009).

2. Julio Feliciano Colón was a sugar cane cutter in Santa Isabel for forty years. He supported his mother and younger brother, then his own wife and children, with two worn hands and a crooked spine. I met him in Santa Isabel, and he recounted a lifetime of struggle, dreams, and despair. For further information about life and work on a sugar cane plantation in early-twentieth-century Puerto Rico, see Sidney W. Mintz, "The Culture History of a Puerto Rican Sugar Cane Plantation: 1876–1949," *Hispanic-American Historical Review* 33, no. 2 (May 1953): 224–251. See also Sidney W. Mintz, *Sweetness and Power: The Place of Sugar in Modern History* (New York: Penguin Books, 1985); Ayala, *American Sugar Kingdom*.

3. *Congressional Record*, 74th Cong., 1st Sess., May 6, 1936, Representative Vito Marcantonio (D-NY). Specifically, Representative Marcantonio stated the following:

Puerto Rico, taken as the booty of war from Spain in 1898, has been successively ruined. Four large American sugar corporations own over half the good sugar land and produce over half the total crop. Sugar now composes about 75 percent of the exports of the island, whereas tobacco and coffee have been relegated to the background. The once landowning farmers, dispossessed by the huge sugar plantations, today work the unfertile mountain soil or are landless. Only 7 percent of the native dwellers in the rural regions are landowners in Puerto Rico, an agrarian country. Over the heads of these small farmers hangs a total mortgage debt of about $25,000,000. For years they have been unable to pay taxes.

The landless peasants have been converted into a great army of colonial slaves in the sugar plantations, or are unemployed. The reports of the Puerto Rican Department of Labor for 1935 show an average wage for male workers in the sugar fields of $3.34 per week, and for female workers of $1.96 per week. This same wage scale runs through the other island industries, and in tobacco and coffee they are much worse.

4. *Congressional Record*, 76th Cong., 1st Sess., May 11, 1939, Representative Vito Marcantonio (D-NY). Specifically, Representative Marcantonio stated the following:

The needletrade industry in Puerto Rico is the most disgraceful situation ever permitted under the American flag. You have down there 15,000 workers who work in factories, needletrade factories, and the factory workers receive all the way from 12 1/2 cents an hour down to as low as 2 cents an hour. In one case— and I quote from Claiborne's memorandum to me—a 13 year old child was receiving 25 cents a week.

So much for the factory workers. Let me explain the system they have for home workers; that is, those who work at home. These chiselers from New York, my own home town, the worst type of labor exploiters, who ran away because in New York they had to pay decent wages, because we forced them to clean up their sweatshops and establish decent working conditions, brought their work to Puerto Rico. Then they gave the work to a contractor. Then the contractor gave it to a subcontractor, and the subcontractor gave it to another sub-subcontractor, and it goes all the way down the line through many subcontractors, each of them receiving a profit from the toil of poor women and children. The poor woman at home receives the following pay: She gets as low as 3 to 5 cents a dozen for hand-rolled handkerchiefs of the best type. They retail for $3 a dozen in Macy's in New York. This means they are paid from 8 to 15 cents a day, and no more. It means a total income of about $30 a year.

5. Julio Feliciano Colón recounted this conversation in the sugar cane field with Don Tomás and the other macheteros.

6. Juan Antonio Corretjer, *Albizu Campos and the Ponce Massacre* (New York: World View Publishers, 1965), 2–4.

7. Charles H. Allen, *First Annual Report of Governor of Porto Rico* (Washington, DC: Government Printing Office, 1901), 65.

8. Corretjer, *Albizu Campos and the Ponce Massacre*, 2–4.

9. Allen, *First Annual Report*, 149–187.

10. Corretjer, *Albizu Campos and the Ponce Massacre*, 2–4. See also Manuel Maldonado-Denis, *Puerto Rico: A Socio-historic Interpretation* (New York: Random House, 1972), 74; Truman R. Clark, *Puerto Rico and the United States, 1917–1933* (Pittsburgh, PA: University of Pittsburgh Press, 1975), 107.

11. Ayala, *American Sugar Kingdom*, 45–47. See also "Federal Attack on Sugar Trust," *New York Times*, November 29, 1910; Leonard J. Arrington, *Beet Sugar in the West, 1891–1966* (Seattle: University of Washington Press, 1966), 54–55; "Charles Allen Resigns," *New York Times*, June 15, 1915; "Sold Beet Sugar Stock: President Allen Says Sugar Trust Tried to Conform to the Law," *New York Times*, April 1, 1914.

12. *Balzac v. Porto Rico*, 258 US 298 (1922). The US Supreme Court held that Sixth Amendment protections (i.e., trial by jury) and, in fact, the entirety of the US Constitution did not apply to Puerto Rico since the island was an unincorporated territory (a possession); Puerto Ricans therefore did not have standing to assert privileges and immunities or to claim constitutional protections.

13. Calvin Coolidge to Vincent M. Cutter, President of United Fruit Company, February 16, 1926; Everett Sanders (secretary of Coolidge) to Secretary of War Dwight F. Davis, February 16, 1926; Davis to Coolidge, February 25, 1926, Calvin Coolidge Papers, File 400ZB, Series 1, Manuscript Division, Library of Congress.

14. Ayala, *American Sugar Kingdom*, 139, 140, 185, 187, 225.

15. Thomas Aitken, *Poet in the Fortress: The Story of Luis Muñoz Marín* (New York: Signet Books, 1964), 60–62.

16. Memorandum by General Frank D. McIntyre, chief of US Bureau of Insular Affairs (BIA), on large landholdings in Puerto Rico, October 20, 1927, BIA Files, File 94–70.

17. Aitken, *Poet in the Fortress*, 60–62.

18. Bailey W. Diffie and Justine Whitfield Diffie, *Porto Rico: A Broken Pledge* (New York: Vanguard Press, 1931), 199–200.

19. Ibid.

20. Ibid.

21. "The Sad Case of Porto Rico," *American Mercury* 16, no. 62 (February 1929); reprinted in Kal Wagenheim and Olga Jiménez de Wagenheim, *The Puerto Ricans: A Documentary History* (Princeton, NJ: Markus Wiener Publications, 1973), 153–161.

22. Rich Cohen, in *The Fish That Ate the Whale: The Life and Times of America's Banana King* (New York: Farrar, Straus & Giroux, 2012), 14–67, documents the pattern of Central and South American expropriation of farmland:

> In 1912 the Cayumel Banana company, a United States corporation, orchestrated the military invasion of Honduras in order to obtain hundreds of thousands of acres of Honduran land and tax-free export of its entire banana crop.
>
> By 1928 the United Fruit Company (also a United States corporation) owned over 200,000 acres of prime Colombian farmland. In December of that year, its officials savagely ended a labor strike in what was called the Banana Massacre, resulting in the deaths of 1,000 persons, including women and children.
>
> By 1930 United Fruit owned over 1,000,000 acres of land in Guatemala, Honduras, Colombia, Panama, Nicaragua, Costa Rica, Mexico and Cuba.
>
> By 1940, in Honduras alone, United Fruit owned 50 percent of all private land.

By 1942, United Fruit owned 75 percent of all private land in Guatemala—plus most of Guatemala's roads, power stations and phone lines, the only Pacific seaport, and every mile of railroad. (See "United States expansion in Latin America" at "Pedro Albizu Campos," Wikipedia, http://en.wikipedia.org/wiki/Pedro_Albizu_Campos; Howard Zinn, *A People's History of the United States* [New York: HarperCollins, 2005], 439; Oliver Stone and Peter Kuznick, *The Untold History of the United States* [New York: Simon & Schuster, 2012], xxviii, xxix, xxx, 262–265, 279.)

Historian Manuel Maldonado-Denis provided a similar, highly detailed study of Puerto Rican economic development during the first half of the twentieth century:

The first four decades of U.S. foreign domination in Puerto Rico (1898–1940) mark a period during which inch by inch our country gradually fell into the hands of U.S. industrial and financial capitalists. Consequently, all the elements indicating the exploitation of a colony occurred here during this period: the captive market; an increase in the values of goods due to an abundant work force and the payment of subsistence-level salaries; the exploitation of native natural resources by a handful of foreign investors; the predominance of finance capital from the colonial power; latifundism and monoculture; the military occupation of the territory; the superimposition of an administrative structure responsible only to the colonial power; the systematic attempt to bring about the cultural assimilation of the colony . . . and the devaluation of money by the North American authorities. (*Puerto Rico*, 72–73)

CHAPTER 5: A GOOD CAREER MOVE

1. Ray Quintanilla, "Welcome to the Town Viagra Built," *Orlando Sentinel*, December 19, 2004. See also Matt Wells, "Puerto Rico's Viagra Town," BBC, February 17, 2005.

2. "Manufacturing at a Crossroads," *Caribbean Business*, December 22, 2013. See also "Puerto Rico: A Hotspot for Pharmaceutical Manufacturing," *Puerto Rico Industrial Development Company*, December 2013.

3. Quintanilla, "Welcome to the Town Viagra Built."

4. Harriet B. Presser, "The Role of Sterilization in Controlling Puerto Rican Fertility," *Population Studies* 23, no. 3 (November 1969): 343–361.

5. Kathryn Krase, "Sterilization Abuse: The Policies Behind the Practice," National Women's Health Network, January/February 1996.

6. Claude M. Fuess, *Creed of a Schoolmaster* (1939; rpt. Freeport, NY: Books for Libraries Press, 1970), 192–193.

7. "Birth Rate Fall Held Dangerous," *Kitchener Daily Record*, January 19, 1934, 16.

8. *Buck v. Bell*, 274 US 200 (1927). Justice Oliver Wendell Holmes Jr. wrote the majority opinion.

9. Kent C. Earnhardt, *Development Planning and Population Policy in Puerto Rico* (San Juan: Editorial de la Universidad de Puerto Rico, 1982), 28.

10. *New York Times*, April 13, 1928, 3.

11. Truman R. Clark, *Puerto Rico and the United States, 1917–1933* (Pittsburgh, PA: University of Pittsburgh Press, 1975), 152–153.

12. "Service for Dr. Rhoads: Memorial for Sloan-Kettering Director Here Tomorrow," *New York Times*, August 24, 1959. See also US Department of Defense, *Report on Search for Human Radiation Experiment Records, 1944–1994*, 1:211. As director of the Sloan-Kettering Institute for Cancer Research, and with his name appearing in all the contract documentation, Dr. Cornelius Rhoads bore professional responsibility for the protocols and results of this postirradiation syndrome study. However, a summary report for this project seems a model of deceit and denial.

The report stated it was funded by US Army contracts DA-49-007-MD-533 and DA-49-007-MD-669, then by Armed Forces Special Weapons Project contract DA-49-146-XZ-037. The report then states that patients "received total body irradiation" at dosages up to 4,000 roentgens. According to the US Nuclear Regulatory Commission (NRC), humans exposed to 500 roentgens of radiation will likely die without medical treatment.

The report makes it clear that medical treatment was not provided and flatly states, "There is no record of clinical follow-up beyond the 75 day post-exposure period."

As if anticipating raised eyebrows, the report adds an odd disclaimer: "Since the primary intent of the study was to treat cancer and provide a direct benefit to the subjects, apparently the Nuremberg Code and the Declaration of Helsinki were complied with."

Even sixty years later, the hypocrisy of this report is chilling. Since lethal levels of radiation were used (800 percent higher than the NRC fatality threshold), and since there was "no clinical follow-up" with the irradiated victims, there was clearly no "intent to benefit the subjects," who most likely died.

It is apparent that this study, funded by the US Army and the Armed Forces Special Weapons Project, was a radiological warfare project that needed several human lab rats on which to perform target practice.

On a final chilling note, the report stated, "Certain records are missing."

CHAPTER 6: CADETS OF THE REPUBLIC

1. Federico Ribes Tovar, *Albizu Campos: Puerto Rican Revolutionary* (New York: Plus Ultra Publishers, 1971), 49.

2. FBI Files, Subject: Pedro Albizu Campos, File Number 105-11898, Section 2, 43. See also Marisa Rosado, *Pedro Albizu Campos: Las Llamas de la Aurora*, 5th ed. (San Juan: Ediciones Puerto, 2008), 182–190. The strikingly high enrollment of cadets—roughly 10,000 by 1936—may have contributed to a sense of general alarm on the part of the United States and to the rapid militarization of the Insular Police under General Blanton Winship. Ironically, the early popularity and visibility of the Cadets of the Republic contributed to their surveillance and infiltration by the FBI, which compromised their ultimate effectiveness.

3. Through his contact with Éamon de Valera and his organizing efforts on behalf of Irish liberation while at Harvard, Albizu became aware of Irish resistance efforts and Sinn Féin party history. Albizu recognized the symbolic value of the 1916 Easter Rising in Ireland: though not successful per se, it set the moral tone for ongoing dissent and ultimate independence of the Irish Republic. See John F. Boyle, *The Irish Rebellion of 1916: A Brief History of the Revolt and Its Suppression* (n.p.: HardPress Publishers, 2012); Francis X. Martin, *Leaders and Men of the Easter Rising: Dublin 1916* (Ithaca, NY: Cornell University Press, 1967). Albizu prepared for his own uprising by establishing the Cadets of the Republic. See Osvaldo Torres Santiago, *El Evangelio de Don Pedro Albizu Campos* (Lexington, KY: Letras de America, 2013), 35–41.

The US government was also aware of the Easter Rising and took steps to suppress a corresponding movement in Puerto Rico. After Albizu's imprisonment in 1936 and the shock of the Ponce Massacre in 1937, cadet enrollment dropped precipitously. Later, eleven years after the Ponce Massacre, several hundred policemen surrounded the main campus of the University of Puerto Rico (UPR) in Río Piedras from April 15, 1948, until early November. During those seven months they used tear gas, clubbing, and mass arrests to overcome the University Crusade, a student movement protesting the university administration. On September 23, 1948, the Insular Police blocked the passage of several hundred students, then clubbed them fiercely until two were beaten unconscious and had to be hospitalized. At this point it became evident that the police violence was politically motivated. The Insular Police had been instructed to prevent any contact between the university students and the Nationalist Party. This included a prohibition against Albizu's speaking anywhere, to anyone, on the UPR campus. See Ruth Mary Reynolds, *Campus in Bondage* (New York: Research Foundation of the City of New York, 1989), 1, 97–158, 235–240.

The police shooting of cadets and the clubbing and harassment of college students had a chilling effect on youth involvement in the independence movement. On October 12, 1948, in a public speech in Ponce broadcast over WORP (Ponce) and WCMN (Arecibo), Albizu stated that he could no longer find youths "capable of defying the Yankee empire." See FBI Files, Subject: Pedro Albizu Campos, File Number 105-11898, Section 12.

4. FBI Files, Subject: Pedro Albizu Campos, File Number 105-11898, Section 1, 20.

5. Ibid., 107–110.

6. Ibid., 113.

7. A. W. Maldonado, *Luis Muñoz Marín: Puerto Rico's Democratic Revolution* (San Juan: Editorial Universidad de Puerto Rico, 2006), 138.

8. Ramón Bosque Pérez, *Puerto Rico Under Colonial Rule* (New York: State University of New York Press, 2006), 71.

9. FBI Files, Subject: Nationalist Party of Puerto Rico, File Number SJ 100-3, Vol. 23, 128–129.

10. Ibid.

11. Ibid., 24, 101, 103.

Chapter 7: The Ponce Massacre

1. Marisa Rosado, *Pedro Albizu Campos: Las Llamas de la Aurora*, 5th ed. (San Juan: Ediciones Puerto, 2008), 210–215.

2. Federico Ribes Tovar, *Albizu Campos: Puerto Rican Revolutionary* (New York: Plus Ultra Publishers, 1971), 56–64.

3. Rosado, *Pedro Albizu Campos*, 227–228.

4. A. W. Maldonado, *Luis Muñoz Marín: Puerto Rico's Democratic Revolution* (San Juan: Editorial Universidad de Puerto Rico, 2006), 152. See also Miñi Seijo Bruno, *La Insurrección Nacionalista en Puerto Rico, 1950* (Río Piedras, PR: Editorial Edil, 1989), 14; Stephen Hunter and John Bainbridge Jr., *American Gunfight: The Plot to Kill Harry Truman—and the Shoot-Out That Stopped It* (New York: Simon & Schuster, 2005), 109.

5. Ribes Tovar, *Albizu Campos*, 56–64. See also Rosado, *Pedro Albizu Campos*, 227–228.

6. "La Borinqueña" is the official anthem of the Commonwealth of Puerto Rico. The title refers to the aboriginal Taíno name for the island of Puerto Rico: Borinkén or Borinquén. The music was originally credited to Félix Astol Artés in 1867. The following year, Lola Rodríguez de Tió wrote a poem in support of the Puerto Rican revolution of 1868, known as El Grito de Lares. The poem was set to the Astol Artés music and called La Borinqueña. Here is an excerpt of the original 1868 revolutionary lyrics:

¡Despierta, Borinqueño	Arise, Boricua
que han dado la señal!	The call to arms has sounded!
¡Despierta de ese sueño	Awake from the slumber
que es hora de luchar!	it is time to fight!

El Grito de Lares	The Cry of Lares
se ha de repetir	must be repeated
y entonces sabremos:	and then we will know:
vencer o morir.	victory or death.

After US occupation in 1898, the popular revolutionary lyrics were deemed too subversive, and nonconfrontational lyrics were written in 1903. The tune was officially adopted as the commonwealth's anthem in 1952, using the softer lyrics. However, until that time, the singing of "La Borinqueña" was suppressed in Puerto Rico. In 1937 it enraged the police and helped to provoke the Ponce Massacre. From 1948 until 1957 (under Public Law 53), the singing of "La Borinqueña" was a felony and grounds for several years' imprisonment.

7. Photographer Ángel Lebrón Robles; published in *El Mundo*, March 22, 1937, 5.

8. "Puerto Rico Case Speeded," *New York Times*, February 9, 1938, 10.

9. Photographer Carlos (Aguilita) Torres Morales; published in *El Imparcial*, April 1, 1937, 1.

10. A. Castro Jr., "Once Muertos y Mas de Ciento Cincuenta Heridos en Ponce," *El Mundo*, March 22, 1937, 1, 5. See also Ribes Tovar, *Albizu Campos*, 84.

11. Manuel de Catalan, *Florete*, March 27, 1937, 11.

12. Carlos Torres Morales, "Lo Que Vi en Ponce," *El Imparcial*, April 2, 1937, 28, 29.

13. Juan Antonio Corretjer, *Albizu Campos and the Ponce Massacre* (New York: World View Publishers, 1965), 16–23; Juan Ortiz Jimenez, *Nacimiento del Cine Puertorriqueño* (San Juan: Editorial Tiempo Nuebo, 2007), 43–58.

14. Rafael V. Pérez-Marchand, *Reminiscencia Histórica de la Masacre de Ponce* (San Lorenz, PR: Partido Nacionalista de Puerto Rico, Movimiento Libertador de Puerto Rico, 1972), 24.

15. Juan Antonio Corretjer, *Albizu Campos and the Ponce Massacre* (New York: World View Publishers, 1965), 23; Carmelo Rosario Natal, "Luis Muñoz Marin, Arthur Garfield Hays y la Masacre de Ponce: Una Revelación Documental Inedita," in *Kálathos—Revista Transdisciplinaria* (San Jose: Universidad Interamericana de Puerto Rico, Recinto Metro, 2007), 10; Rosado, *Pedro Albizu Campos*, 278–279; Katherine Rodríguez-Pérez, *Reports on the Ponce Massacre: How the U.S. Press Protected U.S. Government Interests in the Wake of Tragedy* (Middletown, CT: Wesleyan University, 2010), 86–93.

16. Photographer Carlos (Aguilita) Torres Morales; published in *El Imparcial*, April 4, 1937, 7.

17. "7 Die in Puerto Rico Riot, 50 Injured as Police Fire on Fighting Nationalists," *New York Times*, March 22, 1937, 1, 11.

18. "Puerto Rico Riot Toll Reaches 10; Others Near Death," *Washington Post*, March 23, 1937, 14.

19. "Puerto Ricans Riot, 7 Killed," *Detroit News*, March 22, 1937, 1.

20. Rodríguez-Pérez, *Reports on the Ponce Massacre*, 66.

21. "Puerto Rican Riot Seen as Planned," *New York Times*, March 23, 1937, 9; R. Menendez Ramos, "From Puerto Rico," *Washington Post*, May 1, 1937, 8.

22. "Puerto Rico Riot Toll Reaches 10; Others Near Death," 14; "First Photograph of Fatal Riot in Puerto Rico," *New York Times*, March 24, 1937, 5; Harwood Hull, "Clash Rekindles Puerto Rico Feud," *New York Times*, March 28, 1937, 63; "A. G. Hays at Puerto Rico," *New York Times*, May 14, 1937, 7.

23. "A. G. Hays at Puerto Rico," 7.

24. "Lets in Plot Evidence at Puerto Rican Trial," *New York Times*, September 18, 1937, 8.

25. Ibid.

26. "Puerto Rico: Guns Blaze Afresh," *Washington Post*, March 28, 1937, 3.

27. "Puerto Rico Fears New Liberty Riots." *Washington Post*, March 28, 1937, 13.

28. J. M. Clark, "What Destiny?," *Washington Post*, November 3, 1937, 9.

29. Arthur Garfield Hays and the Commission of Inquiry on Civil Rights in Puerto Rico, *Report of the Commission of Inquiry on Civil Rights in Puerto Rico*, New York, 1937, 41.

30. Castro, "Once Muertos y Mas de Ciento Cincuenta Heridos en Ponce," 1, 5; José E. Pujals and Castro-Combas, "Aumentan a Quince los Muertos en Ponce," *El Mundo*, March 23, 1937, 1, 5; "Gruening Pide Informe por Cable Sobre los Sucesos de Ponce," *El Mundo*, March 23 1937, 1; "Para Que las Investigaciones se Hagan con Prontitud y Energía," *El Mundo*, March 23, 1937, 1,10; "¡Al Gesto Altivo, la Tración a Tera!," *El Imparcial*, April 1, 1937, 1; Cayetano Coll y Cuchí, "Falsa Leyenda de una Foto," *El Imparcial*, April 1, 1937, 1, 2; "El Pueblo Relata los Crimenes de Ponce," *El Imparcial*, April, 1, 1937, 3, 25; "Ejercite Su Juicio en Bien de la Justicia," *El Imparcial*, April 2, 1937, 2; Torres Morales, "Lo Que Vi en Ponce," 28, 29.

31. *El Imparcial*, April 4, 1937, 19.

32. *El Mundo*, May 24, 1937, 9.

33. Hays and the Commission of Inquiry, *Report of the Commission of Inquiry on Civil Rights in Puerto Rico*, 62.

34. Ribes Tovar, *Albizu Campos*, 84.

Chapter 8: It's Only Chinatown

1. Federico Degatau, the first resident commissioner from Puerto Rico, speaking to the US Congress in 1899. See 41 *Congressional Record*, 55th Cong., 2nd Sess, 1905, 4467.

2. Manuel Maldonado-Denis, *Puerto Rico: A Socio-historic Interpretation* (New York: Random House, 1972), 77.

3. Roberto H. Todd, a founder of the Puerto Rico Republican Party and mayor of San Juan for twenty years (1903–1923), wrote the most comprehensive treatment of this subject. Todd had a front-row seat to the decisions and actions of the early US-appointed governors. A reader of his book emerges convinced that the colonial governors who filed through Puerto Rico during the first four decades of the twentieth century were with very few exceptions a living illustration of ineptitude, insolence, and a lack of respect for the entire island. See Roberto H. Todd, *Desfile de Governadores de Puerto Rico*, 2nd ed. (Madrid: Ediciones Iberoamericanas, 1966).

4. Charles H. Allen, *First Annual Report of Governor of Porto Rico* (Washington, DC: Government Printing Office, 1901), photographs facing 12, 13, 15.

5. Ibid., photographs facing 14, 15.

6. Ibid., photographs facing 16, 17.

7. Ibid., photograph facing 17.

8. Ibid., 55–80, 137–305. See also Thomas Aitken, *Poet in the Fortress: The Story of Luis Muñoz Marín* (New York: Signet Books, 1964), 60–62; Maldonado-Denis, *Puerto Rico*, 70–76.

9. Allen, *First Annual Report*. See also Aitken, *Poet in the Fortress*, 60–62.

10. Allen, *First Annual Report*, 97–98.

11. Ibid., 29.

12. Ibid., 41.

13. Ibid., 99.

14. Ibid., 99.

15. Ibid., 39.

16. Ibid., 39.

17. Ibid., 40.

18. Ibid., 39.

19. Second Annual Report of William H. Hunt, Governor of Porto Rico, 1902.

20. Cesar J. Ayala, *American Sugar Kingdom* (Chapel Hill: University of North Carolina Press, 1999), 45–47.

21. "Federal Attack on Sugar Trust," *New York Times*, November 29, 1910. See also Leonard J. Arrington, *Beet Sugar in the West, 1891–1966* (Seattle: University of Washington Press, 1966), 54–55.

22. "Charles Allen Resigns," *New York Times*, June 15, 1915; "Sold Beet Sugar Stock: President Allen Says Sugar Trust Tried to Conform to the Law," *New York Times*, April 1, 1914.

23. *New York Times*, November 21, 1921, 1, 5.

24. In his personal correspondence with President Warren Harding, Reily claimed to have been "Warren Harding's pre-convention Western campaign manager" and to have personally contributed $11,000 to the Harding campaign fund. See Reily to Harding, September 21, 1921, E. Mont. Reily Papers, Manuscript Division, New York Public Library, New York City.

25. *La Democracia*, July 19, 1921, 4. See also *Congressional Record*, 67th Cong., 2nd Sess., March 2, 1922, 3302; *Congressional Record*, 67th Cong., 4th Sess., March 1, 1923, 5030.

26. *El Tiempo*, July 30, 1921, 2. See also Marisa Rosado, *Pedro Albizu Campos: Las Llamas de la Aurora*, 5th ed. (San Juan: Ediciones Puerto, 2008), 210–215.

27. Bureau of Insular Affairs Files, War Department Records, National Archives, "P" Files, E. Mont. Reily. Brigadier General Frank McIntyre had tried to warn Reily about this plural phraseology in his speech. He sent Reily a note warning, "I notice you refer to 'these islands.' It is usual to refer to Porto Rico as a single island."

28. *La Democracia*, August 1, 1921, 1.

29. *La Correspondencia*, August 1, 1921, 1; August 2, 1921, 1.

30. *El Mundo* (San Juan), August 1, 1921, 1.

31. *El Tiempo*, July 30, 1921, 2. Interestingly, the *New York Times* presented a completely different outlook on Reily's inaugural speech. The *Times* headline is self-explanatory: "E. Mont. Reily Brings Cheers When He Says Old Glory Is Only Flag for Island," *New York Times*, July 31, 1921, 8.

32. *La Democracia*, October 29, 1921, 4.

33. Todd, *Desfile de Gobernadores de Puerto Rico*, 66–69.

34. Reily to Harding, April 19, 1922, Reily Papers.

35. Ibid., May 3, 1922.

36. Ibid., September 28, 1921.

37. Ibid., May 10, 1922.

38. Ibid., October 19, 1922.

39. E. Mont. Reily, *Twenty-First Annual Report of Governor of Porto Rico* (Washington, DC: Government Printing Office, 1921), 42.

40. This was a slight exaggeration. Records show that of the 642 days from taking the oath of office as governor of Puerto Rico (May 16, 1921) until the date of his letter of resignation (February 16, 1923), Reily was absent from the island 204 days. This was 31.8 percent of the time, or roughly one-third. See Truman R. Clark, *Puerto Rico and the United States, 1917–1933* (Pittsburgh, PA: University of Pittsburgh Press, 1975), 60.

41. Córdova Dávila to Harding, December 23, 1921, Warren G. Harding Papers, Box 252, Ohio State Historical Society, Columbus, Ohio.

42. Weeks to Harding, December 29, 1921, Harding Papers, Box 252.

43. Reily to Harding, December 17, 1921, Reily Papers.

44. Reily, *Twenty-First Annual Report*, Exhibit "B."

45. *New York Times*, April 8, 1922, 1; April 11, 1922, 3.

46. *New York Times*, June 1, 1922, 2; June 4, 1922, 12.

47. Reily to Harding, April 19, 1922, Reily Papers; Harding to Reily, August 2, 1922, Reily Papers.

48. Alfonso Lastra Charriez, "I Accuse," *Nation* 115, no. 2983 (September 6, 1922): 236–237.

49. Towner to Harding, April 11, 1922, Harding Papers, Box 252.

50. Weeks to Reily, December 29, 1921, Harding Papers, Box 252.

51. *New York Times*, November 26, 1921, 8; April 3, 1922, 1.

52. Thomas George Mathews, *Puerto Rican Politics and the New Deal* (Gainesville: University of Florida Press, 1960), 56.

53. A. W. Maldonado, *Luis Muñoz Marín: Puerto Rico's Democratic Revolution* (San Juan: Editorial Universidad de Puerto Rico, 2006), 69.

54. This is especially true in Latin American cultures, where one of the worst things you can do to a male authority figure is to make him an object of ridicule. See the discussion of the value of *dignidad* by John P. Gillin in "Some Signposts for Policy," *Social Change in Latin America Today*, ed. Richard N. Adams et al. (New York: Vintage Press, 1960), 29–33.

55. Clark, *Puerto Rico and the United States*, 60.

56. Mike McCormick, "Man Wanted to Transform Newspaper," *Terra Haute Tribune Star*, September 23, 2001.

57. Mike McCormick, "Schools, Churches Were Beneficiaries of Post Editor's Wealth," *Terra Haute Tribune Star*, September 30, 2001.

58. Luis Muñoz Marín, *Memorias: 1898–1940* (San Juan: Fundacion Luis Muñoz Marín, 2003), 116.

59. Hubert Herring, "Rebellion in Puerto Rico," *Nation* 137 (November 29, 1933): 618–619.

60. Stuart McIver, "Book Review: Past the Edge of Poverty," *Fort Lauderdale Sun-Sentinel,* March 31, 1991.

61. Aitken, *Poet in the Fortress,* 101.

62. Maldonado, *Luis Muñoz Marín,* 102–103.

63. Aitken, *Poet in the Fortress,* 102.

64. Maldonado, *Luis Muñoz Marín,* 107.

65. Aitken, *Poet in the Fortress,* 102.

66. Maldonado, *Luis Muñoz Marín,* 107–108.

67. Muñoz Marín, *Memorias,* 114. See also Maldonado, *Luis Muñoz Marín,* 108–109.

68. Paul A. Gore, *Past the Edge of Poverty: A Biography of Robert Hayes Gore.* Rpt. ed. (Notre Dame, IN: University of Notre Dame, 1993).

69. McCormick, "Schools, Churches Were Beneficiaries."

70. Herring, "Rebellion in Puerto Rico," 618–619.

71. Maldonado, *Luis Muñoz Marín,* 108, 109. See also Arturo Morales Carrión, *Puerto Rico: A Political and Cultural History* (New York: Norton Press, 1983).

72. Maldonado, *Luis Muñoz Marín,* 119.

73. Ibid., 111.

74. Wesley E. Higgins and Paul A. Gore, "Robert H. Gore: An Orchid Legacy," American Orchid Society, January 2009.

75. Maldonado, *Luis Muñoz Marín,* 119.

76. Muñoz Marín, *Memorias,* 127. See also Maldonado, *Luis Muñoz Marín,* 121.

77. Cesar J. Ayala and Rafael Bernabe, *Puerto Rico in the American Century: A History Since 1898* (Chapel Hill: University of North Carolina Press, 2007), 136. See also "A Death Penalty Case in Puerto Rico," *New York Times,* February 4, 2013; Aitken, *Poet in the Fortress,* 105; Ivan Roman, "U.S. Judge Kills Death Penalty in Puerto Rico," *Orlando Sentinel,* July 19, 2000. In 1994, a federal district court judge ruled that the federal death penalty could not be applied to Puerto Rico since a death penalty ban is currently written into the Constitution of Puerto Rico. However, the First Circuit Court of Appeals overturned this decision, and the US Supreme Court affirmed the First Circuit. See *Acosta-Martinez v. United States,* 535 US 906 (2002). At present, though the Constitution of Puerto Rico prohibits capital punishment, the United States has reserved the right to impose it.

78. Rosado, *Pedro Albizu Campos,* 235. See also Federico Ribes Tovar, *Albizu Campos: Puerto Rican Revolutionary* (New York: Plus Ultra Publishers, 1971), 61.

79. Public Works Administration, Puerto Rico, PWA PR1012-F, Graving Dock, July 1, 1936–June 30, 1941 (National Archives Microfilm Publication PM0007, Roll 8504); Blanton Winship to Hon. Harold L. Ickes, January 19, 1937, Record Group 135, National Archives College Park, Maryland.

80. The scope of Winship's project was increased far beyond the naval air base to a total of 771 projects throughout the island, authorized with "a final estimated cost of

$112,570,000, exclusive of fee and the cost of excess material." See USN-SMA, *Final Report and Factual Survey*, Vol. 1, General Report, Contract NOy-3680, Madigan-Hyland Co., March 22, 1943, general forward and introduction, 2. Commander H. W. Johnson, officer in charge of construction of Navy Contract NOy-3680, as well as commander of the Tenth Naval District, immediately assumed oversight of most of the projects. This resulted in the usual corporate graft, influence peddling, and back-scratching. While the work employed many local laborers and some local firms, references throughout the contractors' correspondence construct a backstory of preference for US expatriate workers and contractors. Commander Johnson reported in May 1940, "Approximately 90 employees have been transported from the U.S. for the work at San Juan to fill positions as supervisors, machine operators, and as mechanics in certain skilled trades." See Officer-in-Charge, Contract NOy-3680, NAS, San Juan to Chief of BuDocks, *Report of Progress and Procedures*, May 17, 1940, BuDocks, Contract NOy-3680, RG 71, Box 548, Vol. 11. He also characterized the "native labor" as relatively inefficient but "generally satisfactory" after a moderate amount of training.

This pattern of preferring imported US expatriate labor for higher-paying positions and characterization of Puerto Rican laborers as somewhat lazy would be repeated across the building projects that extended over the next three years to Vieques and Ensenada Honda. In the same letter, Commander Johnson also reported hiring the Baltimore firm Standard Dredging Corporation after unceremoniously dumping the local subcontractor, F. Benitez Rexach, who was contracted on December 30, 1939, and fired on March 4, 1940, after only two months on the job.

The big-money items on the contracts began to elide the local economy as the money started drifting toward US continental corporations with connections to Commander H. W. Johnson and his business cronies. These large-scale "public works projects" were of limited benefit in the form of providing short-term jobs to the lowest-paid laborers, while the navy and stateside corporations gained massive profits in the form of property, hegemony, and capital.

81. Aitken, *Poet in the Fortress*, 105–106; Maldonado, *Luis Muñoz Marín*, 118–120.

82. "Nature Ramblings: Admirals Wearing Spurs," *Science News-Letter* (Society for Science and the Public) 27 (March 30, 1935): 29.

83. On the floor of the US House of Representatives, on August 14, 1939, Congressman Vito Marcantonio stated,

> In his 5 years as Governor of Puerto Rico, Mr. Blanton Winship destroyed the last vestige of civil rights in Puerto Rico. Patriots were framed in the very executive mansion and railroaded to prison. Men, women, and children were massacred in the streets of the island simply because they dared to express their opinion or attempted to meet in free assemblage. Citizens were terrorized. The courts became devoid of any prestige because of the evil influence exerted upon them by politicians who acted with the connivance and consent of Mr. Winship. American workers were persecuted and shot down whenever they sought to exercise

their right to strike, or to organize and protest against the abominable wages that were paid to them by Mr. Winship's pals. (See *Congressional Record*, 76th Cong., 1st Sess., August 14, 1939, Representative Vito Marcantonio [D-NY]).

84. Rosado, *Pedro Albizu Campos*, 225–228. See also Ribes Tovar, *Albizu Campos*, 56–57.

85. Maldonado, *Luis Muñoz Marín*, 138.

86. Ibid.

87. Miñi Seijo Bruno, *La Insurrección Nacionalista en Puerto Rico, 1950* (Río Piedras, PR: Editorial Edil, 1989), 14. See also Ribes Tovar, *Albizu Campos*, 61; Ronald Fernandez, *Los Macheteros: The Wells Fargo Robbery and the Violent Struggle for Puerto Rican Independence* (New York: Prentice Hall, 1987), 144.

88. "Two in Puerto Rico Kill Police Head and Are Shot Dead," *New York Times*, February 24, 1936.

89. Rosado, *Pedro Albizu Campos*, 232–235.

90. Ibid., 234.

91. "Disparen para que Vean Como Muere un Hombre," *El Imparcial*, February 25, 1936.

92. Ribes Tovar, *Albizu Campos*, 59.

93. On the floor of the US House of Representatives, on August 14, 1939, Congressman Vito Marcantonio described Winship's growing police state: "The Insular police was militarized and transformed from an honest police organization to an organization of provocateurs and murderers, such as existed in the darkest days of czaristic Russia. Nero played the fiddle while Christians were massacred in the days of ancient Rome. Winship drank cocktails and danced in the Governor's palace while the police ruthlessly killed and persecuted Puerto Rican citizens." See *Congressional Record*, 76th Cong., 1st Sess., August 14, 1939, Representative Vito Marcantonio (D-NY).

94. *El Imparcial*, February 25, 1936.

95. Ibid., February 26, 1936.

96. Ribes Tovar, *Albizu Campos*, 57 63.

97. Report to Commanding General, Second Corps Area, Governors Island, New York (July 16, 1936), 230–231.

98. Rosado, *Pedro Albizu Campos*, 256–258.

99. Ribes Tovar, *Albizu Campos*, 63 75.

100. Rosado, *Pedro Albizu Campos*, 224–238.

101. Maldonado, *Luis Muñoz Marín*, 145.

102. "Continúa Investigándose la Trágica Muerte del Coronel Riggs," *El Mundo*, February 25, 1936, 1.

103. Juan Antonio Corretjer, *Albizu Campos and the Ponce Massacre* (New York: World View Publishers, 1965), 23. See also Rafael V. Pérez-Marchand, *Reminiscencia Histórica de la Masacre de Ponce* (San Lorenz, PR: Partido Nacionalista de Puerto Rico, Movimiento Libertador de Puerto Rico, 1972), 24.

104. Rosado, *Pedro Albizu Campos*, 279–281. See also Maldonado, *Luis Muñoz Marín*, 145.

105. Ribes Tovar, *Albizu Campos*, 88–89; Maldonado, *Luis Muñoz Marín*, 153.

106. *Congressional Record,* 76th Cong., 1st Sess., May 11, 1939, Representative Vito Marcantonio (D-NY).

107. *Congressional Record,* 76th Cong., 1st Sess., August 14, 1939, Representative Vito Marcantonio (D-NY).

108. Albor Ruiz, "U.S. Forgot That an All-Volunteer Puerto Rican Unit, the Borinqueneers, Fought Bravely," *New York Daily News,* May 29, 2011.

109. Captain Matthew Firing, "JAG Celebrating Its 233rd Anniversary Today," *Gold Standard,* July 30, 2008. See also US Army, Judge Advocate General's Corps, *The Army Lawyer: A History of the Judge Advocate General's Corps, 1775–1975* (Washington, DC: US Government Printing Office, 1975), 149–151.

CHAPTER 9: *CARPETAS*

1. "The Sad Case of Porto Rico," *American Mercury* 16, no. 62 (February 1929), reprinted in Kal Wagenheim and Olga Jiménez de Wagenheim, *The Puerto Ricans: A Documentary History* (Princeton, NJ: Markus Weiner Publications, 1973), 153–161.

2. "G-Men Federales Enviados a Puerto Rico," *El Imparcial,* February 20, 1936. See also Ramón Bosque-Pérez and J. J. Colón Morera, eds., *Las Carpetas: Persecución Política y Derechos Civiles en Puerto Rico: Ensayos y Documentos* (Río Piedras, PR: Centro para la Investigación y Promoción de los Derechos Civiles, 1997), 56–57.

3. The five chiefs of police who attended the FBI National Academy were Astol Caero Toledo and Salvador T. Roig (class of 1946), Luis Maldonado Trinidad (1961), Jorge L. Collazo (1965), and Desiderio Cartagena Ortiz (1968). See Bosque-Pérez, *Las Carpetas,* 58.

4. César J. Ayala, "Political Persecution in Puerto Rico: Uncovering Secret Files," *Solidarity* 85 (March–April 2000). Ayala also wrote an incisive study of the international sugar economy during the early twentieth century. See César J. Ayala, *American Sugar Kingdom* (Chapel Hill: University of North Carolina Press, 1999).

5. Bosque-Pérez, *Las Carpetas,* 58.

6. David M. Helfeld, "Discrimination for Political Beliefs and Associations," *Revista del Colegio de Abogados de Puerto Rico* 25, no. 1 (November 1964). See also Bosque-Pérez, *Las Carpetas,* 61. The Insular Police's bureaucratic deference to the FBI was rooted in the overall command structure of US intelligence organizations throughout Latin America. On June 24, 1940, President Franklin Roosevelt ordered that "the FBI should be responsible for foreign intelligence work in the Western Hemisphere," whereas "the Army Military Intelligence Division (MID) and the Office of Navy Intelligence (ONI) branches should cover the rest of the world." See G. Gregg Webb, "The FBI and Foreign Intelligence: New Insights into J. Edgar Hoover's Role," *Studies in Intelligence* 48, no. 1 (2004): 45–58.

FBI director Hoover wasted no time in implementing this presidential directive. Just one week later, on July 1, 1940, Hoover established the Special Intelligence Service (SIS) and created an administrative framework for it, appointing his assistant director,

Percy "Sam" Foxworth, as the first SIS chief. See Webb, "The FBI and Foreign Intelligence." On January 16, 1942, President Roosevelt formalized the Western Hemisphere jurisdiction of the SIS with a signed presidential directive, followed on October 14, 1942, by a signed jurisdictional agreement between the FBI, MID, and ONI. See Webb, "The FBI and Foreign Intelligence."

7. Bosque-Pérez, *Las Carpetas*, 154.

8. John Marino, "Apology Isn't Enough for Puerto Rican Spy Victims," *Washington Post*, December 28, 1999.

9. Bosque-Pérez, *Las Carpetas*, 181–192.

10. Ayala, "Political Persecution in Puerto Rico."

11. Cynthia López Cabán, "Compañía de Seguridad en la UPR Viene a Carpetear, Según la FUPI," *El Nuevo Día*, February 12, 2012.

12. Mireya Navarro, "Decades of FBI Surveillance of Puerto Rican Groups," *New York Times*, November 28, 2003.

13. Ibid.

14. Ibid.

15. FBI Files, Subject: COINTELPRO, File Number FBIHQ 105-93124, Section I, 2. See also Ward Churchill and Jim Vander Wall, *The COINTELPRO Papers* (Cambridge, MA: South End Press, 2002), 68.

16. FBI Files, Subject: COINTELPRO, File Number FBIHQ 105-93124, Section I, 20. See also Churchill and Wall, *The COINTELPRO Papers*, 69.

17. Ibid., 21.

18. A. W. Maldonado, *Luis Muñoz Marín: Puerto Rico's Democratic Revolution* (San Juan: Editorial Universidad de Puerto Rico, 2006), 266–268; Marisa Rosado, *Pedro Albizu Campos: Las Llamas de la Aurora*, 5th ed. (San Juan: Ediciones Puerto, 2008), 332–333; Ivonne Acosta-Lespier, "The Smith Act Goes to Washington: La Mordaza, 1948–1957," in *Puerto Rico Under Colonial Rule*, ed. Ramón Bosque-Pérez (Albany: State University of New York Press, 2005); Stephen Hunter and John Bainbridge Jr., *American Gunfight: The Plot to Kill Harry Truman—and the Shoot-Out That Stopped It* (New York: Simon & Schuster, 2005), 173, 211; Pedro A. Malavet, *America's Colony: The Political and Cultural Conflict Between the United States and Puerto Rico* (New York: New York University Press, 2004), 93.

19. FBI Files, Subject: Nationalist Party of Puerto Rico, File Number SJ 100-3, Vol. 3, Section I, 7–8.

20. "Arrestos en Masa," *El Imparcial*, November 3, 1950, 1–5. See also Letter to David Helfeld, Esq., Counsel to Human Rights Commission, "Information on Discrimination and Persecution for Political Purposes," 1989, 49, as cited in Rosado, *Pedro Albizu Campos*, 364. See also Bosque-Pérez, *Las Carpetas*, 43–44. See also José Trias Monge, *Como Fue: Memorias* (San Juan: Editorial Universidad de Puerto Rico, 2005), 154, 214-215. The FBI files themselves contain references to Governor Muñoz Marín using the October 1950 revolution as "a pretext to carry out wholesale arrests in Puerto Rico of leaders of all opposition parties." See FBI Files, Subject: Luis Muñoz Marín,

File Number 100-5745, Section III, 285–291. See also "Jail 170 in Puerto Rico Terror Raid," *Daily Worker*, November 8, 1950, 9.

21. FBI Files, Subject: Luis Muñoz Marín, File Number 100-5745, Section I, 109.

22. Helfeld, "Discrimination for Political Beliefs and Associations."

23. Marino, "Apology Isn't Enough for Puerto Rican Spy Victims."

24. Navarro, "Decades of FBI Surveillance of Puerto Rican Groups." US Congressman José Serrano (D-NY) is a key figure in the ongoing investigation of *carpetas*. In "Dialogue Open About FBI Carpeta Questions," *Puerto Rico Herald*, April 9, 2000, Serrano wrote,

> As the ranking Democrat on the CJSJ subcommittee [the Commerce, Justice, Judiciary and Related Agencies Subcommittee of the House Appropriations Committee], which funds the FBI and other federal agencies, I have an obligation to ensure that we appropriate funds in a responsible manner.
>
> And if at one time the FBI was using government monies illegally to target a given group, it is our obligation to ensure that history does not repeat itself. . . . As ugly as it is, the FBI/*carpetas* issue is a part of Puerto Rico's history.

25. The use of *carpetas* continued well into the latter half of the twentieth century. The head of the FBI Intelligence Division, D. Milton Ladd, acknowledged that there were 10,763 Security Index cards on Puerto Rican "Communists" and Nationalist Party members as of 1946. The index was continued, and in a July 26, 1961, report to President John F. Kennedy, presidential adviser McGeorge Bundy defined it as "the list of individuals to be considered for apprehension and detention . . . in a period of emergency." See *Final Report of the Select Senate Committee to Study Governmental Operations with Respect to Intelligence Activities*, 94th Cong., 2nd Sess., Report No. 94-755, April 14, 1976, 422, 465, 466.

Many of these Security Index cards were still in use during a massive island-wide raid conducted by over two hundred SWAT-equipped agents, beginning before dawn on the morning of August 30, 1985. Operating out of the Roosevelt Roads Naval Base, the raiders invaded thirty-seven homes and offices, arresting nearly fifty *independentistas* on "John Doe" warrants that specified no charges. Considerable personal property was destroyed, impounded, or "lost." See Alfredo Lopez, *Dona Licha's Island: Modern Colonialism in Puerto Rico* (Boston: South End Press, 1988), 140–141. See also Ronald Fernandez, *Los Macheteros: The Wells Fargo Robbery and the Violent Struggle for Puerto Rican Independence* (New York: Prentice Hall, 1987), xi–xiv; Churchill and Wall, *The COINTELPRO Papers*, 82–90.

Among those arrested was Coquí Santaliz, a reporter for the *San Juan Star*, novelist, poet, and former president of the Puerto Rican chapter of PEN. As reported by the *New York Times*, Santaliz stated that "a dozen or so armed agents descended on her apartment shortly after 6 o'clock that Friday morning, occupying the premises for almost 13 hours and impounding her typewriter, thousands of negatives, numerous cassettes of interviews and the draft of a novel." See Edwin McDowell, "Writers Assail

FBI Seizures in Puerto Rico," *New York Times*, October 2, 1985; Lopez, *Dona Licha's Island*, 140–141.

A number of writers rallied around Santaliz in New York City. Norman Mailer and Allen Ginsberg held a news conference in the New York PEN headquarters. William Styron, Kurt Vonnegut, Gay Talese, and PEN officers and board members also expressed their "outrage at the . . . violations of civil rights of writers and intellectuals in Puerto Rico." Mailer was "singularly shock[ed]" that the novel Santaliz was writing "was taken from her and has not been returned." See McDowell, "Writers Assail FBI Seizures in Puerto Rico." Only after this high-profile press conference with stateside celebrities did the FBI return Coquí Santaliz's property.

26. The repressive FBI *carpetas* were not written and wielded in a vacuum. They were created with the complicity of hundreds (perhaps thousands) of informants over several decades. See Navarro, "Decades of FBI Surveillance of Puerto Rican Groups." This includes Puerto Ricans who were tortured, threatened, bribed, or placed on the FBI payroll.

During the mass arrests following the October 1950 revolution, some police informants who had been posing as Nationalists for many years were arrested and jailed alongside the Nationalists. This enabled the FBI to continue spying and informing on them from within the prison system itself. See FBI Files, Subject: Pedro Albizu Campos, File Number 105-11898, Section X, 102–103 (FBI Radiogram); ibid., 25 ("State of Subject Pedro Albizu Campos' Health Prior to Commencement of Trial"). The arrested "double agents" included attractive women who were paid to romance and extract information from the Nationalists. The fictitious arrest of these women added to the credibility of their cover stories. These Caribbean Mata Haris are discussed (some with photographs) in José Martínez Valentín, *La Presencia de la Policia en la Historia de Puerto Rico: 1989–1995* (San Juan: Producciones Luigi, 1995), 97–101.

For a more genteel level of betrayal, one might view the career and writings of José Trías Monge. A graduate of Harvard Law School (JD, 1943) and Yale University (PhD, 1947), Trías Monge was the quintessential government insider for nearly forty years. He served as undersecretary of justice of Puerto Rico (1949), secretary of justice (1953–1957), and chief justice of the Puerto Rico Supreme Court (1974–1985). He was also a member of the group that defended the commonwealth status of Puerto Rico at the United Nations in 1953 and 1954 and a close personal friend of and adviser to Governor Muñoz Marín during the entirety of the latter's sixteen-year administration. When Muñoz Marín rammed Public Law 53 (the Gag Law) through the Puerto Rican legislature in 1947, and when he used fourteen-year old "FBI lists" to imprison over 3,000 Puerto Ricans in 1950, the Honorable José Trías Monge was there, looking over his shoulder. At no point did he resign, dissent, or attempt to restrain the governor from these brutal assaults on the civil liberties of an entire island population.

In his memoir, written during the last year of his life, Trías Monge finally admitted that Public Law 53 was "unconstitutional" and "unwise" and that "great injustices" and "grave errors were committed" under the Gag Law. The memoir also describes how Trías Monge stood by while the governor opened "two or three shoe boxes of cards" containing the names of people who had "attended this or that celebration . . . or attended a public meeting of Nationalists . . . or who wrote this or that article . . . and then the Governor arrested all of them." It also describes how, as secretary of justice, Trías Monge stood by when thirteen innocent men were denounced as Communists and imprisoned (some of them for three years), even though they were all acquitted of every charge against them. Instead of resigning as secretary of justice to protest this monstrous constitutional abuse, Trías Monge stayed on so that he could "effectuate change from within." See Trías Monge, *Como Fue: Memorias*, 215, 218.

In the last years of his life, Trías Monge also penned *Puerto Rico: The Trials of the Oldest Colony in the World* (New Haven, CT: Yale University Press, 1997), which denounced Puerto Rico's "commonwealth" status as fraudulent, thinly disguised colonialism—even though Trías Monge himself had helped to write the commonwealth constitution and had argued before the United Nations (in 1953–1954) that Puerto Rico was no longer a colony.

This last-minute attack of conscience is a frequent phenomenon in colonial politics: career opportunism and a lifelong Stockholm syndrome often afflict the colonial upper classes. These are followed by a convenient deathbed conversion, just in time to face St. Peter and to diffuse some of the lingering animosity toward the traitor's children. Sadly, Monge's deathbed conversion did little for thousands of people who were arrested, hundreds who were sentenced and imprisoned, hundreds more whose careers were ruined, and a countless number of *desaparecidos* who were tortured and killed while he was Puerto Rico's secretary of justice (aka attorney general), Senate president, and chief justice.

CHAPTER 10: THE GOVERNOR

1. Edwin J. Emerson Jr.—an American spy who toured the island, then delivered a detailed map for use by the US Army—provided a vivid firsthand account of the physical effects of the bombing of San Juan in "Alone in Porto Rico" (*Century Magazine* 56, no. 5, September 1898):

> The older forts and towers had suffered severely. . . . [M]ore than a score of houses had gaping holes and clefts in their walls. The fragments of one shell alone . . . shattered the roof of the building, went through the so-called throne room . . . and finally disfigured the front and rear walls of several adjoining buildings, injuring and wounding two other persons. One old man was blown to pieces. . . . [T]he larger stores and shops stood empty and open, with none to buy and none to do the selling. . . . All available carriages, carts, and wagons, as well as horses, donkeys, and even bicycles, had been seized upon to carry the fleeing citizens into the hills. (668–669)

2. A. W. Maldonado, *Luis Muñoz Marín: Puerto Rico's Democratic Revolution* (San Juan: Editorial Universidad de Puerto Rico, 2006), 22.

3. Luis Muñoz Marín, *Memorias: 1898–1940* (San Juan: Fundacion Luis Muñoz Marín, 2003), 26.

4. Thomas Aitken, *Poet in the Fortress: The Story of Luis Muñoz Marín* (New York: Signet Books, 1964), 52.

5. Carmen T. Bernier-Grand, *Poet and Politician of Puerto Rico: Don Luis Muñoz Marín* (New York: Orchard Books, 1995), 10; Maldonado, *Luis Muñoz Marín*, 28.

6. Mack Reynolds, *Puerto Rican Patriot: The Life of Luis Muñoz Rivera* (Springfield, OH: Crowell-Collier Press, 1969).

7. Muñoz Marín lived with several Cuban socialists on Thirty-Ninth Street and Broadway. This started in 1918 and continued, off and on, for thirteen years. Muñoz Marín told them about his childhood, including his "accident" in art class while at Collegiate. Years later these socialists met my father in New York City and stayed in touch with me after my father was exiled to Cuba. They spoke at length about Muñoz Marín and had an extremely low opinion of him. See also Bernier-Grand, *Poet and Politician of Puerto Rico*, 9–10.

To place these Cubans in context, the Cuban Socialist Party, founded by Diego Vicente Tejera in 1899, dissolved quickly within a matter of months. See Mario Averhoff Purón, *Los Primeros Politicos* (Havana: Instituto Cubano del Libro, 1971), 29–30; Ciro Bianchi Ross, "Elections in Cuba Before the Revolution," *Juventud Rebelde*, October 3, 2007. In 1925 the Communist Party of Cuba was formed; it evolved circa 1944 into the Popular Socialist Party. See Dieter Nohlen, *Elections in the Americas: A Data Handbook* (Cary, NC: Oxford University Press, 2005), 1:211. The Cuban socialists in New York were loosely affiliated with the Cuban Communist Party/Popular Socialist Party and supported Eugene Debs's campaign for US president in 1920, while Debs was in prison.

8. Bernier-Grand, *Poet and Politician of Puerto Rico*, 15, 18–19; Maldonado, *Luis Muñoz Marín*, 30–33.

9. Aitken, *Poet in the Fortress*, 56.

10. Truman R. Clark, *Puerto Rico and the United States, 1917–1933* (Pittsburgh, PA: University of Pittsburgh Press, 1975), 8, 12.

11. Ibid., 56–57.

12. Ibid., 59; Maldonado, *Luis Muñoz Marín*, 29–30; Bernier-Grand, *Poet and Politician of Puerto Rico*, 12.

13. Bernier-Grand, *Poet and Politician of Puerto Rico*, 12; Maldonado, *Luis Muñoz Marín*, 29.

14. Muñoz Marín, *Memorias*, 29–33; Bernier-Grand, *Poet and Politician of Puerto Rico*, 14. See also Jesus Rexach Benitez, *Vida y Obra de Luis Muñoz Marín* (San Juan: Editorial Edil, 1989).

15. Bernier-Grand, *Poet and Politician of Puerto Rico*, 14.

16. Muñoz Marín, *Memorias*, 30. See also Carmelo Rosario Natal, *La Juventud de Luis Muñoz Marín* (San Juan: Editorial Edil, 1989).

17. Maldonado, *Luis Muñoz Marín*, 31; Bernier-Grand, *Poet and Politician of Puerto Rico*, 14.

18. Muñoz Marín, *Memorias*, 34.

19. Ibid., 34. The uptown dance hall, on 145th Street and Broadway, was very popular with the Cuban community. It was called the Happy Hills Casino. In *Memorias*, Muñoz Marín wrote, "I was more interested in the dance hall in upper Broadway and spending Sundays at the beach on Coney Island than in the Kaiser's armies or President Wilson's proclamation" (32).

20. Despite its unpleasant name, Nigger Mike's became a well-known music and entertainment venue. It featured a singing waiter named Izzy Baline who later became famous as Irving Berlin. It had a "back room" notorious for illegal gambling and opium smoking. At one point, "the notoriety of Nigger Mike's saloon had traveled as far as Europe." See Stephen Birmingham, *The Rest of Us: The Rise of America's Eastern European Jews* (New York: Little, Brown & Co., 1984), 184–185. See also "Nigger Mike's Funeral: Bowery and Chinatown Notables Attend," *New York Times*, December 18, 1922.

21. Muñoz Marín himself told this to the Cuban socialists.

22. Bernier-Grand, *Poet and Politician of Puerto Rico*, 19. A few years later, the Cuban socialists noticed Muñoz Marín's constant nose scratching after he had smoked opium. This began to infuriate the socialists when Muñoz Marín increasingly failed to pay his share of the rent.

23. Maldonado, *Luis Muñoz Marín*, 33; Bernier-Grand, *Poet and Politician of Puerto Rico*, 19. See also Benitez, *Vida y Obra de Luis Muñoz Marín*.

24. Muñoz Marín, *Memorias*, 34–35; Maldonado, *Luis Muñoz Marín*, 33–36.

25. Maldonado, *Luis Muñoz Marín*, 33; Bernier-Grand, *Poet and Politician of Puerto Rico*, 19. See also Benitez, *Vida y Obra de Luis Muñoz Marín*.

26. Maldonado, *Luis Muñoz Marín*, 38–39. See also Reynolds, *Puerto Rican Patriot*.

27. Aitken, *Poet in the Fortress*, 71.

28. Ibid., 68. See also Bernier-Grand, *Poet and Politician of Puerto Rico*, 25.

29. Muñoz Marín, *Memorias*, 57; Maldonado, *Luis Muñoz Marín*, 49–50. See also Natal, *La Juventud de Luis Muñoz Marín*.

30. FBI Files, Subject: Luis Muñoz Marín, File Number 100-5745, Section I, 16, 18.

31. The Cuban socialists deemed this especially low. To them, Muñoz Marín's abandonment of his wife and children showed worse character than his addiction to opium. When they heard about it in August 1931, they evicted him from their apartment on Thirty-Ninth Street and Broadway. That same month, Muñoz Marín sailed back to Puerto Rico.

32. Kendall Taylor, *Philip Evergood: Never Separate from the Heart* (Cranbury, NJ: Associated University Presses, 1987), 72. See also "Mme Blanchard of 'Village' Dead," *New York Times*, January 10, 1937.

33. In Muñoz Marín's own words, while his wife was raising their two children, he lived four years of "Bohemian life and indigence" from 1927 to 1931. See Muñoz

Marín, *Memorias*, 87; Muñoz Marín, *Memorias* (unedited draft) (San Juan: Fundacion Luis Muñoz Marín, 1974), 73; Maldonado, *Luis Muñoz Marín*, 70.

34. The Cubans took these "Greenwich Village Safari Tours" several times—not for the tours per se but to be physically present when Muñoz Marín collected his fee. In this way they ensured that Muñoz Marín paid his share of the rent before squandering it in Georgie Yee's opium den. The Cubans also met Joe Gould and found him amusing but grew tired of buying him drinks. See also Allen Churchill, *The Improper Bohemians: Greenwich Village in Its Heyday* (New York: Ace Books, 1959), 103–121; Albert Parry, *Garrets and Pretenders: Bohemian Life in America from Poe to Kerouac* (Mineola, NY: Dover Publications, 1960), 255–328.

35. Ibid.

36. FBI Files, Subject: Luis Muñoz Marín, File Number 100-5745, Section I, 17.

37. Maldonado, *Luis Muñoz Marín*, 70–71.

38. Aitken, *Poet in the Fortress*, 82, 90.

39. Parry, *Garrets and Pretenders*, 316–319; Churchill, *The Improper Bohemians*, 318–325.

40. This recollection comes from the Cuban socialists.

41. People have ascribed a variety of motives to Muñoz Marín's return to Puerto Rico. Some said he wanted "to help his people." Others said he wanted to help his mother. See Benitez, *Vida y Obra de Luis Muñoz Marín*; Bernier-Grand, *Poet and Politician of Puerto Rico*, 47–49; Aitken, *Poet in the Fortress*, 94–95. The Cuban socialists took a more prosaic view. According to them, they had grown tired of Muñoz Marín's drug habit and failure to pay his share of the rent. When they found out his wife and children were penniless in Puerto Rico, they kicked him out of their apartment. Homeless and broke, Muñoz Marín returned to the island.

42. Cesar J. Ayala, *American Sugar Kingdom* (Chapel Hill: University of North Carolina Press, 1999), 139, 140, 185, 187, 225.

43. Ibid., 116–120.

44. Aitken, *Poet in the Fortress*, 60; Victor S. Clark, ed., *Porto Rico and Its Problems* (Washington, DC: Brookings Institution, 1930), 13, 21, 27; Manuel Maldonado-Denis, *Puerto Rico: A Socio-historic Interpretation* (New York: Random House, 1972), 74.

45. Maldonado, *Luis Muñoz Marín*, 79, 99; Aitken, *Poet in the Fortress*, 87.

46. Bernier-Grand, *Poet and Politician of Puerto Rico*, 50.

47. Muñoz Marín, *Memorias*, 117–127; Bernier-Grand, *Poet and Politician of Puerto Rico*, 49–56; Maldonado, *Luis Muñoz Marín*, 79–116; Aitken, *Poet in the Fortress*, 95–99.

48. Muñoz Marín, "The Sad Case of Porto Rico," *American Mercury* 16, no. 62 (February 1929).

49. Aitken, *Poet in the Fortress*, 98; Muñoz Marín, *Memorias*, 107–108; Maldonado, *Luis Muñoz Marín*, 50, 94–95. Muñoz Marín's drug addiction was a recurring theme throughout his career. Here are several reference points:

- Shortly after his father's death, Muñoz Marín wrote a play about Julio Herrera Reisseg, a morphine-addicted poet from Uruguay. See Muñoz Marín, *Memorias*, 107.
- Rumors of his opium habit in Greenwich Village wafted down from New York.
- On March 12, 1932, at a Liberal Party convention, Muñoz Marín stormed onstage to deny that he was a morphine addict. See Muñoz Marín, *Memorias*, 107–108; Maldonado, *Luis Muñoz Marín*, 94–95; Aitken, *Poet in the Fortress*, 98.
- An April 1943 FBI report stated that, according to a confidential informant, Muñoz Marín was "a narcotics addict." See FBI Files, Subject: Luis Muñoz Marín, File Number 100-5745, 109.
- Another FBI report stated that Muñoz Marín was "involved in an important narcotics case, but nothing was being done." See ibid., 111.
- Another FBI report cited his reputation as El Moto de Isla Verde (the Junkie of Isla Verde); this was a common nickname for the governor, who frequently retreated to his second home in Isla Verde. See ibid., Section III, 285–291.
- On June 11, 1948, in a major public speech in Manatí, Puerto Rico, Albizu Campos condemned "the tools and parasites who . . . hide themselves in castles and drug themselves with morphine and drink rum continuously." The FBI recorded this speech and included it in its permanent files. See FBI Files, Subject: Pedro Albizu Campos, File Number SJ 3-1, 7. The speech was also reported twice by *El Imparcial* on June 13 and June 15, 1948.
- After the prison breakout that instigated the October 1950 revolution, a poem circulated with a direct reference to Governor Muñoz Marín as a drug addict. The El Moto de Isla Verde reference also surfaced in FBI Files, Subject: Luis Muñoz Marín, File Number 100-5745, Section III, 285–291:

Me dicen que Correa Cotto	They say that Correa Cotto
esta buscando al otro moto	is looking for the other junkie
el moto de Isla Verde	the junkie of Isla Verde
el moto que cada noche pierde	the junkie who every night loses
su sobriedad y sus dentaduras	his sobriety and his dentures
en el culo de Harry Truman	in Harry Truman's ass

- In his memoirs Muñoz Marín discussed the morphine addiction that kept resurfacing throughout his career. He denied being a *morfinómano* (morphine maniac). See Muñoz Marín, *Memorias*, 107–108.

50. The principle issue in Muñoz Marín's first Senate campaign was Puerto Rican independence. He won the election but did not pursue the independence issue. See Maldonado, *Luis Muñoz Marín*, 99.

51. H. L. Mencken coined the phrase "dogs barking idiotically through endless nights" in his description of the prose style of President Warren G. Harding. It is

especially apt in describing the Puerto Rican legislature during the early twentieth century. After the American occupation, Puerto Rican legislators became increasingly adept at surrealistic filibusters and playing the Puerto Rican independence card to extort benefits from the United States. The insular Republican Party assumed the role of vigorous proponent of "North Americanization" and ultimate annexation of Puerto Rico as a US state. See Maldonado-Denis, *Puerto Rico*, 93.

The Union Party took the opposite route: it would demand independence for Puerto Rico, threaten every colonial governor with revolution, and then negotiate with those same governors for government contracts, franchises, and political appointments. Governor E. Montgomery Reily was so stupid that he took the Unionists seriously, declared an "anti-Communist" war against them, and was forced to resign in utter embarrassment. See *New York Times*, November 26, 1921, 8; April 3, 1922, 1; Thomas George Mathews, *Puerto Rican Politics and the New* Deal (Gainesville: University of Florida Press, 1960), 56; Maldonado, *Luis Muñoz Marín*, 69; Clark, *Puerto Rico and the United States*, 60.

Unfortunately, the legislature's "partnership" with American interests sometimes degenerated into outright complicity. Shortly after Governor Blanton Winship's police force murdered seventeen people in the Ponce Massacre, the legislature declared him "an adopted son of Puerto Rico" and blamed the Nationalists for the massacre. See Maldonado-Denis, *Puerto Rico*, 126. Eleven years later, in 1948, this same legislature passed Public Law 53, which stripped Puerto Ricans of their First Amendment rights and allowed thousands to be arrested on suspicion of "disloyalty" to the United States.

52. In addition to his memoirs, Muñoz Marín published *Borrones*, a collection of poems, short stories, and a one-act play. Two biographies about him are titled *Poet in the Fortress: The Story of Luis Muñoz* and *Poet and Politician of Puerto Rico: Don Luis Muñoz Marín*.

53. Muñoz Marín's 1940 campaign was extremely well orchestrated, with an island-wide newsletter (*El Batey*), a targeted electoral base (the rural *jíbaros*), a grassroots organization (with committees in all 768 rural districts), and a noble slogan: "Pan, Tierra, Libertad." The slogan was especially adept, with promises that matched Abraham Maslow's hierarchy of human needs:

Libertad = Liberty = Self-actualization
Tierra = Land = Security
Pan = Bread = Food

To Muñoz Marín's credit, and as testament to his political acumen, this 1940 slogan predated Maslow's theory of human motivation by three years. See Abraham Maslow, "A Theory of Human Motivation," *Psychological Review* 50, no. 4 (1943): 370–396.

54. Maldonado, *Luis Muñoz Marín*, 241–244, 247–248, 251–252; Marisa Rosado, *Pedro Albizu Campos: Las Llamas de la Aurora*, 5th ed. (San Juan: Ediciones Puerto,

2008), 321–324; Federico Ribes Tovar, *Albizu Campos: Puerto Rican Revolutionary* (New York: Plus Ultra Publishers, 1971), 97–99. After he became governor, the Dwight D. Eisenhower administration quietly approached Muñoz Marín in late 1953 and early 1954 with a renewed offer of independence for Puerto Rico. See Ronald Fernandez, *The Disenchanted Island: Puerto Rico and the United States in the Twentieth Century*, 2nd ed. (Westport, CT: Praeger Publishers, 1996), 187–191.

The Eisenhower Presidential Library contains an extensive file—meeting records of President Eisenhower and UN Ambassador Henry Cabot Lodge Jr., letters from Ambassador Lodge, telephone records of Secretary of State John Foster Dulles, a State Department memo—documenting these two offers of independence for Puerto Rico, both made to enhance America's standing during the Cold War. The Eisenhower Library contains no response from Governor Muñoz Marín. Presumably he understood that given his eight-year advocacy of commonwealth, a shift to independence would spell the end of his political career. See the Dwight D. Eisenhower Presidential Library for the following:

- President's appointments for Friday, November 20, 1953, and a letter from Ambassador Lodge to the president dated November 28, 1953. This letter can be found in the files of Ann Whitman, Administrative Series, Box 23.
- Papers of Secretary of State Dulles, Telephone Call Series, Box 2; this is a summary account of a telephone conversation between Ambassador Lodge and Secretary of State Dulles.
- State Department memo by Mr. Mason Sears dated January 8, 1954, and stamped "Top Secret." This memo appears in the Ann Whitman files, Administrative Series, Box 23.

CHAPTER 11: HOW TO RULE A COUNTRY WITH A ONE-PAGE REPORT

1. FBI Files, Subject: Luis Muñoz Marín, File Number 100-5745, Section I, 3.
2. Ibid., 11.
3. Ibid., 16.
4. Ibid., 32.
5. Ibid., 112.
6. Ibid., 18.
7. Ibid., 4.
8. Ibid., 2.
9. Ibid., 62.
10. Ibid., 18.
11. Ibid., 31.
12. Ibid., 109.

13. Ibid., 18.

14. Ibid., 110.

15. Ibid., 112.

16. Ibid., 113.

17. Ibid., 110.

18. Ibid., 19.

19. Ibid., 5, 6, 12, 13, 24.

20. Ibid., 59–61, 87–104.

21. Ibid., 109.

22. Ibid., Section III, 285–291.

23. Ibid., Section I, 111.

24. Ibid.

25. Ibid., 122.

26. A. W. Maldonado, *Luis Muñoz Marín: Puerto Rico's Democratic Revolution* (San Juan: Editorial Universidad de Puerto Rico, 2006), 142; Frank Otto Gatell, "Independence Rejected: Puerto Rico and the Tydings Bill of 1936," *Hispanic American Historical Review* 38 (February 1958): 31–32. It is deeply ironic that three months after Tydings submitted his 1936 bill for Puerto Rican independence, Albizu Campos and eight other Nationalists were imprisoned for demanding this same independence. Following this logic, if Puerto Ricans had voted yes in favor of the 1936 Tydings bill, then the entire island of Puerto Rico would have to be arrested and imprisoned.

27. José Trias Monge, *Puerto Rico: The Trials of the Oldest Colony in the World* (New Haven, CT: Yale University Press, 1999), 95; Marisa Rosado, *Pedro Albizu Campos: Las Llamas de la Aurora*, 5th ed. (San Juan: Ediciones Puerto, 2008), 239–243; Gatell, "Independence Rejected," 33, 34; Thomas Aitken, *Poet in the Fortress: The Story of Luis Muñoz Marín* (New York: Signet Books, 1964), 172–173; Maldonado, *Luis Muñoz Marín*, 241–243.

28. Aitken, *Poet in the Fortress*, 172–173; Gatell, "Independence Rejected," 38; *La Democracia*, May 20, 1936; Maldonado, *Luis Muñoz Marín*, 174–175, 241–243.

29. Maldonado, *Luis Muñoz Marín*, 241; Aitken, *Poet in the Fortress*, 172.

30. Maldonado, *Luis Muñoz Marín*, 248; Ronald Fernandez, *The Disenchanted Island: Puerto Rico and the United States in the Twentieth Century*, 2nd ed. (Westport, CT: Praeger Publishers, 1996), 154; Carlos Zapata Oliveras, *United States–Puerto Rico Relations in the Early Cold War Years* (PhD diss., University of Pennsylvania, 1986), 131–132.

31. Monge, *Puerto Rico*, 108–110; Cesar J. Ayala and Rafael Bernabe, *Puerto Rico in the American Century: A History Since 1898* (Chapel Hill: University of North Carolina Press, 2007), 156–157.

32. Ayala and Bernabe, *Puerto Rico in the American Century*, 157.

33. Juan Angel Silén, *Historia de la Nación Puertorriqueña* (Río Piedras, PR: Ediciones Edil, 1973), 276–277, 293–295. See also Roberta Ann Johnson, *Puerto Rico:*

Commonwealth or Colony? (New York: Praeger, 1980), 35; James L. Dietz, *Economic History of Puerto Rico* (Princeton, NJ: Princeton University Press, 1986), 235.

34. The flag of Puerto Rico has a turbulent and politically charged history. For four hundred years the colonial Spanish flag presided over every municipality. During the anti-Spanish Grito de Lares revolt of 1868, Puerto Ricans assaulted the civil guard building in the town of Lares and declared the Republic of Puerto Rico, with its own revolutionary flag. The revolt was quickly suppressed, and the woman who sewed the flag, Mariana Bracetti, was thrown in jail. In 1892 Puerto Rican rebels seeking independence from Spain designed another flag; on April 24, 1897, this flag flew during a second anti-Spanish revolt known as the Intentona de Yauco. After that revolt failed, this flag was also outlawed, though the penalties were not heavily enforced. In 1948, Public Law 53 made ownership of this flag—no matter how small and even if kept in a closet, box, attic, or basement—punishable by several years' imprisonment. Puerto Rican homes were searched and people were jailed. The Gag Law was in force until 1957. In 1952, however, after Puerto Rico was declared a US Commonwealth, Muñoz Marín relaxed the flag restrictions of Public Law 53 and adopted the very 1892 flag (with slight color adjustments to match the American flag) that, from 1948 to 1952, had sent many Puerto Ricans to prison. This suppression of a basic human symbol—the flag of one's own homeland—has created a special affection for the Puerto Rican flag. It is also the basis for an enduring popular song:

Que Bonita Bandera

Que bonita bandera	What a beautiful flag
que bonita bandera	what a beautiful flag
que bonita bandera	what a beautiful flag
es la bandera Puertorriqueña	is the flag of Puerto Rico

Singing this song, of course, would have landed you in jail between 1948 and 1957.

35. *El Universal*, May 22, 1948. See also Ruth Mary Reynolds, *Campus in Bondage* (New York: Research Foundation of the City University of New York, 1989), 188–194.

36. *El Imparcial*, May 27, 1948. *El Imparcial*'s writers were among the most "leftist" on the island. They solidified this reputation when one of their photographers, Carlos Torres Morales, took the critical photo of the Ponce Massacre that ignited the Hays Commission investigation and ended Governor Blanton Winship's political career. A 1941 FBI report stated that *El Imparcial* was "reputed to be owned and operated by members or people in sympathy with the Nationalist Party." FBI Files, Subject: Nationalist Party of Puerto Rico, File Number SJ 100-3, Vol. 23, 4.

37. Reece B. Gonzalez Bothwell, *Puerto Rico: Cien Años de Lucha Politica* (Río Piedras, PR: Editorial Universitaria, 1979), 3:516.

38. Pedro Albizu Campos disclosed Luis Muñoz Marín's personal and recreational habits in the governor's mansion in a public speech on June 11, 1948 in Manatí, Puerto Rico. Albizu obtained this information from individuals on the staff of La Fortaleza.

Two Cuban socialists who had lived with Luis Muñoz Marín confirmed the stories, as did two Nationalists from Caguas, Puerto Rico. See also FBI Files, Subject: Luis Muñoz Marín, File Number 100-5745, Section III, 285–291, providing additional discussion and references to the personal drug habits of Luis Muñoz Marín.

39. Discussion of Muñoz Marín's alcohol and drug use was becoming so rampant that an FBI report contained references to his nickname as El Moto de Isla Verde. See ibid., 285–291. Various FBI files reported that when on "protracted drunks," he would "take nothing to eat unless forced to by his friends"; that he "indulged in excessive drinking in public places and became quite intoxicated"; and that on his visit to El Escambrón Beach Club, he "swept all the drinks from the table with his arm" and "became so intoxicated he was hardly able to walk when he left the place." See ibid., Section I, SJ 100-302, 18, 31, 113.

40. Jean Cocteau, *Opium: Journal d'une Désintoxication* (Paris: Editorial Stock, 1930), quoted in Steven Martin, *Opium Fiend: A 21st Century Slave to a 19th Century Addiction* (New York: Villard/Random House, 2012), 345. Muñoz Marín admired French symbolist poets, writers, and surrealists. He had a special fondness for Jean Cocteau and the Uruguayan poet Julio Herrera y Reisseg, who died of a morphine addiction. See Luis Muñoz Marín, *Memorias: 1898–1940* (San Juan: Fundacion Luis Muñoz Marín, 2003), 50–52, 57, 61, 107.

CHAPTER 12: THE NATIONALIST

1. Thomas Aitken, *Poet in the Fortress: The Story of Luis Muñoz Marín* (New York: Signet Books, 1964), 34.

2. A Nationalist who knew Albizu Campos from their earliest days in Ponce witnessed and conveyed this childhood experience during the arrival of General Miles.

3. Albizu Campos's precise birth date has been debated. One biographer lists it as September 12, 1891. See Federico Ribes Tovar, *Albizu Campos: Puerto Rican Revolutionary* (New York: Plus Ultra Publishers, 1971), 17. In honor of this birth date, Los Macheteros, a Puerto Rican revolutionary group, stole $7 million from a Wells Fargo depot in West Hartford, Connecticut, precisely on September 12, 1983—the ninety-second anniversary of Albizu's birth. However, other evidence—his 1922 marriage certificate, his 1918 US Army induction papers, and his application to Harvard Law School—suggests that Albizu Campos was born on June 29, 1893. Albizu's law school application is unambiguous: it is handwritten (presumably by him) and declares June 29, 1893, as his birthday. Another biographer found this evidence to be persuasive. See Marisa Rosado, *Pedro Albizu Campos: Las Llamas de la Aurora*, 5th ed. (San Juan: Ediciones Puerto, 2008).

4. Rosado, *Pedro Albizu Campos*, 40–52.

5. See "Albizu Was a Child Prodigy," *Boston Globe*, November 3, 1950, in which Dr. José Padín, Puerto Rico's commissioner of education, stated, "He was a child prodigy

who led his classes in high school and became an oratorical spellbinder at an early age." See also Rosado, *Pedro Albizu Campos*, 45–47.

6. Andrew Schlesinger, *Veritas: Harvard College and the American Experience* (Chicago: Ivan R. Dee, 2005), 153. See also John T. Bethell, *Harvard Observed* (Cambridge, MA: Harvard University Press, 1998), 99–101.

7. Schlesinger, *Veritas*, 140; Bethell, *Harvard Observed*, 54–56. See also Waldron Kintzing Post, *Harvard Stories: Sketches of the Undergraduate* (New York: G. P. Putnam's Sons, 1895).

8. John T. Bethell, Richard M. Hunt, and Robert Shenton, *Harvard A to Z* (Cambridge, MA: Harvard University Press, 2004), 56–59.

9. Albizu spoke fluent English and Spanish. He could also speak French, Italian, Portuguese, and German. See Rosado, *Pedro Albizu Campos*, 60.

10. Instituto de Cultura Puertorriqueña, *Imagen de Pedro Albizu Campos* (San Juan: Instituto de Cultura Puertorriqueña, 1973), 14–16; Rosado, *Pedro Albizu Campos*, 58–61.

11. Laura Meneses de Albizu Campos, *Albizu Campos y la Independencia de Puerto Rico* (Hato Rey, PR: Publicaciones Puertorriqueñas, 2007), 19–33.

12. A number of sources, including the recently released FBI reports, assert that Albizu Campos was "anti-American" due to racism he endured while serving in the US Army. See FBI Files, Subject: Pedro Albizu Campos, File Number SJ 3-1, 2. See also Earl Parker Hanson, *Transformation: The Story of Modern Puerto Rico* (New York: Simon & Schuster, 1955), 83. That allegation is wrong on several levels. First, Albizu was not anti-American; he was against American ownership of Puerto Rico. This is a reasonable distinction, along the lines of "I don't mind your hand, but please take it out of my pocket." Second, the US Army would not have been Albizu's first encounter with racism. Surely one year at the University of Vermont (1912–1913) and four years at Harvard University (1913–1917), prior to joining the army, gave him ample exposure to overt and subtler forms of racism and discrimination. Third, to brand Albizu's politics as a personal response to racism is to trivialize and ignore the larger issue: US appropriation of Puerto Rico's land, natural resources, legal system, and right to self-determination. To resist this is not a "personal" vendetta. It is common sense.

13. Pedro Albizu Campos, *La Conciencia Nacional Puertorriqueña*, ed. Manuel Maldonado-Denis (Cerro del Agua, Mexico: Siglo Veintiuno Editores, 1972), 89–92, 121–190.

14. Ribes Tovar, *Albizu Campos*, 22–23; Rosado, *Pedro Albizu Campos*, 70–72.

15. Instituto de Cultura Puertorriqueña, *Imagen de Pedro Albizu Campos*, 16.

16. Ibid., 16–17; Ribes Tovar, *Albizu Campos*, 29; Rosado, *Pedro Albizu Campos*, 92–93.

17. In view of the career options offered to Albizu, this willful embrace of poverty for the sake of a higher principle weighed heavily on him and his family. On several occasions he was forced to ask others for assistance. In an undated letter from the early 1930s, he wrote the following to a friend:

Dear Pepe,

We just had a terrible night with my little girl. I beg you to send me a bottle of milk of magnesia, a packet of lactose, and five cents of bicarbonate. If at all possible, please send $10, or whatever you can.

Sincerely,

Albizu

See Rosado, *Pedro Albizu Campos*, 94.

On another occasion, Albizu invited three visitors to join his family for supper, but his daughter Rosita informed him that they did not have enough to eat. See Casandra Rivera de Irizarry, "Anécdotas de la Vida de Don Pedro Albizu Campos," *Claridad*, September 17, 1972. At another point, they could not afford the public bus fare for his son, Pedro. See Rosado, *Pedro Albizu Campos*, 97. His undergoing these privations after graduating from Harvard College and then Harvard Law School indicates a firm commitment to his core beliefs. Unfortunately his family paid the price as well. An entirely different book needs to be written about the quiet heroism of his wife, Laura Meneses de Albizu Campos, who raised three children in extreme poverty and in the face of FBI surveillance and death threats, while her husband spent twenty-five years in jail. Her life was suffused with suffering.

18. FBI Files, Subject: Pedro Albizu Campos, File Number 100-3906, Letter to FBI Director J. Edgar Hoover from FBI agent A. C. Schlenker, 1–3.

19. Albizu Campos, *Albizu Campos y la Independencia*, 61.

20. Albizu Campos, *La Conciencia Nacional Puertorriqueña*, 62–81.

21. Rosado, *Pedro Albizu Campos*, 192–194. See also *New York World Telegraph*, June 30, 1932; *Enquirer-Sun* (Columbus, Georgia), July 11, 1932. The *Enquirer-Sun* article expressed a strong opinion about the Puerto Rico Republic bonds: "The federal authorities should stop the sale of these bonds and arrest the junta, if for no other reason than to protest those who might become victims. America has swindlers enough of its own."

22. Ribes Tovar, *Albizu Campos*, 51–54.

23. Cesar J. Ayala, *American Sugar Kingdom* (Chapel Hill: University of North Carolina Press, 1999), 238.

24. *El Imparcial*, January 15, 1934.

25. Pablo Neruda, *Canción de Gesta* (Chile: El Siglo Ilustrado, 1964). See also Pablo Neruda, *The Poetry of Pablo Neruda*, ed. Ilan Stavans (New York: Farrar, Straus & Giroux, 2005).

26. The Citizens Committee of One Thousand for the Preservation of Peace and Order was so intent on breaking the agricultural strike that it demanded a declaration of martial law in Puerto Rico. On December 29, 1933, a hysterical cable to President Roosevelt stated, "A state of actual anarchy exists. Towns in a state of siege. Citizens unable to leave home. Police impotent. Business paralyzed." The cable worked. Exactly two weeks later, on January 12, 1934, Roosevelt appointed an Army general, Blanton

Winship, as the new governor of Puerto Rico. See A. W. Maldonado, *Luis Muñoz Marín: Puerto Rico's Democratic Revolution* (San Juan: Editorial Universidad de Puerto Rico, 2006), 119.

27. Two Nationalists who were with Albizu in Guánica confirmed this phone call from Police Chief Riggs, the conversation with Albizu, and the invitation to lunch.

28. The Riggs Bank continued its "embassy banking" operations well into the twenty-first century, until it serviced one dictator too many. In January 2005, Riggs Bank admitted that it had laundered money for Chilean dictator Augusto Pinochet and officials of Equatorial Guinea and agreed to civil and criminal fines totaling $41 million. See Terence O'Hara, "Riggs Bank Agrees to Guilty Plea," *Washington Post*, January 28, 2005. See also Timothy O'Brien, "A Washington Bank in a Global Mess," *New York Times*, April 11, 2005; Glenn R. Simpson, "Riggs Bank Had Long-Standing Link to the CIA," *Wall Street Journal*, December 31, 2004; Jack Shafer, "The CIA and Riggs Bank," *Slate*, January 7, 2005; Jonathan O'Connell, "Former Riggs Bank Headquarters Near White House Up for Sale," *Washington Post*, December 6, 2013.

29. An example of Riggs Bank financing for the military interventions of United Fruit is provided in Anthony R. Carrozza, *William D. Pawley: The Extraordinary Life of an Adventurer, Entrepreneur, and Diplomat Who Cofounded the Flying Tigers* (Washington, DC: Potomac Books, 2012), 201. As Carrozza reports, in 1954 the Riggs Bank supplied $150,000 in cash for the purchase of three US fighter planes that were stored in a Puerto Rico air base. The planes were quickly turned over to Guatemalan rebel pilots, who flew the planes into combat on the very next day, against democratically elected president of Guatemala Jacobo Árbenz Guzmán. See also Geoffrey G. Jones and Marcelo Bucheli, "The Octopus and the Generals: The United Fruit Company in Guatemala," *Harvard Business Review*, May 27, 2005; Diane K. Stanley, *For the Record: The United Fruit Company's Sixty-Six Years in Guatemala* (Guatemala City: Editorial Antigua, 1994); Rich Cohen, *The Fish That Ate the Whale: The Life and Times of America's Banana King* (New York: Farrar, Straus & Giroux, 2012), 190–211.

30. Jorge Rigau, *Puerto Rico Then and Now* (San Diego, CA: Thunder Bay Press, 2009), 46.

31. The waiter who served Albizu and Police Chief Riggs at El Escambrón spoke and understood English quite well and proudly called himself "Mr. 17-17." He was proud of being born a US citizen in 1917 (under the new Jones Act) and of being on hand, at age seventeen, to witness a representative of the US government's offering Albizu Campos $150,000 to run for public office. That the $150,000 was a bribe did not matter to Mr. 17-17. He considered it a sign of progress, an indication of "how far we've come." He was still talking about it nearly fifty years later, when I met him in the town of Caguas.

32. The luncheon conversation between Albizu Campos and Police Chief Riggs was described to me by the employee who served them at El Escambrón and was also confirmed by several Nationalists. Albizu's wife also discusses the luncheon, as well as the

$150,000 bribe, in her book. See Albizu Campos, *Albizu Campos y la Independencia*, 63. The meeting was also reported on January 19, 1934 (the day after it occurred), in *El Imparcial*. It is further discussed in Rosado, *Pedro Albizu Campos*, 215, and Ribes Tovar, *Albizu Campos*, 50.

33. Ribes Tovar, *Albizu Campos*, 55–57; Albizu Campos, *Albizu Campos y la Independencia*, 63–66; Rosado, *Pedro Albizu Campos*, 218–224, 229.

34. Albizu's wife is very detailed in her recollection of these assaults. Here is a translation from her own book about the armed assaults on their home in 1935: "[Police Chief] Riggs sent agents to our home in Río Piedras. When we moved to Aguas Buenas in 1935, we had to live day and night with an armed guard. . . . [A]rmed American agents watched our house during the night. But they didn't stop there. They tried to assault the house four times. . . . [O]ur guards held them off with gunfire." Albizu Campos, *Albizu Campos y la Independencia*, 64–65.

35. Ibid., 63–64; Ribes Tovar, *Albizu Campos*, 56; Rosado, *Pedro Albizu Campos*, 224–228.

36. *La Democracia*, October 28, 1935.

37. Ribes Tovar, *Albizu Campos*, 63–64.

38. Ronald Fernandez, *Los Macheteros: The Wells Fargo Robbery and the Violent Struggle for Puerto Rican Independence* (New York: Prentice Hall, 1987), 145; Ribes Tovar, *Albizu Campos*, 63–64; *La Acción*, November 20, 1937, 12; Rosado, *Pedro Albizu Campos*, 251–269. If Kent's story is true, this was a blatant denial of the constitutional right to due process.

39. *Albizu Campos et al. v. United States*, 88 F. 2d 138 at 140, 141 (1st Cir., 1937).

40. Rosado, *Pedro Albizu Campos*, 256–261.

41. Ibid., 259–261.

42. Ibid., 613–614.

43. Ibid., 287.

44. Between 1934 and 1950, Vito Marcantonio represented East Harlem for seven terms. See John J. Simon, "Rebel in the House: The Life and Times of Vito Marcantonio," *Monthly Review* 57, no. 11 (April 2006). Marcantonio was especially popular with his Puerto Rican constituents for his defense of their interests both in New York City and on the island of Puerto Rico. This included the cause of Puerto Rican independence. Marcantonio visited Albizu Campos and the Nationalist prisoners six times during their imprisonment in the Atlanta penitentiary and persuaded warden James Bennett to allow Albizu Campos to receive additional medication from outside. See Gerald J. Meyer, "Pedro Albizu Campos, Gilberto Concepcion de Gracia, and Vito Marcantonio's Collaboration in the Cause of Puerto Rico's Independence," *Centro Journal* 23, no. 1 (spring 2011): 98, 100.

45. General Smedley D. Butler, "I Was a Gangster for Capitalism," *Common Sense* 4, no. 11 (November 1935): 8–12.

46. General Smedley D. Butler, *War Is a Racket* (1935; rpt. Los Angeles, CA: Feral House, 2003), 27–32.

47. Rosado, *Pedro Albizu Campos*, 300. See also FBI Files, Subject: Pedro Albizu Campos, File Number SJ 3-1, 15.

48. Ibid., 299. For Congressman Marcantonio's threat to produce the FBI wire on the congressional floor, see Meyer, "Pedro Albizu Campos," 11.

49. As a measure of the FBI's surveillance of Albizu and penetration of his personal life, an report written in early 1948 discusses someone snooping through his wardrobe trunk: "T-1, a highly confidential and reliable source having access to the wardrobe trunk of the subject at the time of his departure . . . furnish[ed] information regarding same to Special Agents JOSEPH V. WATERS and ALFRED B. NOVAK." See FBI Files, Subject: Pedro Albizu Campos, File Number NY 100-47403, 4. This could have been an employee of the Bull Steamship Lines, which owned the SS *Kathryn*, or an FBI agent placed onboard the ship. That this was a "highly confidential and reliable source," assigned Confidential Informant Number T-1, suggests it was someone inside Albizu's circle.

50. Ivonne Acosta, *La Mordaza: Puerto Rico, 1948–1957* (San Juan: Editorial Edil, 1987), 38. See also "The Return of Albizu Campos: Reception Ceremonies and Speech," in FBI Files, Subject: Pedro Albizu Campos, File Number SJ 3-1, 18–19. On December 20, 1947, Hoover sent this report of Albizu's arrival to the US secretary of the interior. FBI Files, Subject: Pedro Albizu Campos, File Number SJ 3-1.

51. Rosado, *Pedro Albizu Campos*, 325, 328–329, 335.

52. The eight days of Octavitas, the final installment of the Puerto Rican yuletide season, commence the day after El Día de los Magos (Three Kings Day) and continue for eight days through January 14. This effectively extends Puerto Rico's Christmas season into the middle of January. In Puerto Rican tradition, if you receive a visit from a friend or relative on Three Kings Day, you return the visit eight days later. Often this visit is accompanied by a *parranda* (troubadours) singing *aguinaldos* (Puerto Rican Christmas carols). Some writers have stated that Puerto Ricans are the happiest people on earth because they celebrate Christmas (*las Navidades*) longer than anyone. Other writers view this extended season as an effort to combat an underlying melancholy.

53. Albizu noticed this change all over the island and spoke openly about it. One of his speeches was radio broadcast over WORP and WCMN in Ponce and Arecibo on October 12, 1948. In that speech, he lamented the change that had occurred on the island during the years he was imprisoned. He said that he could no longer find youths capable of defying the American empire. See FBI Files, Subject: Pedro Albizu Campos, File Number SJ 1-3, 12.

54. During its post–World War II peak, the United States had over two dozen military installations in Puerto Rico. The largest were the Roosevelt Roads Naval Station in Ceiba, the Ramey Air Force Base in Aguadilla, the Atlantic Fleet Weapons Training Facility in Vieques, the National Guard training facility at Camp Santiago in Salinas, Fort Allen in Juana Diaz, and Fort Buchanan and the Puerto Rico Air National Guard in San Juan. See Humberto Garcia Muñiz, "U.S. Military Installations in Puerto Rico: Controlling the Caribbean," in *Colonial Dilemma*, ed. Edgardo Meléndez and Edwin

Meléndez (Boston, MA: South End Press, 1993), 53–66. Together with nearly two hundred other missile silos, ordnance depots, and safe houses, these US military facilities occupied 14 percent of the island's territory. See Juan Gonzalez, *Harvest of Empire: A History of Latinos in America* (New York: Penguin Books, 2000), 286. For late-twentieth-century numbers, see OSD, Washington Headquarters Services, Directorate for Information Operations and Reports (DIOR), "Atlas/Data Abstract for the United States and Selected Areas," FY 1997, Department of Defense, 1998.

55. Garcia Muñiz, "US Military Installations in Puerto Rico: Controlling the Caribbean," 53–66.

56. The Caribe Hilton Hotel received a no-fee, tax-free casino license worth millions of dollars per year, a deal engineered by the governor himself. Through the Puerto Rico Industrial Development Company, the insular government built the three-hundred-room hotel at a cost of $7 million ($69 million in current dollars) and then handed the entire resort—the building, casino, and swimming pools—to Conrad Hilton on a twenty-year lease. One year after the hotel opened, in 1950, the people of Puerto Rico and even Representative Vito Marcantonio (D-NY) were still waiting for the governor to disclose the terms of that lease. The congressman called this part of the governor's "Operation Booby Trap" economic plan for the island.

57. José Trías Monge, *Puerto Rico: The Trials of the Oldest Colony in the World* (New Haven, CT: Yale University Press, 1997), 107–118.

58. Mireya Navarro, "Decades of FBI Surveillance of Puerto Rican Groups," *New York Times*, November 28, 2003. The lights around Albizu's house were fixed after his arrest.

59. Acosta, *La Mordaza*. See also Rosado, *Pedro Albizu Campos*, 332–335; Maldonado, *Luis Muñoz Marín*, 266–267.

60. Gerald Meyer, "Vito Marcantonio and the Puerto Rican Nationalist Party," *Signos* 1, no. 1. (January–March 1980).

61. As noted in the "Sources and Methodology" section of this book, customers, barbers, and members of the 65th Infantry Regiment (the "Borinqueneers") who frequented the Salón Boricua barbershop confirmed this and other conversations. Albizu's reference to "40 FBI men on my tail" was no exaggeration—in fact, it was a slight understatement. The FBI assigned a ten-man detail to conduct surveillance on Albizu and his family twenty-four hours a day, seven days a week. In order to maintain this ten-man rotation at all times, the FBI committed forty-two men, each working forty hours a week. Albizu referred to these "40 FBI men" again in a public speech in Ponce on March 21, 1949, which was broadcast over the WPRP and WCMN radio stations in Arecibo and WITA in San Juan. Ironically, the FBI agents themselves generated the transcript in which Albizu states, "The matter of 40 detectives following behind Albizu Campos, even to the toilet, is going to stop some day." FBI Files, Subject: Pedro Albizu Campos, File Number SJ 3-1, 34. The FBI files show that as early as 1934, Police Chief Riggs had informants in the Nationalist Party. Beginning

April 21, 1948, Albizu was under constant surveillance. A film crew followed him throughout the island and took footage of all his speeches and public appearances, and official police photographers photographed him in thirty-three towns from 1947 through 1950. See ibid., 27, 23, 43; File Number SJ 100-3906, Letter from Jack West to FBI Director Hoover, December 17, 1947. Over time this FBI surveillance of Albizu Campos, the Nationalist Party, and "suspected Nationalists" generated nearly 1.8 million pages of FBI surveillance transcripts. See Navarro, "Decades of FBI Surveillance of Puerto Rican Groups."

62. Two Borinqueneers who frequented the Salón Boricua reported this question-and-answer sequence. According to them, Captain Astro sent them over every week to "help the business a little." Specifically, this meant joking with any FBI personnel in the area and distracting them as much as possible while people met in the room adjacent to the barbershop.

63. At the outset of his career, Albizu was known for diplomacy and not speaking harshly of other people. But after a decade in prison, disbarment, death threats, and constant FBI surveillance, he started to call things as he saw them. For example, the Gag Law was passed on June 10, 1948. The very next day, June 11, 1948, in a speech in the town of Manatí, Albizu referred to Governor Muñoz Marín as a "parasite" who used morphine and drank rum continuously. This speech was also broadcast over radio stations WITA in San Juan and WCMN in Arecibo. See FBI Files, Subject: Pedro Albizu Campos, File Number SJ 3-1, 7.

64. Just a few days later, during the siege of his home from October 30 until November 2, Albizu shared these thoughts with Alvaro Rivera Walker, a Nationalist with him during the final hours before his arrest. Albizu also shared these reflections with the Nationalist prisoners in La Princesa penitentiary. Heriberto Marín Torres later published them in his book *Eran Ellos* (Río Piedras, PR: Ediciones Ciba, 2000). Albizu Campos also wrote about the disappearance of Puerto Rican culture under a mountain of tourist traps in *La Conciencia Nacional Puertorriqueña*. Finally, his wife's book, *Albizu Campos y la Independencia de Puerto Rico*, contains repeated discussion of Albizu's concern for an island long gone, dominated by foreign "developers."

65. The New York Yankees swept the Philadelphia Phillies in the 1950 World Series. They won Game 4 in Yankee Stadium on October 7, 1950. Albizu communicated the irony of this moment (FBI agents saying, "The Yankees won") to Alvaro Rivera Walker and to the Nationalist prisoners in La Princesa.

CHAPTER 13: THE ARTIST

1. In the early 1900s, the three major theaters were San Juan's Cine de la Plaza and Cine Tres Banderas and Ponce's Cine Habana. Until 1919 they showed many Mutual Film Company productions (Charlie Chaplin, Harold Lloyd, Fatty Arbuckle, the Keystone Cops). After the formation of United Artists, Douglas Fairbanks became a

huge favorite, and many considered him an honorary Puerto Rican for his title roles in *The Mark of Zorro* (1920), *Don Q, Son of Zorro* (1925), *The Gaucho* (1927), and *The Private Life of Don Juan* (1934). Juan Emilio Viguié not only attended the films in these local theaters but read foreign film magazines at a very early age. See Juan Ortiz Jimenez, *Nacimiento del Cine Puertorriqueño* (San Juan: Editorial Tiempo, 2007), 15–18.

2. Siegmund "Pop" Lubin was America's first Jewish movie mogul. Despite constant litigation with Thomas Edison, his company was one of the most profitable early film enterprises. By 1913 Lubin was operating studios in Florida, California, New Mexico, and Pennsylvania. See Joseph P. Eckhardt, *The King of the Movies* (London: Fairleigh Dickinson University Press, 1997).

3. Tom Jicha, "HBO Look at Villa Is True Fun," *Sun Sentinel*, September 6, 2006.

4. Juan Emilio Viguié and actor Juano Hernández recounted this conversation to the author. Viguié discussed the scene after a screening of his own film *Vecinos*. Juano Hernández also played a role as a Mexican revolutionary in Raoul Walsh's *The Life of Pancho Villa*. Hernández was present during the filming of the "drunken *Federales* scene."

5. The Smithsonian Insitution wrote a fine article about the Mutual Film Company's *The Life of General Villa*. See Mike Dash, "Uncovering the Truth Behind the Myth of Pancho Villa, Movie Star," *Smithsonian Magazine*, November 6, 2012, http://www.smithsonianmag.com/history/uncovering-the-truth-behind-the-myth -of-pancho-villa-movie-star-110349996. The actor Juano Hernández had a role as a Mexican revolutionary in Raoul Walsh's *The Life of Pancho Villa*. He observed the interactions between Juan Emilio Viguié, Raoul Walsh, and Pancho Villa; he also accompanied them to the Jesse James movie in Ciudad Juárez. According to Hernández, Walsh's filming and financing of the Mexican Revolution were the craziest thing he had ever seen and sealed his love affair with filmmaking. I met Mr. Hernández in the late 1960s, and he shared his memories of *The Life of Pancho Villa*. At the time, he was trying to produce a film about the boxer Sixto Escobar.

6. The entire text of the Jones-Shafroth Act appears in the *American Journal of International Law* 11 (1917): 66–93. It was passed by the 64th Congress as HR 9533.

7. Manuel Maldonado-Denis, *Puerto Rico: A Socio-historic Interpretation* (New York: Random House, 1972), 104–109; Pedro Albizu Campos, ed. Manuel Maldonado-Denis, *La Conciencia Nacional Puertorriqueña* (Mexico: Siglo Veintiuno Editores, 1972), 163–165; Ronald Fernandez, *The Disenchanted Island: Puerto Rico and the United States in the Twentieth Century*, 2nd ed. (Westport, CT: Praeger Publishers, 1996), 70–73.

8. Maldonado-Denis, *Puerto Rico*, 108.

9. Lev Kuleshov, *Kuleshov on Film* (Berkeley: University of California Press, 1975)

10. Ortiz Jimenez, *Nacimiento del Cine Puertorriqueño*, 8.

11. Ralph Ince had directed well over 110 films by the time he filmed *Tropical Love*. See "Ralph Ince (1887–1937)," IMDB, http://www.imdb.com/name/nm0408433/?ref_=tt

_ov_dr. Reginald Denny had been the heavyweight boxing champion of the British Royal Air Force. See Lemuel F. Parton, "Robot Planes Is Ex-Pug Denny's Hobby Business," *Philipsburg Mail*, December 30, 1938. See also *Los Angeles Times*, December 16, 1922. The two men had massive arguments on the set of *Tropical Love*, with Denny challenging Ince to a fight, which brought production to a standstill. See Eduardo Rosado, *La Llegada del Cine Puertorriqueño* (San Juan: Cinemovida Entertainment, 2012). Juan Emilio Viguié witnessed these arguments.

12. Juan Emilio Viguié himself confirmed the rumors about Eusebio after a screening of his film *Vecinos*. The fact that they were filming in the town of Loíza Aldea amplified the concern. In Puerto Rico, Loíza Aldea and Guayama are known as the "witch doctor towns." Guayama currently has two professional teams, one for baseball and one for basketball, both named the Brujos de Guayama (Guayama Witch Doctors). Satchel Paige pitched for the Brujos de Guayama during the 1939–1940 winter baseball season. In one famous game, Paige left the stadium in a hurry, claiming that a ghost was standing next to him on the pitcher's mound.

Founded by freed or escaped African slaves, Loíza Aldea has a strong Yoruba tradition, encompassing both Santería and Palo spiritualist practices, and is also famed for its *Vejigante* spirit masks, which represent evil, the devil, and Moors. The town's cult, Santiago Matamoros, worships Matamoros as the son of thunder with the power to bring fire from the sky down on any Moors or foreign invaders (the word *Matamoros* means "killer of Moors"). See Nigene González-Wippler, *Santería, the Religion* (New York: Crown Publishers, 2008), 291–294. See also Carlos Mendez-Santos, *Por Tierras de Loiza Aldea: Estudios de Antropología Cultural* (San Juan: Producciones Ceiba, 1973). Given this sensitivity to foreign invasion and that the *Tropical Love* producers were hiring virtually no locals from Loíza Aldea among either the cast or the crew, the resentment embodied by Eusebio was not merely understandable but almost inevitable.

13. Rosado, *La Llegada del Cine Puertorriqueño*.

14. Ortiz Jimenez, *Nacimiento del Cine Puertorriqueño*, 48.

15. David B. Hinton, *The Films of Leni Riefenstahl*, 3rd ed. (Lanham, MD: Scarecrow Press, 2000), 23–46.

16. Juan Emilio Viguié conveyed this after a screening of his film *Vecinos*. According to Viguié, he took long walks to observe people, landscapes, and architecture, particularly in Ponce and San Juan. Viguié stated that the island's trees, landscapes, ocean, and people had as much narrative power as any of the elements of Leni Riefenstahl's megaproduction, if not more. This view on Viguié's part was confirmed by his forty years of newsreel and documentary photography of Puerto Rico as well as by an interview with his son, Juan E. Viguié Jr.

17. In 1962, Juan Emilio Viguié visited our home in Washington Heights and provided a Saturday night screening of his film *Vecinos*, which had been sponsored by the Puerto Rico Department of Education. He then screened his thirteen-minute film of the Ponce Massacre. It was one continuous master shot taken from a window on the

corner of Marina and Aurora Streets. The carnage was impossible to forget. Viguié himself had suffered nightmares over it. He then discussed Assistant District Attorney (ADA) Pedro Rodriguez-Serra's attempts to bully, threaten, and extort people into fabricating evidence against the Nationalists. Viguié talked about the ADA's unannounced visit to his home. He remembered their conversation vividly since, as Viguié put it, "The man had my tripod in one hand and my freedom in the other." According to Viguié, the Ponce Massacre was the central political event in his life; it had converted him from a disengaged "artist" into a documentarian of his island's struggle for dignity and independence.

18. Viguié was allowed to film these events because of his recognized position as the island's preeminent news photographer. Viguié was under contract with MGM and Fox News and supplied newsreel footage to both. According to Viguié, whenever he filmed Albizu Campos or the Nationalists, he took two additional precautions. First and foremost, Viguié always brought another person as a witness (often his son, Juan Viguié Jr.) in case anyone tried to arrest him or confiscate his film. Second, Viguié was always courteous to the FBI cameraman filming Albizu's speeches and public events and always assisted him with any technical problems. On several occasions, when the FBI cameraman had had a "rough night" and was unable to attend an event, Viguié gave him a duplicate copy of his own footage. The FBI files confirm that the bureau had a film crew follow Albizu Campos and the Nationalist Party all over the island. Agent Jack West was responsible for filming Albizu's speeches and public appearances. The FBI would then make six-by-eight-inch still photos of individuals appearing in these films (such as the Cadets of the Republic) for distribution to agents throughout the island and for the opening of police files (*carpetas*) on those individuals. See FBI Files, Subject: Pedro Albizu Campos, File Number SJ 100-3906, Letter from Jack West to FBI Director Hoover, December 17, 1947.

19. Several conversations with Viguié's son, Juan Viguié Jr., reaffirmed the account given to me by Viguié regarding his filming of Albizu Campos and Nationalist events. They were all part of a much larger catalog of news and sporting events, press conferences, public ceremonies, Christmas specials, celebrity interviews, concerts, hurricane reports, and documentary news footage from all over the island. Today, the newsreels of Noticiero Viguié (Viguié News) are recognized as the single greatest visual record of historical events in Puerto Rico.

20. The transformative power of socially engaged cinema became evident throughout the last century. Films such as *Battleship Potemkin, Strike, October, Titicut Follies, Battle of Algiers, JFK, Salvador, Z, State of Siege, Medium Cool, Putney Swope, Memories of Underdevelopment,* and *Investigation of a Citizen Above Suspicion* showed the possibilities for meaningful examination of significant political issues. With the exception of *A Show of Force* (1990), financed externally by Paramount Pictures, this cinema has yet to develop in Puerto Rico.

Chapter 14: The OSS Agent

1. "Waller Beale Booth '26," *Princeton Alumni Weekly* 86, no. 39 (April 23, 1986): 19. See also "Princeton Triangle Club Puts on Brilliant *Fortuno*," *Indianapolis News*, December 25, 1925, 10.

2. "Princeton Opera 'Fortuno' a Winner," *New York Times*, December 14, 1925.

3. See the author's biography in Waller B. Booth, *Mission Marcel Proust: The Story of an Unusual OSS Undertaking* (Philadelphia: Dorrance & Co., 1972).

4. Several Borinqueneers who served with Booth during Operation Portrex recounted the phone call from Dulles.

5. Booth's OSS memoir *Mission Marcel Proust* reads like a *Who's Who in America*, as Booth entered the upper ranks of the OSS along with Michael Burke (president of the New York Yankees), John Haskell (vice president of the New York Stock Exchange [NYSE]), D. Christian Gauss (senior partner at Shearman & Sterling), and J. Russell Forgan (an investment banker at Glore-Gorgan & Co. with his own seat on the NYSE).

6. Located near the town of Whitby on the northwestern shore of Lake Ontario, Camp X was the first training school for clandestine operations in North America. It was founded in 1941 and decommissioned in 1969. See David Stafford, *Camp X: OSS, Intrepid, and the Allies' North American Training Camp for Secret Agents, 1941–1945* (New York: Dodd Mead, 1987).

7. Established in Puerto Rico in 1908, the 65th Infantry Division is also known as the Borinqueneers, in recognition of the original Taíno name for the island of Puerto Rico, which was *Borinquen*. The Borinqueneers served with distinction in both world wars and the Korean War and were deployed into active service as recently as 2009. See Larry Brystan, "Legendary Borinqueneers Deserve the Congressional Gold Medal," Fox News Latino, January 8, 2013; David A. Hurst, *65th Infantry Division* (Nashville, TN: Turner Publishing, 1993). Over the past century, members of the Borinqueneers have earned ten Distinguished Service Crosses, hundreds of Silver and Bronze Stars, and thousands of Purple Hearts. Until September 1950, the Borinqueneers trained and bivouacked in Camp Las Casas in Santurce, Puerto Rico. See Johnny J. Burnham, "Push to Honor Puerto Rican Regiment Gains Momentum," *New Britain Herald*, August 13, 2013; Denise Oliver Velez, "The Borinqueneers: Award Them the Gold," *Daily Kos*, May 27, 2013. In May 2014, the US House and Senate passed a bill granting the Borinqueneers the Congressional Gold Medal. Together with the Presidential Medal of Freedom, this is the highest civilian honor awarded by the United States. See Kevin Mead, "Borinqueneers Bill Reaches the White House," *Caribbean Business*, May 24, 2014.

8. On April 18, 1911, the *New York Times* reported a cigar factory strike with the headline "Anarchists Behind Porto Rico Strike." It reported the "assassination" of a foreman, the arrest of many anarchists, and threatening letters warning that "other

heads of factories will be killed and the factories set afire." Over the ensuing weeks the "anarchists" were released for lack of evidence, and no factories or factory heads were harmed—while the workers received a meager increase of twenty-five cents per 1,000 cigars. By the time Waller Booth arrived in Puerto Rico, he had tens of thousands of FBI *carpetas* to choose from. They contained wild accusations, including a rumor about the impending murder of American sugar cane plantation owners. Quite wisely, Booth opened a saloon and listened for himself. See FBI Files, Subject: Nationalist Party of Puerto Rico, File Number SJ 100-3, Vol. 23. See also A. W. Maldonado, *Luis Muñoz Marín: Puerto Rico's Democratic Revolution* (San Juan: Editorial Universidad de Puerto Rico, 2006), 92.

9. Gilberto N. Villahermosa, *Honor and Fidelity: The 65th Infantry in Korea, 1950–1953* (Washington, DC: Center of Military History, US Army, 2009).

10. Waller B. Booth, "The Battle of the Sheep: One of the Most Unusual Engagements of World War II," *News and Courier*, December 6, 1964, 12,14.

11. The theft of Colonel Klaus von Strobel's papers was a real intelligence coup. Booth and his men accomplished it one week before the 45th US Infantry Division landed its 18,000 soldiers on the beaches of northern France. The papers contained complete information regarding von Strobel's command, including troop strength and deployment; armament; equipment; supply status; names, grades, and assignments of all officers; casualty reports; locations of field and base hospitals; oil depots; warehouses; tank repair stations; phone lines; railroad schedules; and highway routes—in short, just about everything that von Strobel himself could have known. This enabled the French Resistance to interrupt railways, damage bridges, cut off German communication lines, and create general confusion just days before the Allied landing. See Booth, *Mission Marcel Proust*, 127–128.

12. Some people (mostly Cubans) swear that the "Sun Sun Babae" number was developed in 1952 by choreographer Roderico Neyra at the Sans Souci nightclub in Havana. See Peter Moruzzi, *Havana Before Castro: When Cuba Was a Tropical Playground* (Layton, UT: Gibbs Smith, 2008), 110–111. Others swear they saw it first at the Club with No Name. One thing is certain: "Sun Sun Babae" was a smash hit on both islands.

13. Due to the nostalgia of the *Casablanca* screenings, the members of the 65th Infantry Regiment were the most loyal patrons of the Club with No Name. Nationalists also frequented the club due to its reputation as a safe zone where the Insular Police did not dare to arrest or harass people. From these two groups, I received multiple consistent accounts of the events at the Club with No Name, including about the one-liners hurled at the *Casablanca* movie screen and the staged arguments between Waller Booth and the FBI.

14. This dramatic confrontation between Booth and the FBI men was witnessed and described by both Borinqueneers and customers at the Club with No Name and corroborated by multiple witnesses.

15. For an excellent account of Operation Portrex and Waller Booth's role in it, see US Brigadier General Edwin L. Sibert, "Operation PORTREX," *Studies in Intelligence* 4, no. 2 (1960): A1–A9. General Sibert commanded all defending land forces and had a firsthand view of Booth's counterespionage and fifth column tactics. According to Sibert, Booth was a former OSS officer living in San Juan who "organized and directed an undercover net of counterespionage agents among the native residents of Vieques, and who prepared a group of stay-behind guerrillas to operate within the invaders' beachhead." Booth's "unorthodox" techniques were so successful that, according to Sibert, "I am told that one result from our efforts at Vieques was the establishment of an Army school to teach the kind of operations Wally demonstrated there. If that is true, one of the buildings at the school should be called Booth Hall."

16. See Booth, *Mission Marcel Proust.*

17. In later years, after teaching counterinsurgency techniques in Latin America, Vietnam, and throughout the Third World, Booth developed a philosophical side. He published a book of poetry titled *Booth's Truths* (Kendallville, IN: Kendallville Publishing, 1976), which contained numerous epiphanies about personal ethics ("A Lesson in Ethics"), corporate responsibility ("A Suggestion to Manufacturers"), the perils of big government ("Point of View" and "The Economy, or Lack of It"), and inequities in our legal system ("Justice and Legality").

Chapter 15: The Barber

1. Vidal Santiago Díaz was arrested along with 3,000 other Puerto Ricans in the weeks following the Nationalist revolt of 1950. He was tried for treason, sentenced to eighteen years, and imprisoned in La Princesa along with Albizu Campos and dozens of other Nationalists. See Miñi Seijo Bruno, *La Insurrección Nacionalista en Puerto Rico, 1950* (Río Piedras, PR: Editorial Edil, 1989), 172–173; Federico Ribes Tovar, *Albizu Campos: Puerto Rican Revolutionary* (New York: Plus Ultra Publishers, 1971), 107–110; FBI Files, Subject: Pedro Albizu Campos, File Number 105-11898, Sections 1, 2; FBI Files, Subject: Puerto Rican Nationalist Party, File Number SJ 100-3, Vol. 23. Vidal became great friends with another Nationalist in La Princesa, Juan Jaca Hernández, who was also a barber. See Heriberto Marín Torres, *Eran Ellos* (Río Piedras, PR: Ediciones Ciba, 2000), 93.

2. Jesus Colón, *A Puerto Rican in New York and Other Sketches* (New York: International Publishers, 1982), 11–13. See also Araceli Tinajero and Judith E. Greenberg, *El Lectór: A History of the Cigar Factory Reader* (Austin: University of Texas Press, 2010); Nilo Cruz, *Anna in the Tropics* (New York: Dramatists Play Service, 2005).

3. Ybor City, Florida, was a major cigar-producing center until the Tampa cigar makers' strike of 1931. Unfortunately, the factory owners decided that the *lectóres* were organizing and inciting the workers, and the Ybor City cigar factories banned all *lectóres* permanently. See "Tampa Cigar Makers to End Strike," *New York Times,*

November 30, 1931; "Tampa Cigar Strike Ends," *Wall Street Journal*, December 15, 1931; "Tobacco Men Ban Strikes," *Wall Street Journal*, December 28, 1931.

4. Cesar J. Ayala, *American Sugar Kingdom* (Chapel Hill: University of North Carolina Press, 1999), 45–47, 139, 140, 185, 187, 225. See also Manuel Maldonado-Denis, *Puerto Rico: A Socio-historic Interpretation* (New York: Random House, 1972), 74; Juan Antonio Corretjer, *Albizu Campos and the Ponce Massacre* (New York: World View Publishers, 1965), 2–4; "Federal Attack on Sugar Trust," *New York Times*, November 29, 1910; Leonard J. Arrington, *Beet Sugar in the West, 1891–1966* (Seattle: University of Washington Press, 1966), 54–55; *New York Times*, April 1, 1914; Thomas Aitken, *Poet in the Fortress: The Story of Luis Muñoz Marín* (New York: Signet Books, 1964), 60–62.

5. Sidney W. Mintz, *Sweetness and Power: The Place of Sugar in Modern History* (New York: Penguin Books, 1985), xviii–xix. See also Gillian McGillivray, *Blazing Cane* (Durham, NC: Duke University Press, 2009), 2–4; Ayala, *American Sugar Kingdom*, 121–148.

6. A picaresque rogue, Captain Astro presents a moral quandary. With one hand he stole rations from Puerto Rican soldiers for personal profit; with the other he helped fifty Puerto Rican families fend off starvation. According to several Nationalists, Captain Astro was not a patriot—he was a sharp businessman who calculated every risk and reward and never sold on credit. Before judging him too harshly, one might consider him within a larger ethical framework. Equal parts Damon Runyon, Robin Hood, and Sammy Glick, Captain Astro is a familiar cultural archetype: the protean trickster who overcomes oppression by abusing and outwitting his colonial masters.

In American society, Astro has many cultural correlatives: Milo Minderbinder in *Catch-22* (novel, film), Hawkeye Pierce and Trapper John in *M*A*S*H* (film, TV), Will Stockdale in *No Time for Sergeants* (novel, Broadway play, film, TV), Corporal King in *King Rat* (novel, film), Alec Leamas in *The Spy Who Came in from the Cold* (novel, film), Joe Keller in *All My Sons* (Broadway play, film), J. J. Sefton in *Stalag 17* (Broadway play, film), Major Archie Gates in *Three Kings* (film), Private Kelly in *Kelly's Heroes* (film), Colonel Robert E. Hogan in *Hogan's Heroes* (TV), Sergeant Bilko in *The Phil Silvers Show* (TV), and virtually every character in *McHale's Navy* (TV).

On the island of Puerto Rico, Captain Astro had the most compelling role model of all: the US government. Throughout the 1940s, the cost of building a US naval base somehow ballooned from an initial budget of $4 million to a "final estimated cost" of $112.57 million, exclusive of "fees" and the cost of "excess material." In current dollars, this represents $1.5 billion. This massive transfer of wealth to US military contractors does not excuse the larceny of Captain Astro, but it may have inspired it.

7. El Águila Blanca (the White Eagle) is a legendary figure among Puerto Rican Nationalists and *independentistas*. He was born José Maldonado Roman, but everyone called him Don Pepe or El Águila. Throughout his youth, Spanish authorities repeatedly arrested him for stealing cows and farm animals and giving them to hungry *jíbaros*. On March 24, 1897, El Águila and a man named Fidel Vélez led the Intentona

de Yauco, a revolutionary attack on the Spanish Civil Guard barracks in the town of Yauco. When the revolt failed, El Águila escaped to Cuba and fought the Spanish as a soldier in the Cuban Liberation Army. When he returned to Puerto Rico, he continued to wage a guerilla war against Spain. Just before the US invasion, he helped an American spy named Edwin Emerson Jr. avoid capture and return to the United States. When it became apparent to El Águila that the Yankees were worse than the Spanish, he waged guerilla warfare against them. He attacked US soldiers in Ponce and Jayuya and set fire to a plantation in Juana Díaz. During one of these offensives, he lost the sight in one of his eyes.

El Águila eventually married, settled down, and became a barber. He continued his "Robin Hood" activities, albeit in a more orderly and clandestine manner, using his barbershop as a front for the exchange of information, food, funds, and weapons. He was one of Albizu Campos's earliest and most trusted friends and helped connect him with some of the most hardened *independentistas* on the island.

Half a century after his death, on September 12, 1983, a Puerto Rican revolutionary organization called Los Macheteros stole $7 million from a Wells Fargo depot in Hartford, Connecticut—at the time, it was the largest robbery in American history. The Macheteros code-named the operation "El Águila Blanca." See Reynaldo Marcos Padua, *Águila* (San Juan: Ediciones Huracan, 2008); Loida Figueroa, *Breve Historia de Puerto Rico*, Vol. 1 (San Juan: Editorial Edil, 1979); FBI Files, Subject: Pedro Albizu Campos, File Number 105-11898, Sections 1, 2; FBI Files, Subject: Puerto Rican Nationalist Party, File Number SJ 100-3, Vol. 23; *La Democracia*, May 22, 1899. José Maldonado Roman's granddaughter, Margarita Maldonado, wrote an essay about him titled "El Águila Blanca y la Memoria Colectiva." At the time of this writing, it could be read in Spanish at http://margaritamaldonado.tripod.com/memoria.htm.

8. A barber who worked at the Salón Boricua reported this conversation to the author. Vidal Santiago Díaz had confided this conversation to him. It was also confirmed by a Nationalist prisoner from La Princesa, who learned of the conversation and its contents directly from Vidal. See http://margaritamaldonado.tripod.com/memoria.htm. For a good overview of the life and views of José Maldonado Roman, see Padua, *Águila.*

9. Marisa Rosado, *Pedro Albizu Campos: Las Llamas de la Aurora*, 5th ed. (San Juan: Ediciones Puerto, 2008), 201–203; A. W. Maldonado, *Luis Muñoz Marín: Puerto Rico's Democratic Revolution* (San Juan: Editorial Universidad de Puerto Rico, 2006), 91.

10. The FBI hotly pursued the weapons stored by Vidal Santiago Díaz. See FBI Files, Subject: Puerto Rican Nationalist Party, File Number SJ 100-3, Vol. 23, 104–134; FBI Files, Subject: Pedro Albizu Campos, File Number 105-11898, Section 1, 20. It is a credit to both El Águila Blanca and Vidal that they managed to keep this arsenal a secret for nearly twenty years. Its existence is beyond question. Vidal Santiago Díaz waged a three-hour gunfight against thirty National Guard troops and Insular Police officers, which was broadcast live via radio throughout the island and heard

by millions of people. Santiago Díaz could not have sustained this three-hour battle without significant ammunition. The FBI finally discovered and provided proof of the arsenal. Shortly after the October 1950 revolution, a report identified the Salón Boricua barbershop as the location of a major weapons cache "recovered by the Insular Police while disarming Nationalists during the revolt." FBI Files, Subject: Nationalist Party of Puerto Rico, File Number SJ 100-3, Vol. 23, 149.

11. As the personal barber of Albizu Campos, Vidal Santiago Díaz received years of FBI attention. See FBI Files, Subject: Puerto Rican Nationalist Party, File Number SJ 100-3, Vols. 23, 26. The "drunk" in front of Vidal's barbershop was an FBI agent working as part of the ongoing surveillance of the Nationalist Party. This "drunk" was a nuisance but he didn't fool anyone—since a new one seemed to arrive every eight hours.

CHAPTER 16: THE ACADEMY OF TRUTH

1. Pursuant to a Freedom of Information Act request, the US Department of Defense admitted that it had stationed nuclear weapons in Puerto Rico during the 1950s, 1960s, and 1970s. See Carmelo Ruiz-Marrero, "Puerto Rico: Surrounded by Nuclear Missiles?," Inter Press Service News Agency, November 8, 1999. For late-twentieth-century nuclear deployments in Puerto Rico, see Ivelaw L. Griffith, *Strategy and Security in the Caribbean* (New York: Praeger Publishers, 1991), 36–42.

2. The Ramey Air Force Base has been replaced by a US military facility on the island of Diego Garcia. Located in the Indian Ocean, it was purchased by Great Britain and leased to the United States for fifty years (1966–2016), with an option to extend until 2036. The principal construction of Diego Garcia (1972–1978), at a cost of over $400 million, coincided precisely with the closure of Ramey Air Force Base in 1973. See Richard Edis, *Peak of Limuria: The Story of Diego Garcia and the Chagos Archipelago* (Chippenham, UK: Antony Rowe, 2004), 90.

At Diego Garcia, the US Navy currently operates an air base and a naval support facility for large ships and submarines. See Diego Garcia Integrated Natural Resources Management Plan, US Naval Support Facility Diego Garcia (September 2005, par. 2.4.3). US bombers from Diego Garcia have bombed enemy targets in Iraq, Kuwait, and Afghanistan. See Edis, *Peak of Limuria*, 94, 96.

But there is much more to Diego Garcia. In 2007, the *Guardian* reported, "The existence of the CIA's black site prisons was acknowledged by President George Bush in September last year. . . . Bush did not disclose the location of any prison, but suspicion that one may have been located on Diego Garcia, some 1,000 miles off Sri Lanka's southern coast, has been building for years." See "Claims of Secret CIA Jail for Terror Suspects on British Island to Be Investigated," *Guardian*, October 18, 2007. The *Huffington Post* also reported that British members of Parliament were conducting an investigation into CIA "crimes against humanity of disappearance, torture and prolonged incommunicado detention" at Diego Garcia Island. See "British MPs to Probe Claims of CIA Island Prison in Indian Ocean," *Huffington Post*, March 28, 2008.

Historian Eduardo Galeano provided the most memorable description of Diego Garcia Island in *Children of the Days: A Calendar of Human History* (New York: Nation Books, 2013):

> This paradise of white sand in the middle of the Indian Ocean became a military base, a station for spy satellites, a floating prison and torture chamber for suspected terrorists, and a staging ground for the annihilation of countries that deserve to be punished.
>
> It also has a golf course. (301)

3. The Aguadilla facility has disappeared, as has the Ramey Air Force Base that surrounded it. This is logical and to be expected. It would be poor tradecraft to leave such a massive and damning international footprint just a few years after the Nuremberg Trials.

4. As reported by the Nationalist prisoners I interviewed, Captain Rolf made a point of keeping doors open and screaming loudly during the interrogations so that his voice echoed through the corridors. This was Rolf's tactic for instilling fear in the prisoners.

5. The sources for this chapter include Nationalists who knew Vidal Santiago Díaz from his barbershop days, five Nationalist prisoners from La Princesa, two Nationalist prisoners from El Oso Blanco penitentiary, three Nationalist prisoners who were interrogated in the Aguadilla facility near Ramey Air Force Base, and a medical assistant from the Aguadilla facility. The three Nationalists were confined during the same time as Vidal and witnessed his treatment. All these Nationalist testimonies were provided via repeated interviews conducted longitudinally, over the course of forty years, from 1974 to 2014. As the years progressed, the Nationalist prisoners never calibrated their testimonies or embellished their recollections. Their statements regarding the Aguadilla facility provided a dense and consistent pattern of information. The medical assistant was also consistent over time. He was so shocked by the events at Aguadilla that he became a lifelong *independentista*—though not a Nationalist, for fear of having a *carpeta* opened on him and becoming a prisoner himself.

6. Vidal Santiago Díaz shared the details of this torture and all the other "sessions" with his fellow Nationalist prisoners at La Princesa. According to the other prisoners, these tortures cemented Vidal's resolve as a Nationalist and his courage during the uprising of October 1950.

7. Captain Rolf repeatedly asked Vidal about the location of guns and ammunition. This was the focus of his interrogation sessions with Vidal.

8. The waterboarding and other tortures Vidal endured are shocking to contemplate, but they were not new or exclusive to Puerto Rico. The behavior of US intelligence forces—both before and after the October 1950 revolution—has shown a

consistent pattern throughout Latin America and even globally. Much of that behavior is discussed in two CIA manuals: *KUBARK Counterintelligence Interrogation* (Washington, DC: US Government Printing Office, 1963) and *Human Resource Exploitation Manual* (Washington, DC: US Government Printing Office, 1983). At the time of this writing, both manuals were still viewable in the National Security Archives at http://www2.gwu.edu/~nsarchiv/NSAEBB/NSAEBB122/index.htm#hre. Both are quite detailed. For instance, "the electric current [at an interrogation site] should be known in advance, so that transformers and other modifying devices will be on hand if needed." See *KUBARK Counterintelligence Interrogation*, 46. There are chapters on debility, dread, fear, intense fear, deprivation of sensory stimuli, anxiety, threats, hypnosis, narcosis, pain, intense pain, and torture. The pain chapter details how to achieve various levels of pain (*KUBARK Counterintelligence Interrogation*, 93–95; *Human Resource Exploitation Manual*, K-9 through K-11). The manuals also recommend using extremities of heat, cold, and moisture; sleep and sensory deprivation; the water tank (i.e., waterboarding); and the iron lung.

Beyond the two CIA manuals, seven additional Spanish-language manuals were used for decades in Latin America. See "Memorandum to the Deputy Secretary of Defense from Werner S. Michel, Asst. to the Secretary of Defense," March 10, 1992, viewable in the National Security Archives at http://www2.gwu.edu/~nsarchiv/NSAEBB /NSAEBB122/920310%20Imporper%20Material%20in%20Spanish-Language%20 Intelligence%20Training%20Manuals.pdf. These manuals were even more explicit than the counterintelligence interrogation and human resource exploitation manuals, providing detailed instructions on the use of beatings, false imprisonment, extortion, truth serums, and executions. They were distributed to thousands of military officers in ten South and Central American countries: Bolivia, Columbia, Costa Rico, Dominican Republic, Ecuador, Guatemala, Honduras, Mexico, Peru, and Venezuela. According to Werner's memo, a review of the seven manuals showed that five of them contained language regarding the use of executions, beatings, false testimony, bounty payments for enemy dead, truth serums, motivation by fear, and false imprisonment. The memo further states, "We were told by USCINCSO [the US commander in chief of the Southern Command] that one of his major priorities is the adherence to human rights policies by Latin American armed forces. Obviously, the offensive and objectionable material in the manuals contradicts this policy, undermines U.S. credibility, and could result in significant embarrassment." See "Memorandum to the Deputy Secretary of Defense from Werner S. Michel," 3.

9. Darkness and sensory deprivation are covered in the CIA interrogation manuals. See "Deprivation of Sensory Stimuli" (*KUBARK Counterintelligence Interrogation*, 87; *Human Recourse Exploitation Manual*, L-10).

10. This film was probably taken by an FBI cameraman. The FBI had a film crew follow Albizu Campos and the Nationalist Party all over the island. See: FBI Files, Subject: Pedro Albizu Campos, File Number SJ 100–3906, Letter from Jack West to FBI Director Hoover, December 17, 1947.

11. An Aguadilla Nationalist who slept in a cell next to Vidal's told him about the Nationalist who was fed his own son, and about Governor Muñoz Marín's opium addiction. This addiction was already well known to Vidal, from the many people who passed through his barbershop.

12. Margaret Bourke-White took this photo, titled "The American Way of Life," in front of a relief station in Louisville, Kentucky, in the days after the Great Ohio River Flood of 1937. Vidal had seen it before, in *Life* magazine, just one month before the Ponce Massacre.

13. Guns, ammunition, and their location were the focus of Vidal's interrogation sessions at the Aguadilla facility.

14. The medical assistant was present during the drug-enhanced interrogation of Vidal and during some of the more brutal interrogations at the Academy of Truth. According to this medical assistant, everyone referred to the visiting interrogator as "Dr. Hebb." Though this may have been a code name, the medical assistant remembered Dr. Hebb's mention of the Yerkes Center, which creates an interesting historical possibility. Dr. Donald O. Hebb worked at the Yerkes National Primate Research Center in Orange Park, Florida, from 1942 to 1947 and developed sensory-deprivation techniques used in interrogations conducted by the CIA. If the doctor who interviewed Vidal was indeed this Dr. Hebb, then the CIA was using him as a roving collector of information.

CHAPTER 17: LAST DAYS

1. Marisa Rosado, *Pedro Albizu Campos: Las Llamas de la Aurora*, 5th ed. (San Juan: Ediciones Puerto, 2008), 340; Ruth Mary Reynolds, *Campus in Bondage* (New York: Research Foundation of the City University of New York, 1989), xv. As reported in Reynolds's book, in 1950 "President Truman sent his Secretary of Defense, Louis Johnson, to Puerto Rico with instructions for the military authorities there to pass on to Luis Muñoz Marín, the first elective governor of Puerto Rico, that he should utilize the insular police force to liquidate the Nationalist Party of Puerto Rico and arrest its leadership and, should such arrests prove difficult, that leadership should be assassinated" (xv).

2. Rosado, *Pedro Albizu Campos*, 357; A. W. Maldonado, *Luis Muñoz Marín: Puerto Rico's Democratic Revolution* (San Juan: Editorial Universidad de Puerto Rico, 2006), 304; "Muñoz Certain Reds Back Plot," *Times Picayune*, November 2, 1950.

3. Maldonado, *Luis Muñoz Marín*, 247, 267.

4. FBI Files, Subject: Luis Muñoz Marín, File Number 100-5745, Letter from Governor Luis Muñoz Marín to FBI agent A. C. Schlenker.

5. Ibid., Letter from Governor Luis Muñoz Marín to FBI agent A. C. Schlenker.

6. J. Edgar Hoover had a love-hate relationship with Governor Muñoz Marín. He would investigate him as a Communist on one day, then praise him as a beacon of democracy the next. See FBI Files, Subject: Luis Muñoz Marín, File Number 100-5745,

Section I, 2, 4, 62. Hoover would also provide him with a personal FBI security detail, an armored car, and background investigations of Muñoz Marín's personal and political enemies. Muñoz Marín returned these favors by repeatedly inviting Hoover down to Puerto Rico as his own personal guest. See ibid. 100-5745-42X4, 144–148, 167; August 6 and 25, 1953 ; May 29, 1952; July 6, 1953. There is no record of Hoover ever taking him up on this invitation. In view of the Nationalists' feelings toward J. Edgar Hoover, this comes as no surprise.

7. Jack West was one of the San Juan FBI agents assigned to Albizu Campos and the Nationalist Party of Puerto Rico. He wrote frequent reports that went into the secret FBI Files (the *carpetas*) of Albizu and the Nationalists. He also conducted personal surveillance all over the island. Among his responsibilities were the filming of Albizu's speeches and public appearances. The FBI would then make six-by-eight-inch still photos of individuals appearing in these films (such as the Cadets of the Republic) for distribution to FBI agents throughout the island and for the opening of a police file (a *carpeta*) on them. See FBI Files, Subject: Pedro Albizu Campos, File Number SJ 100-3906, Letter from Jack West to FBI Director Hoover, December 17, 1947.

8. José Trías Monge was the undersecretary of justice (i.e., assistant attorney general, 1949) and the secretary of justice (i.e., attorney general, 1953–1957) of Puerto Rico. He later became a senator and the chief justice of the Supreme Court of Puerto Rico. The FBI office in Washington, DC, kept him informed of significant communications and actions with respect to the surveillance and arrest of Albizu Campos and the Nationalists. For example, Monge was informed of Hoover's call with respect to Vidal Santiago Díaz. Years later, during a visit to Yale Law School, Monge shared some of his recollections of that period.

9. Vidal Santiago Díaz later communicated this and other experiences to fellow Nationalist prisoners at La Princesa.

10. This Nationalist later shared his experiences at La Princesa prison.

11. *El Imparcial*, October 30, 1950, 1.

12. Ibid.

13. Albizu Campos and the Nationalists could not appeal to the government of Puerto Rico for any protection since Governor Luis Muñoz Marín and his party—the same politician and party that had enacted the Gag Law—dominated the politics of the island. In 1950 the Puerto Rican Senate consisted of seventeen senators from the Popular Democratic Party (Partido Popular Democrático, PPD) and two senators from the Republican Statehood Party (Partido Estadista Republicano, PER). As leader of the PPD and governor of Puerto Rico, Luis Muñoz Marín had an iron hold on Puerto Rican politics, power, and patronage.

Although the PPD and PER held every seat in the legislature, other political parties vied for influence on the island:

Nationalist Party of Puerto Rico	Partido Nacionalista de Puerto Rico	PNP
Puerto Rican Communist Party	Partido Comunista de Puerto Rico	PCP
Socialist Party	Partido Socialista de Puerto Rico	PSPR
Puerto Rican Republican Union	Unión Republicana	PUR

The Tripartite Party (Socialist-Republican-Liberal) had some success in the early 1940s but disappeared after the PPD landslide of 1944. The Union Party, founded by Luis Muñoz Marín's own father in 1904, had been a party of great subtlety and expedience. Every time a new governor arrived on the island, its members threatened a revolution and demanded Puerto Rican independence—then withdrew their demands after securing government contracts and political appointments. By 1950 this party had evolved into the Republican Union. The Nationalist, Socialist, and Communist parties were highly marginalized, particularly after the 1947 enactment of the Gag Law, which enabled Governor Muñoz Marín to brand them all as "subversive" and prompted the FBI to create *carpetas* on all their members. As of June 2012, Puerto Rico had six registered electoral parties:

Popular Democratic Party	Partido Popular Democrático	PPD
New Progressive Party	Partido Nuevo Progresista	PNP
Independence Party	Partido Independentista	PIP
Puerto Ricans for Puerto Rico Party	Partido Puertorriqueños por Puerto Rico	PPR
Sovereign Union Movement	Movimiento Unión Soberanista	MUS
Working People's Party	Partido del Pueblo Trabajador	PPT

Currently in Puerto Rico, the PPD remains the dominant party. The governor, the majority of both the Senate and the House of Representatives, and more than half of the island's mayors are all PPD.

14. Mark Harrison, *The Economics of World War II: Six Great Powers in International Comparison* (Cambridge: Cambridge University Press, 1998), 15, 17, 81–117.

CHAPTER 18: REVOLUTION

1. The October 30 revolution has been dubbed a "Nationalist revolt" and the "Jayuya uprising." However, given the repressive machinery of the FBI and Insular Police, the use of secret police dossiers against tens of thousands of Puerto Ricans, the bombing of two towns in broad daylight by the US military, the deployment of 5,000 US National Guardsmen into those towns, the arrest of 3,000 Puerto Ricans within a matter of days, the use of Public Law 53 (the Gag Law) to stifle all forms of patriotic expression on the island, and armed conflict in eight towns, the events of October 30 to November 3, 1950, emerge as a revolutionary expression of underlying and widely held sentiment in Puerto Rico. The term "revolution" is thus an appropriate designation for the October 30 uprising.

2. "Motín en el Presidio," *El Imparcial*, October 29, 1950, 1. Correa Cotto was killed in a gunfight with the Insular Police in 1952. However, the testimony of two prisoners who participated in the escape from El Oso Blanco prison, Otilio Robles Ventura and Gregorio Lebron Martinez, confirmed that the mass escape was planned and timed jointly by the Nationalists and the Oso Blanco prisoners. See *El Imparcial*, November 3, 1950, 7; *El Imparcial*, November 7, 1950, 3; Miñi Seijo Bruno, *La Insurrección Nacionalista en Puerto Rico, 1950* (Río Piedras, PR: Editorial Edil, 1989), 78–86.

3. "Motín en el Presidio," *El Imparcial*, October 29, 1950, 3.

4. Only five feet, six inches tall, weighing 135 pounds, with cold eyes and scars across his lips, eyebrow, and forehead, Correa Cotto was a career criminal serving a life sentence for multiple murders. After breaking out of prison in October 1950, he killed ten more people and led the police on a wild chase through the entire island. He became a legendary figure—a cross between John Dillinger and Kilroy—who was "seen" in almost every town in Puerto Rico; some theorists had him in New York, Chicago, and even Korea, disguised as a Borinqueneer. Four Florida policemen, including J. A. Youell, assistant chief of the Miami Police, flew down with specially trained bloodhounds to join the island-wide man hunt. Cotto was finally caught and killed near Ponce on May 16, 1952. See "Puerto Rican 'Dillinger' Bad Man Has Island on Deadly Man Hunt," *Times-News* (Hendersonville, NC), March 19, 1952, 29.

5. *El Imparcial*, October 30, 1950, 3, 50.

6. José Trías Monge, who became the attorney general of Puerto Rico the following year, was present during this conversation. In 1980, Monge discussed it in a private forum at Yale Law School.

7. Bruno, *La Insurrección Nacionalista*, 86–93.

8. *El Mundo*, October 31, 1950, 10; *El Imparcial*, October 31, 1950, 30.

9. Testimony of Ramón Pedrosa, in Bruno, *La Insurrección Nacionalista*, 92–93.

10. This story of Guillermo González Ubides patrolling the field of battle after his death was passed down by farmers and Nationalists.

11. Bruno, *La Insurrección Nacionalista*, 122; *El Mundo*, October 31, 1950, 4.

12. Heriberto Marín Torres, *Eran Ellos* (Río Piedras, PR: Ediciones Ciba, 2000), 63.

13. Testimony of Elio Torresola, in Bruno, *La Insurrección Nacionalista*, 121.

14. *El Mundo*, October 31, 1950, 4.

15. *El Mundo*, November 12, 1950; *El Vocero*, March 3, 1979, 6.

16. Marín Torres, *Eran Ellos*, 40.

17. Ibid., 64; Bruno, *La Insurrección Nacionalista*, 123–126.

18. "Aviación Bombardea en Utuado," *El Imparcial*, November 1, 1950, 1. The United States bombed both Jayuya and Utuado in broad daylight. The number of planes used were reported as ten in Jayuya and four in Utuado. Marisa Rosado, *Pedro Albizu Campos: Las Llamas de la Aurora*, 5th ed. (San Juan: Ediciones Puerto, 2008), 353–354. See also Bruno, *La Insurrección Nacionalista*, 78–86; Laura Meneses de Albizu Campos,

Albizu Campos y la Independencia de Puerto Rico (Hato Rey, PR: Publicaciones Puertorriqueñas, 2007), 82. Despite the presence of Associated Press and United Press International reporters on the island, this extraordinary event was barely reported on the US mainland. No contemporaneous reports of this bombing were found in any of the major papers (e.g., *New York Times, Washington Post, Wall Street Journal, Boston Globe, Los Angeles Times, Chicago Tribune, Denver Post*).

19. Testimony of Elio Torresola, in Bruno, *La Insurrección Nacionalista*, 126.

20. Pedro Aponte Vázquez, *El Ataque Nacionalista a la Fortaleza* (San Juan: Publicaciones René, 2014), 7.

21. FBI Files, Subject: Nationalist Party of Puerto Rico, File Number SJ 100-3, Vol. 23, 128–129.

22. Testimony of José Angel Medina Figueroa, in Bruno, *La Insurrección Nacionalista*, 140–141.

23. Testimony of Angel Colón Feliciano, in Bruno, *La Insurrección Nacionalista*, 143–144.

24. Ibid., 144–145.

25. Ibid., 145.

26. Ibid., 145–146.

27. Ibid., 144.

28. Ibid., 144–145.

29. Testimony of José Angel Medina Figueroa, in Bruno, *La Insurrección Nacionalista*, 147–148.

30. Ibid., 146.

31. Testimony of Angel Colón Feliciano, in Bruno, *La Insurrección Nacionalista*, 145.

32. Testimony of Pedro Matos Matos, in Bruno, *La Insurrección Nacionalista*, 150–151.

33. "Aviación Bombardea en Utuado," 1, 2, 35. See also Rosado, *Pedro Albizu Campos*, 353–354; Bruno, *La Insurrección Nacionalista*, 78–86; Albizu Campos, *Albizu Campos y la Independencia*, 82.

34. José Martínez Valentín, *La Presencia de la Policia en la Historia de Puerto Rico: 1898–1995* (San Juan: Producciones Luigi, 1995), 180.

35. Testimony of Ismael Díaz Matos, in Bruno, *La Insurrección Nacionalista*, 110.

36. "Aviación Bombardea en Utuado," *El Imparcial*, November 1, 1950, 1; *El Imparcial*, November 5, 1950, 4; *El Imparcial*, November 7, 1950, 2, 31; *El Mundo*, November 2, 1950, 3.

37. Testimony of Amado Eulogio, in Bruno, *La Insurrección Nacionalista*, 197.

38. Testimony of Irvin Flores, in Bruno, *La Insurrección Nacionalista*, 198.

39. Testimony of Juan Medina Acosta, in Bruno, *La Insurrección Nacionalista*, 95.

40. *El Mundo*, October 31, 1950, 7.

41. Testimony of Ramón Pedrosa, in Bruno, *La Insurrección Nacionalista*, 92.

42. *El Imparcial*, November 11, 1950, 7, 38.

43. *El Imparcial,* November 18, 1950, 35; November 19, 1950, 2, 34.

44. Testimony of José Antonio Negrón, in Bruno, *La Insurrección Nacionalista*, 220.

45. FBI Files, Subject: Nationalist Party of Puerto Rico, File Number SJ 100-3, Vol. 23, 128–129.

46. Testimony of Angel Colón Feliciano, in Bruno, *La Insurrección Nacionalista*, 141. The infiltration and betrayal of the Nationalist Party is evident from the dozens of FBI reports based on information provided by confidential informants from within the party. It is also evident from the speed and surgical precision with which the Insular Police discovered all the following weapons caches during and immediately after the revolt: a cave in Sitio Viafara (Arecibo), the woods near Barrio Cedro Abajo (Naranjito), a sugar cane field in Barrio Miraflores (Arecibo), three farms (Naranjito, Dorado, and Cayey), a gasoline station (Naranjito), and six homes in five towns (Ponce, Utuado, Arecibo, Naranjito, Mayagüez). FBI Files, Subject: Nationalist Party of Puerto Rico, File Number SJ 100-3, Vol. 23, 149.

47. Bruno, *La Insurrección Nacionalista*, 80, 87.

48. Vázquez, *El Ataque Nacionalista a la Fortaleza*, 115, 130, 132–134; Rosado, *Pedro Albizu Campos*, 354–356; Carlos Nieves Rivera, "Seis Nacionalistas Intentaron Tomar por Asalto la Fortaleza," *El Mundo*, October 31, 1950.

49. According to the testimony of Gregorio Hernández, the only Nationalist who survived the attack on La Fortaleza, all the Nationalists in the car were aware that they were on a suicide mission with very little chance of escaping alive. This was especially true for Raimundo Diaz Pacheco. According to Hernández, as they drove through Old San Juan toward La Fortaleza, Raimundo told everyone in the car to look at all the soldiers and snipers on the rooftops and to prepare "to be massacred." Vázquez, *El Ataque Nacionalista a la Fortaleza*, 115, 130, 132–134.

50. Vázquez, *El Ataque Nacionalista a la Fortaleza*, 71–72; Stephen Hunter and John Bainbridge Jr., *American Gunfight: The Plot to Kill Harry Truman—and the Shoot-Out That Stopped It* (New York: Simon & Schuster, 2005), 32.

51. *El Mundo*, October 31, 1950, 1, 10; Vázquez, *El Ataque Nacionalista a la Fortaleza*, 7.

52. Vázquez, *El Ataque Nacionalista a la Fortaleza*, 77–111 (interview with Gregorio "Goyito" Hernández Rivera).

53. Hunter and Bainbridge, *American Gunfight*, 31.

54. FBI director J. Edgar Hoover, "Joint Report to the National Security Council Regarding the Recent Outbreak of Violence by Puerto Rican Nationalists," US Department of Justice, Washington DC, January 18, 1951.

55. The conversation between Governor Muñoz Marín and General Sibert was reported by the attorney general of Puerto Rico, Vicente Géigel Polanco. Attorney General Polanco was in the governor's mansion with Muñoz Marín at the precise time of both the attack and the subsequent conversation with General Sibert. See Cesar

Andréu Iglesias and Samuel A. Aponte, "Vicente Géigel Polanco Revela Incidentes de Su Relación con Luis Muñoz Marín," *La Hora*, April 26, 1972. The phone call to General Sibert was reported in Rosado, *Pedro Albizu Campos*, 356–357. It was also reported in the FBI's *Report to the National Security Council Regarding the Recent Outbreak of Violence by Puerto Rican Nationalists*, US Department of Justice, January 18, 1951.

56. Efraín Lopez Corchado was one of the fugitives from El Oso Blanco prison. According to Insular Police sources, he had an escape plan for Albizu: some other fugitives had commandeered a boat in San Juan Harbor and were waiting for Albizu to break free. See Archives of the Puerto Rico Department of Justice, Office of the Attorney General, Nationalist Series, Box 5.

57. "Aviación Bombardea en Utuado," *El Imparcial*, November 1, 1950, 1, 3; *El Imparcial*, November 2, 1950, 2–3, 34–35; *El Mundo*, October 31, 1950, 1, 10; *El Mundo*, November 2, 1950, 2–3.

58. Hunter and Bainbridge, *American Gunfight*, 267; Rosado, *Pedro Albizu Campos*, 360.

59. Testimony of Alvaro Rivera Walker in Rosado, *Pedro Albizu Campos*, 361–365; Bruno, *La Insurrección Nacionalista*, 170–172; Hunter and Bainbridge, *American Gunfight*, 269.

60. Testimony of Alvaro Rivera Walker, in Bruno, *La Insurrección Nacionalista*, 170–172. See also Rosado, *Pedro Albizu Campos*, 361–365; Hunter and Bainbridge, *American Gunfight*, 34, 269. The local and US authorities were aware of the symbolic value of Albizu's death and did not want to make a martyr of him. In addition, the siege of Albizu's home was occurring in the capital city of the entire island, just a few hundred feet from the governor's mansion, with a great deal of newspaper and radio attention. This accounts for the restraint shown by the National Guard, FBI, and Insular Police. Even as they bombed the towns of Utuado and Jayuya and machine-gunned Nationalist prisoners in Utuado, they treated Albizu with kid gloves (relatively speaking). Rather than demolish the entire building, they lay siege to it for three days.

61. *El Mundo*, October 31, 1950, 1, 10; *El Imparcial*, November 1, 1950, 1, 3. See also Hunter and Bainbridge, *American Gunfight*, 267; Rosado, *Pedro Albizu Campos*, 358–361.

62. Juan Antonio Ocasio Rivera, "Puerto Rico's October Revolution," *New York Latino Journal*, November 3, 2006.

63. Testimony of Alvaro Rivera Walker, in Bruno, *La Insurrección Nacionalista*, 170–172. I had the opportunity to speak with Rivera Walker at his restaurant in Canovanas, Puerto Rico, in 1974. He remembered the last hours before their arrest as Albizu's personal Gethsemane. He said that Albizu, who had already spent seven years in a federal penitentiary, knew that he was about to be arrested and sentenced to many more years in prison. He was trying to find personal strength to face this arrest and the ordeal that would follow.

64. "Albizu en La Princesa," *El Imparcial*, November 13, 1950, 1; Federico Ribes Tovar, *Albizu Campos: Puerto Rican Revolutionary* (New York: Plus Ultra Publishers, 1971), 112; Rosado, *Pedro Albizu Campos*, 365; Bruno, *La Insurrección Nacionalista*, 171–172.

65. "Assassin Slain Another Shot at Truman's Door Puerto Rican Terrorists Kill Guard, Wound 2; President Glimpses Battle's End from Window," *Washington Post*, November 2, 1950, 1.

66. "2 Die, 3 Shot as Pair Try to Kill Truman," *New York Daily News*, November 2, 1950, 1.

67. "2 Puerto Rican Revolutionists Try to Kill Truman at Home," *Baltimore Sun*, November 2, 1950, 1.

68. In addition to the three above-referenced articles from the *Washington Post*, *Baltimore Sun*, and *New York Daily News*, see "Truman's Guards Shoot 2!," *New York Journal American*, November 2, 1950; "Gunmen Try to Kill Truman: Pair, Pistols Blazing, Rush Mansion Guards," *Long Beach Press-Telegram*; "Two Gunmen Shot in Effort to Kill Truman," *Tacoma New Tribune*, November 2, 1950; "Two Shot Trying to Kill Truman," *Times Picayune*, November 2, 1950.

69. "Blair House: The Afternoon Quiet Erupted on Pennsylvania Avenue," Associated Press, November 2, 1950.

70. "Assassin Slain, Another Shot at Truman's Door," *Washington Post*, November 2, 1950, 1.

71. "Two Shot Trying to Kill Truman," *Times Picayune,* November 2, 1950, 1.

72. "Muñoz Certain Reds Back Plot," *Times Picayune,* November 2, 1950. Muñoz Marín also cabled US Secretary of the Interior Oscar L. Chapman about a Nationalist collaboration with "Communists on the island." See Rosado, *Pedro Albizu Campos*, 357.

73. "The Truman Assassination Attempt," *New Republic*, November 13, 1950.

74. "Puerto Rico Revolt Endangers Truman," *Life*, November 13, 1950.

75. "The Presidency," *Time*, November 13, 1950.

76. Hunter and Bainbridge, *American Gunfight*, 86.

CHAPTER 19: SALÓN BORICUA

1. As they had around Albizu Campos's house at 156 Calle Sol, the Insular Police broke the traffic lights around the Salón Boricua. This provided them an excuse to detain any motorists in the vicinity and to question, ticket, harass, or arrest them. The lights were fixed after the October 1950 revolt.

2. Vidal Santiago Díaz shared these thoughts and recollections with other Nationalists, while he was imprisoned with them in La Princesa.

3. Marisa Rosado, *Pedro Albizu Campos: Las Llamas de la Aurora*, 5th ed. (San Juan: Ediciones Puerto, 2008), 356–357.

4. Ramon Medina Ramirez, *El Movimiento Libertador en la Historia de Puerto Rico* (Santurce, PR: Imprenta Borinquen, 1958), 5:313.

5. *El Imparcial*, November 2, 1950, 2, 35.

6. Vidal Santiago Díaz discussed the radio shows, sponsors, and commercial spots with his fellow Nationalist prisoners.

7. Miñi Seijo Bruno, *La Insurrección Nacionalista en Puerto Rico, 1950* (Río Piedras, PR: Editorial Edil, 1989), 173.

8. Vidal Santiago Díaz particularly remembered the irony of "If I Knew You Were Comin' I'd've Baked a Cake" in view of his situation. As he related to the Nationalist prisoners at La Princesa, he felt that the cake in the song represented the whole island of Puerto Rico. Interestingly, director Francis Ford Coppola engaged this same symbolism in the film *The Godfather: Part II* in the scene where Hyman Roth cuts a birthday cake in the shape of Cuba and shares it with his gangster friends.

9. Rosado, *Pedro Albizu Campos*, 358.

10. *El Mundo*, October 31, 1950. The sequence of events at the battle of Salón Boricua, the Albizu Campos radio speeches, the exclamations, and Vidal Santiago Díaz's singing and his colloquy with Luis "El Bibí Marrero" were additionally confirmed in a 2004 interview with journalist Miguel Ángel Álvarez, who went on to a successful career as a radio and TV actor. He also directed four feature films for Columbia Pictures, including the infamous *Natas es Satan* in 1977.

11. Medina Ramirez, *El Movimiento Libertador*, 313; *El Imparcial*, November 2, 1950, 2, 35. This was additionally confirmed in a 2004 interview with journalist Miguel Ángel Álvarez and a separate interview with Luis "El Bibí" Marrero.

12. *El Mundo*, October 31, 1950. This was additionally confirmed personally by Luis "El Bibí" Marrero and by journalist Miguel Ángel Álvarez.

13. Vidal Santiago Díaz shared these thoughts and recollections with other Nationalists while imprisoned with them in La Princesa. See also Heriberto Marín Torres, *Eran Ellos* (Río Piedras, PR: Ediciones Ciba, 2000).

14. Journalists Miguel Ángel Álvarez and Luis "El Bibí" Marrero overheard this exchange and reported it live via radio, as eyewitnesses. The author interviewed both Álvarez and Marrero, who provided consistent recollections of the conversation. It was also reported by Vidal Santiago Díaz to the other Nationalist prisoners at La Princesa. The author interviewed several of these prisoners, who confirmed the conversation.

15. *El Imparcial*, November 2, 1950, 2, 35; *El Mundo*, October 31, 1950; additionally confirmed by journalist Miguel Ángel Álvarez.

16. Miguel Angel Alvarez and Luis "El Bibí" Marrero were among the reporters who heard these speeches. The radio stations maintained tape-recorded archives of every speech. The FBI notified the radio stations that these recordings were not to be destroyed, as they might be required as evidence in possible court proceedings (that is, to document Public Law 53 violations by Albizu Campos).

17. Albizu Campos's speech in Manatí, Puerto Rico, on June 11, 1948, recorded and transcribed by the FBI. The speech was also broadcast over WITA and WNEL (San

Juan), WCMN (Arecibo), and other stations in Ponce and Mayagüez. See FBI Files, Subject: Pedro Albizu Campos, File Number 105-11898, Section XII. A complete list of Albizu Campos's speeches and press conferences as recorded and transcribed by the FBI is available at ibid., ii–iii (Table of Contents). This list contains over forty speeches and press events from December 15, 1947, to March 2, 1954.

18. Albizu Campos's speech in Río Piedras, Puerto Rico, on November 19, 1948, recorded and transcribed by the FBI. See FBI Files, Subject: Pedro Albizu Campos, File Number 105-11898, Section XII. According to this FBI report, the speech "was radio broadcast and recordings of which are retained in the files of the Insular Police of Puerto Rico" (15nb7c).

19. Albizu Campos's speech in Manatí, Puerto Rico, on June 11, 1948, recorded and transcribed by the FBI. The speech was also broadcast over WITA and WNEL (San Juan), WCMN (Arecibo), and other stations in Ponce and Mayagüez. See ibid.

20. Albizu Campos's speech in Santurce, Puerto Rico, on April 16, 1948, recorded and transcribed by the FBI. The speech was also radio broadcast over WITA (San Juan). See ibid.

21. Albizu Campos's speech in Ponce, Puerto Rico, on July 25, 1948. This speech was delivered on the fiftieth anniversary of the US occupation of Puerto Rico and, in addition to being recorded and transcribed by the FBI, was broadcast over WPRP (Ponce), WCMN (Arecibo), and WPBP (Mayagüez). See ibid.

22. Albizu Campos's speech in Ponce, Puerto Rico, on March 21, 1949, recorded and transcribed by the FBI. The speech was also radio broadcast over WPRP (Ponce), WCMN (Arecibo), and WITA (San Juan). See ibid.

23. This spontaneous *aguinaldo* by Vidal Santiago Díaz was confirmed in a 2004 interview with journalist Miguel Ángel Álvarez.

24. Vidal Santiago Díaz recounted these last moments at Salón Boricua to two Nationalists imprisoned with him in La Princesa.

25. Journalists Miguel Angel Alvarez and Luis "El Bibí" Marrero reported the soldier's words. *El Imparcial*, November 2, 1950, 2, 35; Medina Ramirez, *El Movimiento Libertador*, 313.

26. In *Albizu Campos: Puerto Rican Revolutionary* (New York: Plus Ultra Publishers, 1971), Federico Ribes Tovar summarized the battle of Salón Boricua as follows:

> It was perhaps the most colorful and dramatic episode of the Nationalist uprising . . . [with Vidal Santiago Díaz] holding at bay, singlehanded and from the inside of his barber shop, a whole detachment of police and soldiers of the National Guard . . . who had him completely surrounded and were firing at him from every angle with all manner of automatic weapons. . . .
>
> The heroic barber waged a tremendous battle, like a caged tiger, refusing to give in. . . . [L]ike a brave bull goaded to renewed savagery, and apparently unaware of the overwhelming odds he faced, [Vidal] fired ceaselessly at his attackers from the windows and the very doorway of his shop. . . .

The whole island followed the drama of Vidal Santiago's capture, which was broadcast direct over the radio. (108–109)

27. Juan Emilio Viguié's reputation as a newsreel photographer, his press pass, and his respectful demeanor toward the FBI cameraman usually averted problems and deflected suspicion. For the battle of Salón Boricua he took some extra precautions: he filmed it from a remote rooftop using a long zoom lens. See also chapter 13 of this book, notes 18 and 19.

CHAPTER 20: *LA CAJA DE CHINCHAS*

1. "Arrestos en Masa," *El Imparcial*, November 3, 1950, 1–5. See also Letter to David Helfeld, Esq., Counsel to Human Rights Commission, "Information on Discrimination and Persecution for Political Purposes," 1989, 49, as cited in Marisa Rosado, *Pedro Albizu Campos: Las Llamas de la Aurora*, 5th ed. (San Juan: Ediciones Puerto, 2008), 364.

2. "Intentan Quemar Edificios Utuado," *El Mundo*, November 1, 1950. See also Heriberto Marín Torres, *Eran Ellos* (Río Piedras, PR: Ediciones Ciba, 2000), 109–110.

3. James Fowler, "Diez Poblaciones Están Envueltas en Rebelión," Associated Press, November 1, 1950.

4. Ruth Mary Reynolds was an American educator and civil rights activist who developed a profound commitment to Puerto Rican independence. In 1943, while performing social work with children in El Barrio (East Harlem), she met Pedro Albizu Campos, who was interned in Columbus Hospital. Shortly afterward, Reynolds cofounded and became executive secretary of the American League for Puerto Rican Independence. In 1946 and 1947, she appeared before the US Congress and the United Nations to speak on behalf of that cause. In 1948, Reynolds wrote in *Campus in Bondage* (New York: Research Foundation of the City of New York, 1989),

> Several hundred policemen surrounded the environs and inhabited the grounds of the University of Puerto Rico on April 15, 1948, and did not retire until early November. During the intervening months they used—in addition to the influence of their own presence—tear gas, clubbing, and mass arrests to overcome the University Crusade, a student movement protesting against the University Administration. After we learned that on September 23, 1948, the passage of several hundred students had been blocked by police[,] . . . that the police proceeded to club these students when they refused to disband, and that two of them had been beaten unconscious and had to be hospitalized. . . . I was dispatched to Puerto Rico to carry out the investigation. (1)

After a four-month investigation and hundreds of interviews, Reynolds concluded that the police violence was politically based, with the sole purpose of preventing both the Nationalist Party of Puerto Rico from having any contact with the college students and Albizu Campos from speaking anywhere on campus.

At that point, she decided to stay in Puerto Rico and write a book about it: *Campus in Bondage*. The book was ready for publication in 1950, when on October 31 of that year, she was arrested for violation of Gag Law 53 and for conspiracy to overthrow the US government. In a letter to her sister Helen, Reynolds described this arrest:

> I was asleep in my bed at 2 a.m. . . . And then, more than forty policemen and National Guardsmen, armed with rifles, machine guns, and revolvers, came to the house where I was living alone. . . . With more machine guns pointed at me than I had ever before seen in one place, I did not resist. After stealing all my books and papers, they told me that they had no paper, but that they did have orders to arrest me.

Reynolds was released in June 1952, after nineteen months in prison. The manuscript of *Campus in Bondage* had mysteriously "disappeared," but she wisely had kept another copy of it in New York.

Despite the government harassment and imprisonment, Reynolds never abandoned her principles. She presented a petition to the UN General Assembly in late 1952 and again testified before the UN Committee on Decolonization in 1977 on behalf of Puerto Rican independence. She continued to work, speak, and organize on the issue for the rest of her life. *Campus in Bondage* was finally published in 1989, the year of her death. The Ruth Reynolds Papers were preserved in the Archives of the Puerto Rican Diaspora, Centro de Estudios Puertorriqueños, Hunter College, City University of New York.

5. Margaret Pour, "Puerto Rican Women Nationalists vs. US Colonialism: An Exploration of Their Conditions and Struggles in Jail and Court," *Chicago-Kent Law Review* 87, no. 2 (2012): 467–468.

6. Rosado, *Pedro Albizu Campos*, 364–365.

7. Reece B. Bothwell, *Cien Años de Lucha Política*, 5 vols. (San Juan: Editorial Universitaria), 503. See also Rosado, *Pedro Albizu Campos*, 363; FBI Files, Subject: Nationalist Party of Puerto Rico, File Number SJ 100-3, Vol. 3, Section I, 7–8.

8. Rosado, *Pedro Albizu Campos*, 364.

9. Ibid.

10. Laura Meneses de Albizu Campos, *Albizu Campos y la Independencia de Puerto Rico* (Hato Rey, PR: Publicaciones Puertorriqueñas, 2007), 86.

11. Marín Torres, *Eran Ellos*, 13–34.

12. Ibid., 20–23.

13. Ibid., 13.

14. Ibid., 14–15.

15. Ibid., 29–31.

16. FBI Files, Subject: Luis Muñoz Marín, File Number 100-HQ-5745, Section III, 294.

17. Ibid., 106.

18. Ibid., 125.

19. Ibid., 122–123.

20. Ibid., 72.

21. Ibid., 73.

CHAPTER 21: ATOMIC LYNCHING

1. Heriberto Marín Torres, *Eran Ellos* (Rio Piedras, PR: Ediciones Ciba, 2000), 49.

2. Ibid.

3. Laura Meneses de Albizu Campos, *Albizu Campos y la Independencia de Puerto Rico* (San Juan: Edición del Partido Nacionalista de Puerto Rico, 2007), 126–128.

4. Marisa Rosado, *Pedro Albizu Campos: Las Llamas de la Aurora*, 5th ed. (San Juan: Ediciones Puerto, 2008), 372–374.

5. Pedro Aponte Vázquez, *¡Yo Acuso! Y lo que Pasó Despues* (Bayamón, PR: Movimiento Ecuménico Nacional de PR, 1985), 41.

6. FBI Files, Subject: Pedro Albizu Campos, File Number 105-11898, Section XI, 83.

7. Rosado, *Pedro Albizu Campos*, 374.

8. FBI Files, Subject: Pedro Albizu Campos, File Number 105-11898, Section VIII, 51.

9. Ibid., 50–51.

10. Ibid., 51.

11. Ibid., 46–51.

12. FBI Files, Subject: Pedro Albizu Campos, File Number 105-11898, Section X, 9.

13. Rosado, *Pedro Albizu Campos*, 386.

14. FBI Files, Subject: Pedro Albizu Campos, File Number 105-11898, Section X, 30.

15. Laura Meneses de Albizu Campos, *Albizu Campos y la Independencia de Puerto Rico* (Hato Rey, PR: Publicaciones Puertorriqueñas, 2007), 126–128.

16. "Albizu Campos Alleges That They Are Directing Light Rays at Him," *El Mundo*, February 2, 1952.

17. *El Mundo*, May 3, 1953.

18. "Albizu Told the Story of Atomic Torture to the Press," *El Mundo*, October 1, 1953.

19. *El Imparcial*, May 12, 1953.

20. "Linchamiento Atomico de un Martir de la Libertad," *Verdad*, February 1953, 1, 24–27.

21. *Correo Indoamericano de Mexico*, August 15, 1953.

22. Alfonso Granados, *Tiempo en Cuba*, February 6, 1953. See also FBI Files, Subject: Pedro Albizu Campos, File Number 105-11898, Section VIII, 67.

23. Rosado, *Pedro Albizu Campos*, 383–386.

24. Vicente Cubillas Jr., "El Martírio de Pedro Albizu Campos," *Bohemia*, October 18, 1953. A woman named Herminia Rijos also visited Albizu. She said he presented a most unusual sight. Lying on a cot, surrounded on all sides by cold bottles of water, the man was covered in a dripping bedsheet, his body wrapped in an assortment of cold, wet towels. He draped two more towels around his head, like an Arab sheik.

Asking her forgiveness, he explained that he needed a moment to recover from the latest attack. As she sat on a small chair and waited, she saw that the entire floor was covered with water. An empty tube of Jergens lotion floated around the room.

A few minutes later the man smiled and said he wanted to show her something. He removed several towels from his body and, with great effort, sat up and faced her. His thighs were burned. His calves and feet were swollen red balloons. She touched one of the calves: it was hard as a rock and hot, as if the leg had a fever. He showed her the heels of his feet and the palms of his hands: all were raw and peeling, as if with second-degree burns. He pulled up his shirt. Two hard lumps jutted out of his stomach. His chest and back were striped, as if someone had flipped him over on a grill. His head was swollen. She reached out and touched his forehead: it was boiling. In every way, from every angle, he looked like he was burning alive.

The man told her he was being subjected to constant "atomic rays" throughout the day, with the greatest concentration in the afternoon. He could only protect himself by wrapping himself in wet towels, smothering his skin in cold cream, and moving continuously, as much as possible, around the tiny space. (Also see Marín Torres, *Eran Ellos*, Appendix B, 93.)

It all sounded fantastic to her. She promised to visit him again, but as she walked out, she noticed that her tongue felt thick and her eyes were irritated. It was enough to dissuade her from returning. (Declaration of Herminia Rijos to Ruth Reynolds, Herbert H. Lehman College Archives, Partido Nacionalista Records, 1950–1962, Box 1.)

Herminia Rijos was not a Nationalist. She was a family friend who visited Albizu in La Princesa and in his home in late 1953 (when he was briefly pardoned due to his failing health before being rearrested in 1954). Rijos repeated this testimony during an on-camera interview with reporter Sylvia Gomez on Channel 2 San Juan. The interview appeared in a documentary, aired in August 1985, titled *Albizu Campos: Rompiendo el Silencio* (*Albizu Campos: Breaking the Silence*).

25. FBI Files, Subject: Pedro Albizu Campos, File Number 105-11898, Section VIII, 66–67.

26. Ibid., Section X, 112, 113. See also ibid., Section XI, 25.

27. Rosado, *Pedro Albizu Campos*, 378.

28. FBI Files, Subject: Pedro Albizu Campos, File Number 105-11898, Section X, 112, 113.

29. Rosado, *Pedro Albizu Campos*, 378. The signatories to the letter were Gaspar Mortillaro, R. E. Montes Bradley, and Dardo Cúneo (Argentina); Mauricio Magdaleno, Raúl Cordero Amador, José Vasconcelos, Salvador Azuela, and Gonzalo Chirino Rangel (Mexico); Ofelia Machado Bonet, Carlos Sabat Ercasty, and Atilio Giacosa Bertoli (Uruguay); Rosalía de Segura and Isbert Montenegro (Costa Rica); Juan José Orozco Posadas, Marco Antonio Villamar, Alberto Velázquez, Enrique Chaleleu Gálvez, David Vela, and Manuel Galich (Guatemala); Ernesto Alvarado García (Honduras); Justo Pastor Benítez (Paraguay); Miguel Gutiérrez Corrales (Nicaragua); Manuel I. Mesa

Rodríguez, Rafael Argilapos, Lilia Castro, and Emilio Roig de Leuchsenring (Cuba); Jouvert Douge (Haiti); and Augusto Arias (Ecuador).

30. Laura Meneses de Albizu Campos, "Pedro Albizu Campos as I Knew Him," *El Día*, October 2, 1957. See also Federico Ribes Tovar, *Albizu Campos: Puerto Rican Revolutionary* (New York: Plus Ultra Publishers, 1971), 139; Albizu Campos, *Albizu Campos y la Independencia*, 126–128. The FBI took a serious interest in Dr. Daumy's findings and reported them verbatim in FBI Files, Subject: Pedro Albizu Campos, File Number 105-11898, Section XVI, 33.

31. Rosado, *Pedro Albizu Campos*, 398.

32. See Vázquez, *¡Yo Acuso!*, 42–43. See also Juan Gonzalez, "A Lonely Voice Finally Heard," *New York Daily News*, January 12, 1994. The pardon of Albizu Campos ended on March 6, 1954, when Lolita Lebrón led three other Nationalists into the gallery of the US Congress and opened fire on several congressmen. See Rosado, *Pedro Albizu Campos*, 397–398.

33. FBI Files, Subject: Pedro Albizu Campos, File Number 105-11898, Section XI, 48, 71. See also ibid., Section X, 70, 103, 123, 133.

34. Vázquez, *Yo Acuso!*, 37–54. See also Gonzalez, "A Lonely Voice Finally Heard"; Rosado, *Pedro Albizu Campos*, 374–386.

35. FBI Files, Subject: Pedro Albizu Campos, File Number 105-11898, Section XI, 25.

36. Ibid., Section X, 124.

37. Ibid., Section XVI, 33.

38. Ibid., Section XV, 2. See also Albizu Campos, *Albizu Campos y la Independencia*, 123–124. Albizu's wife, Laura, claims that the period of medical inattention was longer and that the prison authorities waited five days before transferring her husband to Presbyterian Hospital in Santurce, Puerto Rico.

39. Albizu Campos, *Albizu Campos y la Independencia*, 124.

Chapter 22: Weird Science in Puerto Rico

1. Subcommittee on Energy Conservation and Power, US House of Representatives, "American Nuclear Guinea Pigs: Three Decades of Radiation Experiments on U.S. Citizens," 99th Cong., 2nd Sess., November 1986, 1–17.

2. Ibid.

3. Philip J. Hilts, "U.S. to Settle for $4.8 Million in Suits on Radiation Testing," *New York Times*, November 20, 1996.

4. "Count of Subjects in Radiation Experiments Is Raised to 16,000," *New York Times*, August 20, 1995.

5. Keith Schneider, "Secret Nuclear Research on People Comes to Light," *New York Times*, December 17, 1993.

6. Matthew L. Wald, "Rule Adopted to Prohibit Secret Tests on Humans," *New York Times*, March 29, 1997.

7. Ibid.

8. Hilts, "U.S. to Settle for $4.8 Million."

9. FBI Files, Subject: Pedro Albizu Campos, File Number 105-11898, Section XV, 2. See also Laura Meneses de Albizu Campos, *Albizu Campos y la Independencia de Puerto Rico* (Hato Rey, PR: Publicaciones Puertorriqueñas, 2007).

10. Pedro Aponte Vázquez, ¡*Yo Acuso! Y lo que Pasó Despues* (Bayamón, PR: Movimiento Ecuménico Nacional de PR, 1985), 41.

11. Ibid., 103.

12. Ibid., 109.

13. Ibid., 106.

14. Ibid., 117, 121.

15. Ibid., 118–119.

16. Ibid., 120.

17. "U.P.R. Prueba Abono con Materia Radioactiva," *El Imparcial*, October 7, 1953. Later that month, on October 23, *El Imparcial* reported about prisoners in Chicago who were used in a radiation experiment.

18. Eileen Welsome, *The Plutonium Files* (New York: Random House, 1999), 208, 357–361.

19. Ibid., 359.

20. US Department of Defense, *Report on Search for Human Radiation Experiment Records, 1944–1994* (Springfield, VA: Department of Commerce, Technology Administration, National Technical Information Service, 1997), 1:61. See especially Cornelius Rhoads, director, *Study of Post-Irradiation Syndrome on Humans* (Sloan-Kettering Contract, Contract DA-49-07), 125.

21. Ibid., appendix 1, 1:211.

22. "Service for Dr. Rhoads: Memorial for Sloan-Kettering Director Here Tomorrow," *New York Times*, August 24, 1959.

23. US Department of Defense, *Report on Search for Human Radiation Experiment Records, 1944–1994*, 1:211. As Director of the Sloan-Kettering Institute for Cancer Research, and with his name appearing in all the contract documentation, Dr. Cornelius Rhoads had a professional responsibility for the protocols and results of this "Post-Irradiation Syndrome" study. However, a summary report for this project seems a model of deceit and denial.

The report stated it was funded by US Army contracts DA-49-007-MD-533 and DA-49-007-MD-669, and then an Armed Forces Special Weapons Project (AFSWP) contract DA-49-146-XZ-037. The report then states that patients "received total body irradiation" at dosages up to 4,000 roentgens. However according to the US Nuclear Regulatory Commission (NRC), humans exposed to 500 roentgens of radiation will likely die without medical treatment.

The report makes it clear that medical treatment was *not* provided. It flatly states that "there is no record of clinical follow-up beyond the 75 day post-exposure period."

As if anticipating raised eyebrows, the report adds an odd disclaimer: "since the primary intent of the study was to treat cancer and provide a direct benefit to the subjects, apparently the Nuremberg Code and the Declaration of Helsinki were complied with."

Even sixty years later, the hypocrisy of this report is chilling to any reader. Since lethal levels of radiation were used (800 percent higher than the NRC fatality threshold), and since there was "no clinical follow-up" with the irradiated victims, there was clearly no "intent to benefit the subjects," who most likely died.

It is apparent that this study—funded by the US Army and the "Armed Forces Special Weapons Project," was a radiological warfare project that needed several human lab rats on which to perform target practice.

On a final chilling note, the report stated that "certain records are missing."

This is the type of research that Dr. Cornelius P. Rhoads was conducting and supervising at the Sloan-Kettering Center, during the same time period (1954–1955) as Albizu's imprisonment.

24. Welsome, *The Plutonium Files*, 481–486.

25. Tomás Stella, "40,000 Pay Tribute to Albizu," *San Juan Star*, April 26, 1965. See also Ruben Arrieta, "Piden Investigar la Muerte de Albizu Campos," *El Nuevo Día*, April 22, 1986; Juan Gonzalez, "A Lonely Voice Finally Heard," *New York Daily News*, January 12, 1994; Ivonne García, "Author Calls for Release of Albizu Records," *San Juan Star*, January 20, 1994; Sara Del Valle, "Reclaman Justicia por Tortura a Albizu," *Claridad*, January 21–27, 1994.

The investigation into what happened to Albizu Campos is ongoing. US Congressman José Serrano wrote in the pages of the *Puerto Rico Herald*, "As the ranking Democrat on the CJSJ subcommittee [Commerce, Justice, Judiciary and Related Agencies Subcommittee of the House Appropriations Committee], which funds the FBI and other federal agencies, I have an obligation to ensure that we appropriate funds in a responsible manner." In the same article, he asked, "Did the FBI play any role in torturing the leader of the independence movement, Dr. Pedro Albizu Campos, while he was in federal prison? The rumor persists among people in the Puerto Rican government, and elsewhere, that the FBI participated with federal prison officials in torturing Albizu Campos." See Rep. José Serrano (D-NY), "Dialogue Opens About FBI/Carpeta Questions," *Puerto Rico Herald*, April 9, 2000. In addition to Representative Serrano, Representatives Nydia Velasquez and Luis Gutierrez (each with twenty-two years of service in the US Congress) have demanded answers and accountability with respect to the life and death of Pedro Albizu Campos.

CHAPTER 23: THE KING OF THE TOWELS

1. Pedro Aponte Vázquez, "An Interview with Laura Albizu," *El Imparcial*, November 9, 1955, 6.

2. Ramón Bosque Pérez and José Javier Colón Morera, *Las Carpetas: Persecución Política y Derechos Civiles en Puerto Rico: Ensayos y Documentos* (Río Piedras, PR: Centro para la Investigación y Promoción de los Derechos Civiles, 1997), 249.

3. Laura Meneses de Albizu Campos, *Albizu Campos y la Independencia de Puerto Rico* (Hato Rey, PR: Publicaciones Puertorriqueñas, 2007), 124–125.

4. "Albizu Campos Jailed on Wall Street's Order," *Daily Worker*, August 17, 1951.

5. The FBI reports on Albizu were largely built on information from informants. This did not change once Albizu was imprisoned. He was surrounded by informants in La Princesa, as he had been everywhere else. For example, one FBI report states, "A Federal prisoner detained at the San Juan District Jail [La Princesa] had occasion to talk with ALBIZU and to observe him rather closely. . . . [He] complains of seeing North Americans shooting cosmic rays into his head." FBI Files, Subject: Pedro Albizu Campos, File Number 105-11898, Section X, 25. Elsewhere the report states, "T-1, who is familiar with activities in the San Juan District Jail, is convinced that Albizu's allegation that he is being subjected to atomic rays is just an act." See ibid., 123. Yet another prison informant reported, "Albizu has more bluish marks on his body. . . . [P]risoners swear these bluish marks are the result of 'atomic rays.' . . . [A]ll of the Nationalist prisoners in the San Juan District Jail believe Albizu's story about the atomic rays." See ibid., 113.

Epilogue

1. The Nineteenth General Assembly of the United Nations, December 11, 1964, reprinted in David Deutschmann, *The Che Guevara Reader: Writings on Politics and Revolution*, 2nd ed. (North Melbourne, Australia: Ocean Press, 2003).

2. Marisa Rosado, *Pedro Albizu Campos: Las Llamas de la Aurora*, 5th ed. (San Juan: Ediciones Puerto, 2008), 420–426. The outpouring of grief and sympathy at the passing of Albizu Campos was striking. Political leaders, writers, artists, academics, and intellectuals arrived from every country in Latin America. The leaders of every political party in Puerto Rico made highly publicized and suitably grief-stricken appearances. The following is a partial list of the organizations that participated in the funeral ceremonies: Ateneo Puertorriqueño, Acción Patriótica Unitaria, Logia Sol de Libertad, Logia Masónica Independencia, Cruzada Patriótica, Partido Independentista Puertorriqueño, Liga Socialista, Colegio de Abogados, Estudiantes Independentistas de la Universidad de Puerto Rico, Partido Comunista, Juventud del MPI, Cadetes de la Republica, Confraternidad de los Pueblos, Congreso de Poesía, Consejo Puertorriqueño de la Paz, Secretaría Acción Femenina, Congreso Federación de Universitarios Pro Independencia, and Logia Simón Bolivar. Hundreds of cables and letters poured in from throughout the Western Hemisphere. To maintain law and order, the Insular Police deployed large security units to protect all federal buildings, US corporate office buildings, and banks.

3. Theodore Roosevelt, *Thomas Hart Benton* (New York: Charles Scribner's Sons, 1906), reprinted in Noam Chomsky, "Presidential 'Peacemaking' in Latin America," *In These Times*, January 5, 2010.

4. Ibid.

5. Ray Suarez, *Latino Americans: The 500-Year Legacy That Shaped a Nation* (New York: Penguin Group, 2013). See also Brett Bowden, *The Empire of Civilization: The Evolution of an Imperial Idea* (Chicago: University of Chicago Press, 2009), 233; De-Wayne Wickham, "U.S., Like Russia, Exercises Hegemony," *USA Today*, March 31, 2014.

6. *Congressional Record*, 56th Cong., 1st Sess., April 2, 1900, 3612.

7. Smedley D. Butler, *War Is a Racket* (Los Angeles: Feral House, 2003), 10.

8. Charles H. Allen, *First Annual Report of Governor of Porto Rico* (Washington, DC: Government Printing Office, 1901), 99.

9. Larry Russmussen, ed., *Reinhold Niebuhr: Theologian of Public Life* (New York: Harper & Row, 1989), 84–85.

10. James L. Dietz, *Economic History of Puerto Rico* (Princeton, NJ: Princeton University Press, 1986), 190. See also James L. Dietz, *Puerto Rico: Negotiating Development and Change* (London: Lynne Rienner, 2003), 44.

11. The 81st Cong., 2nd Sess., March 16, 1950, Report of Congressman Vito Marcantonio before the US House Committee on Public Lands.

12. Ibid.

13. Ronald Fernandez, *Los Macheteros: The Wells Fargo Robbery and the Violent Struggle for Puerto Rican Independence* (New York: Prentice Hall, 1987), 189. See also Dietz, *Economic History of Puerto Rico*, 206–218; Virginia E. Sanchez Korrol, "The Story of U.S. Puerto Ricans: Part IV," Centro de Estudios Puertorriqueños, Hunter College, City University of New York, http://centropr.hunter.cuny.edu/education /puerto-rican-studies/story-us-puerto-ricans-part-four.

14. Fernandez, *Los Macheteros*, 192. See also Clare E. Rodriguez, *Puerto Ricans: Born in the USA* (Boulder, CO: Westview Press, 1989), 9–21.

15. Juan Gonzalez, *Harvest of Empire: A History of Latinos in America* (New York: Penguin Books, 2000), 280–282.

16. Lizette Alvarez, "Economy and Crime Spur New Puerto Rican Exodus," *New York Times*, February 8, 2014; Al Yoon, "Puerto Rico Downgrade Puts Bond Deal in Spotlight," *Wall Street Journal*, February 8, 2014; Danica Cotto, "Puerto Rico Rushes to Cut Budgets and Renegotiate Loans After Being Downgraded to Junk Status," *Huffington Post*, February 5, 2014.

17. Dietz, *Puerto Rico*, 139–147; Gonzalez, *Harvest of Empire*, 280–282.

18. Eduardo Galleano, *Open Veins of Latin America: Five Centuries of the Pillage of a Continent* (New York: Monthly Review Press, 1997), 227.

19. Fernandez, *Los Macheteros*, 1–30. See also Armando Andre, "Los Macheteros: El Robo de $7 Millones de la Wells Fargo," *La Crónica Gráfica*, 1987; Edmund H. Mahony, "Wells Fargo Fugitive Captured," *Hartford Courant*, February 8, 2008.

20. Danica Cotto, "Puerto Rico Rushes to Cut Budgets and Renegotiate Loans."

21. "Census: Puerto Rico Poverty Up, Income Down," *Caribbean Business*, September 23, 2012.

22. Alvarez, "Economy and Crime Spur New Puerto Rican Exodus."

23. Ibid.

24. Yoon, "Puerto Rico Downgrade Puts Bond Deal in Spotlight."

25. David Greene, "Puerto Ricans Wrestle with High Crime," NPR, February 7, 2013.

26. Eric Lichtblau, "28 Puerto Rico Police Caught in Drug Smuggling," *Los Angeles Times*, August 15, 2001.

27. American Civil Liberties Union, *Island of Impurity: Puerto Rico's Outlaw Police Force*, June 2012, 12.

28. Alvarez, "Economy and Crime Spur New Puerto Rican Exodus."

29. American Civil Liberties Union, *Island of Impurity*, 10.

30. Michael Connor, "Puerto Rico's Population Drops as Economy Wobbles," Reuters, September 10, 2013.

BIBLIOGRAPHY

BOOKS

Acosta, Ivonne. *La Mordaza: Puerto Rico, 1948–1957*. San Juan: Editorial Edil, 1987.

Adams, Richard N. *Social Change in Latin America Today*. New York: Vintage Press, 1960.

Aitken, Thomas. *Poet in the Fortress: The Story of Luis Muñoz Marín*. New York: Signet Books, 1964.

Albizu Campos, Pedro, and Manuel Maldonado-Denis, ed. *La Conciencia Nacional Puertorriqueña*. Mexico: Siglo Veintiuno Editores, 1972.

Allen, Charles H. *First Annual Report of Governor of Porto Rico*. Washington, DC: Government Printing Office, 1901.

Alsop, Stewart, and Thomas Braden. *Sub Rosa: The OSS and American Espionage*. New York: Reynal & Hitchcock, 1946.

Amnesty International. *Proposal for a Commission of Inquiry into the Effect of Domestic Intelligence Activities on Criminal Trials in the United States of America*. Nottingham, UK: Russell Press, 1981.

Anderson, Robert. *Party Politics in Puerto Rico*. Stanford, CA: Stanford University Press, 1965.

Arce de Vásquez, Margot. *Pedro Albizu Campos: Reflexiones Sobre Su Vida y Su Obra*. Río Piedras, PR: Editorial Marién, 1991.

Arrington, Leonard J. *Beet Sugar in the West, 1891–1966*. Seattle: University of Washington Press, 1966.

Ayala, César J. *American Sugar Kingdom*. Chapel Hill: University of North Carolina Press, 1999.

Ayala, César J., and Rafael Bernabe. *Puerto Rico in the American Century: A History Since 1898*. Chapel Hill: University of North Carolina Press, 2007.

Bacchus, Kassim. *Utilization, Misuse and Development of Human Resources in the Early West Indian Colonies.* Waterloo, Ontario: Wilfred Laurier University Press, 2000.

Berbusee, Edward. *The United States in Puerto Rico 1898–1900.* Chapel Hill: University of North Carolina Press, 1966.

Bernays, Edward. *Propaganda.* New York: Ig Publishing, 2005.

Bernier-Grand, Carmen T. *Poet and Politician of Puerto Rico: Don Luis Muñoz Marín.* New York: Orchard Books, 1995.

Bethell, John T. *Harvard Observed.* Cambridge, MA: Harvard University Press, 1998.

Bethell, John T., Richard M. Hunt, and Robert Shenton. *Harvard A to Z.* Cambridge, MA: Harvard University Press, 2004.

Black, Ruby. *Eleanor Roosevelt: A Biography.* Whitefish, MO: Kessinger Publishing, 1940.

Blum, William. *Freeing the World to Death: Essays on the American Empire.* Monroe, ME: Common Courage Press, 2005.

————. *Killing Hope: U.S. Military and CIA Interventions Since World War II.* Monroe, ME: Common Courage Press, 1995.

Booth, Waller B. *Booth's Truths.* Kendallville, IN: Kendallville Publishing Co., 1975.

————. *Mission Marcel Proust: The Story of an Unusual OSS Undertaking.* Philadelphia: Dorrance & Co., 1972.

Bosque-Pérez, Ramón, and J. J. Colón Morera, eds. *Las Carpetas: Persecución Política y Derechos Civiles en Puerto Rico: Ensayos y Documentos.* Río Piedras, PR: Centro para la Investigación y Promoción de los Derechos Civiles, 1997.

————, eds. *Puerto Rico Under Colonial Rule: Political Persecution and the Quest for Human Rights.* Albany: State University of New York Press, 2006.

Bothwell, Reece B. Gonzalez. *Puerto Rico: Cien Años de Lucha Politica.* Río Piedras, PR: Editorial Universitaria, 1979.

Bowden, Brett. *The Empire of Civilization: The Evolution of an Imperial Idea.* Chicago: University of Chicago Press, 2009.

Boyle, John F. *The Irish Rebellion of 1916: A Brief History of the Revolt and Its Suppression.* N.p.: HardPress Publishers, 2012.

Bruno, Miñi Seijo. *La Insurrección Nacionalista en Puerto Rico, 1950.* Río Piedras, PR: Editorial Edil, 1989.

Butler, Smedley D. *War Is a Racket.* Los Angeles: Feral House, 2003.

Cabán, Pedro A. *Constructing a Colonial People: Puerto Rico and the United States, 1898–1932.* Boulder, CO: Westview Press, 1999.

Carrión, Arturo Morales. *Puerto Rico: A Political and Cultural History.* New York: Norton Press, 1983.

Carrión, Juan Manuel, Teresa C. Garcia Ruiz, and Carlos Rodríguez Fraticelli. *La Nación Puertorriqueña: Ensayos en Torno a Pedro Albizu Campos.* San Juan: Editorial de la Universidad de Puerto Rico, 1993.

Castro Arroyo, María de los Ángeles. *La Fortaleza de Santa Catalina*. San Juan: Patronato del Palacio de Santa Catalina, 2005.

Central Intelligence Agency. *The CIA Document of Human Manipulation: KUBARK Counterintelligence Interrogation Manual*. Washington, DC: US Government Printing Office, 1963; acquired pursuant to Freedom of Information Act (FOIA) by Thousand Oaks, CA: BN Publishing, 2012.

———. *Human Resource Exploitation Manual*. Washington, DC: US Government Printing Office, 1983.

Che Guevara, Ernesto. *Guerrilla Warfare*. Thousand Oaks, CA: BN Publishing, 2007.

Churchill, Allen. *The Improper Bohemians: Greenwich Village in Its Heyday*. New York: Ace Books, 1959.

Churchill, Ward, and Jim Vander Wall. *The COINTELPRO Papers*. Cambridge, MA: South End Press, 2002.

Clark, Truman R. *Puerto Rico and the United States, 1917–1933*. Pittsburgh, PA: University of Pittsburgh Press, 1975.

Clark, Victor S., ed., *Porto Rico and Its Problem*. Washington, DC: Brookings Institute, 1930.

Cohen, Rich. *The Fish That Ate the Whale: The Life and Times of America's Banana King*. New York: Farrar, Straus & Giroux, 2012.

Colón, Jesus. *A Puerto Rican in New York and Other Sketches*. New York: International Publishers, 2002.

Congressional Record, 64th Cong., 1st Sess., May 5, 1916, 7473.

Congressional Record. 56th Cong., 1st Sess., April 2, 1900, 3612 (William B. Tate, D-TN.)

Corretjer, Juan Antonio. *Albizu Campos*. Montevideo: El Siglo Ilustrado Pub., 1965.

———. *Albizu Campos and the Ponce Massacre*. New York: World View Publishers, 1965.

Crawford, James, ed. *Language Loyalties*. Chicago: University of Chicago Press, 1992.

Crumpton, Henry A. *The Art of Intelligence: Lessons from a Life in the CIA's Clandestine Service*. New York: Penguin Press, 2012.

Cruz, Nilo. *Anna in the Tropics*. New York: Dramatists Play Service, 2005.

Davis, James K. *Spying on America: The FBI's Domestic Counter-Intelligence Program*. New York: Praeger Publishers, 1992.

de Moral, Solsiree. *Negotiating Empire: The Culture and Politics of Schools in Puerto Rico, 1898–1952*. Madison: University of Wisconsin Press, 2013.

Diaz, Nilda. *I Was Never Alone: A Prison Diary from El Salvador*. North Melbourne, Australia: Ocean Press, 1992.

Dietz, James L. *Economic History of Puerto Rico*. Princeton, NJ: Princeton University Press, 1980.

———. *Puerto Rico: Negotiating Development and Change*. London: Lynne Rienner, 2003.

Diffie, Bailey W., and Justine Whitfield Diffie. *Porto Rico: A Broken Pledge*. New York: Vanguard Press, 1931.

Earnhardt, Kent C. *Development Planning and Population Policy in Puerto Rico*. San Juan: Editorial de la Universidad de Puerto Rico, 1982.

Eckhardt, Joseph P. *The King of the Movies: Film Pioneer Siegmund Lubin*. Cranbury, NJ: Associated University Presses, 1997.

Fernandez, Ronald. *The Disenchanted Island: Puerto Rico and the United States in the Twentieth Century*. 2nd ed. Westport, CT: Praeger, 1996.

————. *Los Macheteros: The Wells Fargo Robbery and the Violent Struggle for Puerto Rican Independence*. New York: Prentice Hall, 1987.

Ferrao, Luis Angel. *Pedro Albizu Campos y el Nacionalismo Puertorriqueño, 1930–1939*. Harrisburg: Editorial Cultural, Banta Co., 1990.

Figueroa, Loida. *Breve Historia de Puerto Rico*. Vol. 1. San Juan: Editorial Edil, 1979.

Freire, Paulo. *Pedagogy of the Oppressed*. New York: Bloomsbury Academic, 2000.

Fuess, Claude M. *Creed of a Schoolmaster*. Freeport, NY: Books for Libraries Press, 1970.

Galeano, Eduardo. *Open Veins of Latin America: Five Centuries of the Pillage of a Continent*. New York: Monthly Review Press, 1977.

García Ochoa, Asunción. *La Política Española en Puerto Rico Durante el Siglo XIX*. Río Piedras, PR: Editorial de la Unversidad de Puerto Rico, 1982.

Garcia-Crespo, Naida. *Company of Contradictions: Puerto Rico's Tropical Film Company*. Vol. 23. Bloomington: Indiana University Press, 2011.

Gill, Leslie. *The School of the Americas: Military Training and Political Violence in the Americas*. Durham, NC: Duke University Press, 2004.

Gonzalez, Juan. *Harvest of Empire: A History of Latinos in America*. New York: Penguin Books, 2000.

Gore, Paul A. *Past the Edge of Poverty: A Biography of Robert Hayes Gore*. Rpt. ed. Notre Dame, IN: University of Notre Dame, 1993.

Gould, Lyman, J. *La Ley Foraker: Raíces de le Política Colonial de los Estados Unidos*. Río Piedras, PR: Editorial Universidad de Puerto Rico, 1969.

Grosfoguel, Ramon. *Colonial Subjects: Puerto Ricans in Global Perspective*. Berkeley: University of California Press, 2003.

Haines, Gerald K., and David A. Langbart. *Unlocking the Files of the FBI: A Guide to Its Records and Classification System*. Wilmington, DE: Scholarly Resources, 1993.

Hanson, Earl Parker. *Transformation: The Story of Modern Puerto Rico*. New York: Simon & Schuster, 1955.

Harbury, Jennifer K. *Truth, Torture and the American Way: The History and Consequences of U.S. Involvement in Torture*. Boston: Beacon Press, 2005.

Harris, W. W. *Puerto Rico's Fighting 65th U.S. Infantry: From San Juan to Chorwan*. San Rafael, CA: Presidio Press, 1980.

Harrison, Mark. *The Economics of World War II: Six Great Powers in International Comparison.* Cambridge: Cambridge University Press, 1998.

Hays, Arthur Garfield, and the Commission of Inquiry on Civil Rights in Puerto Rico. *Report of the Commission of Inquiry on Civil Rights in Puerto Rico.* New York, 1937.

Herman, Edward S., and Noam Chomsky. *Manufacturing Consent: The Political Economy of the Mass Media.* 1st ed. New York: Pantheon Books, 1988.

Hinton, David B. *The Films of Leni Riefenstahl.* 3rd ed. Lanham, MD: Scarecrow Press, 2000.

Hoftsadter, Richard, William Miller, and Daniel Aaron. *The Structure of American History.* Upper Saddle River, NJ: Prentice Hall, 1964.

Holm, Richard L. *The Craft We Chose: My Life in the CIA.* Mountain Lake, MD: Mountain Lake Press, 2011.

Holmes, Oliver Wendell, Jr. *Buck v. Bell* 274 US 200 (1927) (majority opinion).

Hopkins, Ralph D. *Chapters: Confessions of a Military/CIA Retiree.* Bloomington, IN: First Books Library, 2004.

Hunt, William H. *Second Annual Report of Governor of Porto Rico.* Washington, DC: Government Printing Office, 1902.

Hunter, Stephen, and John Bainbridge Jr. *American Gunfight: The Plot to Kill Harry Truman—and the Shoot-Out That Stopped It.* New York: Simon & Schuster, 2005.

Jimenez, Juan Ortiz. *Nacimiento del Cine Puertorriqueño.* San Juan: Editorial Tiempo Nuevo, 2007.

Jimenez de Wagenheim, Olga. *Puerto Rico's Revolt for Independence: El Grito de Lares.* Boulder, CO: Westview Press, 1985.

Johnson, Haynes. *The Age of Anxiety: McCarthyism to Terrorism.* Orlando: Harcourt, 2005.

Johnson, Roberta Ann. *Puerto Rico: Commonwealth or Colony?* New York: Praeger, 1980.

Jones, Ishmael. *The Human Factor: Inside the CIA's Dysfunctional Intelligence Culture.* Jackson, TN: Encounter Books, 2010.

Katz, Friedrich. *The Life and Times of Pancho Villa.* Stanford, CA: Stanford University Press, 1998.

King, John. *Magical Reels: A History of Cinema in Latin America.* London: Verso, 2000.

Kuleshov, Lev. *Kuleshov on Film.* Berkeley: University of California Press, 1974.

Laguerre, Enrique A. *La Llamarada.* Río Piedras, PR: Editorial, 1977.

Lait, Jack, and Lee Mortimer. *New York Confidential: The Low-Down on the Big Town.* Chicago: Ziff Davis, 1948.

Lewis, Gordon K. *Puerto Rico: Colonialismo y Revolución.* Mexico City: Ediciones Era, 1977.

Lopez, Alfredo. *Dona Licha's Island: Modern Colonialism in Puerto Rico.* Boston: South End Press, 1988.

Malavet, Pedro A. *America's Colony: The Political and Cultural Conflict Between the United States and Puerto Rico.* New York: New York University Press, 2004.

Maldonado-Denis, Manuel. *Puerto Rico: A Socio-historic Interpretation.* New York: Random House, 1972.

———. *Puerto Rico: Mito y Realidad.* San Juan: Ediciones Peninsula, 1969.

Martin, Francis X. *Leaders and Men of the Easter Rising: Dublin 1916.* Ithaca, NY: Cornell University Press, 1967.

Mathews, Thomas George. *Puerto Rican Politics and the New Deal.* Gainesville: University of Florida Press, 1960.

McCoy, Alfred W. *A Question of Torture: CIA Interrogation, from the Cold War to the War on Terror.* New York: Henry Holt and Co., 2006.

———. *The Politics of Heroin in Southeast Asia.* New York: Harper & Row, 1972.

Medina Ramírez, Ramón. *El Movimiento Libertador en la Historia de Puerto Rico.* San Juan: Imprenta Nacional, 1970.

Medina Vazquez, Raul. *Verdadera Historia de la Masacre de Ponce.* Ponce: Instituto de Cultura Puertorriqueña, 2001.

Meléndez, Edgardo, and Edwin Meléndez. *Colonial Dilemma.* Boston: South End Press, 1993.

Meneses de Albizu Campos, Laura. *Albizu Campos y la Independencia de Puerto Rico.* Hato Rey, PR: Publicaciones Puertorriqueñas, 2007.

Merrill-Ramirez, Marie A. *The Other Side of Colonialism: COINTELPRO Activities in Puerto Rico in the 1960s.* PhD diss., University of Texas, Austin, 1990.

Mintz, Sidney W. *Sweetness and Power: The Place of Sugar in Modern History.* New York: Penguin Books, 1985.

———. *Worker in the Cane: A Puerto Rican Life History.* New York: W. W. Norton, 1974.

Moraza Ortiz, Manuel E. *La Masacre de Ponce.* Hato Rey, PR: Publicaciones Puertorriqueñas, 2001.

Morison, Samuel Eliot. *Three Centuries of Harvard.* Cambridge, MA: Belknap Press, 1936.

Moruzzi, Peter. *Havana Before Castro: When Cuba Was a Tropical Playground.* Layton, UT: Gibbs Smith, 2008.

Muñoz Marín, Luis. *Memorias: 1898–1940.* San Juan: Fundación Luis Muñoz Marín, 2003.

Murillo, Mario A., ed. *Islands of Resistance: Puerto Rico, Vieques, and U.S. Policy.* New York: Seven Stories Press, 2001.

Natal, Carmelo Rosario. *La Juventud de Luis Muñoz Marín.* San Juan: Editorial Edil, 1989.

———. "Luis Muñoz Marin, Arthur Garfield Hays y la Masacre de Ponce: Una Revelación Documental Inedita." In *Kálathos—Revista Transdisciplinaria.* San Jose: Universidad Interamericana de Puerto Rico, Recinto Metro, 2007.

Negroni, Héctor Andrés. *Historia Militar de Puerto Rico*. Madrid: Sociedad Estatal Quinto Centenaria, 1992.

Nohlen, Dieter. *Elections in the Americas: A Data Handbook*. Vol. 1. Cary, NC: Oxford University Press, 2005.

O'Donnell, Patrick K. *Operatives, Spies and Saboteurs: The Unknown Story of World War II's OSS*. New York: Kensington Publishing, 2004.

O'Toole, G. J. A. *The Spanish War: An American Epic, 1898*. New York: W. W. Norton & Co., 1984.

Ojeda Reyes, Felix. *Vito Marcantonio y Puerto Rico por los Trabajadores y por la Nación*. Río Piedras, PR: Ediciones Huracán, 1978.

Padua, Reynaldo Marcos. *Águila*. San Juan: Ediciones Huracán, 2008.

Paláu Suárez, Awilda. *Veinticinco Años de Claridad*. 1st ed. Río Piedras, PR: Editorial de la Universidad de Puerto Rico, 1992.

Parry, Albert. *Garrets and Pretenders: Bohemian Life in America from Poe to Kerouac*. Mineola, NY: Dover Publications, 1960.

Pérez-Marchand, Rafael V. *Reminiscencia Histórica de la Masacre de Ponce*. San Lorenzo, PR: Partido Nacionalista de Puerto Rico, Movimiento Libertador de Puerto Rico, 1972.

Piñero, Enrique Bird. *Don Luis Muñoz Marín: El Poder de la Excelencia*. San Juan: Luis Muñoz Marín Foundation, 1991.

Post, Waldron Kintzing. *Harvard Stories: Sketches of the Undergraduate*. New York: G. P. Putnam's Sons, 1895.

Poveda, Tony G. *Lawlessness and Reform: The FBI in Transition*. Pacific Grove, CA: Brooks/Cole Publishing Co., 1990.

Purón, Mario Averhoff. *Los Primeros Políticos*. Havana: Instituto Cubano del Libro, 1971.

Ramos-Perea, Roberto. *Revolución en el Infierno: La Masacre de Ponce de 1937*. San Juan: Ediciones Mágica, 2005.

Redmond, Charles F. *Selections from the Correspondence of Theodore Roosevelt and Henry Cabot Lodge, 1884–1918*. New York: Scribner's, 1925.

Rexach Benítez, Jesus. *Vida y Obra de Luis Muñoz Marín*. San Juan: Editorial Edil, 1989.

Rexach Benítez, Roberto F. *Pedro Albizu Campos: Leyenda y Realidad*. San Juan: Publicaciones Coquí, 1961.

Reynolds, Mack. *Puerto Rican Patriot: The Life of Luis Muñoz Rivera*. Springfield, OH: Crowell-Collier Press, 1969.

Reynolds, Ruth Mary. *Campus in Bondage*. New York: Research Foundation of the City of New York, 1989.

Ribes Tovar, Federico. *Albizu Campos: Puerto Rican Revolutionary*. New York: Plus Ultra Publishers, 1971.

Rigau, Jorge. *Puerto Rico Then and Now*. San Diego: Thunder Bay Press, 2009.

Rivero, Angel. *Crónica de la Guerra Hispanoamericana en Puerto Rico*. New York: Plus Ultra Publishers, 1973.

Roosevelt, Theodore. *Thomas Hart Benton*. New York: Charles Scribner's Sons, 1906.

Rosado, Marisa. *Pedro Albizu Campos: Las Llamas de la Aurora*. 5th ed. San Juan: Ediciones Puerto, 2008.

Roure Marrero, Juan. *Don Pedro Albizu Campos: El Partido Nacionalista*. Perth Amboy, NJ: L&A Quick Printing, 1996.

Rouse, Irving. *The Taínos: The Rise and Decline of the People Who Greeted Columbus*. New Haven, CT: Yale University Press, 1992.

Rudgers, David F. *Creating the Secret State: The Origins of the Central Intelligence Agency, 1943–1947*. Lawrence: University of Kansas Press, 2000.

Russmussen, Larry, ed. *Reinhold Niebuhr: Theologian of Public Life*. New York: Harper & Row, 1989.

Salinas, Pedro. *Aprecio y Defensa del Lenguaje*. San Juan: Editorial Universitaria, 1974.

Sandburg, Carl. *Always the Young Strangers*. New York: Harcourt, Brace, 1953.

Schlesinger, Andrew. *Veritas: Harvard College and the American Experience*. Chicago: Ivan R. Dee, 2005.

Seijo Bruno, Miñi. *La Insurrección en Puerto Rico, 1950*. San Juan: Editorial Edil, 1997.

Silén, Juan Angel. *Historia de la Nación Puertorriqueña*. Río Piedras, PR: Ediciones Edil, 1973.

———. *Pedro Albizu Campos*. Río Piedras, PR: Editorial Antillana, 1976.

Smith, Bradley F. *The Shadow Warriors: OSS and the Origins of the CIA*. New York: Basic, 1983.

Stafford, David. *Camp X: OSS, Intrepid, and the Allies North American Training Camp for Secret Agents, 1941–1945*. New York: Dodd Mead, 1987.

Suarez, Ray. *Latino Americans: The 500-Year Legacy That Shaped a Nation*. New York: Penguin Group, 2013.

Taber, Robert. *War of the Flea: The Classic Study of Guerrilla Warfare*. Washington, DC: Potomac Books, 2002.

Talbot, David. *Devil Dog: The Amazing True Story of the Man Who Saved America*. New York: Simon & Schuster, 2010.

Taylor, Kendall. *Philip Evergood: Never Separate from the Heart*. Cranbury, NJ: Associated University Presses, 1987.

Theoharis, Athan G. *FBI (Federal Bureau of Investigation): An Annotated Bibliography and Research Guide*. New York: Garland Publishing, 1994.

Tinajero, Araceli, and Judith E. Greenberg. *El Lectór: A History of the Cigar Factory Reader*. Austin: University of Texas Press, 2010.

Todd, Roberto H. *Desfile de Governadores de Puerto Rico*. 2nd ed. Madrid: Ediciones Iberoamericanas, 1966.

Torres, Heriberto Marín. *Eran Ellos*. Río Piedras, PR: Ediciones Ciba, 2000.

Trias Monge, José. *Como Fue: Memorias*. San Juan: Editorial Universidad de Puerto Rico, 2005.

———. *Puerto Rico: The Trials of the Oldest Colony in the World*. New Haven, CT: Yale University Press, 1999.

US Department of Defense. *Report on Search for Human Radiation Experiment Records, 1994–1994*. Vol. 1. Springfield VA: Department of Commerce, Technology Administration, National Technical Information Service, 1997.

Valentín, José Martínez. *La Presencia de la Policia en la Historia de Puerto Rico: 1989–1995*. San Juan: Producciones Luigi, 1995.

Vásquez, Pedro Aponte. *¡Yo Acuso! Y lo que Pasó Despues*. Bayamón, PR: Movimiento Ecuménico Nacional de PR, 1985.

Villahermosa, Gilberto N. *Honor and Fidelity: The 65th Infantry in Korea, 1950–1953*. Washington, DC: Center of Military History, US Army, 2009.

Wagenheim, Kal. *Cuentos: Stories from Puerto Rico*. Princeton, NJ: Markus Weiner Publishers, 2008.

———. *Puerto Rico: A Profile*. New York: Praeger, 1970.

Warner, Michael. *The Office of Strategic Services: America's First Intelligence Agency*. Washington, DC: Central Intelligence Agency, 2001.

Wayne, Mike. *Political Film: The Dialectics of Third Cinema*. London: Pluto Press, 2001.

Weiner, Tim. *Legacy of Ashes: The History of the CIA*. New York: Doubleday, 2007.

Welsome, Eileen. *The Plutonium Files*. New York: Random House, 1999.

Zeno-Gandía, Manuel. *La Charca*. Princeton, NJ: Markus Wiener Publishers, 2010.

Zinn, Howard. *A People's History of the United States*. New York: HarperCollins, 2005.

Historic Newspaper Articles

"7 Die in Puerto Rico Riot, 50 Injured as Police Fire on Fighting Nationalists." *New York Times*, March 22, 1937, 1, 11.

"40,000 Pay Tribute to Albizu." *San Juan Star*, April 26, 1965, 1.

"Albizu Told the Story of Atomic Torture to the Press." *El Mundo*, October 1, 1953.

"Aviación Bombardea en Utuado." *El Imparcial*, November 1, 1950, 1.

"Count of Subjects in Radiation Experiments Is Raised to 16,000." *New York Times*, August 20, 1995, http://www.nytimes.com/1995/08/20/us/count-of-subjects-in-radiation-experiments-is-raised-to-16000.html.

"Disparen para que Vean Como Muere un Hombre." *El Imparcial*, February 25, 1936, 1.

"E. Mont. Reily Brings Cheers When He Says Old Glory Is Only Flag for Island." *New York Times*, July 31, 1921, 8.

"El Informe del Comité Hays Inculpa a Winship." *El Imparcial*, May 24, 1937, 3, 4, 5, 6, 11, 14, 19, 23, 25, 27.

"G-Men Federales Enviados a Puerto Rico." *El Imparcial*, February 20, 1936.

"La Masacre de Ponce y la Sangre de los Mártires de la Historia." *El Imparcial*, April 3, 1937, 20, 21.

"Linchamiento Atomico de un Martir de la Libertad." *Verdad*, February 1953, 1, 24–27.

"Lo Que Vi en Ponce." *El Imparcial*, April 2, 1937, 28, 29.

"Los Insulares Son Desalojados de Jayuya y Utuado; Gran Parte de Jayuya Fue Destruida por las Llamas." *La Prensa*, November 2, 1950, 1.

"Motín en el Presidio." *El Imparcial*, October 29, 1950, 1.

"Once Muertos y Mas de Ciento Cincuenta Heridos en Ponce." *El Mundo*, March 22, 1937, 1, 5.

"Our Flag Raised in Puerto Rico." *New York Times*, July 27, 1898, 1.

"Pueblo en Actitud Respetuosa." *El Imparcial*, April 24, 1965, 1.

"Puerto Rican Riot Seen as Planned." *New York Times*, March 23, 1937, 9.

"Puerto Rico: Guns Blaze Afresh." *Washington Post*, March 28, 1937, 3.

"Secret Nuclear Research on People Comes to Light." *New York Times*, December 17, 1993.

"Seven Killed in Puerto Rico Riot, 50 Hurt in Nationalist Clash with Police." *Washington Post*, March 22, 1937, 1.

"Two in Puerto Rico Kill Police Head and Are Shot Dead." *New York Times*, February 24, 1936.

"US to Settle for $4.8 Million in Suits on Radiation Testing." *New York Times*, November 20, 1996.

"¡Viva la Republica! ¡Abajo las Asesinos!" *El Imparcial*, March 23, 1937, 1.

"Winship Quits Island with Report on Riot." *New York Times*, May 28, 1937, 4.

FBI FILES

FBI Files. Subject: Luis Muñoz Marín. File Number SJ 100-302. Office of Public and Congressional Affairs, Washington, DC, 1943.

FBI Files. Subject: Luis Muñoz Marín. File Number 100-5745, Sections I, III. Office of Public and Congressional Affairs, Washington, DC, 1965.

FBI Files. Subject: Nationalist Party of Puerto Rico. File Number SJ 100-3, Vols. 23, 26. Office of Public and Congressional Affairs, Washington, DC, 1951.

FBI Files. Subject: Pedro Albizu Campos. File Number 105-11898, June Mail. Office of Public and Congressional Affairs, Washington, DC, 1952.

FBI Files. Subject: Pedro Albizu Campos. File Number 105-11898, Part 1 of 8. Office of Public and Congressional Affairs, Washington, DC, 1952.

FBI Files. Subject: Pedro Albizu Campos. File Number 105-11898, Section Sub A. Office of Public and Congressional Affairs, Washington, DC, 1952.

FBI Files. Subject: Pedro Albizu Campos. File Number 105-11898, Serial 194 EBF 260, 260 EBF A-B, 260 EBF D, 325 EBF, 445 EBF, 585 EBF. Office of Public and Congressional Affairs, Washington, DC, 1952.

FBI Files. Subject: Pedro Albizu Campos. File Number 105-11898, Sections VI, VII, XII, XIII. Office of Public and Congressional Affairs, Washington, DC, 1952.

Other Government Publications and Reports

Central Intelligence Agency. *Human Resource Exploitation Manual.* Washington, DC: US Government Printing Office, 1983.

Human Radiation Interagency Working Group. *Building Public Trust: Actions to Respond to the Report of the Advisory Committee on Human Radiation Experiments.* Washington, DC: Government Printing Office, 1997.

Officer-in-Charge, Contract NOy-3680, NAS, San Juan to Chief of BuDocks. *Report of Progress and Procedures,* May 17, 1940. BuDocks, Contract NOy-3680, RG 71, Box 548, Vol. 11.

Standard, J. Newell. *Radioactivity and Health: A History.* 3 vols. Oak Ridge, TN: Office of Science and Technical Information, 1988.

Task Force on Human Subject Research. *A Report on the Use of Radioactive Facilities Within the Commonwealth of Massachusetts from 1943 Through 1973.* Commonwealth of Massachusetts, Office of Health and Human Services, Department of Mental Retardation, 1994.

University of California, San Francisco (UCSF), Ad Hoc Fact Finding Committee. *Report of the UCSF Ad Hoc Fact Finding Committee on World War II Human Radiation Experiments.* San Francisco: UCSF, February 1995.

US Congress, House Committee on Energy and Commerce, Subcommittee on Energy Conservation and Power. *American Nuclear Guinea Pigs: Three Decades of Radiation Experiments on U.S. Citizens.* 99th Cong., 2nd Sess., November 1986.

US Congress, House Committee on Energy and Commerce, Subcommittee on Energy and Power. *Radiation Testing on Humans.* 103rd Cong., 2nd Sess., January 18, 1994.

US Congress, House Committee on Science and Technology, Subcommittee on Investigations and Oversight. *Human Total Body Irradiation (TBI) Program at Oak Ridge.* Hearings. 97th Cong., 1st Sess., September 23, 1981.

US Congress, House Committee on the Judiciary, Subcommittee on Administrative Law and Government Relations. *Government-Sponsored Testing on Humans.* Hearings. 103rd Cong., 2nd Sess., February 3, 1994.

US Congress, Joint Hearing Before the Subcommittee on Oversight and Investigations and the Subcommittee on Energy and Power of the Committee on Commerce. *Department of Energy: Misuse of Federal Funds.* Hearings. 104th Cong., 1st Sess., November 17, 1995.

US Department of Defense. *Report on Search for Human Radiation Experiment Records, 1994–1994.* Vol. 1. Springfield VA: Department of Commerce, Technology Administration, National Technical Information Service, 1997. See especially

Contract DA-49-07, 125 (Sloan-Kettering Contract, Cornelius Rhoads Dir., *Study of Post-irradiation Syndrome on Humans*).

US Department of Energy. *Human Experimentation: An Overview on Cold War Era Programs*. Washington, DC: US Government Accounting Office, 1994.

———. *Human Radiation Experiments Associated with the U.S. Department of Energy and Its Predecessors*. Springfield, VA: Department of Commerce, Technology Administration, National Technical Information Service, 1995.

———. *Human Radiation Experiments: The Department of Energy Roadmap to the Story and the Records*. Springfield, VA: Department of Commerce, Technology Administration, National Technical Information Service, 1995.

USN-SMA, *Final Report and Factual Survey*. Vol. 1, General Report, Contract NOy-3680, Madigan-Hyland Co., March 22, 1943, General Forward and Introduction, 2.

Scientific Articles

"Acute Clinical Effects of Penetrating Nuclear Radiation." *JAMA* 168, no. 4 (September 27, 1958): 381–388.

"Acute Radiation Death Resulting from an Accidental Nuclear Critical Excursion." *Journal of Occupational Medicine* 3, no. 3, special supplement (March 1961).

Duany, Jorge. "Nation on the Move: The Construction of Cultural Identities in Puerto Rico and the Diaspora." *American Ethnologist* 27, no. 1 (February 2000): 5–30.

"Element of Consent in Surgical Operations." *JAMA* 15 (September 13, 1980): 401–402.

Evans, Robley. "Radium Poisoning: A Review of Present Knowledge." *American Journal of Public Health* 23, no. 10 (October 1933): 1017–1023.

Gautier Mayoral, Carmen. "Notes on the Repression Practiced by US Intelligence Agencies in Puerto Rico." *Revista Jurídica de la Universidad de Puerto Rico* 52, no. 3 (1983): 431–450.

Harkness, Jon. "Nuremberg and the Issue of Wartime Experiments on U.S. Prisoners." *JAMA* 276, no. 20 (November 27, 1996): 1672–1675.

Helfeld, David M. "Discrimination for Political Beliefs and Associations." *Revista del Colegio de Abogados de Puerto Rico* 25, no. 1 (November 1964): 5–276.

Heublein, Arthur C. "A Preliminary Report on Continuous Radiation of the Entire Body." *Radiology* 18, no. 6 (June 1932): 1051–1062.

"The History and Ethics of the Use of Humans in Medical Experiments." *Science* 108 (July 1948): 1–5.

Ivy, A. C. "Nazi War Crimes of a Medical Nature." *JAMA* 139, no. 3 (January 1949): 131–135.

Jacobs, Melville L., and Fred J. Marasso. "A Four-Year Experience with Total-Body Irradiation." *Radiology* 84 (March 1965): 452–465.

Macklis, Roger. "The Great Radium Scandal." *Scientific American* 269 (1993): 94–99.

Maslow, Abraham. "A Theory of Human Motivation." *Psychological Review* 50, no. 4 (1943): 370–396.

McCaffrey, Katherine T. "Struggle Against the U.S. Navy in Vieques, Puerto Rico: Two Movements in History." *Latin American Perspectives* 33 (January 2006): 83–101.

Medinger, Fred G., and Lloyd Craver. "Total Body Irradiation." *American Journal of Roentgenology* 48, no. 5 (1942): 651–671.

Report by the Committee Appointed by Governor Dwight H. Green. "Ethics Governing the Service of Prisoners as Subjects in Medical Experiments." *JAMA* 136, no. 7 (February 1948): 457.

West-Durán, Alan. "Puerto Rico: The Pleasures and Traumas of Race." *Centro Journal* 17 (spring 2005).

INDEX

NELSON A. DENIS was the editorial director of *El Diario*, the largest Spanish-language newspaper in New York City, and won the Best Editorial Writing Award from the National Association of Hispanic Journalists. A graduate of Harvard University and Yale Law School, Denis served as a New York State assemblyman (1997–2001) and has written for the *New York Daily News*, *Newsday*, and *Harvard Political Review*. Denis also wrote and directed the feature film *Vote for Me!*, which premiered at the Tribeca Film Festival.